HOW
CELTIC CULTURE
INVENTED SOUTHERN
LITERATURE

HOW
CELTIC CULTURE
INVENTED SOUTHERN
LITERATURE

James P. Cantrell

PELICAN PUBLISHING COMPANY
Gretna 2006

The word "Pelican" and the depiction of a pelican are trademarks
of Pelican Publishing Company, Inc., and are registered in the
U.S. Patent and Trademark Office.

Library of Congress Cataloging-in-Publication Data

Cantrell, James P.
  How Celtic Culture Invented Southern Literature / by James P. Cantrell.
    p. cm.
  Includes bibliographical references (p.   ) and index.
  ISBN-13: 978-1-58980-330-5 (alk. paper)
  ISBN-10: 1-58980-330-2 (alk. paper)
  1. American literature—Southern States—History and criticism. 2. Scottish
Americans—Southern States—Intellectual life. 3. Irish Americans—Southern
States—Intellectual life. 4. Welsh Americans—Southern States—Intellectual
life. 5. Celts—Southern States—Intellectual life. 6. American literature—
Celtic influences. 7. Southern States—Intellectual life. 8. Southern States—In
literature. 9. Celts in literature. I. Title.
  PS261.C34 2005
  810.9'8916075—dc22
                                        2005013762

Printed in Canada

Published by Pelican Publishing Company, Inc.
1000 Burmaster Street, Gretna, Louisiana 70053

Contents

"Men can always be blind to a thing so long as it is big enough."
—G. K. Chesterton, "The Story of the Vow,"
The Superstition of Divorce

"At any given moment there is an orthodoxy, a body of ideas of which it is assumed that all right-thinking people will accept without question. It is not exactly forbidden to say this, that or the other, but it is "not done" to say it. . . . Anyone who challenges the prevailing orthodoxy finds himself silenced with surprising effectiveness. A genuinely unfashionable opinion is almost never given a fair hearing, either in the popular press or in the high-brow periodicals."
—George Orwell, 1945, Introduction to *Animal Farm*

"To see what is in front of one's nose needs a constant struggle."
—*The Collected Essays, Journalism and Letters of George Orwell: In Front of Your Nose, 1945-1950*

"A truth's initial commotion is directly proportional to how deeply the lie was believed. . . . When a well-packaged web of lies has been sold gradually to the masses over generations, the truth will seem utterly preposterous and its speaker a raving lunatic."   —Dresden James

Preface

The thesis that propelled me to undertake this study of Southern literature is that Celtic folkways and heritage formed a significant basis in the
development of white Southern culture and in certain parts of the South
became predominant. At the time I first began to consider that as a possibility I had read no contemporary theory of language, literature, and
culture, but I sensed the spirit of the age critically to be one moving
toward a recovery and an examination of the cultural heritages and
accomplishments of peoples other than those dozen or so, beginning with
the Sumerians and Egyptians, traditionally emphasized in Western
Civilization surveys (which virtually exclude at least half of the various
European ethnic and cultural groups). Years later I would find the
essence of the age's best intents summed up by David Harvey: "The idea
that all groups have a right to speak for themselves, in their own voice,
and have that voice accepted as authentic and legitimate is essential to
the pluralistic stance of postmodernism" (48).

But from the moment the idea of Celtic heritage as indispensably
defining to Southern culture occurred to me, many of those in the academy with whom I have discussed it have considered it either somehow
intrinsically unworthy of any consideration or as overly idiosyncratic.
This is rather odd considering the volume of recent literary scholarship
and classroom teaching extolling the literary and especially the socio-
moral merits of the likes of Anais Nin, James Baldwin, Armistead
Maupin, and bell hooks, and the now standard classroom teaching and
"mainstream" scholarship predicated principally upon validating postmodern obliquities or asserting absolute cultural relativity, except, of
course, when non-Western superiority is asserted. Eugene Genovese has
written of important works of scholarship ignored or refused the light of
day by university presses, "In decades past, it was books that disturbed

9

liberal complacency that were abused or made to disappear; in these days of the Culture War, it is books that rankle the complacency of the multicultural left" (Foreword 6).

As any claim that culturally Celtic peoples made a significant impact on the development of American cultures cannot be said to promote a Brahmin WASP exclusivity, I was rather shocked to discover that apparently all of those academics who styled themselves adherents of the stand eloquently stated by David Harvey were contemptuous of or downright hostile toward my desire to proceed with my project. While still completing my master's thesis the most revealing attack on my proposed subject was made by an all-but-dissertation graduate student specializing in twentieth-century British literature, and presumably expecting to teach at least Yeats and Joyce among Irish writers. She asked, sincerely, how I could be given foreign language credit for Irish, which she believed to be a mere uneducated, provincial dialect of the English language.

When I was working on my dissertation, another revealing attack also came from a fellow student. This one showed me a quote from Lord Acton, the widely respected nineteenth-century classical liberal:

> The Celts are not among the progressive, initiative races, but among those which supply the material rather than the impulse of history, and are either stationary or retrogressive . . . the Celts of these islands . . . waited for a foreign influence to set in action the rich treasures which in their own hands could be of no avail. . . .

If, the soon-to-be Ph.D. asked me, a widely acknowledged brilliant classical liberal such as Acton, who made security for minorities a key plank in his definition of a free society and who defended the secession of eleven Southern states and the formation of the Confederacy as morally and philosophically just as a legitimate attempt to stifle government tyranny, were so unabashedly dismissive of Celtic peoples, why would I waste my time researching Celtic heritage in the South? For these reasons, the dearth of knowledge about basic matters of Celtic heritage even among many of the post-graduate educated and the often automatic acceptance of the silliest negative stereotypes of Celtic peoples, again often among the more formally and prestigiously educated, I believe the reader of *Celtic Southern Literature* will be well served by knowing something of its genesis.

I began to develop the ideas as a Master of Arts student at the University of North Carolina, where I planned to specialize in the Irish Renaissance. My advisor suggested that I learn Gaeilge because the Irish language informs the use of English by Irish writers, and I also studied

Cymric, or Welsh. My Celtic language teacher required that in addition to grammar and syntax, I learn the folk cultures of the languages by reading anthropological, archaeological, historical, literary, and sociological scholarship.

At some point, this inundation of research on Celtic culture struck me as describing a society that in a number of key and interesting ways was similar to that of the South, most specifically to the rural and small town hill South. My knowledge of both branches of the Celtic language family, rudimentary though it was, allowed me to recognize that a large percentage of the surnames common to my native middle Tennessee from its original settling by peoples other than American Indians are Celtic in origin. In addition, I knew from histories of some longtime middle Tennessee residents (those with ancestries that date back to antebellum days) that at times surnames that appear to mark English families actually are the names of peoples who emigrated from Celtic lands. For example, I knew of one Smith family originally from Scotland and another Smith family originally from Ireland.

Fascinated by the possibility of some kind of deep-culture connection, I began to review literature from both Celtic lands and England in terms of compatibility to the South. I perhaps was most astonished and persuaded by finding that the Celtic sense of history was Southern, that Quentin Compson's thought *"Maybe nothing ever happens once and is finished"* and Gavin Stevens's assertion "The past is never dead. It's not even past" (Faulkner *Absalom, Absalom* 261; *Requiem for a Nun* 92) was Eugene O'Neill's Mary Tyrone's querying declaration, "The past is the present, isn't it? It's the future, too" (87).[1]

After reading accounts of Celts refusing to bow to ruthlessly skilled conquerors from Alexander the Great and his successors to Julius Caesar and his successors to England's Edward I, his grandson Edward III, and Oliver Cromwell, I had an answer to Faulkner's Isaac McCaslin's question concerning Southerners and the Confederate secession:

> Who else could have declared a war against a power with ten times the area and a hundred times the men and a thousand times the resources, except men who could believe that all necessary to conduct a successful war was not acumen nor shrewdness nor politics nor diplomacy nor money nor even integrity and simple arithmetic but just love of land and courage? (*Go Down, Moses* 288-89)

Celts from any era of history and any locale not only could have but would have under the same circumstances.

I concluded from my comparative reading that while medieval Celtic literature revealed family and social structures, an emphasis on man's relationship to nature, and an interest in women's often paradoxically powerful roles in an aristocratic warrior and hunting society similar to those of the South, old English literature revealed few, if any, such direct comparisons. Moreover, while the English fictive worlds of Samuel Richardson, Fanny Burney, Jane Austen, Virginia Woolf, and D. H. Lawrence appeared as alien to my Southern sensibilities as the works of German writers, the fictive worlds of Maria Edgeworth, Walter Scott, William Butler Yeats, and James Joyce all seemed comfortably familiar. The writings of Elizabeth Gaskell, Charles Dickens, William Thackery, and, to a lesser degree, George Eliot I found unlike those of Southern writers in their treatments of family, community, and history, but the works of the Brontë sisters, daughters of an Irish immigrant to England who spoke with Irish accents as children (Chitham 1), I found similar to Southern works.[2] These findings, these feelings of like and unlike or of similarity and dissimilarity, though based on considerable reading and running against the grain of the prejudices that had been indoctrinated into me by both formal schooling and the media, signify nothing by themselves; they are valuable only as starting points.

At the time, this "discovery" of cultural connections was being used primarily to help me understand Irish literature. I was in the early stages of plotting a thesis on the novels of Liam O'Flaherty, a study I planned to expand into a dissertation discussing the stories as well. In my naive desire that my linguistic skills would improve significantly, I hoped it would be the first book-length study of O'Flaherty to feature a chapter on *Dúil*, his lone Irish-language volume. But an accidental discovery pulled me into Southern literature. I helped finish cataloging the papers of the late Guy Owen in the Southern Historical Collection, and I decided to let O'Flaherty wait while I made use of these papers, which included unpublished fiction that I wanted to pursue. The primary setting of Owen's fiction, the tobacco and cotton country of southeastern North Carolina, is unique in the South in that it is an area near the Atlantic coast in which the original European settlement was preponderantly by the Scots-Irish and Scottish Highlanders, not Anglo-Normans and Anglo-Saxons, and Owen's stories kept drawing my attention back to the descendants of Celtic immigrants in the South and to Celtic folk culture surviving in the South.

As I was completing my thesis and armed with this sense of a cultural connection between Celtic lands and the South, I began exploring the possibilities for a study of Southern literature as influenced by literature from Celtic lands. I then stumbled upon the historical scholarship of Grady McWhiney and Forrest McDonald. Their thesis is that the descendants of the hundreds of thousands of immigrants from Celtic lands to the South in the seventeenth and eighteenth centuries were the primary determinants of white Southern folk culture. The Celtic-Southern thesis provided an important foundation, and I began a re-reading of Southern literature to determine the validity of the thesis in the realm of literary studies.

My research was considerably more fruitful than I imagined. Originally, I expected that my work would require chapters revealing the extensive intentional borrowing from Irish literature by Southern writers. I tentatively projected a chapter discussing the influence of Yeats's Abbey Theatre on the Carolina Playmakers, and from there to Thomas Wolfe, and another chapter on the allusions to Irish literature in the works of Eudora Welty. While informative, such scholarship merely reveals that Southern writers have learned and borrowed from great Irish literature as they have from great Greek, Roman, English, French, and German literatures. What is more important, it seems to me, is to find authors whose works acknowledge and reveal a deep-culture connection between the South and Celtic lands, or who use characters of Celtic ancestry to suggest thematically the South's strengths and weaknesses, origins and declines, senses of family and spirituality. And I have found them galore, to use a Southern colloquialism straight from Gaeilge.

Readers violently hostile to the possibility that Celtic folk culture could underpin a great Germanic language-family literature need only look to Iceland. While some scholars in America and England continue to teach medieval Icelandic literature as the essence of pristine Germanic culture,[3] scholars in Iceland know better:

> It has been long known that the Norsemen took Irish wives and slaves on their way to Iceland, but it is now thought possible *that as many as half of the early settlers may have been Christian Irish Celts* [my emphasis]. Some scholars attribute the flowering of Icelandic literature in the 12th to 14th centuries to this unique blending of cultures. "The Irish brought to Iceland their learning—of which the Scandinavians had nothing," said Halldor Laxness, Iceland's Nobel Prize-winning author. (Levanthes 202)

In her study of medieval Irish social structure, Nerys Patterson finds "close parallels that exist between early medieval Irish and Icelandic institutions," one of which was that the Icelandic evaluation of property for church tithes was the Irish pattern, not the Norwegian (15, 204). If Icelandic scholars and writers, including a Nobel laureate, can move beyond Teutonphilia (and readers should be aware that the word *Teuton* is Celtic in origin, related to the ancient Celtic *teuta*, Modern Irish *tuath*, meaning people or tribe) to recognize Celtic folkways and heritage, and the story-telling methods that derive from that folk culture, as indispensable to the development of Icelandic culture and its literature in its medieval Golden Age, and a Harvard sociologist can perceive the defining legacy of Irish Christian culture in Iceland, then surely scholars of the South and America, where immigration records mark conclusively the influx of hundreds of thousands of people native to Celtic lands whose ancestors numbered in the millions by the 1850s, likewise can reexamine their specialties to determine the extent of Celtic cultural influence on and survivals in these United States.

For many, perhaps most, readers the problem with this plea is that it never has been done. Recognizing Celtic heritage in the modern world, much less that it could be significant, lies outside the paradigms operative in today's education establishment; the few chance recognitions are tabbed as anomalies and forgotten. We have been trained to accept without any question the centrality of the Anglo-Saxon, Puritan, New England cultural experience to all subsequent American literature, or at least to all works written in English and especially by white authors. And the recent emphasis on minority cultural contributions to the American experience has sensitized us to the once widely neglected heritage of non-white peoples. As a result, we now generally accept as valid any non-white cultural readings of American literature, whether the work in question was written by a white or a non-white author.

Celtic peoples and their cultural contributions and assessments, however, have not been included in the academy's gadarene rush to endorse and then to declare dogmatic American multi-racial multiculturalism. There is a modicum of scholarship on the Irish American experience, but it has not been translated into any significant number of college courses and inside-the-Pale status.[4] Furthermore, a considerable percentage of the scholarship on Irish American culture is rife with regional and religious exclusions, which may reveal deep-seated bigotries. Charles Fanning's focus in *The Irish in America*, the seminal study of Irish American fiction, is on the northern, urban, Catholic experience, which largely neglects the Irish in the South, Irish Protestants, and non-denominational Christians of Irish heritage. The only unequivocally Southern novel that Fanning treats is John Kennedy Toole's *Confederacy of*

Dunces, which he dismisses as a work in which "the dialogue is hilarious but hollow" (344). Fanning apparently is incapable of seeing, or unwilling to see, Irish American experiences as being much greater than the stereotype of Irish Catholic immigrants huddled in tenements in northern urban centers and making it in America through northern big city politics and higher education. Through his inclusions and exclusions, Fanning all but dismisses an Irish American reading of the works of Southern writers. In his article on Irish American fiction in *The Irish in America,* the companion book to the PBS documentary, Eamonn Wall does not mention a single work by a Southern writer or a writer whose religious background is other than Catholic, thereby validating the prejudices for a mass audience.

"The fact that it remains easy to think of a reading that most of us would dismiss out of hand," Stanley Fish says, "does not mean that the text excludes it but that there is as yet no elaborated interpretive procedure for producing that text" (345). Using an inventive hypothetical case to assert his point, Fish declares that there could be an "Eskimo" reading of "A Rose for Emily" if someone were to discover "a letter in which Faulkner confides that he has always believed himself to be an Eskimo changeling" (346). Outside the rarefied, hermetic, self-reflective walls of postmodern academia, few of us would accept as valid, certainly fully so and particularly valid beyond the work itself, a cultural reading based upon an author's mystical or drug-induced imaginings, but, considering the emphasis now widely placed on non-white ethnic heritage as virtually an interpretive procedure itself, I believe that a knowledge of the significant emigration from Celtic lands to the South in its culturally formative period and of the Celtic ancestry of many influential white Southern writers should persuade readers that certain works of Southern literature can be, and perhaps need to be, read in terms of Celtic heritage.

Continental Europeans are leading the current drive to recover and understand Celtic heritage. The most impressive recent display of the paramount significance of Celtic culture to the development of European cultures, ancient and modern, was the 1991 Venice exhibition titled "The Celts, the Origins of Europe." The President of Palazzo Grassi's "introduction to the exhibition catalogue *The Celts*" asserts, in something of an overstatement if for no other reason than the omission of the Greeks, that Celtic heritage is one of the three principal defining contributors to Europe.

> This exhibition is a tribute both to the new Europe which cannot come into fruition without a comprehensive awareness of its unity, and

to the fact that, in addition to its Roman and Christian sources, today's Europe traces its roots from the Celtic heritage, which is there for all to see. (Cunliffe 19)

North America may be lagging behind Europe in this long overdue recognition, but commentators on and analysts of what is usually labeled popular culture are beginning to perceive the distinctive importance of Celtic heritage to America, especially the South. Paddy Moloney, world-renowned musician and authority on Irish folk music, writes in the notes for the Chieftains' 1992 Grammy-winning album *Another Country,* "The concept of recording a Country music album has been on my mind for several years; in fact, 30 years ago I presented a radio series based on the influence of Irish music to Country music." In his notes to the 1998 BMG soundtrack of the PBS documentary *Long Journey Home: The Irish in America,* Moloney reveals that the classic country-and-western tune "The Streets of Laredo" is actually the Irish tune "The Bard of Armagh."[5] "This song," Moloney writes, "is a perfect example of the music that the immigrants brought with them and which eventually became an important part of American culture." Eminent country music critic and historian Robert K. Oermann writes in the liner notes to the Chieftains' 2002 RCA Victor compact disc *Down the Old Plank Road,* "When I lived in rural Ireland, I was impressed with how musical every-day life was and how 'Country' the music seemed. . . . This album 'connects the dots' between our cultures [Ireland and the South] by digging for the shared roots of an Irish shamrock and a Tennessee mountain laurel." In a review of the impact of Mel Gibson's Oscar-winning film *Braveheart,* Richard Grenier says of the eighteenth century, "A massive immigration of mostly Scots and Scots-Irish brought the Celtic heritage [Grenier, unlike most scholars and journalists, does not simplistically confuse English rule and language use with English folkways and heritage] and its flamboyant military tradition to America, particularly the South" (69).

This study is intended for two audiences. First, I hope that scholars and teachers of American studies will read it and, if they have not previously, acknowledge in their course offerings and anthologies and other textbooks the importance of Celtic heritage to the cultures of these United States, particularly the South. Second, knowing that the academy is often slow to, I present this study to the general reader interested in either the South or Celtic heritage. I first became certain there was an audience outside the walls of the ivory tower for such scholarship when

I spoke to an Elder Hostel group. I emphasized to these senior citizens the basic cultural positions detailed in this study. Afterwards, two Catholic Irish American women, one a native of Boston and the other of Chicago, talked with me at some length, each saying that after living for years in the South she had come to believe there was some kind of cultural tie or similarity between Ireland and the South and now saw how the sense of relation could be valid though the South had never been filled with Irish Catholics. Hopefully this book will help readers see the importance of Celtic heritage to the South; the academy may follow with course offerings when it has been shown the path by general, educated readers.[6]

At this point I think I should make it clear what this book is not. I believe that it falls into neither of Barry Cunliffe's division of two groups discussing Celtic studies in Europe, both of which he feels "contain some threads of value but in their extremity . . . are sterile" (19). Though like Cunliffe I recognize that the term *Celt* is laden with centuries of stereotyping, both that of Matthew Arnold presenting Celts as childlike players in nature and that of Rudyard Kipling presenting Celts as violently simpleminded (the pair forming the two-sided English coin of anti-Celtic bias that is seen as the justification for Anglo-Saxon Empire conquering and ruling Celts), I do not believe it to be so tainted as to be unusable, nor is my work part of what Cunliffe labels the "New Celtomania" because it does not see Celtic heritage as some kind of soothing umbrella under which Europeans might unite. Stereotypes, regardless of duration and unfounded viciousness, neither destroy nor invalidate a cultural heritage, and two things that study of Celts will show are their fierce resistance to being amalgamated and homogenized and their uniqueness, both positive and negative.

Furthermore, this book is not a Celtophilic version of the Afrocentric writings that claim the ancient Egyptians were black and sailed across the Atlantic and built the step pyramids in what is now Mexico and Guatemala and thereby were the cultural origin of the glories of Central American native civilizations. It should be noted, however, that the Afrocentrists seem happily willing to allow us to believe that the mass human sacrifices and cannibalism in pre-conquest Meso-America were autochthonous. This work is not one of attempted academic usufruct defended on the ground of helping a people long discriminated against feel good about its history. Nor do I suggest that all American literature, even all of Southern literature, must be read in terms of Celtic heritage. That would be as foolish and simpleminded as claiming that all of the American literary heritage can be understood by studying the New England Puritan heritage and applying it to all works of American literature or that virtually all of American literature can be understood through the prism of racism or sexism. What this work does is ask readers to move beyond the simplistic notion of black and (or versus) white in Southern studies and recognize the obvious: Ireland and Scotland are no more England than Poland and Lithuania are Prussia, and all white peoples are far from the same in folkways and cultural attitudes. And where there is difference there will be conflict and comparison; there will be literary examination. Eugene Genovese has written that opposition to black studies often proceeds from a desire "to assimilate that experience to the experiences of European, Asian, and Latin American immigrants and thereby to deny its claims to being unique" (*Southern Front* 222). Opposition to academic acknowledgment of Celtic peoples as being both non-Anglo-Saxon in cultural heritage and significant contributors to the American experience proceeds from the same basis and is equally false.

Thomas Sowell has asserted, "Some books are written for the pleasure or the zest of it. Other books are written as a painful duty, because there is something that needs to be said—and because other people have better sense than to say it" (Pappas 21). This book has been written because its principle assertions need to be heard and others who might have written it more persuasively or entertainingly have chosen the easy, safe path of not offending the current academy prejudices, which are grounded far more in political assumptions than in intellectual rigorousness. Such could be the source of the needed paradigm shift that will include Celtic heritage, especially that of the South, in American education.

Dario Fernandez-Morera, accepting the assessment of Jacob Neusner that the academy is run according to the spirit of the medieval guild with its built-in protections against truly free competition, notes how peer review can be used to "prevent the success or even the admission of anyone holding political ideas and moral values different from those officially or unofficially supported by the guild" (175).[7] Two decades earlier, Alexander Solzhenitsyn had observed the same phenomenon. Though the West lacked official government censorship, Solzhenitsyn recognized,

> fashionable trends of thought and ideas are fastidiously separated from those that are not fashionable, and the latter, without ever being forbidden, have little chance of finding their way into periodicals or books or being heard in college. Your scholars are free in the legal sense, but they are hemmed in by the idols of the prevailing fad. . . . This gives birth to strong mass prejudices, to a blindness which is perilous in our dynamic era. (54-55)[8]

Introduction

How Celtic Culture Invented Southern Literature in its first drafts was titled *The Matrix and the Nexus: Celtic Heritage in Southern Literature.* It struck me while reading that William Gilmore Simms had sensed that somehow the birth of Southern culture and its connecting tissue were both Celtic, and thus I had an unwieldy title. *How Celtic Culture Invented Southern Literature* opens with a review of what historians have said about culturally Celtic peoples and their descendants in the South and then features a reading of the thematic use of Celts and their progeny in the works of Southern novelists from the prolific antebellum Charlestonian William Gilmore Simms to the current best-selling writer Pat Conroy and Simms-scholar-become-novelist James Everett Kibler and beyond. What I have found is that from the beginnings of a consciously Southern literature (one that saw itself as representing something other and more than just a regional variant of English language literature) until today, Southern novelists have recognized the indispensable contribution of Celtic immigrants and their descendants to the development, expansion, and perpetuation of Southern culture. Melvin Backman believes that you need only "scratch the veneer of the aristocrat of the Deep South and you would find a frontiersman" (94). The works of these novelists suggest that more often than not, certainly in the upper hill South from the eastern flank of Appalachia through the Ozarks and down into east Texas, but also in the non-coastal Deep South, that frontiersman was of Celtic ancestry.

Will Campbell, a Mississippi born author and National Council of Churches race relations worker during the Civil Rights movement of the 1950s and 1960s, reveals in an essay that in his Mount Juliet, Tennessee, home he keeps "an original Allen and Hatley" political cartoon on the wall. It shows two men: One is black and one is white. The black man says to the white, "Here's why I worry about liberals, Lester.

What do you call a poor person from Puerto Rico?"

"A Hispanic-surnamed American."

"How about an illiterate Sioux?"

"A disadvantaged Native American, of course."

"And a dirt farmer of Scots-Irish ancestry?"

"A redneck, naturally" (92).

This prejudice against the mass of white Southerners, the "naturally" affixing pejoratives and assuming of negative traits that Campbell finds endemic throughout these United States, perhaps especially in academia and journalism,[1] may well explain the primary reason that most scholars have ignored the importance of Celtic immigrants and their descendants to Southern culture. Quite simply, to emphasize the Celtic heritage is, to the national psyche, or at least to that privileged part of it that controls formal education and publishing, "naturally" to proclaim *redneck* status, which Campbell sees as being equated by most Americans with violent racism against non-whites. Eugene Genovese says of the costs of the past thirty years of "modernization" in the South, "That price includes a neglect of, or contempt for, the history of southern whites, without which some of the more distinct and noble features of American national life must remain incomprehensible" (*Southern Tradition* xi).

That contempt is far from restricted to unending jokes, pronouncements of Southern inferiority and inherent moral turpitude, and curtailing the teaching of Southern literature and history save by those who use academic pulpits to castigate Southerners and Southern culture. Vanderbilt University professor Jonathan Farley, black and the child of two immigrants, declares in a November 20, 2002 *Nashville Tennessean* editorial, "Every Confederate soldier, by the mores of his age and ours, deserved not a hallowed resting place at the end of his days but a reservation at the end of the gallows." Farley makes certain that no reader could harbor doubts as to his genocidal meaning: "Indeed, the race problems that wrack America to this day are due largely to the fact that the Confederacy was not thoroughly destroyed, its leaders and soldiers executed and their lands given to the landless freed slaves."

Considering that some 1.5 million men served the Confederacy and its state and local governments, in the military or in civil government, Farley's pronouncement, which was defended by masses of academics and journalists, is a clear indication that political correctness is erected upon a Holocaust-level hatred of Southerners and Southern culture. Southerners are the principal Kulaks and Christian Monarchists to America's cultural Marxists and their liberal fellow-travelers, fit only for eternal poverty, incessant apologizing for all the sins of the world, life in the Gulag, or the hangman's noose, all of it done to combat "evil" and save the world through "freedom" and "tolerance" and "diversity."

Thomas Sowell has written of the modern leftist prepossession to see evil as belonging to and/or caused by groups (upper and middle classes, Caucasians, Christians, cultural and moral and fiscal conservatives, etc.) rather than to accept ancient wisdom that evil is something to which all men are susceptible, "This localization of evil is one of the hallmarks of the unconstrained vision. There must [modern leftists believe] clearly be some cause for evils, but insofar as these causes are not so widely diffused as to be part of human nature in general, then those in whom the evils are localized can be removed, opposed, or neutralized, so as to produce a solution" (*Conflict* 155). This localization of evil leads the self-righteously reform-minded to take up weapons to destroy the humans who carry the evil, thereby saving all other humans from the workings of evil. In that, Jonathan Farley is at moral, philosophical one with French Revolutionaries and War Between the States and Reconstruction Republicans.

In listing reasons why he believes Southern culture not only has survived to the final decade of the twentieth century but will continue to thrive, Dennis Covington, himself a novelist, journalist, and creative writing professor, says, "I'm talking about the scorn and ridicule the nation has heaped on poor Southern whites, the only ethnic group in America not permitted to have a history" (xiv). Covington's assertion becomes especially interesting in light of the facts that the Oxford English Dictionary declares the term *red-neck* to date from the seventeenth-century English-Scottish border country as a slur on those dissenting against the State Church, the Anglican Episcopal Church, all were forced to subsidize through taxes. *Redneck* was first recorded in American print in 1830-31 when Anne Royall used it to disparage non-wealthy Carolina Piedmont Presbyterians (Bultman 12). In addition, Eric Partridge has found that *redneck* has been used in England to label Catholics disparagingly (692). In short, historically the slur *redneck* is one usually tossed against non-wealthy white people opposing government activism they see as being against them and in favor of other ethnic and religious groups, and the term is one that became closely tied to a particular ethnic group: American peoples of Scottish and Irish ancestry, most particularly those who are Southern and are not Episcopalian.

The slur *redneck* even has been brought back to America in recent decades by at least one Englishman. In his biography of Alexander Solzhenitsyn, award-winning poet, novelist, and translator of Russian literature, D. M. Thomas castigates the Ford administration for refusing to greet officially the exiled author on his first visit to the United States and reveals that Simon Winchester of the "politically correct," leftist English *Guardian* had praised Ford for his decision to slight the "darling of the redneck population" (433). As Thomas points out, the "sensitive" periodical would not have printed, much less approved of, such a bigoted slur against other ethnic groups, but the alleged *redneck* section of the American populace was fair game for any slur by the Western cultural left that was then discovering that Solzhenitsyn's views on local democracy, free enterprise, family, traditional values, and Christianity were almost as antithetical to their preconceptions and procrustean machinations as they were to Soviet Marxism.

Documentary filmmaker and journalist Bethany Bultman, an unapologetic card-carrying member of the ACLU, faced the reality of widespread prejudices against the ethnic/class rednecks as a result of her time assigned to cover David Duke's campaign for governor of Louisiana. She discovered at the Duke rallies not the overt, militant, racist hatred she expected but what she describes as a generally polite working-class people wearing the term *redneck* (which was the standard condemnation of Duke and his supporters) with something akin to ethnic pride. These so-called racists were focused principally on working-class issues, particularly those that gave government-decreed advantages over them to members of other groups in education admission and scholarships and in job hiring and promotions. The feel of the rallies, which were bereft of the labeling of the "other" race as a criminal, evil race that are a staple of certain "Civil Rights" meetings, was summed up for Bultman in one quote from an elderly woman: "I've been waitin' a long time for God to send us rednecks hope of gettin' our freedom and dignity back." The freedom and dignity desired by the woman are from the slurs on being white Southerners, particularly the non-genteel whose ancestries include neither English Coats of Arms nor plantation ownership. Bultman reveals, "This simple expression of vulnerability so devoid of hate and so filled with hope was not what I expected" (5). She had begun her investigation certain these people were what she labeled both ignorant and racist and "determined" to confront their biases; "ironically, I had to confront my own" (4-5). "I was," Bultman confesses, "one of those Southern liberals who go ballistic at the 'n' word yet had no qualms about dishing out the term 'redneck' as a synonym for dumber-than-spit hair-trigger racists" (1).

In his account of his travels through the worlds of Civil War-battle re-enactors and defenders of Southern heritage, Pulitzer prize-winning journalist Tony Horwitz presents an example of why the elderly woman described by Bultman, and Bultman's own self-castigation at her race-based double standards, cannot be dismissed as paranoid or even prone to exaggeration. In Selma, Alabama, Horwitz visits an all-black "alternative school" founded and run by "Harvard educated lawyers" Hank and Rose Sanders. Rose Sanders explains part of the school's mission to Horwitz by saying, "The whites make heroes of killers like [Confederate general Nathan Bedford] Forrest and because of our own ignorance or internalized oppression, we let it happen," and then she declares that her students "were currently studying African empires," leaving readers to wonder if she and her students had come to believe erroneously that empires on the African continent, whether Egyptian and Carthaginian or the much later sub-Saharan, black empires of Ghana and Mali, were built without soldiers who killed and without slaves (364). When Horwitz speaks to Rose's students about his project, one named Jamal asks the title of the book in progress. The student "went to the blackboard and wrote in large block letters, REDNECKS OF THE SOUTH. The others laughed and started shouting their own suggestions. 'Crackers of the South.' 'Bigots!' 'Peckerwoods'" (367). The Harvard-trained, black civil rights worker never calls attention to, much less chastises, the racist slurring and stereotyping of her charges and then after the students have exited, launches into "a tirade against white civil rights workers, black 'sellouts' like Julian Bond, and 'Jews who knock down men like Farrakhan'" (369).[2]

Most pertinent to this study is that Bultman, after prompting by Gonzo journalist and native Southerner Hunter S. Thompson, concludes that *redneck* culture, which she recognizes as including world-renowned writers and performing artists as well as business millionaires, scholars, and presidents (Truman she labels a "Good Ole Boy Redneck" and Jefferson a "Sir Bubba Redneck", and had she continued the fun she could have labeled Carter a "Bleeding-Heart Saint Redneck" and Clinton a "Satyr Redneck"), is an American derivative of Celtic folkways. "Hunter's insights," she writes, "led me to reexamine my own WASP gene pool. My ancestors were from Scotland and Wales, not Anglo-Saxon at all" (23).

Bultman's journalistic foray into this culture concludes with two interesting observations. First, "in many ways," she writes, "rednecks are the last examples of the independent spirit of our founding fathers, with their live-free-or-die philosophy" that she recognizes as at least partly Irish and British Celtic opposition to English style government centralization, as traditional Celtic governmental localism (276, 289). Second, in keeping with her liberalism but having overcome standard American liberal biases against non-genteel white Southerners, Bultman, who acknowledges the long and still extant history of racist slurs, and resulting discriminations in education and employment, against the people she labels *rednecks,* concludes this group should be added to those already receiving affirmative action preferences (277).[3]

Campbell, who bears a Scottish Highland surname, suggests, "there is a real sense in which the redneck has been victimized one step beyond the black." Throughout slavery and Jim Crow segregation, blacks, primarily because of skin pigmentation that forced them to acknowledge their differences, were able to keep "their *head*" but "the job on the redneck was more extensive because he had his *head* taken away. He has been so thoroughly manipulated and deceived that he still hasn't identified his 'Enemy'" (94), and, perhaps consequently, is not certain who he is.[4] Journalist and professor Roy Reed presents the comic twist on this fuzziness of identity in the essay collection *Looking for Hogeye.* After declaring, "my guess is that most of Arkansas's English are not English at all but transmogrified Scotch-Irish," Reed proffers his reasons for this often willful denial of heritage: "snobbery," because in English-speaking lands the English tend to be thought of as genteel and highly cultured and peaceful (even when slaughtering multitudes to expand or maintain their empire) while the Irish are portrayed widely to be drunken and/or mindlessly violent and/or ignorant, and a desire to avoid being linked to contemporary Ulster Protestants. "Who," Reed asks, "wants anything to do with a people whose most inspiring contemporary leader is the Rev. Ian Paisley?" (111).[5]

As Reed's question suggests, the continuing, though now abating, problems in Northern Ireland may define for many people Irish culture and heritage and therefore Celtic culture and heritage. That, of course, is possible only if journalists and professors foster or condone such bigotry. As a prelude to his evaluation of the cultural contributions of the first centuries of Irish Christianity to the rest of Western Europe, Thomas Cahill declares:

> Our history, the history we read in school and refer to in later life, was largely written by Protestant Englishmen and Anglo-Saxon Protestant Americans. Just as certain contemporary historians have been discovering that such redactors are not always reliable when it comes to the contributions of say, women or African Americans, we should not be surprised to find that such storytellers have overlooked a tremendous contribution in the distant past that was both Celtic and Catholic, a contribution without which European civilization would not have been impossible. (5)

I have said that the collective prejudices against the mass of Scots-Irish Southerners serve as the primary reason scholars have been reluctant to emphasize Celtic heritage in the South. A secondary reason is that many scholars prejudicially equate any discussion of Celtic culture and heritage with outlandish forgeries and folk festivals and displays that falsify history, perhaps by compressing time periods and, in the cases of Celtic lands, for nationalist, anti-imperial reasons. Barry Cunliffe, professor of European archaeology at the University of Oxford, acknowledges the Romantic era fabrications of Iolo Morganwy but declares that such "should not detract from the more serious work" of studying ancient Celtic culture (15), that New Age mystics and charlatans, listening to synthesizer music dubbed Celtic and reciting spells they call pagan Celtic, should no more prejudice people against the reality of Celtic heritage and identity than the myriad of black scam artists claiming to be representatives of the ancient African religions should convince people that there are no real black African cultures to study. Nor should anyone assume that Cunliffe, perhaps the foremost authority of our decade on ancient Celtic culture, means to restrict all "serious" study of Celtic heritage to the ancient world. He concludes his most recent book by reviewing the stereotypes of Celts created by Classical writers and declares of Celts, "their diversity in social and cultural terms is beyond dispute. . . . The 'Celt' is a powerful and emotive image which pervades our [European] culture, and it is entirely proper that we should spend time attempting to understand it" (274).

Another secondary reason for the dearth of American scholarly interest in Celtic heritage is the assumption, comforting to both socialist internationalists and imperialists at heart, that a long conquered and politically dependent people could not maintain a separate folk culture to transplant elsewhere, an assumption that many continue to hold in regard to the Irish and other Celts even as they drop it in regard to peoples of non-European heritage. Commenting on his having quoted Edmund Campion, English Jesuit and martyr-to-be, describing the characteristics general among the Irish, traits far from exclusively positive (as one would expect from an Englishman), Thomas Cahill says:

> We can still make out in this Elizabethan group portrait not only the Irish of our own day but the lively ghosts of Irishmen long past. . . . Whether or not Freud was right when he muttered in exasperation that the Irish were the only people who could not be helped by psychoanalysis, there can be no doubt of one thing: the Irish will never change. (150)[6]

Just as most scholars until recently have ignored Irish contributions to European culture and scholars interested in Southern culture have ignored Celtic contributions because the American popular thought, if not the education system, equates the South's Celtic heritage with "redneck behavior," many Southerners of Celtic ancestry also have been loath to proclaim their heritage. Rather than be labeled redneck, ignorantly prejudiced Scots-Irish Southerners, many white Southerners of Celtic ancestry, like Pat Conroy's Lillian Meecham in *The Great Santini,* ignore their actual family histories and attempt to create a genteel Anglo-Norman legacy that society deems socially preferable.

Southern novelists, however, always have recognized the indispensable role of Celtic immigrants and their descendants to the development of Southern culture. William Gilmore Simms, the son of an Irish immigrant, began his career focusing primarily on the Anglo-Norman gentry of the South Carolina low country, but as his politics turned toward Southern nationalism his works began to explore the importance of Celtic immigrants to early South Carolina, culminating in *Paddy McGann,* an allegory in which the Southern cultural prototype is an Irish immigrant. Simms's two chief rivals as premier Southern novelist of the antebellum era, John Pendleton Kennedy and William Alexander Caruthers, also were both Scots-Irish Southerners.[7]

Ellen Glasgow's novels reveal a shift similar in cultural emphasis to those of Simms. Louis Rubin writes of *The Battle Ground* (1902), Glasgow's Civil War novel, "Miss Glasgow was impressed by her boldness in daring to make a Southern mountaineer [the Scots-Irish-dominated majority area of Virginia], who did not own slaves or landed estates, one of her Confederate soldiers. Actually, however, Pine Top, her 'common man,' is treated with much condescension by Miss Glasgow, who sees him entirely through aristocratic eyes" ("Image" 58). When Glasgow saw her Virginia exclusively through the eyes of the eastern Virginia, Anglo-Norman Cavalier legacy of her mother, her work was "conventional." As she began to recognize and explore the importance of the Scotch-Irish "vein of iron," Glasgow's novels, including those like *The Sheltered Life* (1932) and *The Romantic Comedians* (1926) that concern the Richmond social elite, became richer and more complex.

Unlike Glasgow, William Faulkner emphasized the importance of Celtic immigrants to his South from the beginning of his career. Each of his three great tragic families—Compson, McCaslin, and Sutpen—is of Scottish Highland ancestry. Caroline Gordon's tragic Southern family, Llewellyn, is Welsh, and her fictional vision of the opening of the trans-Appalachian South is of Celtic immigrants paving the way, which would lead inevitably to the founding of great antebellum Southern houses such as Penhally. Stark Young's McGehees, Allen Tate's Buchans, and Andrew Lytle's McIvors are all of Scottish heritage. Margaret Mitchell's heroine, who is the best-known and loved character from Southern literature, is the daughter of an Irish immigrant, and Mitchell makes Tara, the symbolic center of Irish culture, essential to Scarlett's well-being. Flannery O'Connor, perhaps the pre-eminent devoutly Christian writer America has yet produced, suggests the Irish cultural origins of fervent Southern Christian belief and practice. Pat Conroy, one of America's most popular contemporary novelists, emphasizes the Southerner of Irish heritage, the white Southerner outside the small, privileged, wealthy Anglo-Norman Pale, as a moral arbiter in the contemporary South. Finally, James Kibler, a scholar of Southern literature with particular interest and expertise in antebellum writers, marks the growing awareness of the truth of the Celtic-Southern thesis: Kibler's creative writings have moved from lyric poetry to fiction emphasizing Celtic, especially Irish, heritage and culture as central to the South in both its formative period and its quest to survive.

Like many of their main characters, each of these novelists is a descendant of immigrants from Celtic lands, and they are far from the only influential Southern writers and thinkers who possess a Celtic heritage. Lewis Leary declares that the political leaders of Revolutionary era Virginia "supplied a literature of power that insures them a place in the history of American thought" (68). Contrary to the prejudices of H. L. Mencken and others, even the intellectual achievements of eighteenth-century Virginia were not exclusively Anglo-Norman. The foremost Virginian of the period, Thomas Jefferson, writes of his heritage, "the tradition in my father's family was that their ancestor came to this country from Wales, and from near the mountain of Snowdon . . . " (3), and Arthur Link reveals that at least occasionally Jefferson referred to himself as Scotch-Irish (19). His biographer writes of Patrick Henry, the most inspiring orator of his day and one of Jefferson's political rivals, "from John Henry and his other Scottish forebears Patrick derived an intellectual and moral heritage no less important because little known" (Meade I 7). Most scholars of the South may have ignored the Celtic heritage of the mass of white Southerners, but Southern novelists, writing a folklore-based belletristic literature, always have seen Celtic immigrants and their descendants as prototypic or thematically indispensable Southerners.

And the awareness of the centrality of Celtic heritage to the South will continue in Southern literature. Charles Frazier, in his 1997 National Book Award-winning novel *Cold Mountain,* presents a Charleston, South Carolina (a place "kinless" in comparison to the Smokies, Ada comes to feel), born and raised preacher influenced by Ralph Waldo Emerson who moves with his daughter to the Smokies after he is diagnosed with tuberculosis. "All of their Charleston friends," Monroe's daughter Ada recalls, "had expressed the opinion that the mountain region was a heathenish part of creation, outlandish in its many affronts to sensibility, a place of wilderness and gloom and rain where man, woman, and child grew gaunt and brutal, addicted to acts of raw violence with not even a nod in the direction of self-restraint" (42). The reader sees the insanity of this centuries-old series of prejudices, born of ethnic differences and English wars to conquer Celtic lands, through Inman's attempts to flee from the horrific carnage of the War Between the States, the Southern genesis of which Inman is aware was driven not by mountain people but by the "genteel" low country, Anglo-Norman Southerners whose stereotypes of hill Southerners were at least as negative as those they held concerning their own black slaves. Frazier also guarantees that the observant reader will understand that the low country assumptions of hill country inferiority are ethnically based. Monroe, on a "quest for ignorance" that his prejudices declare he must find and then forcibly remove (and the influence of Emerson upon a native of the South is telling here), concludes there is not the slightest evidence of Christian knowledge among the mountain people. Their folkways he does recognize—as both barbaric and Celtic. "Esco," one of the wealthier farmers in the area, "was some old relic Celt was what Monroe concluded; what few thoughts Esco might have would more likely be in Gaelic" (44). Esco, offended by Monroe's ignorant prejudices, has led him on a snipe hunt, pretending never to have heard of the Christian story and finding it an outrageous tale, the low country Anglo-Norman gentleman becoming increasingly excited at his finding his preconceived notions verified and at the civilizing work before him. After Monroe's death, Ada would not have been able to survive except that Sally Swanger, Esco's wife, sends the girl Ruby to help her. Ruby, though the poorest of the poor, refuses anything but a level of equality with Ada, teaching her rather than serving her as a maid-farmer. Before long, the illiterate Ruby's vast knowledge of the world around her, knowledge not merely of how to grow food but to live, amazes Ada. Like Esco, and presumably Sally, Ruby, who is necessary for Ada's survival and her education beyond ladylike piano playing and sketching, is of Celtic heritage (270). The lesson seems unavoidable: Knowledgeable

Southerners of Celtic heritage are necessary to the very survival of "genteel" Anglo-Norman Southerners.

On the more popular side of contemporary Southern literature we have the trilogy of Hannibal Lecter novels by Thomas Harris. With boundaries of Baltimore, small farm towns just north of the Ohio River, and St. Louis, Harris's fictive world is the frontier of the South beset by human-hunting monsters, spawns of the modern world so numbed by mindless violence that it accepts serial killers as almost normal and certainly as nothing new or particularly shocking. Harris's protagonist in the latter two novels is West Virginia native Clarice Starling. *Hannibal* (1999) opens with Starling surviving a gunfight with a female drug lord and being attacked in the press as a racist cop. Harris presents her sitting alone, attempting to organize her thoughts, knowing, "for what she needed now, she must consult her blood" (27). But there is a problem:

> What do you have when you come from a poor-white background? And from a place where Reconstruction didn't end until the 1950s. If you came from people referred to on campuses as crackers and rednecks, or condescendingly, as blue-collar or poor-white Appalachian. If even the uncertain gentility of the South, who accord physical work no dignity at all, refer to your people as peckerwoods—in what tradition do you find an example?

Doug Marlette, who is best known as a political cartoonist and the creator of the cartoon strip *Kudzu,* has entered the world of Southern novel writing with *The Bridge.* Narrator Pick Cantrell, fired from his New York City job as newspaper cartoonist for being a typical non-genteel Southerner who tells the truth and holds his ground no matter how many rich and powerful people wish to silence him, describes the central North Carolina house he has purchased:

> An exquisite product of the Federal period in the Colonial style, it stood proud but practical, dignified, yet unpretentious. The restraint and modesty of the Scots-Presbyterians, who settled here in the rolling-wooded terrain of the Piedmont, which reminded them of their beloved homeland, was evident in the understated elegance of all its lines and details. (72)

Though Marlette does not explore it, his work notes the ethnic connection between the Celtic part of Southern culture and the standard contempt for Southern culture and Southerners by other Americans. In chapter one, Marlette presents a TV producer at a fancy New York City dinner party who declares, "southerners just sound so . . . ignorant. I just can't take anything they say seriously. I'm a Democrat, of course, but I must say I could barely bring myself to vote for Jimmy Carter because of that accent of his" (17). Pick Cantrell (whose first name is a perfect description of his work: He picks or mines for the truth) has for a publisher a midwesterner, a "bona fide WASP" who "didn't like my accent." This fine, respectable, tolerant, and predictably liberal Yankee journalist calls Cantrell a "cracker," and the narrator presents one of the best recent fictional summations of the ethnic/cultural/regional hatred that best defines American politically correct multicultural prejudices:

> In our age of political correctness, of mandatory sensitivity, of well-scrubbed and well-policed public discourse, especially in the sanctimonious Northeast, I had noticed that for some reason Yankees like Garvis still freely and without inhibition used insulting epithets for white southerners like myself. Words like *cracker* and *redneck* flowed contemptuously from their lips with an impunity I found appalling, given the tenor of the times and the poverty, powerlessness, and marginalization of my people (28).

Clarice Starling and Pick Cantrell are descendants of the Escos and Rubys, and their abilities and character mean nothing to those who find in the non-Norman, non-genteel white South the perfect scapegoat: The usually non-wealthy Kulaks for the American Left to rail against and assault in the names of tolerance, diversity, and respect for *other cultures*. Esco, Ruby, Clarice, and Pick are good people who are fully knowledgeable about their worlds, and they are the recipients of unrelenting negative prejudices held by those who descry certain other bigotries. We readers see that; likewise, we must recognize the due granted by other Southern novelists to the indispensable significance of Celtic heritage to Southern culture.

HOW
CELTIC CULTURE
INVENTED SOUTHERN
LITERATURE

Chapter I

Celts in the South

According to the standard twentieth-century historical scholarship on the South, white Southerners are culturally, and perhaps genetically, the most pure Anglo-Saxons outside of East Anglia and Kent. This is not to say that scholars of the South fail to recognize the importance of Amer-Indian peoples and those of sub-Saharan African ancestry, as well as new geographies and technologies, in augmenting and altering European cultural attitudes and perhaps patterns in the South. Rather, these scholars, many of whom, certainly over the past three decades, have searched diligently for reasons to assert that increasing amounts of Southern culture are anything but European in origin, have perceived or acknowledged virtually no significant European contributions to the development of Southern culture except by peoples they label Anglo-Saxon, Anglo-Norman, English, or occasionally British.[1] Grady McWhiney provides the most thorough synopsis of this long unquestioned belief:

> How, one might ask, could emphasizing English influence on the South be a mistake when "everyone knows" that the vast majority of southern whites are and always have been of Anglo-Saxon origins; when a distinguished southern historian can insist that the "English influence [on the South] was powerful"; or when another can state that "the South *is* the habitat of the quintessential WASP" and call it "the biggest single WASP nest this side of the Atlantic"? . . . "They were mostly transplanted Englishmen with a scattering of continental Europeans," writes one author. . . . A different writer claims that both the North and the South "were peopled by Englishmen," and two others emphasize "the gap between Anglo-Saxon and African in the South." (*Cracker Culture* 2)

The attitude that McWhiney highlights with "everyone knows," which waves off any need to answer objections, is common to American scholarship on the South, and it is analogous to one operating in past decades that said "everyone knows" the English determined all of American culture, certainly all of it that matters, and "minority" groups, "ethnic" whites as well as non-whites, made precious few, if any, contributions.

The scholars to whom McWhiney refers, who range the gamut from decidedly liberal to the Anglo-American type of conservative, are among the most distinguished historians of the South, and their works among the most widely read, taught, and quoted over the past four decades: Respectively, Clement Eaton in *The Encyclopedia of Southern History*, George B. Tindall's *The Ethnic Southerners*, Monroe Lee Billington's *The American South: A Brief History*, I. A. Newby's *The South: A History*, and *The South in American History* by William B. Hesseltine and David L. Smiley.

The authors of *A History of the South*, Francis B. Simpkins and Charles P. Roland, are criticized by McWhiney for failing to understand differing European ethnicities. They contrast the few German settlers in the South, who possessed "many sterling qualities," with "the wasteful methods of the Anglo-Saxons." Simpkins and Roland not only appear oblivious to the fact that Anglo-Saxons are culturally and linguistically Germanic, but they also label the Scots-Irish as "of the same Anglo-Saxon stock as the people of the coast regions" of the early South. "To contend that the Scotch-Irish came from the 'same Anglo-Saxon stock' as the English," McWhiney continues, "indicates a profound ignorance of the most important cultural conflict in the history of the British Isles" (3). In their confusion between ethnic heritage and imperial citizenship, between folk culture and primary language spoken (especially after centuries of laws designed to destroy native languages), Simpkins and Roland highlight a recurring problem in Southern scholarship: The automatic labeling of any non-Irish-Catholic Southerner whose ancestry derives from any part of the British Isles as ethnically and culturally Anglo-Saxon. To do so means not only that an unreservedly anti-English, Scots-Irish family like that of Andrew Jackson would be lumped under the cultural heading Anglo-Saxon but so would Scottish Gaelic and Welsh speakers and any recent "converts" from Irish Catholicism to any form of Protestantism.

Over the past two decades, this view has been attacked by a few historians. Foremost among them are Grady McWhiney and Forrest McDonald, who, while working together at the University of Alabama, developed the Celtic-Southern thesis: That the primary cultural patterns of the white South were planted and developed by culturally Celtic immigrants (peoples from Ireland, Scotland, Wales, and the English counties bordering Scotland and Wales) and their descendants, certainly not by true Anglo-Saxons, nor by Anglo-Normans, either latter-day Cavalier nobles operating plantations worked by large numbers of black slaves or yeoman farmers and merchants.

Before proceeding with a review of this and related scholarship concerning the importance of Celts to the South, it is necessary to lay a foundation by discussing the European Celts. This is especially requisite because of the glaring ignorance of, and a resulting indifference to, Celtic peoples and folkways in the American academy. In the Modern Language Association collection of essays *Ethnic Perspectives on American Literature,* a volume that does not include a chapter on Irish American literature, editors Robert Di Pietro and Edward Ifkovic declare, "until 1860 the Celtic immigrants entered America from Ireland, Scotland, and Germany" (5). Germany makes sense in this list only if Di Pietro and Ifkovic grossly misdefine "Celtic" as "northern European Catholic peasant" and ignore Lutheran Germans.

Perhaps the best definition of "Celt" and "Celtic" is that of Peter Berresford Ellis. Using the work of Eoin MacNeill, among others, he notes that the many Greek and Roman physical descriptions of ancient Celts were inconsistent. Most were said to be tall, thin, and primarily blond or red haired; a few others were seen as short, stocky, swarthy, and dark haired; still others were presented as combinations of these myriad physical traits. Therefore, Ellis concludes, there is no such group as a "Celtic Race," not if *race* means people who possess the same physical characteristics. Glanville Price, professor of French at the University of Wales at Aberystwyth and a recognized authority on Celtic language literatures, writes, "It cannot be emphasized too strongly that this [Celtic nations and their folkways] has nothing to do with race" (1). Rather, Celts are people who share a common Indo-European language family[2] and a common folk culture: "a Celtic people is by definition a people who speak, or were known to have spoken, in modern historical times, a Celtic language" (Ellis, *The Celtic Revolution* 13).

Ellis's emphasis upon Celtic languages, an emphasis deriving from his own activist work to save them from extermination and his scholarly awareness that language is essential to folk culture,[3] may appear initially to undercut the Celtic-Southern thesis. After all, opponents may claim, Celtic languages being almost extinct, should not then all people in the British Isles and their American descendants be labeled culturally

Anglo-Saxon? The answer is no, for three reasons. First, the basic cultural patterns of the South were in place roughly by the beginning of the nineteenth century, and the seventeenth- and eighteenth-century immigrants from Ireland, Scotland, and Wales came from lands in which the majority of people were fluent in a Celtic language, which has not been the case since the middle of the nineteenth century.

Second, the application is inconsistently applied, for virtually no one declares that the millions of Irish Catholic immigrants to North America in the second half of the nineteenth century and the early years of the twentieth century, after the Great Famine had spurred the process of killing Gaelic as the first language of Ireland's majority rural population, were culturally Anglo-Saxon. Those Irish immigrants were rarely raised speaking Irish, and virtually none received any education in Irish, but they were culturally Irish.

Third, Ellis's definition, far from being an exclusively linguistic one, is primarily cultural, with the language as the matrix, or perhaps merely the most obvious expression, of the particular cultural patterns. But Ellis is content to include as Celts people who may not be Celtic language speakers if their land is one in which a Celtic language exists, or existed "in modern historical times." Not to acknowledge the Celticness of such people would be to exclude Dubliners of the past four or five centuries from Irish culture and to consider them thoroughly Anglo-Saxon, mere western variants of Londoners. Ellis recognizes that even when the language falls into disuse, perhaps is killed by imperial government actions, its attendant folk culture will live on, perhaps for indeterminate centuries if political and economic conditions permit or if the people in question are pugnaciously conservative in folkways.[4]

Similar to Ellis, J.X.W.P. Corcoran declares that the Irish, Scottish, Welsh, Cornish, Manx, and Bretons "are the Celts, something of whose culture, languages, law, and social institutions has survived into modern times. They would seem to be the inheritors of a Celtic way of life which originated in the prehistoric past" (17). Thomas Cahill sees Irish literature evidencing the continuing of Celtic culture across two millennia. "Her ready speech," he writes of Queen Mebh, the female protagonist of the medieval Irish epic *Tain Bo Cuailgne*, "is characteristically Irish. We can imagine her sharp first sentence ("What put that on your mind?") on the lips of many a character in modern Irish drama—and this opens up to us an astonishing continuity: From prehistoric Ireland to the present day" (76). [5]

Staying within the ancient world, we find that the Galatians of the

Bible, Celts who had entered Asia Minor at the opening of the third century B.C., were described, according to Livy, by conquering Roman general Manlius Vulso as a "degenerate, a mixed race, truly described by their name Gallogrecians" (Cunliffe 179). Like other culturally Celtic peoples, the Galatians may have been a truly mixed people in terms of bloodlines, and they certainly would have learned from both Greek and Persian civilizations, borrowing material culture from them, but they remained culturally Celtic in the heart of Asia Minor for a minimum of seven centuries, centuries during which Roman rule first destroyed their independence and then forced them to accept certain Roman practices (including the required use of either Latin or Greek for all official business and for all but exclusively local economic activities), all of which was compounded by the rise of Christianity. Barry Cunliffe writes, "The maintenance of a Celtic social structure, and indeed a sense of ethnic identity implied by the widespread use of the name 'Galatian', are a remarkable reflection of the deep-seated strength of the Celtic tradition." Cunliffe observes that St. Jerome at the end of the fourth century A.D. noted that the Galatian language was similar to that of the Gaulish Trevari at Trier, and the scholar believes that Jerome was "recognizing . . . the Celtic ancestry of both people" (85). Those inclined to believe that Celtic culture could not survive in any appreciable form in America because Celts have never been the majority population of the continent, nor have they ever ruled it as a named Celtic nation, must consider Cunliffe's assessment of the Galatians: "The Galatians [who ruled themselves only for their first century of existence] provide a fascinating example of a Celtic people who maintained a high degree of ethnic identity over several centuries, even though they must have represented a minority in their territory" (180).

Archaeologist T. G. E. Powell is another scholar of Celtic heritage who recognizes that the subject is one not of mere linguistics but of folkways and attendant philosophies. He writes of Herodotus's discussion of Celts:

> Now it is clear that when Herodotus referred to other barbarian peoples, as the Scythians or Getae, he recognized them as distinctive nations or tribal confederations. He was interested in what he could learn of their political institutions, manners and customs. Languages, other than their own, were not esteemed by the Greeks, and linguistic distinctions between the barbarians would not therefore have come into his consideration. It seems reasonable to suppose that the Celts were distinguishable to Herodotus on descriptive grounds, even if he never saw any representatives, in the same way as other barbarian peoples might be

identified. The term *Celts* is therefore justifiable in a proper ethnolog-
ical sense, and should not necessarily be restricted to mean *Celtic-
speaking* which is a concept of academic thought of quite modern times
deriving from the pioneering linguistic studies of George Buchanan
(1506-82) and of Edward Lhuyd (1660-1709). (14-15)[6]

Ancient Celts, across several centuries, Powell says, "were recognizable
to their southern neighbors by their characteristic way of life" (15). This is
an especially important point, for many may find it easy to dismiss studies
of Celtic cultural influence, particularly in the modern world, out of the pre-
sumption the folk culture died with Roman or certainly Williamite and
Hanoverian conquests. Nerys Patterson, Harvard University sociologist and
Celticist, presents the most forceful proclamations of the survivals of Celtic
culture across millennia and repeated conquests:

> Historical-geographical studies based on early modern data, for exam-
> ple, reveal aspects of the rural social landscape that were continuous
> with the early medieval, and indeed the late prehistoric, terrain.
> Superb studies of folk culture by Maire MacNeill, Kevin Danaher, and
> Estyn Evans, also offer information on rural practices, some of which
> may reasonably be viewed as both indigenous and very old. (59)

"So persistent were Irish farmers' attitudes," Patterson writes, "that,
regardless of major social upheavals, the prestige hierarchy [of stock] on
the farms of Donegal in this century corresponded, roughly speaking, to
that which prevailed in early medieval Ireland." She also notes that folk-
lorist Henry Glassie has found the basic aspects of formal medieval Irish
agricultural law in folklore practice in late-twentieth-century Northern
Ireland, among Protestants who are assumed by many to be not merely
culturally non-Celtic themselves but the descendants of non-Celts (72,
167).

In *Race and Culture: A World View,* Thomas Sowell, through a thorough examination of cultures native to all inhabited continents, refutes
claims that environment, either mere geography or favorable and unfa-
vorable actions by governments, determines culture. Basic cultural attitudes, Sowell finds in study after study of emigrant groups around the
globe, "are not erased by crossing a political border, or even an ocean,
nor do they necessarily disappear in later generations which adopt the
language, dress, and outward lifestyle of a country" (4. My emphasis).
The findings of scholars such as Cunliffe and Patterson concerning the
survival of Celtic culture in Europe across more than two millennia, the
English Channel, and the North Sea are then evidence that the same

general cultural patterns and attitudes will be carried by Celtic peoples wherever they might migrate, and that includes the South.

To use another example from the South of the survival of folk cultures, though the pidgin Gullah survived in small enclaves and a handful of West African, or Africanized European or Arabic, words came into Southern speech; no West African language survived the process of forced economic and minimal cultural assimilation of the slaves. But certain aspects of West African folk culture did survive, and to label the descendants of the black slaves completely, or even preponderantly, culturally Anglo-Saxon and to deny categorically the validity of scholarship unearthing West African folk cultural survivals in modern African American communities because the West African languages were taken from the slaves or because they were a conquered people would be ludicrous, if not simplistically racist.

Richard Wright, writing about his first visit to Africa, to the Gold Coast as it was tossing off English colonial rule and fashioning itself a new and more southerly Ghana, says that after watching West African women swaying in a kind of religious-communal dance he had known from black churches in America he was compelled to begin to change his views of racial and ethnic characteristics. For years he had rejected the existence of such out of hand as "myths of prejudiced minds. Then if that were true, how could I account for what I saw," which was black Americans having retained from Africa "such basic and fundamental patterns of behavior and response" (57). For Wright, this recognition was of a form of racism perhaps worse than that of white supremacy claiming sub-Saharan African traits had survived and were inherently devilish and viciously backward; it was the categorical denial of the uniqueness and the resilience of folk culture, which is a necessary tool of colonialists, both mercantilist and internationalist Socialist. The same logic applies to peoples of Celtic heritage and those who would deny the existence, or perhaps the significance, of their cultural contributions.

In a similar vein, Eugene Genovese in *Roll, Jordan, Roll* declares, "to seek, as so many have done, for European antecedents for every feature of black culture is to collapse into absurdity." "The fact remains," Genovese adds, "that a significant thrust in black culture emanated from the African tradition. If that thrust had European counterparts, so be it. If those counterparts reinforced or encouraged certain features of black religion, well and good" (210). I submit that Genovese's argument is valid as much for the descendants of culturally Celtic peoples in the South, and still to some degree to Irish American communities in the

North, as for black people. Rough corollaries in English culture (which like the word *British* could be borrowings from Celtic at least a millennium old) do not prove that Celtic culture made no appreciable impact on and contributions to American and Southern cultures.

Most important to the Celtic-Southern thesis is Genovese's assertion that "no—*pace* all 'scientific' historians—it [the exact percentage of black American culture that is directly sub-Saharan African in origin] cannot be measured" (*Roll* 210). To be incapable of "scientifically" measuring Celtic cultural survivals is no more proof that they do not exist or are not important than is the similar failure in black studies. From a different angle but perhaps equally important to this study is that Genovese acknowledges, "Northern and English travelers to the South repeatedly compared the slaves to the Irish, often to the detriment of the latter, and *hardly a racial stereotype of the blacks poured forth without its being a modest modification of familiar descriptions of the Irish*" (*Roll* 298. My emphasis). Writing about the beginnings of the English part in the cross-Atlantic slave trade, Peter Kolchin acknowledges that the English regarded black Africans as inherently inferior to themselves but that the view was not strictly "racist" for they likewise viewed the Irish. "The Irish were widely perceived as wild, degraded, and of questionable Christianity," he writes, "more uncivil, more uncleanly, more barbarous, and more brutish in their customs and demeanures, then in any other part of the world that is known" (15-16).[7] The origin of these thousand-year-old bigotries against Celts in the English-speaking world lies in Anglo-Saxon conquering of Celtic lands. Hugh Thomas, in his massive study of the cross-Atlantic slave trade, reviews ancient and medieval European slavery before plunging into the heart of his subject. As regards Celts, the most significant statement he makes is that not only did the various Anglo-Saxon leaders war continually among themselves but also against the Celts, they also continued to push westward and northward "wars that often seemed mere manhunts for Celtic slaves" (32).

Martin Bernal, whose *Black Athena* works read to me like the false etymology and wishful, fantasizing, spurious claims of Celtic origins of the Etruscans but are worse in that they are essentially roorbacks, links what he sees as the anti-black racism of nineteenth-century Classics to the racism against Celts:

> It is interesting to note that [John Bagnell] Bury—like many of the leading British Classicists of the turn of the 19th century, including John Pentland Mahaffy and William Ridgeway—came from the

Protestant Ascendency in Ireland. All three men were enthusiastic about the pure northern, and possibly Germanic, blood of the Dorians. Thus, apart from participating in the general racism of the period, it is clear that they saw an analogy between the Teutonic English relationship with the Irish, whom they saw as 'marginally European', and that between the Dorians and their subject populations, the Pelasgian native inhabitants. (293-94)[8]

This awareness notwithstanding, Bernal is indirectly anti-Celtic. In his slurs on and automatic damning of all northern European peoples and their folk heritages and scholarly accomplishments, Celtic lands must be included. He says of Byron, for whom he holds a fierce contempt due to the poet's Hellenism, "It was no coincidence that he was from Scotland: the 18th century links between that *northern* country and Romanticism have already been noticed" (291). Bernal also notes as a chief sign of what he labels the scholar's "Romantic" "racism" Barthold Niebuhr's decision to attend college in Edinburgh "to learn the language of Ossian" (305). Bernal's theory that Europeans could not have been the principal architects of their own high cultures is so intoxicating that he declares James Joyce's *Ulysses,* set exclusively in Dublin, to be "about Jews, not Greeks" (382), which is yet another unintended revelation of anti-Celtic bigotry, for it suggests that Bernal cannot conceive of a world-renowned masterpiece concerned with the Irish and Irish culture and heritage even when the work is written by an Irishman and set in Ireland.[9]

That the then Marxist Genovese and the openly professed anti-Western European multi-culturalist Bernal, both of whom were at the time of writing academic insiders, could each recognize and report the deep-seated, long-standing, violent bigotries against Celts and continue with their work to advance awareness of non-white peoples they see as downtrodden shouts volumes about why Celtic heritage largely has been ignored in formal education. As the conquered by first Romans and then Germanic peoples, Celts and their cultural contributions are seen naturally as peripheral by many, those who associate war victory and empire building with all advanced or preferable culture. As bearers of fair skin, and inheritors of the most important ethnic-cultural front in the saving of early Medieval Christian scholarship, modern Celts cannot become championed by the Marxists and other anti-Western culture Leftists as victims to be advanced at all costs. In short, Celts in our postmodern world have no powerful natural allies, no special-interest group support, and therefore mere truth about their existence and unique folkways and contributions to Western European and American cultures will need to suffice.

Forrest McDonald's prologue to Grady McWhiney's *Cracker Culture* is the ideal short introduction to Celtic culture and history, certainly for anyone interested in how Celtic culture may have impacted America. McDonald summarizes key events in Celtic history, both on the continent and in the British Isles, and highlights aspects of Celtic culture such as the clan, or extended family, structure; the proclivity to enjoy, or gravitate toward when forced to fight, and to honor particularly heroic age, individual combat even in the modern world; the paradoxical emphasis on individualism in a society predicated upon the clan structure, which checks and balances the individualism, making it less likely to become extreme; the emphasis on the local to the exclusion of what many see as the national; preference for the oral word over the written, at least until the modern era when the written came to reflect more closely the oral; a heightened sense of honor imponderable to outsiders; and a preference for a herding, hunting society coupled with a disdain for a more settled, city life. McDonald also notes repeatedly that for all their many local differences from one another, and their many small-scale wars against one another, the various Celtic tribes, or nationalities, have always been much more like one another than they have been like their non-Celtic neighbors. Finally, he demonstrates the strong cultural continuity of Celtic peoples from the classical world until the early modern age and summarizes the massive migration of Celtic peoples in the seventeenth and eighteenth centuries to the South, noting that the preponderance were Irish Protestants, chiefly Presbyterians (xxi-xliii).[10]

The first work of scholarship advocating the Celtic-Southern thesis was written jointly by Forrest McDonald, a preeminent scholar of the intellectual and cultural origins of the United States Constitution, and Grady McWhiney, primarily trained as a Civil War historian and published in 1975. Rory Fitzpatrick calls "The Antebellum Southern Herdsman: A Re-Interpretation" "a landmark in Scots-Irish studies" (120). Fitzpatrick concurs thoroughly that the cattle raising and herding practices of Scotland and Ireland, which were distinct from those of England, were brought to Virginia and the Carolina Piedmont principally by emigrants from Ulster and their descendants, who then took them into and across the Appalachians and eventually across the Mississippi River into the west, where they would come to be seen as uniquely American by many scholars, as an example of frontier cultural adaptation "obviously" bereft of European lineage because no English origin could be found.[11] Fitzpatrick takes pains to make certain that his readers understand that McDonald and McWhiney use the term "Celtic" not in a political sense, which in Northern Ireland may prevent anyone from seeing the obvious, but in a folk-cultural sense (123), and he declares, "the authors could have added that the seventeenth century Scots arriving in Ireland came into a native pastoral culture which could only reinforce their tribal predilections" (120). In other words, Fitzpatrick accepts that the lowland Scots, who would be the bulk and the cultural heart and backbone of the Ulster Protestant community, came to Ireland as agrarian Celts, as a Celtic tribe benefiting from the English Crown's subordination of another Celtic tribe (Ulster Irish Catholics). By the time Fitzpatrick's book appeared in 1989, McDonald and McWhiney had expanded the thesis both back in time and forward through the era of the War Between the States.

Perhaps the first example of the scholarship advocating the Celtic-Southern thesis that should be examined by the interested reader is "The Ethnic Origins of the American People, 1790," by Forrest and Ellen Shapiro McDonald. The article is a critique of the American Council of Learned Societies' study of the national and ethnic origins of white Americans as revealed by the 1790 census, the nation's first. Published in the 1931 *Annual Report of the American Historical Association,* the work was done primarily by Howard F. Barker and Marcus L. Hansen, with Barker devising a method to calculate the numbers of immigrants and their descendants from the Germanic-speaking lands and the British Isles. The mathematical calculations made by Barker, the McDonalds, and other critics of Barker's work are too convoluted to analyze in this work; however, the McDonalds's reassessment suggests that Barker's highly flawed, idiosyncratic system grossly underestimated the number of Americans of Celtic ancestry in 1790, the height of the formative period of the various American regional identities. The McDonalds' analyses indicate that while the American North, especially New England, was overwhelmingly Anglo-Saxon in settlement, and therefore heritage, the area south and west of Philadelphia was comprised of settlers primarily of Celtic background. Acknowledging the preponderance of English on the coast, the McDonalds demonstrate that most late-eighteenth-century white Southerners were of Celtic ancestry (199).

The McDonalds also reveal the nature of the bigotries they found underlying Barker's methodology:

> Among the first kind of errors, he made clear that his interest was not in culture but in "blood," or supposed genetic strains in the population. That approach obscures the centuries of wars, conquests, and other forms of interactions that altered the "blood" of both Celtic and

Anglo-Saxon peoples but left cultures intact and even hardened them. Consequently, Barker was led into making some strange classifications. For instance, he distinguished between "Celtic Irish" and "Ulster Irish," as if the latter, though most were of Scottish origins, were somehow not Celtic. On the other hand, he treated the Welsh as if they were "Cambrian" English; indeed, of the twenty-two names he selected as distinctively English, no fewer than twelve were distinctively Welsh. ("Ethnic Origins" 184)

There are two essential points here that must be addressed. First, the proponents of the Celtic-Southern thesis, similar to Nora Chadwick, Myles Dillon, Peter Berresford Ellis, and other students of Celtic heritage, are not interested in race per se but in the distinctive and defining cultural characteristics, attitudes, and achievements of people. Second, though the McDonalds are loath to proclaim it, the primary bigotry underlying Barker's distinctions that led to his underestimating the number of Celtic immigrants in America by 1790, and thereby undervaluing Celtic contributions to the early development of the United States, appears to be religious. The only possible explanation for labeling not only Irish Presbyterians but also the Welsh as non-Celtic, leaving their numbers and cultural contributions to be usurped under the 'imperial' heading English or Anglo-Saxon, is that both are, or in the case of the Welsh are expected to be, Protestant. Apparently, Barker equated Celtic culture exclusively with Irish Catholicism and Anglophonic Protestantism inextricably with Anglo-Saxon culture.[12]

The ease with which Barker could have thought thus may be seen in sociologist Patrick O'Sullivan's introduction to *Religion and Identity*, the fifth volume of *The Irish World Wide*. O'Sullivan notes that Max Weber's thesis, specifically his "Protestant Work Ethic" postulate, "supports, and draws support from, existing prejudices, especially in the English speaking world" (8). "The example Weber gives," O'Sullivan reveals, "of Cromwell's 'quite specifically capitalist line of thought' is from Cromwell's proclamation of war against the Irish" (7). O'Sullivan then, quoting from Linda Colley's *Britons: Forging the Nation, 1707-1837*, links the origin of the modern "British" nationality, an alliance of Protestants from England, Scotland, Wales, and Ireland against the threats of Catholic France, with the Calvinist doctrine of Providence (9-10). As O'Sullivan asks in a note, "When Britishness is defined as not-Catholic and not-French how then will 'Irishness' be defined?" (20). Perhaps it could be defined most easily as the exclusively impoverished "Celtic" *other* incapable of making significant cultural contributions to the rest of the world, which would justify to many people English colonialism in Ireland.

Whether he chose to do so because of awareness of the pitfalls of designating ethnicity and culture exclusively on surnames or because he was conditioned to select evidence that supported Protestant Anglo-Saxon prejudices, Barker decided to eliminate from his survey names of Celtic origin that were found in more than one country. He deleted Campbell because it also appears in Ireland, and he excised other such distinctively Scottish names as Bruce, Craig, Crawford, Davidson, Ferguson, Graham, Morrison, Murray, Rae, Robertson, Stewart, Thomson, and Wallace (all of which have been found across the South since the Revolutionary era) because some people in the English counties bordering Scotland also bore these names ("Ethnic Origins" 184-185). Because his analysis revealed there were more Americans per capita bearing the distinctively Scottish name (of Pictish origin) Forbes than there were Scots, Barker, who evidently could not imagine the possibility of a major clan emigration, also dropped that name from his study ("Ethnic Origins" 185). Whether they were made consciously or unconsciously, the result of Barker's exclusions was a study that vastly undercounted the number of 1790 Americans who were of Celtic ancestry and likewise declared as Anglo-Saxons many 1790 Americans who were descendants of Celtic peoples.

In 1984, the *William and Mary Quarterly* featured a symposium on the problems with Barker's work as revealed by the McDonalds. Thomas L. Purvis, though skeptical of the Celtic-Southern thesis as a whole, finds that the McDonalds' estimates are closer to his own than to Barker's (100). He also notes that in some ways the McDonalds had handicapped their own efforts by not including in their analysis any distinctively Scottish surnames retaining the Mac or Mc (Irish for "son of"). "Perhaps the most important reason for the McDonalds' exclusion of such names . . .," he writes, "was to ensure that any biases would work *against* their Celtic thesis. Counting the Macs would have increased the percentage of English in New England and of Scots in the Carolinas" (94).

Unlike Purvis, Donald H. Akenson, a recipient of Canada's Molson Prize for lifetime contribution to the nation's cultural life, finds the American Council of Learned Societies study "beyond rehabilitation." His summation of the McDonalds's analysis of Barker's wrangling with numbers to achieve answers that he believed should be correct, which lowered the estimates of Celtic immigrants in eighteenth-century America, reveals the occasionally arbitrary nature of Barker's work more satirically than the McDonalds had done: "When Barker first applied his ethnic-name formula to the people of North Carolina, he found that 100.5 percent of them were English in 1790. Then he combined English and Welsh names and found that only 98 percent of North Carolinians were English. Finally, he decided that 66 percent was about right" (109).

Akenson makes two other worthy points, one in his article and the other in his "Commentary." He reveals, "in a general sense, the ACLS report was occasioned by the federal government's attempts in the 1920s to control the size and character of the stream of migrants into the United States" (103). A scholarly study so tainted by the political situation—by 1927 immigrants were to be in proportion to the "'national origins' of the existing population" (103)—could not help but reflect the (often viciously) anti-Catholic and anti-Celtic biases of the northern WASPs who held mandarin sway over America. Akenson then provides a story to demonstrate the ease with which an "obviously" English name could be Celtic. A Professor John Kelleher had investigated the origins of an Irish family named Oates and

> discovered that their name was originally McQuirk. McQuirk in Irish is Mac Cuirc, "son of Curc," and *curc* in Old Irish is a heroic epithet meaning "purple light." The Old Irish word does not exist in modern Gaelic, however, and would not be understood by speakers of Gaelic. A popular etymology then mistakenly drew a derivation from the modern word *coirce*, meaning "oats," and, by the processes of anglicization, McQuirk became Oates. (127)

Akenson's story reveals the futility that anyone studying transplanted Celtic ethnicity must feel when relying on surnames almost exclusively. The forced Anglicization process left many completely culturally Celtic people bearing surnames that appear to mark them as being "obviously" Anglo-Saxon or Norman. And awareness of this problem is not new. In *A Literary History of Ireland*, published in 1897, Douglas Hyde, who would later serve as Ireland's first president, laments the losses of Gaelic names, which had been spurred by English government decrees and then in his own century by U.K. economic motives, and instructs his readers: "For the wholesale translation of names, such as O'Gara into Love, O'Lavin into Hand, MacRury into Rogers, and so on, see an article by me in 'Three Irish Essays,' published by Fisher Unwin" (636).[13]

Others investigating name changes of peoples from Celtic lands have made discoveries similar to those of Hyde and Akenson. Padraig O Snodaigh, in a work designed to refute the prejudices that Ulster

Protestants are culturally the antithesis of Irish Catholics, discloses that in 1465 England's Edward IV legislated "every Irishman to take as surname the name of an English town, a colour, a trade or an office 'under penalty of forfeiting his goods yearly.' Similar legislation was imposed in Scotland. Hence the number of Ulster surnames which hide a Gaelic origin" (35-36). Roger Blaney, whose chief interest lies in recovering the full cultural heritage of Presbyterianism, details the process by which originally Gaelic surnames became the English sounding names common among Scottish lowlanders and Ulster Presbyterians: "Mac an Ri (McAree) became King; Mac Ruari (McRory) became Rogers; O Loinsigh (Lynch) became Lindsay; O Baoill (Boyle) became Boal; Mac Seain (McShane) became Johnston. Many apparently English surnames can, therefore, hide the [Celtic cultural, ethnic] origins of their bearers, e.g. Armstrong, Baird, Smith, Cromie, Howard, Lambe, Woods, Haire, to name a few" (17).

In their closing response to the articles and commentaries of Purvis and Akenson, the McDonalds make two significant points. First, they refute Purvis's attack on their estimations of Welsh names by noting "that the flow of migration inside the United Kingdom during that century [the nineteenth] was toward metropolitan centers . . .," meaning that "the distribution of Welsh names in England indicates . . . the pattern of migration of Welsh people during the age of industrialization" (129), rather than the fact that Welsh names are somehow not distinctively Welsh, as Purvis suggests.

Of greater importance is the McDonalds's summation of how and why certain immigrant groups retain or lose their unique identities:

> (1) If an immigrant ethnic group is sizeable and its members settle in some proximity to one another and either in separation from others or amidst members of a similar culture, retention of its identity is likely. (2) If such persons settle in close proximity to others in an alien culture in which they are vastly outnumbered, they are likely to be assimilated into the alien culture. (3) *But,* if they can live more or less in isolation (as on the American frontier), they are likely to retain their cultural characteristics no matter how small their relative numbers. (4) *And,* if they live in close proximity to others in an alien culture but are discriminated against (as with the Boston Irish), they are prone to retain their ethnic identity. (135)

This schema demonstrates that the McDonalds believe that Celtic folkways, altered by New World conditions, survived in the South, not because of any alleged innate superiority of the culture over all others, but because of ideal conditions.

Akenson's *Being Had: Historians, Evidence, and the Irish in North America* (1985) is a book-length study further advocating the positions he took in the *William and Mary Quarterly* symposium on the population study. As the book focuses primarily on Canada, Akenson has little to say specifically about the South. He does declare, however, "scholars must overcome an unfortunate piece of *cultural blindness* [my emphasis] embedded in the historiography of the Irish in America, namely that the Protestants from Ireland are not part of that history" (60). Considering the mass migration of Scots-Irish to the South, such an inclusive approach would primarily benefit studies of the importance of Celts to the South. Not only does Akenson support the argument made by the McDonalds but he goes a step further:

> To compare name frequencies in the early United States with those obtaining in England and lowland Scotland after the human displacements of the industrial revolution and with the names predominating in Ireland and the Scottish highlands after the Great Famine of the late 1840s is so outlandish as to be ludicrous. (23)

Akenson has continued his challenging and therefore rebarbative assaults on the prejudicial tendencies of scholarship on the emigrant Irish in *The Irish Diaspora: A Primer* (1993). In this international perspective on Irish settlers throughout the "English-speaking" world, Akenson emphasizes that "Ireland formed everyone who lived in it," and therefore all emigrants from Ireland must be studied as Irish culturally. "They could hate Ireland, love it, hate each other, it mattered not," Akenson declares. "They were of Ireland: hence Irish" (7). Especially pertinent to the Celtic-Southern thesis is Akenson's accentuation on denominational apostasy among Irish immigrants in North America. The common "folk religion" of the Irish, their "primitive Christianity" led them as emigrants to common inter-marriages and church affiliation changes (245-46). This understanding of a common Irish folk heritage that persists across time, space, and church leads Akenson to his most direct support of the tenets of the Celtic-Southern thesis:

> Any serious, non-racist history of the Irish in the United States should spend as much time upon the Baptists (especially the Southern Baptists), Methodists, Anglicans, and Presbyterians, as it does upon the history of the Catholic Church. The life of William Bell Riley (the

founding father of twentieth-century American fundamentalism) should be as well known as, say, that of Cardinal Spellman. And the career of Jimmie Rodgers (the father of American country music) deserves to be as widely known as that of the great tenor John McCormack (224).[14]

If surname analysis, however enlightening, is ultimately flawed both by forced Anglicization and modern population shifts within the United Kingdom, which combine to lessen the numbers of Celtic names in such studies, then an examination of folk cultural characteristics is necessary to suggest whether culturally Celtic peoples have made significant, perhaps indispensable, contributions to the development of modern Anglophonic cultures such as the South's.[15] The first book-length study to be published promoting the Celtic-Southern thesis was *Attack and Die: Civil War Tactics and the Southern Heritage* (1982) by Grady McWhiney and Perry D. Jamieson. Their postulate is that the strategies and fighting styles of the Union and Confederate armies reveal a significant cultural difference between the North and the South. The North, they argue, fought a characteristically English war while the South waged Celtic-style campaigns.[16] Though the book's focus on military tactics may make it difficult for readers lacking such martial interests, it is challenging, especially the last chapter, in which the authors move beyond military tactics to a larger, more general comparison of folk cultures. James Michael Hill's *Celtic Warfare: 1595-1763* (1986) accepts the basic military thesis in *Attack and Die* that there is continuity in Celtic warfare from the ancient world to the modern.

McWhiney and Jamieson argue that "the majority of the white people in the South of the 1860s were of Celtic origins and most of those who were not had become culturally Celticized; the majority in the North were of English origins and many who were not had become culturally Anglicized" (178). This "cultural dichotomy," they suggest, explains not merely the fighting styles of the respective armies but also the clashes that led to war. They posit, "it was no accident that the Confederates adopted as their battle flag the Celtic St. Andrew's cross," (180) which may be seen on the Scottish flag, the colors of which are white, the cross, and cerulean blue, the field. That shade of sky blue, perhaps best known in the United States as the color of the University of North Carolina's athletic teams, is also the color of the Confederate violet and the Bonnie Blue Flag, which was raised on 9 January 1861 in Jackson, Mississippi, to honor the state's secession: "one of the witnesses to this event, an Irish-born actor named Harry Macarthy, was so inspired by the spectacle that he wrote a song entitled 'The Bonnie Blue Flag' which was destined to be the second most popular patriotic song in the Confederacy" (Cannon 31). As evidence that at least some nineteenth-century Southerners recognized the basic English-North, Celtic-South cultural dichotomy, McWhiney and Jamieson quote from an orator contrasting "the Teutonic and Anglo-Saxon North with the Celtic South. . . . Only Southerners, with their Celtic ways, could counterbalance the evils of this business culture, insisted the orator" (173).

Most of the academics who have dismissed or trashed the Celtic-Southern thesis to me have insisted that it lacks merit because no one in the antebellum South recognized Celtic differences from England, much less an awareness of their own Celtic heritage, or indicated any interest in Celtic peoples whatsoever. I think it important to stress not merely this reference and the fact that Mary Noailles Murfree, who, writing as Charles Egbert Craddock, was the best-selling Southern local colorist, chose for her first pen name Robert Emmet (who was an executed Irish nationalist), but also Eugene Genovese's observation:

> Ireland especially caught the attention of southern youth. 'Ireland's misery,' exclaimed Junius Irving Scales in 1853, has ever been England's shame.' Scales recounted the early conquest and the ruthlessness of Cromwell and concluded that, notwithstanding some reforms, the Irish peasants were still starving. (*Southern Front* 99)

Kelly J. O'Grady's *Clear the Confederate Way: The Irish in the Army of Northern Virginia* provides numerous references that support not merely the military thesis of *Attack and Die* but the whole of the Celtic-Southern thesis. "Civil War scholars," he writes, "may find it surprising that even obscure Southern sources often hint at Irish-Confederate alliances" (x). For example, in a note, O'Grady reveals, "Private Azariah Bostwick of the 31st Georgia despaired that the failure of the Confederacy would mean abject slavery for all Southerners. Without Southern independence, Bostwick believed, 'We will be to the North what Ireland is to England, a slave of the darkest kind.'" O'Grady also notes that William Porcher Miles, who was once presented to me by an elderly scholar of the *Old South=Anglo-Norman* school of cultural studies as an example of the English country squire/antebellum Southern gentleman *par excellence,* wrote to Jefferson Davis and stressed the cultural differences between the Irish and the Germans in Kentucky (18-19). More important, Miles declared, "half my blood is Irish" (19).

O'Grady declares of native Irishmen who fought for the Confederacy,

"Their numbers were so great—and their stories so compelling" that he was forced to limit his study to Robert E. Lee's Army (iv). O'Grady also emphasizes the great Irish paradox of the time: That though Irish Catholic immigrants in the north were the group most prone to opposition to the Union war effort and the draft, as well as to insubordination during military service, Irish natives in the South, who were overwhelmingly Catholic, were as wholeheartedly patriotic for their States and secession from the Union as were the Scots-Irish Protestants in the South, whose ancestors had arrived almost totally before the Revolutionary War (iv). O'Grady provides the cultural answer to the paradox: "The Northern cabal of Yankee Puritans, radical abolitionists allied with the world's leading abolitionist state, Great Britain, and nativist [therefore stridently anti-Catholic and anti-Irish culture] Whigs and Know-Nothings [violently anti-Catholic and anti-Irish culture nativists] represented the historic enemies of the Irish people" (14). The hatred of the Irish and Irish culture, the belief that both are inherently the worst of the worst, that deeply marks WASP culture was as prominent among Antebellum Southern Liberals, who invariably saw themselves as walking in the Elected Righteous footsteps of the reforming Anglo-Saxon Puritans, as it was among Yankee WASPs. O'Grady notes, "Even avowedly egalitarian abolitionists held racially prejudiced views toward the Irish. In 1857, Hinton Helper, a North Carolina abolitionist who fled to New York during the war, wrote that the Irish 'are a more brutal race and lower in civilization than the negro'" (14).

In contrast to the northern example of WASP contempt for and persecution of both Catholic religion and Celtic culture, the South presented immigrant Irish with a culture into which they fit naturally and were accepted.[17] This is perhaps best evidenced by Irish Catholic bishops and priests in the South being unequivocally pro-Confederate while Irish Catholic bishops in the north were almost unanimous in their neutrality. In the north, Irish Catholics found a WASP culture that hated who and what they were and was dead-set on assimilating them to its values and identity, but in the South they found a similar Celtic culture:

> Irish allegiance to the Southern cause was never more evident than in the actions and statements of Irish Catholic leaders. Indeed, the Irish leaders of the Church in the South were some of history's truest Confederates. At the same time Irish Protestants in the South were apt to cleave to the Confederacy out of common religious and cultural heritage and similar political sympathies. Thus, Southern Irishmen, Catholic and Protestant, were united in their Confederate allegiance. (22-23)

Some of O'Grady's most insightful commentary concerns John Mitchel, the Young Ireland nationalist leader who had been sentenced to penal servitude in Australia and who had escaped and come to the South. Mitchel, though Protestant, is a quintessential example of the leaders of the Irish in the South who invariably "likened the American war to the Irish struggle they left behind. In their minds, the Civil War was another opportunity to win independence by dissolving a tyrannical union" (19). The cultural parallels are furthered in a note: "Mitchel saw in the Northern States just another example of that 'Anglo-Saxon civilization' which he hated and which he was convinced would end some day in disaster for those who clung to it" (309).[18] Mitchel also saw the War Between the States as being just another theater of a centuries-old culture war, one driven by a complex maze of reformist religion, ethnic contempt by cultural Germans (the worst of whom to Mitchel were Anglo-Saxons) for all other European peoples leading to imperialistic wars to push them off land so that cultural Germans could control more, and economic pirating:

> Mitchel believed that the Civil War, as the wars in Europe had been, was an economic and military conquest couched in religious and moral terms. In the American conflict, the North's conquest targeted the South. The result, he wrote, would be the economic, political and religious subjugation of an entire land. (45)

Thus far, the major contribution to the Celtic-Southern thesis is Grady McWhiney's *Cracker Culture: Celtic Ways in the Old South* (1988). While *Attack and Die* was restricted to military tactics, thereby leaving itself too thin to be fully persuasive in its larger cultural arguments—which, paradoxically, may be necessary to an acceptance of the specific military thesis—*Cracker Culture* approaches the thesis from a myriad of subjects. This study is a comparative examination of folkways as revealed primarily in travel accounts. In short, McWhiney presents innumerable examples from the antebellum period both of foreigners, chiefly English men and women, comparing Southern folkways to those of Celts and Northern folkways to those of the English and of Northerners responding to and condemning Southerners much as Englishmen of the era and pervious ones responded to and condemned Celts.

McWhiney notes that "cracker," long a racial slur on white Southerners that in recent years has been voiced most notably by Malcolm X and other Nation of Islam leaders, is in origin a Scottish term for "boaster" (xiv), and he applies it to the Celtic South. *Cracker Culture* begins with the statement, "historians, in their much-argued efforts to determine the extent to which the antebellum North and South were similar or different, have paid too little attention to the abundant observations of contemporaries" (1). McWhiney's exhaustive study does just that, and through an analysis of the writings of hundreds of antebellum Americans and dozens of Englishmen, he demonstrates that the basic folk cultural patterns of the North and South were indeed different, or certainly were perceived to be different, often antagonistically so. *Cracker Culture* is divided into eleven chapters: "Settlement," "Heritage," "Herding," "Hospitality," "Pleasures," "Violence," "Morals," "Education," "Progress," "Worth," and "Collision." No summary can do justice to McWhiney's accomplishment. For 271 pages the reader is bombarded with evidence that the folk culture characteristics of the old South were largely Celtic in origin and, by contrast, those of the North, especially New England, were Anglo-Saxon.

McWhiney's accomplishment is, I believe, no small part of the problem certain contemporary people have in accepting the fact that culturally Celtic peoples made a significant impact on Southern culture. A principle belief among modern Americans of virtually all political stripes, particularly liberals who glorify government centralization, is that antebellum white Americans North and South were, except for economics, exactly alike; therefore, the War Between the States, which began the process that governmentally culminated in The Great Society, was one between good brother with good morals (for the Union or against slavery or both) and bad brother with bad morals (for the Confederacy or against Abolitionism or for Southern culture or all three). In his study of American slavery, Peter Kolchin, who is in no wise a defender of conservative Southern culture, acknowledges that the war was one "only indirectly linked to the peculiar institution" until the Union's leaders saw the political expediency of turning its war effort into a Holy War. "So long as the Confederates could portray their rebellion as an exercise in national self-determination," Kolchin writes, "their cause aroused considerable sympathy abroad, but much of this sympathy would be likely to dissipate if the war could be redefined as a struggle over slavery" (201-2).[19] McWhiney, by drawing attention to the fact that many antebellum anti-Southern slurs and attitudes had nothing to do with slavery and in fact were directed principally at the vast majority of white Southerners who did not own slaves, demonstrates that Northern hostilities began before the first American slavery crisis surrounding the admission of Missouri to the Union and until the 1850s focused not on slavery but on the perceived ethnic differences and, therefore to Northerners and English visitors, the inferiority of Southerners. McWhiney's work suggests that the "exercise in national self-determination" for the South was one predicated not merely upon differing views of the Constitution, whether the focus be slavery or states' rights, but also upon differing ethnic heritages and their cultures that had come to predominate in the states roughly above and below the Mason-Dixon Line.

It is exactly this that journalist Tony Horwitz finds objectionable about the Celtic-Southern thesis. Horwitz, apparently ignoring Lincoln's First Inaugural Address reassertion that he had neither legal right nor intention to interfere with slavery already existing in sovereign states, makes it clear to his readers that to him the war was about the ending of human slavery in these United States, and he writes as if warning people that if the white South were seen as having been the cultural descendant primarily of Celtic peoples, then the war "was a cultural war in which Yankees imposed their imperialist and capitalist will on the agrarian South, just as the English had done to the Irish and Scots—and as America did to the Indians and the Mexicans in the name of Manifest Destiny" (69). As the potential political fallout from this logic frightens him, he later, without casting any doubt upon the population and folklore survival studies that underlie the thesis, slurs Southerners who accept the validity of the Celtic-Southern thesis as "romantics" whose "poster boy was the Scottish clansman played by Mel Gibson in the splatterfest Braveheart" (290). Note that Horwitz uses a term from Celtic heritage easily and often misused by American leftists as equating with racism and makes no mention of the film's theme: Freedom for a distinct people in national and ethnic terms from a centralized, imperially expanding government happy to obliterate them and their culture in its quest to reign unchallenged. Apparently for Horwitz, as for countless other modern liberals, freedom is too precious to be wasted on the culturally Celtic. They have no right to fight to achieve or preserve national or cultural freedom and survival.

The proponents of the Celtic-Southern thesis and revisionists of Barker's population study are not the only scholars to suggest a prominent role for Celts in the development of Southern culture. David Noel Doyle's *Ireland, Irishmen and Revolutionary America, 1760-1820* (1981) is a study of the importance of Irish immigrants to the early development of the United States. Doyle makes the connection between first generation Irish American and quintessential Southerner in his introduction:

> Andrew Jackson, with piercing blue eyes, face as long as a Lurgan
> spade, high shock of red hair, and lonely resolution, would embark on

the career of frontier soldier, land-speculator, professional English-hater, Southern politician, and national hero that would lead him to the Presidency in 1828, and make of him a symbol of the political reconciliation of the older Ulster Irish stock in America and the incoming thousands of Catholic Irish. (*Ireland* xvii)

A professor at University College, Dublin, Doyle came to several conclusions regarding the Irish in the South that support the Celtic-Southern thesis. He notes both that "the adult generation of 1776 were acutely aware of the Irish element among them" and that regardless of the Calvinism of each, the first Scots-Irish settlers in New England received harsh ethnic-national based treatment from the Anglo-Saxon Puritans, determining that the mass of subsequent Scots-Irish immigrants would settle from Philadelphia south (*Ireland* 51, 53). Doyle, while respecting the specific Scots-Irish identity, also rejects the notion, still powerful among certain circles in both the United States and the United Kingdom, that while Irish Catholics tend to be wildly undisciplined, except perhaps as artists, Scottish Protestants and the Scots-Irish are sober, somber, and inherently pious and philosophical, a belief in antithetical philosophical bents necessary to the continuing failure to acknowledge the cultural Celticness of the Scots-Irish. Such a view, Doyle writes, "is to ignore the record of Scottish Lowland folklore, manners, and balladry. Such creative indiscipline was quite indigenously Scottish, as witness the influence of its greatest exponent, Robert Burns, upon the weaver and farmer poets of Ulster shortly afterwards" (*Ireland* 80).

Doyle's assessment that the Pennsylvania Scots-Irish were more easily "Americanized" than their Southern counterparts primarily due to settlement patterns is exactly that of McWhiney and the McDonalds (*Ireland* 133, 135). He concludes that the cultural differences between the descendants of the Scots-Irish in eastern Pennsylvania and those in the South were due to the easy assimilation of the former to the larger, wealthier, better established non-Celtic community surrounding it and the relative isolation of the latter, which allowed it to retain a considerably larger percentage of its Celtic folkways. "In the South, the seaboard was Anglican and semi-aristocratic, its communities running north-south, not east-west," Doyle says. "This meant that Ulster immigrant communities in the South were probably less Americanised [by which he means a type of Anglicized or Yankeeized] in the cultural sense, while more transformed environmentally in practical matters, than were Ulster Pennsylvanians" (*Ireland* 133).

Though he is not working specifically with folk culture, Doyle establishes a link between Ireland and the South in one of the South's most prominent and important folk cultures that was largely ignored in *Cracker Culture*: Music. Doyle sees Southern mountain music as Celtic in origin:

> Filling the Back Country, the Scottish and Irish pentatonic mode pre-empted the folk music tradition of the entire Appalachian region, as has been noted by musicologists; moreover, Ulster forms of imagery and narrative ballads shaped both the secular and sacred folk poetry fused onto those tunes. (*Ireland* 84)

Doyle also notes that Irish Catholics on the early Southern frontier tended to settle in the same areas as the Scots-Irish Protestants, which "raises the issue of their mutual acceptance which the interpenetration of their folk-music in these regions does" (*Ireland* 104).

Similar to Doyle, Patrick Blessing emphasizes the large scale pre-Great Famine Irish emigration to what would become the United States, which he dates back to the time of Walter Raleigh and therefore before Plymouth and even Jamestown. "The passage of legislation, especially in the southern colonies," Blessing writes, "restricting the arrival of Irish 'Papists' as servants [indentured slaves] suggests the extent of this traffic" (12). Blessing also notes that shortly after the end of the massive eighteenth-century Irish exodus to North America, Ulster Presbyterians and other Irish Protestants and their descendants "began identifying themselves as 'Scotch-Irish' in a successful attempt to divorce themselves from Irish Catholics who were arriving in ever-increasing numbers" and drawing the fiery hatred of anti-Catholic Nativists such as those who founded the Know-Nothing Party that would later serve as one of the most important building blocks of the Republican Party and its Anglophilic anti-Southern animus (13).

Of even greater importance than Doyle's work to the Celtic-Southern thesis is David Hackett Fischer's *Albion's Seed: Four British Folkways in America* (1989). Fischer argues in this tome that the basic regional cultures of the United States, folkways that persist to our own day, were formed by four distinct seventeenth- and eighteenth-century migrations from the British Isles. Two would coalesce to form the Northern culture: the New England Puritans, primarily from East Anglia, therefore truly Anglo-Saxon, and the midlands English and Welsh Quakers who settled in Pennsylvania. The remaining pair would determine Southern culture: Anglo-Normans from the south and west of England who settled in the Tidewater and the peoples of northeastern Ireland, Scotland, and the English border counties who settled in the Southern Piedmont and

Appalachian areas. This last group, which Fischer labels "borderers," was the vast majority of Southern whites, "a mass migration, on a scale altogether different from the movements that had preceded it," and would come to dominate the region in numbers and folk cultural influence (606, 615).

Albion's Seed features but one direct comment on the Celtic-Southern thesis, and that is in a note. Referring to herding practices, Fischer writes, "here again the McWhiney-McDonald thesis grows stronger if it is recast from racial to regional terms" (742). As noted previously, the proponents of the Celtic-Southern thesis have no overriding interest in race; their interest is in folk culture transmissions. Fischer's criticism derives from his essentially English imperial approach to studying cultures within the United Kingdom. Unless the group in question, such as most eighteenth-century Irish Catholics or Scottish Highlanders, speaks a Celtic language with only minimal use of English, Fischer labels it and its members culturally, and perhaps ethnically, English, and then in a type of circular logic he proceeds to define the specific local culture in question as English.

Though initially he may appear to stand on solid linguist, as opposed to folkway, grounds for identifying culture, Fischer evidences little knowledge of Celtic languages. He names the native languages of both Wales and Cornwall as Gaelic, though a person with the most rudimentary Celtic knowledge knows that these languages are P-Celtic or Brythonic, not Q-Celtic or Gaelic, the languages of Ireland, Scotland, and the Isle of Man (239, 620). Furthermore, Fischer's acknowledgment of Celtic culture is so slight that he lumps Welsh Quakers in the same cultural category as English Midlands Quakers, which is analogous to declaring that Huguenots (French Calvinists), Presbyterians (Scottish and Irish Calvinists), and English Puritans belong in the same cultural grouping.[20] This is valid only if the grouping denotes Calvinist religion exclusively, and if true would mean that John Wesley and Desmond Tutu are both pure examples of Anglican Anglo-Saxon culture. Fischer also writes of the "English" settlement of the Tidewater, "the great majority of emigrants from Bristol . . . came from the west of England and South Wales" (237). To Fischer, as to Barker before him, even a Welshman may be declared Anglo-Saxon—because in most United Kingdom documents that is his label.

In a further effort to disprove the culturally Celtic heritage of his "borderers," Fischer avows that in the Carolinas the Scots-Irish and Scots Lowlanders were often at odds with the Scottish Highlanders, suggesting that this means that they were culturally distinct, the former two groups being English and the latter group Celtic (621). But Fischer's own work reveals a flaw in this logic. He notes repeatedly that in the "border" culture he describes, people, divided by family groups and local associations, squabbled and feuded with one another constantly.[21] If "tribal" feuding between Scots-Irish and Highlanders eliminates the former from Celtic classification, then it also eliminates every family and sub-regional group Fischer cites from being "borderers." Another flaw in Fischer's logic is that he sees cultural traits as defined principally, almost exclusively, by geography, not by folk cultural groups.[22] If such is indeed the case, when that geography is radically altered by migration, such as that from Europe to North America, then the basic culture should metamorphose significantly, not remain basically the same for two centuries, as Fischer argues throughout *Albion's Seed*.

Unwittingly, Fischer also strengthens the Celtic-Southern thesis in an important way. Perhaps central to the thesis's majority numbers of immigrants who brought an essentially Celtic folk culture to the South is the postulate that English citizens living in the counties bordering Scotland and Wales in the eighteenth century were considerably more Celtic than Anglo-Saxon in folkways. Because the sources used by McWhiney in *Cracker Culture* principally concern the Irish, Scottish, and Welsh, and only sporadically treat people in England's border counties, this part of his case is somewhat weak. Fischer, presumably in an attempt to further his argument that "borderers" are culturally, and perhaps ethnically, English, refers to several documents from the border counties (621-32, 662-63). What he demonstrates, at least to one versed in both Celtic culture and languages and the Celtic-Southern thesis, is that the English borderers were virtually as Celtic culturally as were the linguistic Celts, which is McWhiney's point.[23] Fischer could move these discussions of "English borderer" culture to the Scottish Highlands or to any part of rural Ireland or to a Cymic-speaking area of Wales and few, if any, readers would find them remotely out of place. Likewise, they would be seen as grotesquely out of place in London, East Anglia, or Kent. Furthermore, while these discussions could be transplanted to any part of the South and be seen as belonging, they would immediately be recognized as out of place if attributed to New England.

Arthurian scholar Geoffrey Ashe, whose focus has been on recovering the historical period of the British fifth and sixth centuries A.D., sums up the origin of the Celtic cultural traits of people in England's border counties. Rather than exterminate the native Celts from these areas as their

Germanic ancestors had done on the southeastern coast, the Saxons, moving west and north past what is now central England, slowly conquered and accepted the non-resisting natives and adopted much of their culture, especially their Christianity and its learning, though that was more from the Irish come east to teach than from British Celts. Ashe labels the scholarship at Jarrow that flowered in Bede as "Anglo-Celtic" and sees Lindisfarne's origins through its first saints as "purely Celtic" (188). He also emphasizes the large number of English border counties place names that are either Celtic in origin or begin with "Weala," the Anglo-Saxon word that meant foreigner or slave or Celt and would become the word *Welsh,* which indicate, in contrast to the near absence of such place names in East Anglia and Kent, that the subdued Celts in the west and north of what would be called England "were allowed to exist in organized communities" where significant folk cultural survivals would be expected (188).

In addition to the Celtic folkways of the P-Celt speakers conquered but not exterminated by the Germanic invaders, northern English borderers have folkways derived from Q-Celts. Padraig O Snodaigh tells of Scottish national hero William Wallace, a native of Selkirk in the Lowlands "(where Gaelic was spoken as late as 1931) raiding the linguistically mixed northern counties of England in 1297 and using language as a factor of differentiation ('he spared no one who spoke the English tongue')" (26). Roger Blaney notes that strong cultural ties of north English border counties folk to Scotland and Ireland did not end before the Industrial Revolution. Presbyterian Reverend Caleb Threlkeld, an eighteenth-century native of England's Cumberland County and sufficiently knowledgeable of Gaelic to include copious Gaelic phrases and words in his scholarship, "was the first person to record in print the tradition that St. Patrick used the shamrock to explain the Trinity" (39-40).

Fischer, like many scholars who do not define culture according to socio-economic class, defines culture almost exclusively according to national boundaries, and to do so all but determines that no Celtic culture can be recognized outside the Republic of Ireland. But folk culture, like nature itself, is fluid, and not determined by centralized imperial or federal governments. Scholars of the South, which is not an independent nation, should know this. In the introduction to the *Encyclopedia of Southern Culture*, Charles Reagan Wilson and William Ferris declare, "the *Encyclopedia*'s definition of 'the South' is a cultural one" (xv). Folk cultures, they insist, have "core zones, where the distinctive traits are most concentrated, and margins, where the boundaries of the culture overlap with other cultural areas" (xv). Just as the Little Dixies north of the Ohio River, most areas of northern Missouri, and parts of southern California, especially Bakersfield, are very much culturally Southern, the English counties bordering Scotland and Wales appear to be the "margins" of Celtic folk culture. Therefore, people from those areas will live and transmit numerous Celtic cultural traits.

This is not the extent of Fischer's inadvertent revelations of the validity of the Celtic-Southern thesis. In listing names of settlements in the Southern backcountry, from the beginning of the Piedmont to the west, that would demonstrate his "borderers" view of culture, Fischer chooses many that begin with "Mc" or "Mac." As already stated, "mac" is Irish for "son," and when used as a prefix means "son of." Fischer also quotes English-born Gen. Charles Lee contemptuously referring to the politics of the Southern backcountry as "'macocracy'—that is, 'rule by the race of Macs'" (772). Of greater harm to Fischer's anti-Celtic view is his definition of "borderer" family structures, structures that in turn determined most of the folk culture. He writes that there were two family rings "which were unique to this culture": The *derbfine* and the clan. What he fails to mention is that both terms are taken from Gaelic, the former translating roughly as "true" or "blood family" and the latter as "child" or "family," both meaning a particular type of Celtic extended family and its relationships. If, in order to label and define the all-important family structure of the "borderers" and the backcountry Southerners, Fischer must turn to a Celtic language, then this unique culture must be Celtic in origin. Otherwise, Anglo-Saxon terms would be fully adequate and readily available. Near the close of his study, Fischer writes, "the North British borderers who came to the backcountry were heartily disliked by Puritans, Cavaliers, and Quakers alike" (821). Though Fischer's myopia concerning Celtic culture prevents his recognizing it, the reason is obvious: Fischer's "borderers" are primarily Celtic in folkways, and the Puritans, Cavaliers, and Midlands Quakers, though separated by religious beliefs, political views, and class, are all English culturally.

Fischer is not the sole scholar who has set out to prove that the South is or is not something only to indicate inadvertently the indispensable importance of Celtic immigrants and their descendants to Southern culture. William R. Taylor's *Cavalier and Yankee: The Old South and American National Character* (1961) ostensibly undercuts the notion that the major difference between the antebellum North and South was that the former had been settled by Puritans, who defined its culture, and the latter by Cavaliers, who defined its culture. As *Albion's Seed* convincingly demonstrates, the Anglo-Saxon Puritans did establish New England culture, which certainly appears to have been the stronger partner in defining the larger Northern culture, and the Anglo-Normans, many of whom could be labeled Cavaliers, did settle the narrow strip of coastal South and define much of its culture. But these Cavaliers were a minority, as Fischer acknowledges as readily as McWhiney and McDonald though under another name, to the majority Celtic immigrants in the South, both in numbers and in geographic distribution, and Taylor's work, which is primarily a reading of antebellum novels, concludes that "few, if any, Southerners, no matter what they said, really believed in the Cavalier—only in the need of him" (323).[24]

The primary proof that Taylor produces to rebut the South's Cavalier legacy is that the Scots-Irish seemed to dominate the late-antebellum South in energy and personal accomplishment, literary as well as military, political, and educational. Taylor notes that the Anglophilic tendencies of the country's power structures (centered in New England, New York, Philadelphia, and the coastal South) were so puissant as to cause "men of such different origins as Paulding, Wirt, and Kennedy" to begin referring to themselves as "English" and "Saxon" (192-93). He also posits, through the case of William Alexander Caruthers, how the Scots-Irish, in order to escape anti-Celtic prejudices that were becoming more violent with the growth of the Irish Catholic population, began to associate themselves with the English Puritans as fellow Calvinists (208).

Taylor recounts the general depression that set in over the Tidewater after the War of 1812, "a blow from which it never fully recovered." This economic impetus induced many Tidewater Southerners to migrate west: "by 1830, it has been estimated, close to a third of those born in Virginia and Maryland around the turn of the century had crossed the Alleghenies" (155). Those Southerners native to coastal states, many of whom may have been born into culturally Anglo-Norman families, would then settle in the Celtic backcountry, which means that the process of acculturation, including marriages to peoples of Celtic ancestry, would foster their children and, especially, grandchildren to become Celticized, thereby further increasing the numbers of Southerners by the outbreak of the Civil War who would fit culturally the McWhiney-McDonald prototype. Taylor's analysis of George Tucker's *The Valley of Shenandoah* (1824) reveals that Tucker, himself no Celt, saw the Tidewater Anglo-Norman hegemony as doomed and the Scots-Irish frontiersmen as the future of the South (317). This view is also presented in Taylor's quoting from Mary Boykin Chesnut: "Of late . . . all of the active-minded men who spring to the front in our [South Carolina] government were the immediate descendants of Scotch or Scotch-Irish; Calhoun, McDuffie, Chever, Petigru—who Huguenotted his name but could not tie up his Irish" (324).

Terry G. Jordon and Matti Kaups, in *The American Backwoods Frontier* (1989), proffer the thesis that the culture of the American frontier was determined largely by immigrants from the Savo-Karelian area of eastern Finland. Their attack on the Celtic-Southern thesis is limited but virulent: "those who seek the origins of the culture in the west, on the Scotch-Irish frontier of 1720-1780, mistake child for parent" (247). Though the Finnish migration occurred during the seventeenth century, ending more than two decades before the beginning of the greatest Celtic wave, the Finns settled in New Sweden, an area from southern New Jersey to northern Delaware. In addition to claiming that this non-Southern migration determined certain aspects of Southern heritage, Jordan and Kaups reveal that the Finnish migration numbered approximately 134 in 1655, with a few hundred more arriving before the end of the century (53, 55). The idea that this minuscule migration of "perhaps 400 or 500," which "lasted for at least a quarter of a century" (58, 59), would culturally preclude the hundreds of thousands of Celts is ludicrous even if the Celts had a history of being pliant and changed easily to anything rather than being fiercely independent and resistant to change. Even Jordan and Kaups seem to recognize this in their conclusion. Though they cling fast to their belief that the "forest colonization techniques" of the Finns were adopted by later settlers on the frontier, Jordan and Kaups acknowledge, in language that is somewhat disparaging, that most of the Southern frontier folk culture was Scots-Irish in origin: "Emotional, atomistic dissenter Protestantism was likely their doing, as were blood feuds, British ballads, and the bagpipe-like squealing of Appalachian fiddles" (252).[25]

Scholars of the South's history other than those who developed the Celtic-Southern thesis also occasionally have recorded the prominence of Celts in the Old South. In *Intellectual Life in Jefferson's Virginia, 1790-1830,* Richard Beale Davis finds that:

> Scottish names are frequent in the colony from the mid-seventeenth century [my emphasis], especially among the Anglican clergy. But in the eighteenth century the several waves of Scotch-Irish and Scottish immigrants . . . came to form a recognized part of the Virginia religious and political mind. (13-14)

The frequent Scottish names among the Anglican clergy suggest that early Southern Episcopalianism featured a strong Celtic contingent.[26] Davis also writes of the importance of Hampden-Sydney and Washington Colleges, "their development symbolizes the growing influence and size of the Scotch-Irish population in the South" (59), and he declares of the Scots-Irish Presbyterians, "believing in education and possessing an educated clergy, they supplied tutors to Anglicans and persuaded several of the latter to send their sons to the Presbyterian grammar schools in Virginia" (14). Davis sees Celtic immigrants as largely determining early Southern education even in most of colonial Virginia, which continues to be presented as the quintessence of unadulterated Anglo-Norman high culture in early America.

Bruce Collins in *White Society of the Antebellum South* records the anti-English sentiment found widely in the Old South, which Eugene Genovese terms "traditional Southern Anglophobia" (*World* 167), and accepts both the Southern family structure as that of Gaels and the Scots-Irish origin of white Southern folk music (71-72, 126, 153). E. R. R. Green finds that middle Georgia was quickly populated by Irish immigrants: "An estimate of the population of the settlement was made about 1770, and at that time there were supposed to be about seventy families in Queensborough and two hundred in the 'environs,' most of them Irish" (199). In *Origins of a Southern Mosaic,* Clarence L. Ver Steeg notes that the anti-black-slavery English Methodist James Oglethorpe "purchased" a boatload of "Irish convicts" to perform the manual labor of the colony[27] and that the leaders of the Georgia colony's "dissatisfied group" were called by the trustees a "Scotch club" (83, 95).[28] Leroy Eid, a proponent of the Celtic-Southern thesis, reveals that "in the recent census returns an amazingly large number of Americans claimed 'Irish ancestry.' The sociologist Marjorie Fallows had earlier emphasized the ethnic paradox that the fiercely possessive Catholic Irish American community formed barely fifty percent of those Americans who claimed to be of Irish descent" ("Irish" 211). Eid also notes that Charles Carroll of Carrollton, the leader of the pro-revolutionary movement in 1776 Maryland, was descended from County Tipperary immigrants (216).

The two most prominent historians of the Irish in America, James Leyburn and Lawrence McCaffrey, both recognize the indispensable role of the Irish in the South. McCaffrey, whose scholarship focuses on the urban Irish Catholics in the North, declares of the predominantly Southern settling Scots-Irish, "Ulster nonconformists brought energy to their new country along with economic and intellectual skills and a commitment to democratic principles that speeded the maturation of

America" (*Irish* 59-60). His assertion that "Irish agriculture traditionally was more a cultural life-style than an economic system" supports McWhiney's definition of transplanted folk culture, and his recognition that "many Confederate officers considered the Irish the best soldiers in the Union Army" coalesces with McWhiney's military thesis (*Irish* 63, 96).[29] Perhaps more important to the Celtic-Southern thesis, McCaffrey notes that many eighteenth-century Irish Catholics came to the South as indentured servants or transplanted felons convicted by the imperial legal system often of little more than poverty or Irish nationalist sentiments and they and their descendants helped form Southern culture:

> After servitude or sentences, both usually for seven years, spent in the plantation economy of the South, they moved to the Appalachian frontier. Because the majority of servants and convicts did not leave Ireland as informed or devout Catholics and the American church lacked the personnel and facilities to minister to people in the outer geographic and social edges of society, they melded into evangelical Protestant or Ulster Presbyterian communities. (*Textures* 11)

A superficial reading of Leyburn, the foremost authority on the American Scots-Irish, may lead a reader to conclude that the Celtic-Southern thesis has little validity. Not only does Leyburn see Scots-Irish identity as dissolving in America, but he believes that there was little cultural exchange and few marriages between the Scots planted in Ulster and the native Irish, with the Irish usually "absorbed into the Presbyterian element" (139). Contrary to the popular misbelief, the Scots-Irish did not need Irish Catholic culture to be culturally Celtic. Leyburn, though he emphasizes the Scottish Reformation and religious wars as paramount in shaping the seventeenth-century Lowland mind, declares, "one can hardly contest the predominance of the Celtic stock in the Lowlander's heritage" (66). The importance of this heritage is well stated by Roger Blaney: "These conservative estimates [of seventeenth-century Ulster Presbyterians] suggest that at least half of all the early Presbyterians in Ulster were Irish/Gaelic speakers" (19). Furthermore, Leyburn rejects the traditional British historians' designation of the Scots-Irish as Ulster Scots, by which they considered them not only non-Irish, but as British in the imperial sense, therefore non-Celtic culturally (142). The assumed loss of the specific Scots-Irish identity in the South is explained by the Celtic-Southern thesis: The descendants of the eighteenth-century Scots-Irish immigrants in the South led the formation of a Southern identity in the early national and antebellum eras. Their folkways since then have been labeled Southern, or perhaps Appalachian and Ozark, rather than Scots-Irish. The Scots-Irish in the North, in Philadelphia and New Jersey, began to forget their actual ethnic and national ancestry before the War Between the States and assimilated to the general type of Anglophonic Yankee culture and then served as junior partners to descendants of New England Puritans and descendants of northeastern English Episcopalians in the formation of the Yankee WASP culture.

Novelist James Webb, the former Secretary of the Navy during the Reagan administration, has forayed into historical and cultural study with *Born Fighting: How the Scots-Irish Shaped America.* Webb's greatest significance, for my study, is that he unequivocally sees the Scots-Irish as being culturally Celtic. And that recognition by Webb is not due to his having focused his research on Irish Catholics and perhaps Scottish Highlanders and then simply transferring his findings to the Scots-Irish, which erroneous attack has been made on me repeatedly. Webb's research focus is almost exclusively on the Scots-Irish, and he does make extensive use of the work of Leyburn among others; unlike me, Webb is not examining how various Celtic "tribes" in the South interacted and together formed the majority white Southern culture and how that is expressed in Southern literature. Instead, Webb sees the Scots-Irish as both the majority of white Southerners and as the ethnic group that most defined, and best defines, all aspects of America's, not merely the South's, blue-collar culture and military traditions.

Nor can anyone assert that Webb unquestioningly has accepted the claims of Grady McWhiney. In fact, Webb makes the case for the Scots-Irish being culturally Celtic, and through them Southern culture being largely culturally Celtic, without a single positive reference to McWhiney's work. Nor is that due to his ignorance of McWhiney's work, for Webb does note it to correct it at one point:

> One learned commentator professed that "Southerners lost the war [between the states] because they were too Celtic and their opponents too English." But in actuality the reverse was true. The South lasted for four horrible years with far fewer men, far less equipment, far inferior weapons, and a countryside that was persistently devastated as the Leviathan army worked its way like a steamroller across the landscape. (231)

Webb opens his history by tracing the Scots-Irish back to ancient Celtic tribes in Britain, and throughout the work he maintains his emphasis that the group is culturally Celtic. For example, he asks of the

Scots-Irish in the tribe's early days in Ireland, before it had any chance to intermarry with Irish Catholics or absorb Celtic cultural traits from them, "For who were the Irish but their own closest blood cousins?" (90). Of Scots-Irish Protestant and Irish Catholic immigrants in America, Webb asserts, "Once removed from Ireland, the common Celtic origins of these two groups brought many similarities, especially in their military traditions, their affinity for politics, and their literary prowess" (16). He also demonstrates how McWhiney's claim that the residents of England's northern border counties were, and are, much more culturally Celtic than Anglo-Saxon is true:

> Although Hadrian's Wall had provided an emotional and historical line of demarcation, the English wanted more, and over time they succeeded, rolling back the Scottish border in the west and especially in the east. The bitter fights during these middle centuries caused many areas that were ethnically and historically Scottish to end up on the English side of the border. (77)

If people being defeated in war and forced to accept foreign rule by their conquerors makes them, *ipso facto*, ethnically and culturally the same as their conquerors, then there are no Amer-Indian cultures, and thus there is no need to study or even to acknowledge what does not exist. Though no one dares apply such absurdity to Amer-Indians or any other non-white people, that very absurdity is not merely applied to Celtic peoples and their cultural heritages but is also seen as dogmatic by many: Putative conservatives, particularly those obsessed with fiscal matters or imperial might and always those who are staunchly Anglophilic, as well as liberals and overt cultural Marxists.

Webb quotes eminent Scottish historian T. C. Smout on late medieval/Renaissance Scottish Lowland senses of kinship and place that Webb asserts survived in the Scots-Irish:

> The poor man did not in fact claim the rank of an earl or a baron. What he claimed was something he valued more, to belong to a family [a Celtic clan of extended family with members of varying wealth] of incomparable nobility and martial valour, and by virtue of that to be as good as any earl, baron or commoner of different family in the land. . . . The whole atmosphere of kinship was a complex one, compounded both of egalitarianism and patriarchal features, full of respect for both while being free from humility. It appeared uncouth beyond Scotland mainly because it was a legacy of Celtic influence unfamiliar to the outside world. (80)

Professor Smout is erroneous in his assertion that such a worldview and clan structure was unfamiliar outside Scotland, for such, with local variations, was also the norm in Ireland, Wales, and Brittany, as it was in many sections of England, France, Spain, or Portugal that retained significant Celtic cultural heritage. Other than that quibble, I not only agree wholeheartedly with Smout's analysis of a cultural pattern that is simultaneously aristocratic and egalitarian marking Scotland but also that it is Celtic. Webb emphasizes that this paradoxical, oxymoronic culture, which is family based and determined and emphasizes sense of place both physical and within the clan, continues to define the Scots-Irish. I emphasize that it is necessary to understand this cultural pattern of the Celtic individual having sense of self and pride through his clan and its history of overcoming and surviving against great odds, and of the Celtic individual expecting, and if necessary demanding, that clan leaders will serve the entire clan and not merely its wealthier and more powerful members, in order to comprehend Southern social relations and Southern literature that treats social relations and class.[30]

Webb also emphasizes that the Scots-Irish should not be lumped with either the Anglo-Normans who predominated on the narrow strip of the Southern coast or with the ethnic Anglo-Saxon Puritans of New England. He rightly delineates among various "British" Protestant groups:

> Many of the most literate observers of American culture tend to lump the Scots-Irish in with the largely English-derivative New England Protestant groups and the original English [primarily Norman: my note] settlers of the vast Virginia colony as "WASPs" (white Anglo-Saxon Protestants) under the rubric of British ancestry. But these were, and are, distinctly separate and different peoples. (13-14)

Webb notes of the southerly settling Anglo-Normans, "the majority of this privileged class was originally granted huge tracts of land by royal decree" (141). He emphasizes several times in his history that the feudalist tendencies that the most privileged of the Anglo-Normans continued to carry culturally at least through the War Between the States were devastatingly crippling of, and perhaps antithetical to, Scots-Irish culture in significant ways. This is especially true as feudalism, based on direct descent and particularly primogeniture, is erected upon *who owns what* and *holds what title* (both of which are tied to governmental favoritism for the elite, protected class), while Celtic culture, based on collateral descent, is erected upon *who is related to whom,* no matter how distantly, no matter how poor, or ethnically mixed, one branch of the clan may be, and upon *who, whether as blood member or assimilated member, is willing and able to strive for the clan militarily, economically, spiritually, educationally, or artistically.* The social effects that accrue from the two systems, the two philosophies, are wildly antagonistic. Feudalism determines that the inheritor of a great estate will look down on his fifth and perhaps even third cousins and younger brothers as inherently beneath him and, depending upon their wealth, perhaps as "white trash,"[31] while the Celtic clan system all but requires the wealthiest and most powerful clan leader to acknowledge and honor kinship across socio-economic and educational levels. The former system ossifies class (both privileged and under class), political power, and, to a slightly lesser degree, wealth, while the Celtic system ameliorates wealth and class distinctions to a significant degree, thus producing a political culture and an economic culture in which talented individuals may rise more easily and often and class warfare is next to impossible.[32]

Webb even more insistently draws distinctions between the Scots-Irish and Anglo-Saxon Puritans. In addition to emphasizing that both groups having been Calvinist did not make them ethnically or culturally identical or interchangeable, Webb, like McWhiney, stresses that the Anglo-Saxon Puritans rather heartily despised as inherent ethnic inferiors the Scots-Irish who came to settle in New England: "This initial, instinctive dislike of the Scots-Irish by the Puritans was a clear harbinger of things to come in future decades and even centuries as the American colonies matured into a nation. The Scots-Irish were the cultural antithesis of those who had founded New England" (134). While McWhiney emphasizes that most of the Scots-Irish who attempted to settle in New England headed south before long, Webb emphasizes that almost all of the Scots-Irish who stayed in New England headed north, into New Hampshire and Maine, where they escaped direct Anglo-Saxon Puritan control for decades or more and created a rural, hill culture that in many ways resembled that of Ulster, southwestern Scotland, and the south's Piedmont and Appalachian areas.[33]

Webb's study, like many produced in recent years, mixes in small discussions of his family history to emphasize key points. Most fascinating to me about these insertions are their relevance to the symbiotic nature of Southern history and literature, each of which begin not with scholars but with large numbers of folks remembering family and local histories and telling them to younger generations and perhaps, if pressed, writing them down. Webb emphasizes that though the Scots-Irish speak of their actual ethnic heritage less than any other group in America, they probably produce more "ardent genealogists that any other cultural group in the country" (124). These amateur genealogists, many writing down the information only in condensed versions in family Bibles and letters, continue to spur the writing of both Southern history and belletristic literature. Webb's description of his grandmother's history-telling and then finally writing it down for him is a passage worthy of a Faulkner novel:

> Still others appear in handwritten notes of people like my maternal grandmother, who when I was twelve years old finally wrote out an amazingly accurate eleven-page summary of her family's movement from Virginia through Tennessee, then down into Mississippi and finally into Arkansas, replete with the dates of births and deaths, marriages, and military enlistments. Granny Doyle had been carrying all of this in her head, passed down from mother to daughter through each generation in singsong verse on the narrow front porch of some latest cabin as the hot summer sun gave way to a sultry, bug-filled evening, or huddled next to the fire place before there ever was such a thing as radio to fill the boredom of a winter night. (124-25)

David T. Gleeson's *The Irish in the South, 1815-1877* focuses on the nineteenth-century immigrant Irish. Gleeson sees Irish immigrants, including Catholics, as natural Southerners. Because he wrote after the promulgation of the Celtic-Southern thesis, Gleeson had to make some acknowledgement of its existence. He dismisses it rather quickly, saying, "McWhiney and McDonald have used the term [Celtic] too broadly, lumping Irish, Scots, Welsh, and even northern English into one homogenous group" (5). His condemnation would be more believable if he had provided a definition of *Celtic* that he asserts is the one scholars all accept and should bind upon us. That he fails to do so suggests that perhaps Gleeson is merely grappling for a way to reject a thesis with no real examination, a thesis that if not condemned could be used to tarnish or destroy an academic career in politically correct times like these. After all, rejecting a study of surviving immigrant Celtic culture because the author uses source material from more than one modern Celtic land is as illogical as rejecting a study of survival of Germanic cultural traits because the author used immigrant Germans native to Prussia, Saxony, Bavaria, Westphalia, Austria, Zurich, and East Anglia. His language does not indicate such as the source of the rejection, but if Gleeson chose to dismiss the Celtic-Southern thesis out of hand because McWhiney includes the citizens of England's Celtic fringe counties of the north and west, then he will need to make a case why those citizens of England cannot be labeled culturally Celtic. If he were to execute a comparative study of the basic cultural attitudes and values of Scottish Lowlanders, Scottish Highlanders, Irish Catholics, Ulster Irish Protestants, northern England's border counties folk, and East Anglians, Gleeson would find that the odd man out is the true Anglo-Saxon. Likewise, if Gleeson were to execute a comparative study of the basic cultural attitudes and values of Americans of several generations' residence in Virginia, West Virginia, Kentucky, Tennessee, Alabama, Missouri Ozarks, east Texas, and Wisconsin, the odd man out would be Wisconsin, and no state's decision regarding secession in 1860-61 could alter that.

The tortured logic people must adopt if they deny the Celtic-Southern thesis yet insist upon acknowledging the large number of Southerners who are of Irish, Scottish, and Welsh ancestry *and* that their ancestors made significant contributions to Southern culture, becoming quintessential and defining members, may be witnessed near the opening of Gleeson's book. He writes partly in opposition to Kerby Miller's *Emigrants and Exiles,* which paints a picture of Irish immigrants in America who are unhappy and yearn for home and would be there if at all possible economically. Miller's book focuses almost exclusively on Irish emigrants to the American north, into the heart of Yankee WASP culture. It is to be expected that even though increasing numbers became economically successful well beyond what was possible in English-ruled Ireland, most Irish emigrants into Yankee WASP cultural zones would hate the prevailing culture in which they lived, would feel depressed and miss relatives terribly, and would continue to bemoan their lot very much as their relatives and friends in Ireland had done when they emigrated—as dead in some great sense. Gleeson's point is that Miller's tome is skewed because the experiences of Irish emigrants to the South are almost diametrically opposed to those in Miller's book:

> Unlike Kerby Miller, however, I believe that this feeling of exile did not hinder Irish integration into southern society. The Irish in the South did not wallow in their exile but used it as a means to an end. Initially, they used it to preserve ethnic awareness within their immigrant enclaves and to reap benefits such as jobs, housing, and social occasions, which accrued from this preservation. Later, this ethnic awareness became even more useful in building bonds with natives when the Irish recognized parallels between Ireland's relationship with Britain and the South's with the North. Paradoxically, then, their retention of a strong "Irishness" actually advanced their integration. (6)

The paradox is explained by the Celtic-Southern thesis: Irish immigrants in the nineteenth-century South, though preponderantly Catholic in a land with a large Protestant majority, literally added to Southern culture without changing it and became quintessential Southerners because the basis of Southern culture was very much culturally Celtic. Irish immigrants to the South did not face the grind of living in a local culture that was defined by all things WASP and anti-Celtic, as did most Irish immigrants in the North. Gleeson, like far too many scholars, has gone well out of his way to avoid the obvious: Irish immigrant experiences in the North and the South were radically different because the cultures that defined North and South were radically different, with the former being Anglo-Saxon and the later being preponderantly Celtic.

Beyond that political-theoretical blindness, Gleeson's book is highly valuable to anyone interested in exploring the long ignored Irish presence in the nineteenth-century South. He notes that the ties with Protestants of Irish ancestry, who would have been the plurality in many parts of the South, allowed for cultural smoothing of any "misgivings or misunderstandings about Catholicism. In 1824, for example, the Protestant president of the Savannah Hibernian Society, John Hunter (note the non-Irish sounding name, which would lead most scholars to conclude his ancestry was pure Anglo-Saxon), solved a dispute between Irish Catholics and the Savannah Free School over compulsory readings of the Protestant Bible" (88-89). The Celtic cultural similarities combined with the Irish Catholic tendency to emphasize Thomism, which philosophy nurtured cultural, moral, and theological conservatism, led the majority of Antebellum Southern Protestants to see the Catholicism of their Irish fellow Southerners as "less 'foreign' than the abolitionist antics of their 'fellow' church members in the northern states" (92, 119).

Those who continue to bleat that the Celtic-Southern thesis cannot be true because no one in the antebellum South had any interest in, much less sympathetic view of, Irish culture need to dwell on this quote:

> Southern newspapers, in fact, were sympathetic to Ireland and its efforts against English dominance. They published poetry that paid homage to "Hibernia's patriot brave" and extolled the "free fair homes of Ireland." They supported Catholic Emancipation and Young Ireland [which called for Irish national independence, through violent stand for freedom, ala the American Revolution, if necessary], hoping that the fight for Irish freedom would "engulf" the United Kingdom [which sounds like typical Celtic calls for decentralization of political power

as well as awareness that Celtic peoples other than the Irish needed to be free of rule from London by the English]. Robert Tyler, the son of Virginia-born [Scots-Irish] President John Tyler, was a great supporter of the Irish repeal movement because he "love[d] Irishmen and hate[d] tyranny in every form." (102)

Gleeson makes certain his readers know that Tyler was far from the only prominent, well-connected antebellum Southerner to display an abiding interest in Irish issues, including seeing Ireland as paradigm for the South beleaguered by self-righteous, social-reforming, Anglo-Saxon Puritans. James Hagan, a protégé of John C. Calhoun and a well-known editor, "enjoyed equating abolitionism with Great Britain, thereby linking Ireland's cause with the South's" (133). Henry A. Wise, a Virginian opponent of the Know-Nothings and a pro-Confederate leader, saw the war to destroy conservative Southern culture as being ethnically born and religiously and philosophically determined: Wise "believed that Americanism [which is antithetical to Southernism] had at its core the Puritan 'plans of Exeter Hall, in old England, acting on Williams Hall, in New England'" (111).

Scholars of the Scottish Highland immigrants in America contribute to the Celtic-Southern thesis by revealing that McWhiney and McDonald were correct in their suggestion that a significant minority of the Scots-Irish feature Highland rather than Lowland surnames. Duane Meyer avows, "Scotch-Irish names cannot easily be separated from the names of Highlanders" (27). J. P. MacLean explains, "the blood of the Highlander, to a great degree, permeated that of the Ulsterman, and had its due weight in forming the character of the Scotch-Irish" (42-43). He proceeds to list Highland surnames found among the Scots-Irish emigrants: "Campbell, Ferguson, Graham, McFarland, McDonald, McGregor, McIntyre, McKenzie, McLean, McPherson, Morrison, Robertson, Stewart, etc, all of which are distinctly Highlander and suggestive of the clans" (43). This integration of Highlanders and Lowlanders to form a new identity, a mutual assimilation leading to a new tribal identity suggested by McWhiney and McDonald, means that even if the Lowlanders had not brought Celtic ethnicity and folkways to the Scots-Irish, which according to Leyburn they did, the Highlanders would have.

Attacks on the Celtic-Southern thesis reveal a good deal about its validity. Dennis Clark's *Hibernia America: The Irish and Regional Cultures* reviews the cultural and political accomplishments of Irish Americans in every area of the country. Clark notes that Irish-born

Virginian John Daly Burke was a popular and influential Revolutionary era patriotic poet (94). Like Doyle, Clark sees Irish Catholics and Protestants settling in close proximity in the Appalachians: "their hardy individualistic lifestyle, their racy Irish music, and their suspicious secretiveness were already a tradition in the Southern mountains from the Smokies of Virginia to the Ozarks before the Civil War" (94, 96). Though Clark is an advocate of promoting the long ignored importance of Irish Americans to the historical development of these United States, he is hostile to the Celtic-Southern thesis:

> The legacy of disillusionment, poverty, and alienation in the South after [my emphasis] the Civil War is a sharp contrast to the euphoric, warlike "Celtic" spirit strangely attributed to the region in a fantasy of hyperbole by Grady McWhiney and Perry D. Jamieson. (106)

As *Attack and Die* deals with War Between the States military tactics and, to a lesser degree, cultural clashes that led to the war, not with the Reconstruction South, which, after all, was not at war, Clark's attack has no validity. His hostility, which is partially his objection to what he sees as the McWhiney overemphasis on Celtic quickness to respond martially, which underlies many continuing prejudices against the Irish especially, is primarily regional. Clark, whose assimilation into Yankee WASP culture is evidenced by his religious moves from traditional working-class Irish Catholic to liberal northern American Catholic allied with liberal Protestants and Jews on social and moral issues to Quaker-leaning, anti-church modern, writes of Irish-born Southerners who supported the Confederacy, "such reactionary spokesmen as John Mitchel, himself a former felon and a man who had been imprisoned and exiled from Ireland by England, strongly supported pro-slavery principles . . ." (105).

Clark fails to note that the Protestant Mitchel, an acclaimed writer whose most fervent admirer in the next generations may have been William Butler Yeats, was a political prisoner arrested for supporting and promoting Irish independence[34] and was perhaps the nineteenth century's sharpest, most clamorous critic of the runaway greed and sterling hypocrisy of Victorian colonialism and the feigned-paternalist racism guiding it. Clark's primary, perhaps only, concept of the nineteenth-century South is of slavery, and therefore Mitchel, a man who became as Southern as he was Irish and who linked the English empire, its soldiers, and its repression of dissent to the Union, its soldiers, and its repression of dissent, personified in his arrest to stop his publishing and speaking against the Union, must be dismissed quickly. The Celtic-Southern thesis, then, must be assaulted because it couples the Irish culturally to a South that Clark, a long-time Northern liberal who had imbibed all of the Yankee WASP prejudices, considers to be inherently and perhaps irredeemably immoral and politically incorrect, which in today's academic climate could abort the efforts to promote Irish and Irish American studies.[35]

A similar attack may be found in Rowland Berthoff's "Celtic Mist Over the South" (1986). Berthoff, evidently either more an apologist for English imperialism than Fischer or merely a modern rendition of an old-fashioned waver of the Bloody Flag of the Union, does not believe that a significant Celtic culture, which he, sounding rather like a Sinophilic Marxist discussing Tibet, terms a mere "sectionalism" of the United Kingdom, survived in the eighteenth century to be transplanted. His primary opposition to the thesis, though, is that he considers it politically incorrect: "perhaps particularly in the South, the substitution, however unintended, of an immutable ethnicity, call it Celtic or Anglo-Saxon, for the old generalized racism demands most careful attention" (524-25). To Berthoff then, any study of the cultural origins and survivals of white Southerners, and by implication to a lesser degree of northern Irish Americans, is virtually taboo because he labels it "racism,"[36] and his flippant hostility may be due to a recognition of the fact that the Celtic-Southern thesis possesses a validity that his theory and his nationalist-regionalism require him to condemn as racism, the ultimate damning in modern academia regardless of lack of foundation.

In discussing what she sees as the loss of emphasis on facts in modern history and cultural studies, Mary Lefkowitz says debate has moved "to perceived motives . . . : if they believe that a person's motivations are good, then what they say will be right" (49). Dario Fernandez-Morera reveals that this approach, which is endemic to postmodernism, is in origin Marxist. "As in materialist [Marxist] discourse," he writes, "so in PC the search for truth is displaced from an interest in the hidden and self-serving motivations of speakers and their determining social circumstances; and therefore to an interest in the collective within which the speaker speaks and from which he presumably derives what and how he speaks" (39). If the speaker's motives are adjudged to be politically out of step or insensitive (as determined by Marxists, postmodernists, and other leftists), the work must be condemned out of hand with slurs on the motives, whether those motives are declared to be intentional or latent. Thomas Sowell writes that for many a "vision" is more relevant than facts and truth, for it, like the Inner Voice speaking to Quakers, "is a special state of grace." Believers are correct factually because within the vision fact equals the vision. "Put differently," Sowell writes, "those who disagree with the prevailing vision are seen as being not merely in error, but in sin" (*Vision* 3). This is Berthoff's approach and method.[37]

If, however, rather than objecting to studies of white Southern cultural origins for fear that they might be used by 'racists,' Berthoff were to consider the matter, he would realize that the Celtic-Southern thesis could be used to undercut white supremacist ideas by revealing the obvious truth that white peoples are not monolithic but are divided into a myriad of ethnic, cultural, religious, and socio-economic groups, some of whom, like Celts, have been victims of a longstanding ethnic-cultural discrimination and violence not all that dissimilar from those of Native Americans, Africans, and Jews.[38] But even if this argument could not be advanced, Berthoff's desire to eliminate such a cultural study of the white South is answered by Louis Rubin in *The History of Southern Literature:* "the Southern identity is important because it is. Whether it ought or ought not to be is irrelevant" (5), and if it is important, it must be examined openly, fully, and fairly, which is impossible when the racist label is tossed rather indiscriminately to stifle research and, ultimately, teaching and publishing that fail to promote, that might thoroughly refute, the left-of-center prepossessions that define the postmodernist education establishment and its journalistic cheerleading section.

Berthoff's attack on McWhiney's belief that a general pan-Celtic folk culture existed at least into the early modern era may appear convincing initially, certainly to anyone unfamiliar with studies, such as that of Nerys Patterson mentioned above, that demonstrate the survival of Celtic culture across more than a millennium and a half. Impugning the concept that some sense of common Celtic folk culture led Irish Catholics and Protestants, Scottish Highlanders and Lowlanders, and the Welsh to coalesce into the predominate white Southern culture, Berthoff inveighs, "were it otherwise, someone would long since have applied the formula for Celtic community to pacifying the embattled peoples of Northern Ireland; by that formula, indeed, the troubles there since the 1650s ought never to have happened" (530). His logic is that peoples sharing a common folk culture do not engage in such blood feuds; therefore, because these groups did, and in one area still do, they could not all share a basic Celtic folk culture.

Those inclined to accept this view need only look to the former Yugoslavia. We know the Orthodox Serbs, Catholic Croats, and Moslem Bosnians have in recent years slaughtered one another at a rate never known in Belfast or Derry. Unless it applies exclusively to Celts, if Berthoff's theoretical analysis were remotely correct all these "tribes" would not be linguistic and cultural Slavs. To move outside the Indo-European family, we have such long-term blood feuds between Arabs and Jews (and in ancient times Hebrews and Canaanites-Phoenicians), both Semites, and South African Zulus and Xhosas, both Bantus. Just as the fights between family members are often the most vicious, and certainly do not prove that the combatants are not related, the squabbles between "tribes" of the same basic folk culture are often the most horrific, the most damaging and defeating. Frantz Fanon writes of the common pattern of the colonialist divide-and-conquer technique of prompting the conquered into fighting one another, "Tribal feuds only serve to perpetuate old grudges deep buried in the memory. By throwing himself with all his force into the *vendetta,* the native tries to persuade himself that colonialism does not exist, that everything goes on as before, that history continues," that he is not a conquered servant of an empire (*Roll* 630). This should be kept in mind when considering the Northern Ireland problems.

The ease with which a common Celtic identity may surface once the politically pro United Kingdom Irish native has left the Northern Ireland battlefront is exhibited in social anthropologist Mary Kell's study of Irish-born women living in London. Of one Protestant from rural Northern Ireland she writes:

> Elizabeth did experience changes in self-identification. For example, she said she would never consider herself Irish in Ireland, though she did in Britain. She also felt that her attitude to the political situation in Northern Ireland had changed. Since coming to England, she said, she had "realised" that the Unionists [those supporting rule from London in lieu of the old Northern Ireland Parliament founded for a "Protestant people" and opposing a united Ireland, virtually all of whom are Protestants] were too "intransigent". She saw things "more objectively", she suggested, and said she could envisage a united Ireland, when in London. She also celebrates St. Patrick in London. (207)

Rory Fitzpatrick recognizes this pattern of Celts of differing religious and UK political affiliations meshing into one new identity on the colonial Southern frontier. He notes, "these Irish settlers were not exclusively Presbyterian; Catholics and Episcopalians were prominent among them if not in large numbers" (67).

In *The Uncounted Irish in Canada and the United States* (1990), Margaret E. Fitzgerald and Joseph A. King provide a different criticism of the Celtic-Southern thesis. Unlike Clark and Berthoff, they reveal no overt anti-Southern bigotries. In fact, they disclose that two prominent

Revolutionary era South Carolinians, "Edward Rutledge, a signer of the Declaration of Independence, and his brother John Rutledge, a governor of South Carolina" were the sons of an Irish immigrant from County Longford, and both were members of the Charleston Friendly Brothers of St. Patrick (263). Fitzgerald and King dislike the Celtic-Southern thesis for two reasons: They see it as diminishing the importance of Irish Americans from other regions to the Celtic immigrant experience in America and as one in which Celts are stereotyped negatively (176). Their first concern is irrelevant to the thesis. Their second, while over-stated, is understandable, for though McWhiney and McDonald do not mean to endorse these views uncritically, they do focus on the beliefs of many Englishmen and Northerners that the differences of Celts and Southerners make the latter groups violently, ignorantly inferior.

Historians are not the only non-creative writers to suggest that the white South's cultural origins are Celtic. The two most controversial Southern gadflies, H. L. Mencken and W. J. Cash, both saw Southern culture as one determined considerably by Celts. In "The Anglo-Saxons," Mencken writes that many of the South's earliest settlers were Anglo-Saxon:

> But their Teutonic blood was early diluted by Celtic strains from Scotland, from the north of Ireland, from Wales, and from the west of England, and today those Americans who are regarded as being most thoroughly Anglo-Saxon—for example, the mountaineers of the Appalachian slopes from Pennsylvania to Georgia—are obviously far more Celtic than Teutonic, not only physically but also mentally. . . . A Methodist revival is not an English phenomenon; it is Welsh. (169)[39]

In "The Sahara of the Bozart," Mencken reveals his thesis on the South's cultural failures. He informs his readers that the eighteenth-century coastal South had a brilliant culture. The German Mencken's idolization of the Anglo-Norman South is fairly predictable, as is his rationale for the later South's alleged cultural failings: "The chief strain down there, I believe, is Celtic, rather than Saxon, particularly in the hill country." Mencken again sees Southern religion, in his estimation the ultimate bane on the South, as Celtic: "the religious thought of the South is almost precisely identical with the religious thought of Wales" (185, 190). Mencken recognized the shift from the colonial, coastal South dominated by Anglo-Normans to the antebellum and modern South increasingly dominated by Celts and their descendants, and his pro-Germanic prejudices led him to condemn the South of his time partly because Celtic cultural traits predominated.

Like Mencken, Cash found much to criticize about the South, and he too labeled much of Southern culture as Celtic in origin. Cash's fictional portrayal of the development of the antebellum planter-gentleman, an attempt to undo the Anglo-Norman false myth, begins with a "stout young Irishman" in the "Carolina upcountry about 1800" (15). Cash writes of the average nineteenth-century Southerner:

> He had much in common with the half-wild Scotch and Irish clansmen of the seventeenth and eighteenth centuries whose blood he so often shared, and from whom . . . he mainly drew his tradition; but with the English squire to whom the legend has always assimilated him, and to whom the Southern Agrarians have recently sought to reassimilate him, not much. (30)

To Cash, the fierce individualism of the Southern farmer was like that of "a Gael Chieftain from his rock-ringed glen, wholly content with his autonomy and jealously guardful that nothing should encroach upon it" (34). The romanticism that Cash deemed the South's "Achilles' heel," a "romanticism" that nurtured the literary flowering of Cash's own era, writings that he largely failed to appreciate or understand, was to him Celtic in origin, except when he saw it as tied to the denial of Celtic heritage.

After reading that various writers, most of them scholars, have in a number of ways drawn attention to the importance of immigrants to the South from Celtic lands and particularly to the descendants of those Celtic immigrants, a fair reader cannot declare that Celtic heritage could not be important to Southern literature. This becomes especially obvious in light of Louis Rubin's assertion, "to all intents and purposes, and with only one or two exceptions, the literature of the Piedmont *is* southern literature" (*William Elliott* 211). For as we have seen, the Piedmont South, the South beyond the narrow strip of Tidewater and low country, is very much the Celtic South.

This lengthy review of historical scholarship has been a necessary preparation for my reading of Southern literature for four reasons. First, readers not directly associated with the world of scholarship (and perhaps many who are) may have no idea that scholars have long recognized the large emigration from Celtic lands into the South during the colonial and early antebellum eras. Without this knowledge, a reader may conclude that significant numbers of peoples of Celtic heritage emigrated only to the northern United States beginning with Ireland's Great Famine, and therefore Celtic heritage could play no significant part in Southern culture, that Southern novelistic treatment of peoples of Celtic ancestry would be nothing more than unfounded fancy, fictional fantasy. Also, a reader aware that there is no disputing the mass emigration from Celtic lands into what would be the South well before the American Revolution and continuing throughout the antebellum era can deny the importance of studying Celtic contributions to the South only by asserting that Celtic heritage intrinsically lacks relevance or should be denied for political reasons.

Second, had I not revealed that numerous historians of the South and of Irish and Scottish America in addition to the proponents of the Celtic-Southern thesis have recognized a prominent role for Celtic immigrants and their descendants in Southern culture, readers pre-disposed against the thesis might reject my reading of Southern literature on theoretical grounds; in fact, one scholar responding to my paper at a conference did just that, claiming that the Celtic-Southern thesis was, he *knew* from a colleague whose work focused on the English yeoman image in Southern literature, theoretically untenable and therefore my reading of *Gone With the Wind* as an Irish American novel lacked foundation. Such a prejudiced, circular response is less likely when the reader knows that numerous scholars other than Grady McWhiney and Forrest McDonald acknowledge peoples living and transmitting Celtic identity and folkways to be important to the South. In brief, the South is not and never was the simplistic pattern of WASPs and blacks with a few Indians that is implied or asserted unquestioningly by the preponderance of academics; immigrants to the South from its earliest European settlement included peoples from Celtic lands who brought their non-English worldview and folkways with them.

The third and fourth reasons are closely related. Without a lengthy review of scholars acknowledging the significant presence in the South in all eras of people whose ancestries were Celtic a reader could declare that the use of characters of Celtic heritage by Southern novelists signifies nothing beyond imagination, means nothing culturally unless the reader accepts the postmodern conceit that everything is fiction. Without this review of scholarship, my cultural analysis of Southern novels might seem to some readers to suggest merely that Southern writers often have utilized characters whose ancestry is Celtic. My reading of Southern literature, however, supports the basic tenets of the McWhiney-McDonald Celtic-Southern thesis. A number of the South's novelists have portrayed characters of Celtic heritage as different from those of English heritage and as indispensable to their fictional meanings and morals. Their fiction should not by itself be called history; rather, the historical studies demonstrate that these novelists knew their region's peoples and their folkways and heritages well indeed, much better in certain key ways than have the vast majority of scholars.

Though *Cracker Culture* is convincing, if not exhaustively inductive, it is flawed by its strength: the almost exclusive use of travel accounts relating folkways to argue its case. McWhiney ignores antebellum Southern literature because he believes that its authors, "the most cosmopolitan and learned of Southerners, were not representative of *Cracker Culture*; indeed, many of them were not Crackers at all." McWhiney notes, and I believe correctly, at least for the antebellum era, "Crackers infrequently took pen in hand, and the resulting documents seldom survived to be examined by scholars" (xviii).

Total acceptance of this view, however, creates a problem for those well versed in Southern literature. Vann Woodward, perhaps the best-known historian of the South, declares of Southern novelists, "they have given history meaning and value and significance as events never do merely because they happen" (39), and Frank Owsley, Jr. affirms, "it is the novel's social and intellectual insights that make it most useful to historians. Perceptions and ideals are difficult to capture in historical narrative, and thus we rely on the novelist to deal with these issues" (5). From the literary vantage, John Pilkington avows, "one begins to suspect that for Faulkner, historical facts tend not to explain anything. Understanding of history can only come through the imaginative reconstruction of the past, and for history to make sense to the present the historian must perform an act of the imagination" (177).

This symbiosis between Southern fiction and Southern history determines that if the Celtic-Southern thesis is valid, a number of Southern novelists will have revealed in their works the importance of Celtic immigrants and their descendants to the development, expansion, and perpetuation of Southern culture. Nor does this present the kind of problem McWhiney believes. Not only are a large number of Southern novelists of Irish and Scottish ancestry, but Southern literature is primarily one predicated on folklore. It is created "out of the rag-tag and bob-ends of old tales and talking" (Faulkner, *Absalom, Absalom* 303), and if the folk culture of the white South is primarily transplanted Celtic, then the novels will reveal not only that Celtic heritage but also its significance. Readers predisposed to assume that Celtic heritage in the modern world or in America can signify nothing will be persuaded by nothing I write or anyone else may write; they will remain like those readers and teachers in, say, 1950 who believed that anyone labeled black could not be used thematically in any significant way by major writers and therefore read Faulkner without focusing on and appreciating the thematic significance of Dilsey, Lucas Beauchamp, or Clytie Sutpen.

Before proceeding with an examination of what McWhiney might call "Cracker literature," novels by and about Southerners of Celtic ancestry, I think it important to note briefly that black Southerners also have recognized both an awareness of Celtic heritage as something set apart and the importance of Celtic heritage to the South. Blyden Jackson reveals that Ralph Ellison's Professor Woodridge, a teacher who focused on Irish writers, was modeled upon one of Ellison's Tuskegee English professors. Ellison's *Invisible Man* narrator, Jackson says, does not emphasize Yeats, Joyce, and O'Casey simply because of artistic excellence "but because they were Irish. As Irish they had own consciousness of what it meant to be a member of a minority group and to try to accommodate that when they wrote" (601).

Ernest J. Gaines' *The Autobiography of Miss Jane Pittman* is an allegory, personified in Jane, of the survival and the thriving of black Southerners from the Emancipation Proclamation to the beginnings of the Civil Rights movement. With the freedom from slavery brought by Union troops, Jane, a child, attempts to walk to Ohio, a land that symbolizes freedom to her. On the journey, she meets an elderly white man who attempts to dissuade her from continuing her exodus. In addition to revealing to Jane that the journey to Ohio will be arduously long and dangerous, the old man warns her that to get to Ohio she must cross through the very center of white Southern culture: the "backward" Tennesseans, "still speaking Gaelic" (52). Gaines' character believes that at the heart of white Southern culture lies the Irish language, and in keeping with Anglophonic prejudices he declares that heritage inferior.

Chapter II

The Father: William Gilmore Simms

Louis Rubin believes that for there to be a "Southern" literature, certain "distinctive" elements must be present in the works. These

> are usually said to be a distinctive awareness of the Past, a firm iden-
> tification with a Place, a preoccupation with one's membership in a
> community, a storytelling bent (as compared with a concern for
> Problems), a strong sense of family and an unusually vivid conscious-
> ness of caste and class, especially race. ("Changing" 226)

In addition to defining "race" as being more than simplistically black-white, I would add to Rubin's list a sense of the omnipotence of religion or spirituality that often is manifested in a recognition of the presence of evil in the world; an abiding interest in women's roles and identities in relation to the senses of community and family seemingly predicated upon patriarchy; an appreciation and celebration of the wildly comic in life; an awareness of man's role as despoiler of God's nature that is decidedly non-transcendental[1]; and, perhaps most important, a sense of the South, and likewise various locales in the South, as something considerably more than a mere region or province of a more significant larger unit.

In noting that by themselves these "hallmarks" are found in other liter-atures as well and that it is "their continuing mutual action upon each other" that demarcates Southern literature, Rubin suggests that "no one writer's work may stress all of them" ("Changing" 227-28). Though his works suffer from the flaws generally common to the early antebellum peri-od, to James Fenimore Cooper among others, William Gilmore Simms' novels feature, if they do not stress, each item on Rubin's list and my addi-tions. For this reason, I label him the Father of Southern Literature.[2] If the Celtic-Southern thesis is applicable to Southern literature, it will be evident in the works of Simms, as are most of the other "distinctive elements."

Simms was born in Charleston, South Carolina, on 17 April 1806, the son of an immigrant from Larne, County Antrim, Ireland (Trent 1).[3] In what is thus far the most comprehensive study to be published of Simms as literary artist, Mary Ann Wimsatt declares that the elder William Simms "made a lasting and vital impression on his son. Celtic to the core, he was—by family testimony and the evidence of his actions— rash, courageous, bold and resolute" (14). She sees the younger Simms as inheriting each of his major personality traits from his Irish father and of possessing both "Celtic fluency" and "Celtic temperament" (14, 183, 258). Though she acknowledges that Simms was essentially culturally Celtic and that his art was influenced by his heritage, Wimsatt only touches lightly upon any aspect of Simms' Celticness as revealed in his novels.[4] From the beginning of his career to its close, however, Simms emphasized the indispensable importance of Celtic immigrants and their descendants to the development and expansion of Southern culture.

The Yemassee, published in 1835 and Simms' best known work, is set in the South Carolina low country in 1715. It concerns a Native American uprising against the European colonization of their land. Simms' primary focuses are the nobility of the doomed race (which is much more a Southern version of Homer's tribute to the Trojans than a Southern version of darker-skinned primitives romanticized as more spiritual and "noble" than European peoples) and the necessity of the proprietary governor to act not as an hereditary lord with autocratic privileges but as a frontier "democrat" who earns the right to lead. It would seem that this novel, set at the beginning of the "greatest wave of immigration to the South" (McDonald, "Prologue" xxxix), would have little room for emphasizing the importance of Celtic peoples to the development of Southern culture. Simms, however, notes that even prior to the great northern Irish Protestant migration to the South, the Irish were prominent in the Carolina colony. In remarking the democratic friendliness of Harrison, who is Governor Craven incognito, Simms, though acknowledging others generally, names but two nations as homelands of the settlers, "merry old England, or hilarious Ireland" (*Yemassee* 218).

Simms is not content merely to suggest that the pre-1715, non-genteel European settlement of South Carolina was perhaps roughly half Irish; he introduces an Irish character to represent the courage and bravery necessary to maintain this colony. Teddy Macnamara, a "poor labourer" who still speaks with a pronounced Irish accent and despite his poverty considers himself a "jontleman," has been captured by the Yemassee and is being tortured. Rather than wilt in the face of horror, Macnamara verbally taunts and challenges his captors. Though beaten and cut and shot with arrows numerous times, Macnamara briefly escapes and makes a defiant run toward freedom before being caught and having his skull smashed.

Louis Rubin believes that the Macnamara scene "obviously bears a symbolic relationship, in the mind of the novelist, to the whole matter of leadership, authority, and the frontier." Rubin further suggests that for Simms "there is something significant involved in the episode for him over and beyond its convenience as plot" (*Edge* 116). Though he believes that the Macnamara scene is Simms' tribute to his father (*Edge* 93), Rubin fails to explain the full significance he senses in the episode. The McWhiney-McDonald Celtic-Southern thesis provides the explanation. The Teddy Macnamara scene is an early attempt by Simms to reveal in his fiction the Celtic qualities that from the beginning of European settlement in the South went into the formation of Southern culture. Not only were the Teddy Macnamaras present and prominent in the earliest European settlements in the South, but their sense of equality, one in which men are great not by birth but by personal character and deeds, would thrive in the frontier South.[5]

Mellichampe (1836) was the second of Simms' Revolutionary Romances to be published.[6] It contains no scene as symbolically significant to the portrayal of Celts in the South as Teddy Macnamara's capture and torture, but it does feature a reinforcement of Simms' *Yemassee* assertion that the Irish were numerous in the South Carolina colony by 1715. Piney Grove, a scene of much of the action in *Mellichampe*, is the Berkeley family estate, and it was built around the time of the Yemassee War. A party of some two hundred Edistohs had attacked it, and "old Marmaduke Berkeley, with the aid of his neighbors, and a few trusty Irish workmen, who had been employed upon the estate, made a sturdy defense" (64). Simms acknowledges that the English held the land grants and commissioned the building of the coastal colony's original Big Houses, but the mass of white laborers were Celts, and the logical inference is that those settlers would reproduce and strive to acquire their own lands, and perpetuate their folk culture. Indeed, historian R. J. Dickson notes that after the Yemassee War approximately five hundred Irish settlers assumed possession of "lands in South Carolina vacated by the Yamassee Indians" (24).

The third Revolutionary Romance, *The Scout* (originally published as

The Kinsman, 1841) is the first Simms novel to describe the role of Irish troops in the Southern theater of the American war for independence. The novel, which focuses on the conflict of half-brothers, one a patriot and the other serving the crown, is set in the area around the Wateree and Congaree Rivers, near what is today Columbia, during May and June of 1781. Jack Bannister, the scout of the title, is the first to observe that the newly arrived redcoats are "a body consisting chiefly of the Irish regiments" (225). When Jack is caught spying, Lord Rawdon, the Irish-born commander of the crown forces, reveals a problem for the English that Simms will explore in greater depth in subsequent novels: The mass desertion of Irish troops from the imperial army to the patriot cause (269). This problem is especially vexing to Simms' Rawdon, for though he has under his command loyalists, Hessians, and a few English, the Irish troops are his best: "Martial in their courage, bold in action, and quite as full of vivacity as courage" (273).

In *Katherine Walton* (1851), Proctor, a loyalist, believes that England will lose the war because "she can get no more subsidies of men from Germany, and her Irish recruits desert her almost as soon as they reach America" (124). General Williamson, the Scottish-born patriot who, upon threat of having his estates confiscated and sold by the English who control the South Carolina low country, had withdrawn from the conflict, declares that the Irish troops in the English army "are better disposed to fight *for* the rebels than fight against them" (160).

In a more indirect way, the importance of the South's Celtic heritage is highlighted in Simms' portrayal of the wedding of Mad Archy Campbell, a Scottish officer in the crown forces. Campbell is, with the exceptions of his being well educated and highly intelligent, apparently the English stereotype of a wild Celt. A fierce fighter, Campbell avows, "peace is not my element. Repose does not refresh me. I prefer a storm any day to a calm" (334). Playing off the anti-Celtic fears of the English, Campbell succeeds in having his marriage ceremony performed when and how he desires both by threatening to shoot the Anglican parson if he does not proceed with haste and by telling his terrified intended, "I will sooner shoot both of us than see you disappointed" (337).

Simms' greatest weakness in characterization is his portrayal of the gentry, the Anglo-Norman elite of Charleston and the low country, who are more often than not wooden.[7] His strength lies in his portrayals of what McWhiney would call "Crackers." No place is this more evident than in his comedy. Simms is able to write convincing backwoods comedy, as well as the comic marriage of a Scottish officer, not merely because of his own Irish heritage, but also because that earthy, exuberant Celtic philosophy of life was pre-dominant in the South, reinforcing Simms' familial tendencies. In attempting to draw genteel Anglo-Normans, Simms was creating falsely, for though such people existed in the South to his own day, they were a distinct minority, and almost as foreign to the everyday lives of the mass of white Southerners as New England Puritans or Pennsylvania Quakers.

In a November 1860 letter to his New York confidant James Lawson, Simms wrote of the secession frenzy: "The fact is that it is a complete landsturm, a general rising of the people, and the politicians are far behind them. And every So. State will follow S.C. The people will not suffer the politicians any longer. They are now neither to be deluded, nor coaxed, nor cheated nor cajoled" (IV 261).

This passage suggests that Simms saw the imminent formation of a Southern national government as one driven not by the politicians, who were principally the wealthy slave owners, but by the masses, most of whom owned no slaves. Simms is not asserting that wealthy owners of slaves failed to support secession; he is asserting that the masses of Southerners, starting with South Carolinians, desired secession not for fear of losing their slaves (which they did not own), nor for more complex reasons regarding the proposed tariff increases (which many would not have understood until their wallets were decimated by it), but because they simply no longer could see that federal government, then dominated by Northerners who were spiritual, intellectual, and often physical heirs of New England Puritans, as representing them and their culture. Though Simms does not here state the reason prompting these masses to endorse secession, a reading of Simms' novels reveals that the author believed a basic cultural difference between North and South did indeed exist. What is important to the Celtic-Southern thesis is that by the mid-1850s, when a succession of political crises had pushed the possibility of Southern secession to the forefront, Simms' novels began to reveal an even greater emphasis than did his previously published novels on the importance of Celts, especially the Irish, in developing Southern culture.

The Forayers (1855) was the sixth Revolutionary War novel published by Simms. It is set in the area around Orangeburg, South Carolina, in 1781, as the English forces are being broken. The novel's protagonist is Major Willie Sinclair, a young patriot whose speeches mark him as a Jeffersonian. Willie's father, however, a man of "pure Saxon-sanguine temperament" (147), supports the king and constantly chastises his rebellious son. Willie, "a man of great woodland resources," divides his time between the semi-regular military service common to the Southern theater of the war and attempts to save his father, sister, and family estate from the marauding banditti, both Whig and Tory.

Simms reveals the importance of the Irish to the winning of independence at the novel's opening. The Irish, he writes of the Carolina settlers, "would be sure to wear Whig colors," but the "English were mostly dogged Loyalists" (10). David Noel Doyle's assessment of the enthusiastic support for American independence by the Irish in South Carolina, a group legally discriminated against by the colonial administration, bolsters Simms' fictional assertion. "Despite almost complete disfranchisement (again by gerrymander) and the recent absence of even skeletal government services," Doyle reveals, "the Scotch-Irish of South Carolina generally supported the Revolution, as did the growing community of Irish-born at Charleston" (*Ireland* 134).

As in both *The Scout* and *Katherine Walton*, the patriot cause in *The Forayers* is aided by Irish deserters from the English forces. Ballou, Willie's chief scout, has commandeered considerable English ammunition, "besides sending thirteen Irish deserters into camp" (33). In explaining to his sister the inevitability of an English loss, Willie asserts that the English plan had been one of divide and conquer, but this, finally, has failed. "Their only resource, for new regiments," he declares, "is Ireland, and the Irish desert their ranks almost as soon as they take the field" (127). When Governor John Rutledge, the son of an Irish immigrant, orders Willie to liberate the Orangeburg jail, which is filled with "refractory Irish" troops arrested for being drunken, probably as a way of avoiding the possibility of dying in service to the maintenance of the English empire, he adds, "You will probably find the Irish, whom you emancipate, willing to take arms against their former owners" (419). Indeed, after the battle, "sixteen wild Irish were extricated from the dungeon, charged with the Irish virtue of mutiny and insubordination" (450), and all of them immediately join the revolution to fight for "fradom, and Ameriky for iver."

Rutledge's reference to English imperial forces as "owners" of the Irish not only raises the issue of a nation's being ruled from afar and by another ethnic/national group as tantamount to slavery, but it also encourages the reader to recall a previous scene. Ireland's Lord Edward Fitzgerald, serving under Lord Rawdon, has visited the Sinclair estate and been smitten by Carrie, Willie's younger sister. After pointing out his father's hypocrisy in promoting this potential match ["there was a time when Irish nobility, and the whole Irish race, found but little sympathy in your thoughts" (156)], Willie queries Fitzgerald's presence in America: "How should he be here, sir, with his own people in bonds at home, fighting the battles of their oppressor! . . . One who calls himself an Irish patriot fighting against the liberties of America" (157).

Willie Sinclair, who has learned from fighting a partisan war for national independence that freedom is never given freely, has no patience for Irishmen who "serve as willing mercenaries of the very sovereign whom they hate, and every blow which they strike in his behalf," Willie avows, "rivets more firmly the chain about their own wrists" (157). The reader familiar with Irish history knows that less than two decades later, Edward Fitzgerald would give his life in an attempt to win national independence for Ireland.[8] In utilizing one of the heroes of the United Irishmen Revolution of 1798, Simms prompts his readers to see connections between all anti-imperialist and anti-forced-governmental-centrist revolutions and between the Irish and the Southern theater of the American Revolution. This linkage is one that many today, who have been educated erroneously to think of early America as being almost exclusively Anglo-Saxon in ethnicity and certainly Anglophilic in attitude, cannot fathom having been made by any American in the antebellum era. But the fact is that Simms, like a sizeable number of antebellum Southerners, was a member of a family that had played no insignificant role in attempts to free a Celtic land from being ruled and exploited colonially by England. Simms scholar James Everett Kibler writes:

> what has not been known is that the Simms family of Ulster, and specifically of the Belfast area, were Irish freedom fighters, at the time our William Gilmore Simms Sr. [the author's father] immigrated to Carolina. The Simms family involvement with the Irish independence movement culminated in the great Irish Rebellion of 1798, which led the English to deport Simms family members, and to execute Simms family friends and co-revolutionaries. ("Simms's Irish" 1)

Kibler, as part of his case that Simms certainly knew his family's Irish nationalist ties and recognized them as central to his religious, political, and cultural views and activities, also notes that at the age of twenty-two, Simms published a poem titled "Song of the Irish Patriot" (5). This three-stanza poem, which names Irish nationalist heroes who were compatriots of the Simms family, predicts Ireland's freedom "in long years to come." The poem's early composition, two decades before the massive influx of Catholic Irish fleeing the Great Famine began, and its not having started a firestorm among the South's literati indicates the strong ties, culturally and emotionally, to Ireland held by many antebellum Southerners, which came from family heritage; Andrew Jackson is merely the best known Jacksonian era Southerner who would have found the young Simm's Irish nationalist poem to speak for his cultural views.[9]

Simms' blind spot in his linkage of nations, peoples, being ruled by foreigners (those of a different nation, ethnicity, and language) to slavery, which perhaps was due as much to his passionate desire to be accepted fully among the Charleston elite as to his purse and his times, is that he did not transfer this understanding to chattel slavery. But in this presentation of Southern Revolutionary views, Simms the writer was accurate. Peter Kolchinz says, "Patriots commonly denounced the 'slavery' they suffered at the hands of the British, and insisted they would rather die than remain slaves; although there was considerable hyperbole in this rhetoric . . . the irony of fighting a war for liberty at the same time that they held one-third of their own population as slaves was not lost on them" (76).

Simms also makes the Irish central to the beginnings of Southern literature. Willie sings a song in praise of the Revolution that opens, "My country is my mistress" (234-35). The poet and composer is George Dennison, one of Francis Marion's men and a character in Simms' previously published Revolutionary novels. After hearing his son's performance and criticizing the work, old Sinclair declares of the poet, "The fellow must be an Irishman, I fancy." Willie replies, "he is of the stock, at all events" (235). Throughout the Revolutionary War series, Dennison is shown to be the folk poet, the natural bard of both the war and South Carolina and its culture.[10] It is significant that the cultural spokesman of Marion's band, men who represent the best Southern qualities and spirit in Simms' work, be of Irish heritage. If the heart of this culture is Irish, an Irish bard is required to record and celebrate it.[11]

In a note to a line in one of Dennison's lyrics, Simms provides an explanation for the reason the Carolina Scottish Highlanders tended to support the crown:

> The exiled rebels of '45, when settled in America, almost wholly proved adherents of that monarch whom, as followers of the Stuarts, they opposed to the knife. The disasters of '45 cured them of all propensity to rebellion. Even the Macdonalds, the famous Hector-Flora who saved the Pretender—all became loyal to George the Third in America, and fought against the patriots. (551)

Rather than their being culturally different from the Scots-Irish, as

David Hackett Fischer posits, the majority of Carolina Highlanders either supported the crown or remained neutral during the American Revolution out of the fearful memory of the cultural genocide inflicted on the Highlands after Culloden. Duane Meyer concludes that the Revolutionary era Carolina Highlanders "did fear the loss of their land—some of it very recently acquired. They knew the crown had seized the land of the rebel clans after the Forty-Five and, as of 1775, that the land still had not been returned to the original owners" (154). The Gaelic-language poetry of the Carolina Highlanders makes this same point. Iain MacMhurchaidh in "Gur Muladach A Tha Mi" ("Lonely Am I"), a poem written at the beginning of the conflict, affirms:

> If mastery were to be gained
> over the redcoats,
> I would take a firm stand
> although my hour may be near.
>   . . .
> This is what will happen
> if you do not all yield;
> when the strongest forces
> from the other side arrive
> there will be hanging and destruction,
> and raiding of your cattle
> Neither law nor reason will prevail
> to protect rebels. (MacDonell 50-51)[12]

Eutaw (1856) is the sequel to *The Forayers,* and it takes that novel's action through the battle of Eutaw Springs, which broke the English military dominance of the South Carolina low country. The role of Irish troops is as important in the sequel as its predecessor. Hating the formal military drills as much as the prospect of dying for England, a number of the Irish troops imbibe freely, and under the influence, they riot. Two of them are shot, and a third is hanged as an object lesson, "by way of encouraging the others in a better taste for innocent water" (130).[13] In an interview with Edward Fitzgerald, old Sinclair refers to the troops as British, prompting Fitzgerald to rejoin, "Irish—not British." In addition to correcting the loyalist about nationality, which as an English imperialist old Sinclair deems irrelevant, Fitzgerald explains that the Irish will fight, but only when their hearts are in it, and they are easily won to the argument of national independence (318-19). Shortly thereafter, a detachment of Irish troops attacked by General Lee surrenders en masse without firing a shot. Lee, accepting the prejudices of the Anglo-Norman dominated coastal South and his own English birth, "ascribed it all to panic," but Simms writes, "we half suspect, there was no hearty good will for the British cause" (334). Porgy, with his characteristic comic flair, informs old Sinclair of the "captured" Irish, "the fellows are no cowards, not a man of 'em; but they had no such love for British rule that you entertain, and gave themselves up to better society" (351). As with the many Irish laborers in early Charleston noted in *The Yemassee* and *Mellichampe,* these deserters from the British army will likely remain in the South and further contribute to its Celticization.

Set in 1684-85, *The Cassique of Kiawah* (1859) might appear to portray an era too early in the South's development to include a discussion of the importance of Celtic immigrants. The novel's primary focus is the relationship between two brothers, Edward Berkeley, who has a plantation on the Ashley River (Kiawah to the Indians), and Harry, who uses the surname Calvert and pirates the Spanish galleons returning to Europe laden with western hemisphere riches. But *The Cassique of Kiawah* also acknowledges the indispensable importance of Celts to the opening of the Southern frontier, and thereby to the genesis and expansion of Southern culture. In relating the social hierarchy of early Charleston, Simms avows:

> The Indian traders of 1684, and down thence to 1770, ranked second to the local noblesse. They did a flourishing business; they ushered in the first merchants. They were bold adventurers, chiefly of the class called Scotch-Irish, who possessed a hardy enterprise, great personal courage; were shrewd, intelligent, cautious; not learned, but possessed of mother-wit; were greedy of gain, and ready to risk life upon it; but ambitious of social position, and not unwilling to peril for that which was more precious than life, money! They aimed at something (and this is a right ambition) of social position for themselves and their children. (134)[14]

Simms does not conclude his praise of Celts here. He continues by declaring:

> Could the court of England have cast off, as so many worthless old slippers, their worthless courtiers to whom they confided most of the colonial governments in America, and given their trusts chiefly to those Scotch or Scoto-Irish adventurers, thousands of lives would have been saved from butchery, millions of dollars kept in the treasury, and the miseries which belong to the caprices of an uncertain Indian war upon a wild frontier would have been escaped. (135)

This general contrast between hard, realistic, accomplishing Celt and vapid, otiose Anglo-Norman is made concrete in the novel when Simms introduces Craven and Cavendish, a pair of Charleston dandies. Unlike the active Celts, who place life and limb in danger in order to achieve goals they have set, the Anglo-Norman fops, trussed by all the might of the imperial British army and secure in their belief of inherent cultural superiority over the "red-headed adventurers," devote their energies to seduction attempts and other vanities. Camille Paglia notes a correlation between Cavaliers playing sex roles and effeminate, narcissistic inactivity. "This was clearly the case with the seventeenth-century Cavaliers," she writes, "whose portraits have a stunning epicene grandeur. The west has persistently and probably correctly associated long male hair with a dangerous because entrancing and self-entranced egotism" (329). Though Simms does not make the explicit analogy in the novel, his previous writings and his personal wars with Charleston's social elite suggest that his negative portrayal in *The Cassique of Kiawah* of the city's original Anglo-Norman Cavalier social mandarins may be a comment on the mid-nineteenth-century South as well: the Anglo-Norman on the coast living and playing solipsistically like Craven and Cavendish, ineffectually like Edward Berkeley, or piratically like Harry, none of whom contributes positively to family or community, while the upland Celts, their names largely lost to history, remained vibrant and vigorous, the heart and the future, as well as the virility, of the culture.[15] It may be read as a warning to the South of what Eugene Genovese sees as actually having happened with the spread of plantation life: "the undercurrent of a seemingly effete tidewater exclusiveness was somehow prevailing over the coarse virility of a democratic people" (*World* 123). If this is so, then someplace deep inside, Simms held serious reservations about his slave-owning world, at least in ethnic/cultural terms. Another hint that this may have been the case lies in Simms' use of the name "Craven" for one of his two Cavalier party boys running amuck in seventeenth-century Charleston, for Lord Craven was not merely one of the original plantation proprietors of the Carolina colony but also headed the committee of six that managed the Royal Adventurers, the forerunner of the Royal Africa Company that held Crown monopoly on the English cross-Atlantic slave trade (Thomas 198-201).

Simms also goes out of his way to introduce the reader of *The Cassique of Kiawah* to an actual historical person: Florence O'Sullivan, who "was destined to make himself still more notorious in after-days, in the colonial regime of Carolina" (455). It was, Simms notes, O'Sullivan's idea to build a defensive castle on the subsequently named Sullivan's Island at the entrance to Charleston's harbor. This man of vision who "spoke with a decided Irish accent" was "a Celt of characteristic courage" (455, 542-43). The great importance he attached to O'Sullivan would be revealed in Simms' *The History of South Carolina* (1860). O'Sullivan would quit his post and join "the discontents of the town" (58), who were demanding reforms from the Anglo-Norman Lords Proprietors and their appointed colonial rulers. Though this was a small revolt, Simms sees it as part of the long process leading inevitably to the Revolution. His emphasis on Florence O'Sullivan is due to his tendency to see Celts as the catalysts of change from an hereditarily aristocratic South ruled by and for Anglo-Normans, at the expense of politically and culturally subdued Celts, to a more "democratic" South in which any free man might succeed and make of himself a gentleman.[16]

Perhaps the most important Simms novel concerning Celts and Southern culture is *Paddy McGann; or The Demon of the Stump*, first published serially in 1863 in *The Southern Illustrated News* (Bush xix). Wimsatt notes that "the figure of Paddy indicates Simms' interest, doubtless partly autobiographical, in the idiosyncracies of Celtic character . . ." (205), but her cultural analysis goes no further. The short novel is a Southwestern humor allegory of the South. Its two framers are Wharncliffe, a gentleman planter, and Stylus, a Southern writer who is the actual transmitter of Paddy's tale. Taken as a pair, Wharncliffe and Stylus represent not only Simms himself but also the class of educated, literary, antebellum Southerners. In the opening chapter, Wharncliffe, who is worried himself, attempts to assuage his friend's fears for the South. He best does so by arguing against the writer who, in accepting the bigotries of the educated, believes that the South has produced little literature because "our people have no past" (223). In order to convince Stylus that the South does have the past necessary to create a great literature, Wharncliffe introduces the writer to Paddy McGann, an uneducated Edisto raftsman who is a natural poet and storyteller. "Paddy McGann at his best," declares Robert Bush, "is an emblem of the essential character of the Southern masses, representing values that Simms wished to see preserved" (xxv). In his rollicking analysis of Southern culture, an allegory that suggests that the seeds of a great Southern literature have already been planted in the folklore of the Paddys, Simms chooses as his quintessential Southerner not an Anglo-Norman with a vast estate and a multitude of slaves, nor an Anglo-Saxon merchant perhaps peddling Methodism as well as dry goods, but an Irishman, a financially insecure worker who owns no slave but is the master of an impressive gift of storytelling.

Wharncliffe advocates the centrality of Celts to Southern culture in refuting Stylus's claim that the South lacks traditions. "All the old British superstitions are retained," he says, "and you may trace them, in different sections, to an English, Scotch, or Irish source; to the Scotch, perhaps, more than either" (226). First, the reader should note that rather than label Southern traditions, hence culture, English, Wharncliffe sees three contributors, two of which are Celtic, the trio grouped under the Celtic label adopted by the English: British. Second, the reader should wonder about the prominence given to the Scots rather than the Irish. After all, the prototypic Southerner in this allegory is a Carolinian of Irish heritage who still speaks with "some of the brogue, which . . . he blends curiously with our native backwoods *patois*" (235). Forrest McDonald and Ellen Shapiro McDonald provide an answer in "The Ethnic Origins of the American People, 1790." They note both the disproportionately high number of Scots, especially post-Culloden Highlanders, to migrate to the Carolinas and a religious bigotry that still exists: that Protestantism is antithetical to Celtic culture, that Anglo-Saxon and Protestant are necessary affinities (183). As Simms had never before attempted to foist Catholicism on his largely American Protestant readers,[17] it could not be expected of him to do so in the midst of a war for Southern national independence. As is generally assumed of Scots, Paddy is a Protestant (281).

The first half of Paddy's tale, which is an allegory about the destruction of the Southern wilderness, may be summarized quickly. Paddy is harassed by a spirit, an Otherworld being he calls the "Devil," that wants him to "l'arn to be sinsible," to not continue a destruction of nature for he sees animals as his "children" (315). Unable to put food on the table by hunting, Paddy attempts to flee from his "Devil" by taking a fleet of rafts down the Edisto. But Paddy is incapable of escape, and he is separated from the other raftsmen only to find himself in the middle of the ocean with "shirks" around his raft.

This is the second point at which Celticness becomes central in Simms' Southern allegory. Robert Bush believes that Paddy's pelagic "ordeal seems to be equated to the wartime ordeal of the Confederacy itself," that "the episode has the didactic function of encouraging the people of the South to hold on in their own struggle, to trust in God's providence" (xxv). Paddy is saved by Captain Wilson, a Scot who instantly takes to his Irish South Carolinian refugee. At dinner in the Captain's cabin, Paddy must listen to Wilson's diatribe against "the Amerikin character." Wilson avows, "It's a nation of rogues and swindlers. Their only idea of vartue is *smartness,* and they uses their smartness only to take a fellow in. The only difference between 'em, any whar, is that one man is a *smarter rogue* than the other" (373). Paddy is upset by what he thinks is an insult to his nation, but Wilson, who sounds like an early Vanderbilt Agrarian,[18] declares, "You're a Southern. . . . The Amerikin charackter . . . is made by the North" (373). A little later Wilson tells Paddy of two New Yorkers on board, "I considers you of a different nation from these people" (374). Wilson, who loves the South, cannot return Paddy to Charleston immediately due to business arrangements that require him to be in New York, a city he despises and one that Paddy comes to consider Hell on earth (376, 382). Wilson later offers to give Paddy free passage to Scotland, where, presumably, he will find a community and a culture similar enough to his own so that he would feel as if he belonged there (442).

It is at this point that the "national allegory" is apparent. Wharncliffe, a gentleman bearing a sonorous Norman-sounding surname, introduces a representative Southerner to his friend Stylus, a writer with an overtly Latin cognomen which suggests not only his classical education but also his separation from the South's folk culture, one determined by the Paddys. Wharncliffe makes the introduction of Paddy, a Southern Everyman, to Stylus to prove to the professional writer that the South does indeed possess the foundation necessary for a grand literature. The allegory primarily concerns the Confederacy, but the emphasis upon Paddy as raconteur suggests that for Simms, Southern nationhood is predicated not on economics, such as slavery or opposition to high tariffs, nor even on political philosophy such as decentralism and states' rights, but on cultural differences. This is borne out by Captain Wilson. He is a Celt who identifies with the Southern prototype; Paddy is his kind of person, and he also despises Yankees. Paddy being saved at sea by a Scot may be seen as allegorical on another level. For the South to be saved, it must accept its Celticness; it can be saved only by its Celtic heritage. It must turn not to the Wharncliffes and Styluses but to the Paddys and Wilsons and, dragging the earlier part of Simms' career into the allegorical meaning of this novel, the descendants of the many Irish and Scottish Carolina settlers. At the heart of Southern culture, this allegory says, is an Irishman, not an Anglo-Norman Cavalier, and the South will not develop an expansive, great literature until the Paddys become the Styluses, when the subject of the South's *belles lettres* is an examination of the reality of the Celticness of the South, with all of its violence and earthiness of language and action, both tragic and comic, with all of its striving to overcome centuries of violent assault from English armies and culture, striving merely to survive culturally.

In a note near the novel's opening, Simms declares that the Appalachians are the "backbone of the country," meaning the South. He continues, "Apalachia should be the poetical name of the Confederacy. This native word, of the red man, cannot be surpassed in equal dignity and euphony" (221). Choosing Appalachia as "the poetical name of the Confederacy" would honor more than American Indians. When we recall that the proponents of the Celtic-Southern thesis, David Noel Doyle, and David Hackett Fischer all recognize that culturally Celtic immigrants settled primarily in the Piedmont and Appalachian regions of the South and then spread westward, we know that any honor of the region must be tied to its people: the descendants of Celtic immigrants. Just as Simms' Paddy is the Southern prototype whose folklore will determine the predicted great Southern literature, McWhiney's Crackers are the cultural backbone of the South; the Appalachians, of course, are its geographic backbone. In honoring those people in this manner, Simms reinforces the point made in the novel that the vibrant Southern folk culture is that of the Paddys, not that of the Wharncliffes and Styluses.

Joscelyn, the last Revolutionary novel written by Simms and the first in chronological order of the material, was published serially in *The Old Guard* in 1867. It portrays the origins of the war in the South Carolina-Georgia border backcountry from July to December 1775. As in *The Cassique of Kiawah,* Simms here emphasizes the importance of the Southern Indian trade and concludes that the best of the traders were Celtic: "we owe to these sources, chiefly of the Scotch-Irish, some of the most eminent men that the country has produced" (11). *Joscelyn* explores the effects of the internecine struggle, one that Simms sees as compounded by the lack of homogeneity in the area (116). This problem would be solved eventually under the leadership of one immigrant group that would spearhead the formation of a South Carolinian, and by implication ultimately a Southern, identity. "The Irish settlements alone," Simms writes "exhibited that flexibility, still so characteristic of that race, which gradually breaks down the social barriers, and accommodates itself to a more various convention" (252-53). Simms acknowledges that several European cultural and national groups, Native Americans, and Africans were all present during the South's colonial period, but the Celts, especially the Irish, his works affirm, served as the matrix and the nexus of Southern culture, one that would reach its belletristic zenith beginning with the Southern Renaissance.

Chapter III

Other Progenitors: "An Hibernian," George Tucker, John Pendleton Kennedy, William Alexander Caruthers, and "Paddy O'Flarrity"

Considering that the antebellum South was, as William Taylor reveals in *Cavalier and Yankee,* a land filled with people, certainly many of its political and educational leaders, attempting to convince themselves that their culture had been founded and determined by Anglo-Norman Cavalier gentlemen, the thematic significance of Celts in the novels of Simms is extraordinary. That the best-known, best-selling, and most pro-lific Southern writer of the era, a man whose chief goal in life after the composition of literature was to be accepted as an equal by the Charleston social elite, emphasized the importance of Irish and Scottish immigrants and their descendants to the development of the Southern culture that he and many of his fellow antebellum Southerners believed to be in the midst of a Golden Age is a serious blow to the Anglo-Norman myth. For Simms' case reveals that both the antebellum Southern intel-lectual, whether he would so acknowledge publicly, and the general pub-lic, as revealed by book sales, knew the Anglo-Norman Cavalier myth of Southern genesis to be false and also, to a significant degree, understood the indispensable prominence of the presumed more plebeian Celts in Southern culture.

If, however, Simms were the only antebellum Southern writer to accentuate the presence and thematic significance of Celts in the early South, his cultural observations could be dismissed as the chauvinistic rantings of the son of a "wild" Irish immigrant angry that the Charleston blue-bloods would not accept him fully. Among the earliest novels writ-ten and published in the South is *The Irish Emigrant, An Historical Tale Founded on Fact,* attributed to "An Hibernian" and published in 1817 in Winchester, Virginia. Charles Fanning notes that *The Irish Emigrant* is "the first Irish-American novel. . . . The author may have been one Adam Douglass, who filed the book with the Virginia state clerk, and the location, at the head of the Shenandoah Valley, was a focal point for immigrants from Ulster" (38).[1]

The Irish Emigrant is poorly constructed and both features a predictable melodramatic love story and contains numerous awkward phrasings. Yet for all these faults, it is an important work historically, perhaps especially in terms of the Celtic-Southern thesis. That "the first Irish-American novel" was published not in a Northern city of the 1850s filled with survivors of the Great Hunger but soon after the War of 1812 in a Southern farm town that was the gateway to Appalachia, and from there into the original Old Southwest of Kentucky, Tennessee, Alabama, and Mississippi, speaks favorably of the McWhiney-McDonald thesis. The novel opens with Owen M'Dermott, a veteran of the failed 1798 Irish revolt for national independence, standing "on the bank of the beautiful Potowmac" (I 6). In having his hero's "end" announced at the novel's beginning, the author prepares the reader for his theme: The violent problems inherent in a colonially ruled Ireland administered by a standing army of occupation loyal to the English Crown and Parliament are so impervious to reform that the Owen M'Dermotts, the most fortunate if not necessarily the best and brightest among the Irish, must emigrate, in this case to the American South, in order to have a future.

The novel's action begins in County Antrim, the northeastern-most Irish county and the home of Simms' father. Antrim's proximity to Scotland has meant that since late in the seventeenth century, when six other Ulster counties were set aside by the monarchy as Protestant plantations, it has had a mostly Protestant population. "An Hibernian" uses fiction to demonstrate how the forces of history coupled with the Celtic sense of honor used irresponsibly could lead to change in religious affiliation and political alliance, which do not require a change of basic cultural attitudes and patterns. The rivals for local leadership in the novel are the Catholic M'Dermotts and the Oniall clan. The use of M'Dermott as the surname of the Catholic leading family is interesting, for most readers will see it as Scottish and therefore as Protestant and therefore as non-Celtic culturally. The Oniall surname may be even more significant. If the reader fails to recognize that these stalwart Protestants bear a distinctive Irish clan cognomen prominent in the resistance to Elizabethan and Cromwellian imperialistic wars in Ireland, the author stresses the significance:

> The family of the Onialls were the most ancient, and respectable, of which Ireland could boast. In consequence, however, of some misunderstanding having arisen, between James the Second, and the grandfather

of Sir Phelin [Oniall], respecting, it is conjectured, the precedence in command of the Irish forces, Sir Phelin collected his vassals and joined the army of William, Prince of Orange. (I 10)

This "conversion" means that the fighting between the M'Dermotts and the Onialls is between people who are culturally identical. Northeastern Ireland's Catholics and Protestants, the "Hibernian" declares, are the same people living the same folk culture, but they are divided by religion and imperial politics, one group being rewarded and the other stifled by the government in London. They also at times are done in by the Celtic sense of honor misused by the vain, the selfish, and the short-sighted. Emigration to the South will free them of these "British" bonds, allowing them to interact, intermarry, and forge a new version of their culture in the Southern back country.[2] Warren, the American who has become entangled in Irish politics, invites Owen and his love, Emma Oniall, to emigrate because "America was the only country on the terrestrial globe, where in he [Owen] could hope to enjoy comfort during the remainder of his life" (II 175).

The "Hiberian" avows of America three decades before the potato blight of the 1840s, "it was a country which contained many of the brave sons of Erin. . . . The Emigration from Ireland to the United States had been vast, indeed so much so that numbers of the inhabitants of that unhappy country actually sold themselves for their passage" (II 176). After spending time in Philadelphia, Owen buys an estate "contiguous" to Warren's in the Winchester, Virginia, area. The exact place is important for two reasons. First, as noted by Charles Fanning, Winchester was the center of the initial Scots-Irish settlement of the Shenandoah Valley and the Blue Ridge and therefore was the starting point for the pioneering of the mountains, just as St. Joseph, Missouri, later would be a principle starting point for settlers heading to and across the Rockies. Owen M'Dermott's settling there symbolizes, as does his marriage, the widespread cultural acceptance between Irish Protestant and Irish Catholic in the colonial and antebellum South. Second, the mountain South was almost as unsuitable for profitable chattel slavery as was New England, and having Owen live there, rather than in the Tidewater, makes it easier, if only to the pocketbook, for the "Hibernian" to condemn "the base doctrine of slavery" (II 199). Like Simms, the "Hiberian" links Ireland's colonial bondage to slavery (I 75-76), but unlike the Charlestonian he could condemn American chattel slavery outright. It is, I believe, significant that this Irish and Southern call for the inhumanity of chattel slavery to cease in North America is made more than a decade before *The Liberator* began to proclaim abolition, which was after New England shippers could no longer grow rich in the trans-Atlantic slave trade.

Donald Noble declares that George Tucker's "life bears directly on his work." Tucker was born in Bermuda and came to America in 1795 at the age of twenty. He enrolled at William and Mary and after graduation married the great-granddaughter of William Byrd II. The good life among the Anglo-Norman Tidewater elite began to dissolve after his wife's death in 1799 (Noble viii-ix). With his 1802 second marriage, to George Washington's great-niece, Tucker began a forty-year residence in non-Tidewater Virginia, allowing him to come to know the Scots-Irish South in depth. In 1806 he and his wife moved to Frederick County, the Winchester area of *The Irish Emigrant*, and in 1808 they moved to Pittsylvania County, which is south of Lynchburg. In 1825, Tucker accepted a post at the University of Virginia, which he kept until his retirement in 1845 (Noble x-xvii).

The Valley of Shenandoah (1824), set at the end of Washington's second administration, features "a somber theme that is seldom to be found in the literature of the plantation tradition" (Noble xx): The necessary death of the Anglo-Norman hegemony as symbolized by the failures of such families. As William Taylor observed, Tucker, in the novel, suggests that the Anglo-Norman coastal South by his time had become largely impotent culturally and that the South's future would lie primarily in the hands of the Scots-Irish. Indeed, the character most like Tucker himself, in both his hostility to the theoretically-driven monstrosities of French Jacobinism and in his financial failures, which trigger moves west, is M'Cullough.

Edward Grayson, Tucker's protagonist, explains the Valley's inhabitants to James Gildon, a friend from New York. Unless they receive land, as did his father, the Tidewater Anglo-Normans apparently do not move into the Valley and beyond. The settlers of German heritage Grayson describes as Southerners typically see Yankees and as Celts typically see the English: "a pains-taking, plodding, frugal people" largely devoid of folk art,[3] uninterested in education that does not produce immediate financial profit, often highly skilled in trade and successful as bustling business men, "the dray-horses of society" who must, primarily because they are too busy earning money to create it themselves, borrow or purchase or plunder culture from others (I 49, 53).

"The Irish character," Grayson declares to Gildon, "presents in almost every thing, a strong contrast to that which I have just placed before you—as ardent and impassioned as the others are cold and phlegmatic—

as imaginative as the others are dull, they run into the most violent extremes" (I 54). Like Simms, Tucker's protagonist considers Celts to be the most successful Southern pioneers, and as the mountains became settled "and broken to the restraints of law and civil government, they have even proved its most conspicuous ornaments" (I 55). They display "the liveliest interest" in government, thereby fostering local democracy, and for each one seeming to live idly or luxuriantly, who might well be composing or transmitting folksongs and thereby contributing to the culture's perpetuation through its native arts, "you may there behold another engaged in a course of rapid and adventurous speculation" of that type that Simms saw among the "redheaded adventurers" (I 56). Whereas the Germans in Tucker's novel are presented as supportive of education only when it is directly applicable to job training and potential wealth, "the Irish everywhere show a ready disposition to encourage learning, and every other liberal institution," including the "dead languages" (I 58).[4] Not only do the Irish create the folk culture of the area, Grayson suggests, but they advance the higher education as well. And the combination of the two will lead eventually to belletristic literature and other artistic and intellectual accomplishments, as Simms suggests in *Paddy McGann.*

Grayson's analysis of Irish political affiliation in this nascent era of American political parties is important for the Celtic-Southern thesis:

> When they are collected in great numbers, they retain their original feelings of resentment to the British government, and zeal for the rights of the people, and they find the principles of the democratic party and its systematic opposition to the existing administration, accord better with the character of this party, than do those of the federalists; but when single, their original political feelings, having to keep them up, die away after a while, and being often regarded as Englishmen, by our countrymen, who are not very nice in their distinctions, and consider every European speaking English, as an Englishmen, and all others as Frenchmen, they gradually get the feelings and predilections of those with whom they are confounded. They thus more naturally associate with the federalists, who view the English with favour, and most of those principles of government differ not widely from those of an Englishman, except in the article of hereditary right. You know an Englishman or a Frenchman always continues the same wherever he may live; but it is otherwise with an Irishman, who feels his country degraded by its dependence; he readily identifies himself with the country he adopts. (I 57)

There are three key points made in this speech. First, Tucker's protagonist's analysis of the maintenance of Scots-Irish identity, in this specific case presented through political affiliation, is that of Forrest and Ellen Shapiro McDonald.[5] Second, the Scots-Irish are tempted to "forget" their heritage by a combination of society conflating all Anglophones into one group—a group that fits the definition of the modern British nation as largely predicated upon anti-Catholicism that Patrick O'Sullivan queried, and the desire to avoid being considered a native of a conquered, and therefore degraded, country. Third, because the Irish immigrant "readily identifies" with America, he will mesh himself into the very heart of the new nation's nascent culture so thoroughly that later scholars will label his contributions, his very presence, English or British.

The bulk of *The Valley of Shenandoah* concerns the romantic interactions of the young characters, especially Edward, in Virginia society. As Ritchie Devon Watson observes, Tucker, very much ahead of his time, "juxtaposes the well-born Graysons with the less-distinguished but solidly middle-class Fawkners and gives this family an important role in the novel" (*Cavalier* 73). The novel's title, however, should recall the reader's attention from young love and betrayal to the Celtic-dominated part of Virginia, which, in direct contrast to the staid, increasingly nonproductive Tidewater, is vibrantly alive, with its culture expanding across the mountains into Kentucky and Tennessee. The decaying Graysons, symbols of Tidewater culture, are failures in both the Tidewater and the mountains, and Edward's praise of the Irish is likewise a symbolic presentation of the South's future.[6] Donald Noble believes "*The Valley* was designed to serve as a warning against . . . such romantic excess" (xviii-xix) as found in sentimental novels. He fails to note that Edward's death, and therefore Mathilda's cloistering, is as much due to acceptance of romantic sentiment as is Louisa's seduction. Edward Grayson (the surname suggests both old and worn-out and a drab colorlessness become familial and thus cultural) is a Tidewater Anglo-Norman gentleman destroying himself and others by playing at Cavalier. Meanwhile, those Irish he admiringly described continue to pioneer, educate their children, foster local democracy, and create an extensive, inspiring folk culture. They live an earthy, fecund life, and the Tidewater English who sneer at them live, rather like the French revolutionists, a life based on a series of abstractions, which must eventually either evaporate or cave in.

John Pendleton Kennedy was born in Baltimore the year George Tucker immigrated to Virginia. "Through his mother," Lucinda

MacKethan writes, "he was allied to a thriving planter clan of old Virginia, aristocratic gentlemen and ladies whose plantations were spread throughout the Shenandoah Valley-Berkeley County regions." Though the Kennedys appeared to have been more plebeian than the Pendletons, John Kennedy having emigrated from northeastern Ireland, "the Kennedys zealously traced their lineage back to Scottish Kings and earls" (MacKethan xii). The importance of Kennedy's ancestry to the Celtic-Southern thesis is that he is tied to the Scots-Irish, not the coastal Anglo-Normans, through both parents, from his father to the city-based merchants and from his mother to the original Scots-Irish frontier, which by Kennedy's childhood had become settled with prosperous farms and was expanding ever westward.

Swallow Barn (1832), Kennedy's first novel, is a lightly humorous presentation of Virginia plantation life. The novel is set in the Tidewater, on the James River, but the inspiration for the congenial plantations described by Kennedy's narrator, Yankee visitor Mark Littleton, lay in the Scots-Irish dominated section of Virginia, in fact, in its most westerly section, which featured the highest percentage of peoples of Celtic ancestry:

> A mountain-bound plantation named The Bower, located near Martinsburg, now in West Virginia, provided the setting that helps create the allure of Kennedy's first novel. Owned by his mother's sister, and her husband, The Bower became his parents home in 1825. Although Kennedy was by then committed to his Baltimore career as lawyer-businessman-politician, his earlier visits to The Bower stirred his desire to capture its way of life. (MacKethan xiii)

Lucinda MacKethan reveals of the novel's composition, "in an early draft, Mark Littleton went directly to western Virginia, but Kennedy in his final draft chose the Tidewater" (xxi). The importance of this setting change is that it suggests the prominence of Celtic heritage to what is assumed to be purely Anglo-Norman in Southern culture. The familial and cultural "allure" that readers assume to be Anglo-Norman Cavalier and Tidewater in *Swallow Barn* is actually in origin Celtic hillbilly, a reality of cultural heritage that readers, and scholars, blinded by Anglophilic prejudices and the glitter of Cavalier romance, often fail to recognize.

Like the Washington Irving works that partially inspired it, *Swallow Barn* is too charming and lightly playful to suggest significant observations on Southern culture. Unlike the works of Simms, and even *The*

Valley of Shenandoah, Swallow Barn is not directly engaged in exploring the future of Southern culture by analyzing its origins, strengths, and weaknesses. It does, however, feature brief scenes and descriptions that indirectly support the Celtic-Southern thesis.

While walking in Richmond, Littleton hears music. "On one side of the street," he writes, "a contumacious clarinet screamed a harsh bravado to a thorough-going violin, which, on the opposite side, in an illuminated barber-shop, struggled in the contortions of a Virginia reel" (19). These dueling instruments, the former screaming and harsh and associated with the symphony, the latter playing a reel that is in all probability a Virginia variation of a Scottish or Irish original, and struggling, may suggest the two cultures vying for supremacy in Virginia and the rest of the South, with the Anglo-Normans importing European high culture, making little of it save a "harsh bravado," and the Celts transforming their native folk culture into an original Southern art.

The plantation house itself is not a mansion created by decree and finished in one project based on the abstract designs of an architect. Its main building dates to the early eighteenth century, but "later buildings have been added to this, as the wants or ambition of the family have expanded. These are all constructed of wood, and seem to have been built in defiance of all laws of congruity, just as convenience required" (27-28). *Swallow Barn* is nothing more than a continually organic farm house, the specific importance of which to the Celtic-Southern thesis becomes increasingly obvious in the works of William Faulkner, Caroline Gordon, and Margaret Mitchell. Mr. Chub, the Presbyterian tutor, is a fictional portrayal of the prominence of Celts in early Southern education. His surname appears to be obviously Anglo-Saxon, but "he was an emigrant from the Emerald Isle." Like Owen M'Dermott, Mr. Chub participated in the 1798 United Irishmen Revolution, the last Irish nationalist uprising to win large support from Ulster Protestants. The "rebellion of 1798 stimulated his republicanism into a fever, and drove the full-blooded hero headlong into the quarrel, and put him, in spite of his peaceful profession, to standing by his pike in behalf of his principles" (65). Like Celtic nationalists before and after him who escaped with their lives, Mr. Chub suffered property confiscation and necessary emigration.

The lawyer, Philpot Wart, who is known as "Philly" and who is well respected for his knowledge, skill, and honesty, uses Irish phrases constantly, suggesting a Celtic prominence in the origins of the colorful language of Southern politics and jurisprudence. He comments on a case, "this looks marvelously like an Irish donkey race, where each man cudgels his neighbor's ass" (187). Maliciously enjoying the effeminate Anglo-Norman gentleman Singleton Oglethorpe Swansdown's fear of snakes, Philly advises, "take St. Patrick's plan, Mr. Swansdown; cut a hazel rod, and if you use it properly you may conjure every snake of them out of striking distance" (205). Before a jury Wart Latinizes the Celtic proverb "what is bred in the bone," thereby giving it social status often denied to Celtic wisdom (335).

In *Horse-Shoe Robinson* (1835), Kennedy reveals why he, unlike Simms, did not explore the Celtic contributions to the development of the antebellum South in detail and by name. As narrator, he declares that the area immediately south of Charlottesville, Virginia, was considerably different at the time of the novel's action in 1780 than at the time of its publication. His list of the region's signs of decay concludes, "such are the mischievous interpolations of the republican system" (15). Those Jeffersonian changes, which further weakened the power of the coastal Anglo-Norman elite, were advanced primarily by the descendants of Celts, personified ultimately in Andrew Jackson. Kennedy's quandary was that his anti-Jacksonian political and economic views clashed with any desire he may have had to use literature to honor his Scots-Irish heritage. The result is that his Revolutionary romance, which is like those of Simms in that it is set primarily in the Scots-Irish Carolina back country, has little to say specifically about the role of Celts.

Also unlike Simms, Kennedy readily acknowledges that South Carolina was the home of a large number of royalists. He reasons this was so due to economics, "being a colony of planters whose products were much in demand in England, neither the regulations of their trade nor the restrictions upon commerce, were likely to be so adjusted as to interfere with the profitable expansion of their labors" (128).

In Kennedy's fictional portrayal, the pro-British party in South Carolina is led by the wealthy landowners, who tend to be concentrated on or near the coast. "The disaffected" (those who oppose the British Empire and are willing to strike for freedom from it) "abounded in the upper country" (129), the Scots-Irish region, the home of Galbraith "Horse-Shoe" Robinson. Like Andrew Jackson, Robinson is a larger-than-life native of the Waxhaws, and it is his intuitive sense of guerilla warfare that saves the low-country gentleman, Arthur Butler.

In 1860, with the nation on the brink of war, Kennedy published his last significant fiction, the story "A Legend of Maryland," which is set in approximately 1680. George Talbot, one of the colony's deputy governors, "was born in Ireland, and from some facts connected with his history I infer that he did not emigrate to Maryland until after his marriage, his wife being an Irish lady" (62). Talbot is not the only Celt in this early "fictional" Maryland. Kennedy informs: "the country between the Susquehanna and the Delaware, that which now coincides with parts of Harford and Cecil counties in Maryland and the upper portion of the State of Delaware, was known in those days as New Ireland, and was chiefly settled by emigrants from the old Kingdom whose name it bore" (62).

Talbot's house is named New Connaught, for the western, and then and now most thoroughly Gaelic-speaking, province of Ireland. Kennedy labels the Irish, "a race whose historical boast is the faithfulness of their devotion to a friend in need and their chivalrous courtesy to woman, but still more their generous and gallant championship of woman in distress" (75). Late in his career, with the South about to secede from the Union he continued to support, Kennedy asserts that the Irish played a prominent role in the development of the best of Southern chivalry, a code of conduct he sees as determined by deeds, not birth into an Anglo-Norman family.

His biographer labels William Alexander Caruthers "the chronicler of the cavaliers." At the onset of "the Covenanter troubles," the Caruthers clan was centered in southwest Scotland. "The family was," Curtis Davis boasts, "among the oldest in Scotland, one of those bellicose Border clans that took delight in the sports of football and rustling (almost equating the two), and leavened its religion with a heaping admixture of superstition" (1). The great-grandfather of the future physician and author was settled in Rockbridge County, near Lexington, Virginia, "at least as early as the spring of 1748" (Davis 3).

Contrary to the inferences readers may make from its title, *The Cavaliers of Virginia* (1834-35) is not a paean to the Tidewater's Anglo-Norman gentry. Caruthers does, however, like far too many commentators, overemphasize the Cavalier settlement in Virginia. Ignoring the original Jamestown pioneers, a group that included many "common" laborers and the gentlemen among whom were often desperate younger sons hoping to escape the curse of primogeniture or members of families whose finances had been lost before their genteel status, Caruthers declares, "first came the Cavaliers who fled hither after the decapulation of their royal master and the dispersion of his army, many of whom became permanent settlers in the town or colony, and ever afterwards influenced the character of the state" (I 3).

Caruthers himself may have believed that this influence was positive, but his novel suggests otherwise. It features three "Cavaliers" who may be seen as symbols. Gideon Fairfax "was one of that remarkable race of men which has so powerfully influenced the destinies of the Ancient Dominion from that day to the present" (I 23). He is the ideal of *noblesse oblige*: well-educated, brave, loyal, honest, generous, compassionate yet firm, devoted to family and retainers, and hostile to true tyranny. But Fairfax, dead from a wound suffered in a hunting fall, is not there to aid his family when troubles arise. Symbolically, Caruthers' novel suggests that the fictional ideal Cavalier is just that: not real, not available to lead against tyranny, and the myth of him is no succor to those faced with life's hardships and terrors.

The other two thematic Cavaliers in the novel are based on actual persons: Governor Berkley and Nathaniel Bacon. Berkley, the epitome of the early Tidewater Anglo-Norman Cavalier, is the novel's villain. Guilty of the worst petty tyrannies and bigotries, Berkley is described as a "choleric old Cavalier" (I 206). His vanities in his sense of familial superiority and his authoritarian right to rule, if left unchecked, would destroy both individuals and, perhaps, the entire colony. Bacon, Berkley's nemesis, is not even a true Cavalier; his father, he discovers, fought for the Puritans (II 212). This half-Cavalier leads the revolt against Berkley that Caruthers considers the first American Revolution: "exactly one hundred years before the American revolution, there was a Virginia revolution based upon precisely similar principles. The struggle commenced between the representatives of the people and the representatives of the King" (II 51). Symbolically, the novel implies that Virginia, hence the rest of America, could not have meaningful self-rule until the hegemony of the Anglo-Norman Cavalier was broken, and that someone other than a bona fide Cavalier would have to lead the charge.[7]

Like Simms, Caruthers displays the prominent role of the Irish in these early Southern battles for a democracy that is essentially against imperial rule and for decentralized, local rule. Bacon is thoroughly English, and he was raised in the home of Gideon Fairfax, but his chief companion is the native Irishman Brian O'Reily. Curtis Davis reveals, "for *The Cavaliers of Virginia* the novelist's principal authority was an Irish political refugee named John Daly Burk," who wrote songs, plays, and a four-volume history of Virginia from a fervently Jeffersonian perspective (147-48). Burk's influence no doubt inspired the creation of O'Reily, who initially appears to be a standard Anglo-Saxon-created stage Irishman—verbose, alternately cowardly and bellicose, given to alcoholic excesses—but who is revealed to possess not only each of the positive traits of Gideon Fairfax but also desirable, perhaps essential, qualities Fairfax lacks: the mettle necessary to survive on the frontier and the courage to act decisively for the good of others. Caruthers calls O'Reily a "son of the Emerald Isle, whose countrymen, it may be remarked, formed no inconsiderable part of the inferior population of the city at that day" (I 28). Like Simms, Caruthers acknowledges that the Irish, however poor and socially subservient, were present in prominent numbers in the early colonial South. Symbolized in Brian O'Reily, they not only save the Virginia colony's savior—O'Reily swam the child Bacon to shore after a shipwreck—but they earn, by the quality of their characters and works, the right to be the right hands of those who initially break the power of the English imperial hold on America by opposing Anglo-Norman Cavalier hegemony, which, Caruthers states, led eventually to national independence and, the reader must certainly infer to be the implication, to the glory of the author's own day.

The Knights of the Golden Horse-Shoe (1841) treats an epic historical event necessary for the Celticization of the Southern backcountry: Alexander Spotswood's 1716 expedition across the Blue Ridge. Caruthers immediately thrusts his readers into the eighteenth-century political wars that drove so many Celts to the South. Spotswood, a native Scot and inclined to support the Stuart royal house of his country, receives the body of his half-brother, General Elliott, who had been executed for his Jacobite conspiracies. The letter sent with the corpse states, "he will be accompanied by a great many ruined families of rather a higher class than that from which your immigrants are generally furnished" (18).[8] English persecutions at that time had begun to force the nobility of Celtic lands to immigrate to America as earlier persecutions had led to Celtic nobility fleeing to France, Spain, and Sweden. Having symbolically dismissed the Anglo-Norman Cavalier gentility in *The Cavaliers of Virginia,* Caruthers proffers a new Southern nobility in his last novel: the dispossessed Celts who will flock to the mountains.

Among the recent Scottish and Irish immigrants to Virginia is a man using the name Henry Hall. He is actually native Virginian Frank Lee, who had gone to Edinburgh to be educated and, like a Scott hero, had become a participant in the Scottish-nationalist/Stuart-restoration struggle, thereby earning a death sentence from the Hanoverian crown. It is Frank Lee, who through education and residence has become almost as Scottish as the natives who helped him escape back to Virginia, who proposes that Spotswood's expedition be composed entirely of volunteers (27). This contributes to the democratization of the expedition, for volunteers will have the chance to win land grants through their efforts. Governor Spotswood, Caruthers' prototype of the colonial Southern gentleman, and leader, concurs. When he learns that some of the Cavaliers intend to propose that only "those of gentle blood should be admitted into" the expedition, "he hoped that no such proposition would be offered. Let the noble objects of our ambition be open to every gentleman of fair fame, and to all the officers of the Rangers" (162). The Scottish Spotswood, like an early Jeffersonian, rejects hereditary nobility holding special rights and privileges for themselves in favor of opening competition so that all men might prove themselves noble in deed and character. Not a hypocrite, Spotswood later submits to being taught "the art of horse-shoeing" by the scout Red Jarvis (212), who, because he is a Presbyterian born "under the covenant," is apparently the son of an ordinary, uneducated Scottish or Irish immigrant.

Caruthers presents as one of Spotswood's primary interests in traversing the mountains their Scottish-like beauty. He tells Chunoluskee, the William and Mary Indian student, that he wants him to show Frank Lee "that there is a finer country beyond your blue hills, than even in old Scotia" (56). As the expedition nears the mountains, Spotswood becomes reminiscent. He would:

> tell of his own boyish adventures in his native land, until his moist eye told of his still clinging affections to that glorious land, rich in whatever delights the heart of the patriot, and richer above all, in a border minstrelsy and traditionary treasures, now consecrated to everlasting love and remembrance, with the name of him who has made them familiar as household words in every civilized family, from the rising to the setting son. (205)

Caruthers further declares of Walter Scott's works, "the visions which his magic wand created before our youthful eyes, rise up in every hill and vale in our own bright and favored land" (205). The most widely accepted view, at least among scholars and since Mark Twain, on the widespread, nineteenth-century, Southern love of Scott is that summarized by Ritchie Watson:

> Goaded by attacks from the North, accused of maintaining an inhuman and immoral social institution, southerners turned in their literature to Scott's romantic rendering, in ballad and novel, of medieval Scottish and English Society. (*Cavalier* 103-04)[9]

Caruthers, however, suggests through fiction written a decade before the fury of the 1850's condemnations of slavery in the South that the Southern love of Scott began not as a defense mechanism, nor as naive, romantic playing, but because Scott evokes the Celtic heritage so common to Southerners and in doing so further stimulates their love of the equally beautiful, dangerous, and paradoxical South.[10]

This may be seen in a slightly different light in a brief passage in the War Between the States reminiscence of William Watson, a Scottish native who had lived in Louisiana for years and, though still a citizen of the United Kingdom, served in the Confederate Army. With the army of the West on the border of what would become the state of Oklahoma, Watson meets a non-fullblood Cherokee man literate in both languages and especially fond of Walter Scott. When Watson reveals his national origin, the Cherokee, "said he had read some books about Scotland, which he liked very much." The Cherokee proceeds to quote Scott, and then "he compared the Gaels to the Indians, and the Saxons to the whites in America, and quoting several passages, drew some very fair comparisons" (250-51).

The Knights of the Golden Horse-Shoe closes with Spotswood's rumination on the Valley of Virginia, "this country will suit admirably for our Scottish and Irish emigrants" (238). The expedition as treated fictionally by Caruthers serves two purposes: The hereditary Anglo-Norman Cavalier is superseded by the Celtic natural nobility and the frontier is opened, a frontier that soon will be filled with Celts whose descendants, by Caruthers' time, will dominate the folkways of the hill South especially and the white South generally, and, considering the careers of Simms, Kennedy, and Caruthers, its nascent belletristic literature as well.

The anonymous *Life of Paddy O'Flarrity* (1834) is a wildly satiric comment on anti-Irish Catholic nativism, American self-made success stories, the westward expansion of Southern culture, and, ultimately, the Southern wealthy elite's preference for living with the false myth of the Anglo-Norman Cavalier. The short novel opens with "Paddy," and this ethnic-religious slur on the immigrant Irish (and later applied to police wagons) is significant, playing with typical Anglophonic Protestant stereotypes of the Irish, especially Irish Catholics. The "youngest of thirty-two children," he "was born in Ireland about 46 years ago, and my parents were both what you Americans call Raw Irish" (1). William Taylor notes, "the single characteristic of the Southerner which Emerson and other Northerners found most troubling can be summed up by the word 'wildness'" (238). Whether the descendants of Celts in the South or immigrant Irish Catholics in the northeast and the midwest, culturally

Celtic Americans are inevitably labeled by the culturally English as inherently inferior due to "wildness," and therefore in need of English "civilization" being foisted upon them, often at gunpoint. The anonymous author of Paddy's tale has fun with that overriding bigotry.

Landing in Baltimore in approximately 1806, Paddy finds both work as a shoeblack and many other Irish Catholics in the vicinity. The date is important, for it is a fictional representation of the significant Irish Catholic presence in the upper coastal South before Jefferson left the White House. Paddy initiates his self-education, the first step in American upward mobility, by reading the classical histories written by Irish native Oliver Goldsmith. After moving to the District of Columbia, he works in the bar owned by Pat Duffy. Like many ambitious Americans lacking connections, Paddy decides to seek his fortune "in Western states" (11). He travels along the Ohio River, the political border between South and North,[11] eventually crossing the Mississippi into Missouri. Having educated himself beyond the levels of most men, Paddy applies for and secures the job of tutor to the family of Judge D____. He loses "that dialect which is so peculiar to my countrymen" (15), because a man could not be considered truly educated in the nineteenth century with an Irish accent.

Four years after Paddy began to work for him, the judge is elected governor of Missouri, and Paddy, now possessing important connections, is soon after elected to the state legislature (17-19). Not content merely to toy with political satire, the author plays with American heroism as well. Like a Daniel Boone or Davy Crockett, Paddy saves Maria, the governor's daughter, from an Indian attack. The governor, knowing that his protégée and his daughter are in love, blesses the marriage but adds, "What say you, Mr. O'Flarrity, have you any objections to taking the name of one of the first families of Virginia, and now the Governor of Missouri?" (25). This Paddy does, and he refuses to reveal the name he now bears, "lest when you see me, you may say, 'there goes the Irish Paddy, the *shoeblack*'" (27). Having shed his accent and his name, Paddy can now avoid anti-Irish prejudices. The adoption of a Virginia Cavalier surname is satirically significant, for it suggests that the anonymous creator of Paddy saw many of the accomplishments of the South as due to Celts who must change their names, who at least felt they must "pass" as ethnically English in order to succeed in the face of bigotries against culturally Celtic peoples; it suggests through fiction that much of what Americans of the Jacksonian era assumed to be English accomplishments on the southwestern frontier are actually Irish.

Paddy's political career flourishes. His natural oratorical skills, combined with his being immortalized as an Indian-fighting hero in a St. Louis wax museum, propel him up the power ladder of state government. He serves as Speaker of the House for six years and then is elected to Congress (37-38). At the narrative's conclusion, Paddy hints at a desire to run for president and closes his instructive tale: "I leave you now to guess who I am" (56). This is the author's mischievous, sly wink at America in the midst of Jacksonian Democracy, encouraging it to look first at and then beyond its anti-Celtic stereotypes and bigotries—which took violent form in race riots against Irish Catholic neighborhoods[12]— to discover the Irish cultural origins of the frontier South of Boone, Crockett, Jackson, Thomas Hart Benton, and Sam Houston, the original "western" culture then redefining the American character. Ritchie Watson suggests that history and politics have combined to skew our view of the development of American western culture so that we no longer recognize what antebellum Americans took for granted: that the West and the trans-Appalachian South shared a "unified western consciousness. Even stranger to Americans living today would be the commonly accepted assumption that the roots of this new western culture were southern" (*Yeoman* 12). Paddy challenges his contemporary audience to guess which of the Southern, and Western, political and intellectual leaders of the day is a descendant of the world of *The Irish Emigrant.*

Chapter IV

The Mother of the
Renaissance: Ellen Glasgow

As the first permanent European settlement that would lead eventually to the formation of Southern culture was in Virginia, it is appropriate that a Virginian would herald the Southern Renaissance. Ellen Glasgow is the novelist who best bridges the post-Reconstruction period with the Southern Renaissance. Her first novel was published in 1897, three decades before the flowering of the 1920s, and the last published during her life, for which she won her only Pulitzer Prize, appeared in 1941, as the second generation of Southern Renaissance writers began appearing. Glasgow's parents represent the two primary, always contrasting and often conflicting, white cultural groups in the South: peoples of Celtic heritage and Anglo-Normans. "Thomas Francis Glasgow, born in western Virginia," notes Anne Goodwyn Jones, "came from Scottish and Irish ancestors." While the paternal heritage was Gaelic, "Glasgow's mother . . . came from Tidewater aristocrats who thought Richmond far enough west to settle" (226-27).

Marcelle Thiebaux claims, "Ellen Glasgow has a permanent significance in American literature as the first writer of the modern South, to which she helped give literary definition in its epoch of societal and industrial change. The Virginia of her fiction becomes a paradigm for the region and its history" (189). In addition to the high quality of Glasgow's canon, her fictive world treats Virginia from the later antebellum days to the Great Depression and examines all social classes in the state during that century. Her scope then is almost identical to that of Faulkner, and Glasgow initiated hers in the year of the Mississippian's birth. This scope, combined with the tendency to see Virginia as the epitome of the Anglo-Norman Cavalier South, means that if Glasgow, a considerably more skilled practitioner of the novel than any of her Southern precursors, sees the descendants of Celtic immigrants as essential in any way to her Virginia, "a paradigm" for the whole South, then the cases made by Simms, a native of the second center of the Southern Anglo-Norman Cavalier, and the antebellum upper South novelists "An Hibernian," Tucker, Kennedy, Caruthers, and "Paddy O'Flarrity," are strengthened.

Life and Gabriella (1916) is, as its subtitle indicates, "The Story of a Woman's Courage." As the novel opens, Gabriella Carr is a young woman in late-nineteenth-century Virginia. Her sister Jane is married to a man who lives the role of Anglo-Norman gentleman, although a drunken, abusive Cavalier. Jane, unquestioningly accepting the mores of her age, flees to her mother during her husband Charley's excesses, only to return home to her proper place once the storm has subsided. While Jane can mutter only a feeble "It wasn't my fault," "'one can always do something if it's only to scream,' rejoins Gabriella" (4).

The allotted place for women in this Victorian society—it is not a straight continuation of antebellum Southern Tidewater culture—is one roughly equivalent to that of children. Mrs. Carr, a widow, tells Jane of her desire to have Cousin Jimmy Wrenn decide what to do, "men know so much more than women about such matters." Somewhat later, Uncle Meriwether wants Gabriella, a maiden, to leave the room while the men discuss Jane's options because "the less women and girls know about such matters, the better" (7, 21). Gabriella's fiancé of two years, Arthur Peyton, reveals the social norm regarding women in his explanation to Gabriella of his opposition to her plan to work outside the home: "You're so sacred to me. . . . I always think of you as apart from the workaday world. I always think of you as a star shining serenely above the sordid struggle—" (36). The eastern Virginia men in this novel, and they are symbolic of the Anglo-Norman South, at least as militarily defeated and subordinate to Yankees, require their women to be secular Madonnas on a pedestal, placed by the men in their lives, fathers and brothers as well as husbands, above "the sordid struggle"; they are not allowed to live so that all can see they are flesh-and-blood human beings.

While such is no obvious concern of Glasgow, who was as secular a writer as Eudora Welty, this philosophy, as Flannery O'Connor could point out, while seemingly conservative and traditional and sex-role and family-based, actually promotes long term secularist cultural liberalism because it smacks of Gnostic views of the flesh and the world and because it replaces adoration for the Mother of God Incarnate with adoration for an unrealistic concept of *Woman*, thereby facilitating the societal move from worshiping the Mother of God's child to worshiping that which increasingly was produced by the idealized, pedestal-sitting, abstraction driven *Woman*: humanistic social reform.

The novel traces Gabriella's development from a young woman who understands instinctively that the chivalric view of women is not merely condescending but impoverishing as well ("I'm tired of being on charity just because we are women") to a mature woman who creates her own life (27). What is most important about Gabriella's development is the ethnic-cultural slant taken by Glasgow. Though Gabriella is native to an eastern Virginia city synonymous with the descendants of the Anglo-Norman first families of Virginia, her background is probably Gaelic. Glasgow provides no history of the Carr family that demonstrates conclusively its cultural ancestry, but in *The Surnames of Ireland,* Edward MacLysaght notes that Carr is the anglicized form of several Irish surnames (43), and in his *More Irish Families* he reveals the semi-Anglicized use of both O'Carr and O'Care in Ireland (52-53). George Fraser Black, in *The Surnames of Scotland,* writes that Carr is a variant spelling of Ker or Kerr, which in Scotland is pronounced Carr (137), and Ronald Macdonald Douglas, a non-academic collector of folklore, suggests that the surname originally may have been an appellation deriving from the Scottish Gaelic *cearr,* meaning left-handed (195). The Scottish Lowland origins of many bearing the surname Carr means that it also could be P-Celtic, Welsh, for the Cymric word for "kinsman" is *car.*

Moreover, the fact that Gabriel Carr's reckless passion appears to have set him apart from most of Richmond society suggests that he is one of Grady McWhiney's Crackers. This, however, is not the extent of Gabriella's Irish ancestry. While waiting for Arthur to arrive to escort her to a party, and mulling over the sexism and hypocrisy endemic to Victorian Richmond society, Gabriella "told herself with grim determination that she would never go to a party again. The Berkeley conscience, that *vein of iron* (my emphasis) which lay beneath the outward softness and incompetence of her mother and sister, held her, in spite of her tempting youth, to the resolution she had made" (30).

As we shall see more explicitly in the novel bearing it as a title, "vein of iron" is the central phrase in Glasgow's later work, and it inevitably refers to the inner strength of character inherent in Southerners of Gaelic cultural heritage. What initially may seem somewhat odd here is that Gabriella's "vein of iron" derives specifically from the distaff Berkeley family. Not only does Berkeley not sound particularly Irish, but both Gabriella's mother and sister appear to be culturally at one with Richmond society. The use of the name Berkeley is intriguing, especially when we recall Church of Ireland theologian and philosopher George Berkeley (1685-1753). His biographer declares, "Berkeley was an

Irishman of English descent," that "born, bred, and educated an Irishman in Ireland," Berkeley not only wrote his greatest works in Ireland, but he also referred to himself as Irish (Luce 25-26).[1]

Because there is no reason to suspect that in *Life and Gabriella* Glasgow intends "vein of iron" to mean something other than what she spells out more specifically in subsequent novels, we are safe to assume that the Berkeley family is Irish. If so, Glasgow's use of the name is subtly suggestive on two levels. First, there is the recognition noted above that Episcopalians may be culturally and nationally Irish. Second, in having an Irish family possessing the "vein of iron" become weakened after it has embraced the Anglo-Norman society of the Virginia Tidewater, Glasgow criticizes not only the mandarin minority Southern culture but the genteel, often a-doctrinal Episcopalianism that typically accompanies it, or perhaps that often accompanied it in past decades. As demonstrated already, Glasgow equates the Southern "chivalric" subjugation of women to Anglo-Norman culture, and as Gabriella frees herself of that culture's tentacles, she will re-discover fully her Irish "vein of iron."

The seductive sway of the society's beliefs is revealed when Gabriella meets George Fowler. She is enthralled by this apparent paragon of gallantry: "In his eyes, which said enchanting things, she could not read the trivial and commonplace quality of his soul—for he was not only a man, he was romance, he was adventure, he was the radiant miracle of youth!" (87). True to his culture, George "abhorred independence in a wife," declaring that a knowledge of and interest in business made her "a mannish woman" (99, 102). Seduced by what she should have recognized to be frippery, Gabriella will be forced to locate and embrace the "vein of iron" lying largely dormant in her in order to make her life fulfilling.

Gabriella's marriage to George is an abysmal failure. Raised primarily in New York, George has had no direct access to the Virginian "Scotch-Irish inheritance" that has made his father such a good man (153). George drinks, squanders money, and attempts to hide his actions from both his wife and his family. Not only does he have an affair, but George eventually leaves his wife and children, forcing Gabriella to assume the full responsibility not only for her own life, but for the lives of her children as well.

At each crisis in her life, the "vein of iron" saves Gabriella. Before her marriage, when George refuses to allow her mother to live with them, Gabriella finds the strength to defy the man she sees as a romantic knight in a storybook: "Something stronger than herself—that vein of iron in her soul—would not bend, would not break though every fibre of her being struggled against it. . . . The vein of iron held her firm in spite of herself" (112). When her mother writes and asks for $400 to go to Florida for her health, Gabriella must face the consequences of having lied to protect her worthless husband because:

> custom exacted that a wife should be willing to lie in defense of her husband. Some obscure strain of dogmatic piety struggled in the convulsed depths of her being, as if she had been suddenly brought up against the vein of iron in her soul—against the moral law, stripped bare of clustering delusions, which her ancestors had known and fought for as "the Berkeley conscience." The Berkeley conscience, bred for centuries on a militant faith, told her now that she was punished because she had lied to her mother. (187-88)

Gabriella is a modern woman who is only nominally Christian, but she retains a familial "moral law," the Gaelic "vein of iron," that wars with the customs of modern society, customs that have no respect for her as an individual, that take no account of her family and its heritage unless to war against them.

George's affair with Florrie prompts Gabriella to look inward for strength in order to avoid becoming a lifetime martyr like her sister: "Thanks to the vein of iron in her soul she would never—no, not if she died fighting—become one of the victims of life" (242). Glasgow does not use the phrase "vein of iron" when Gabriella is faced with George's leaving her, but she has her heroine turn immediately to Madame Dinard, "who had been born an O'Grady," for employment (212, 253). Not only is it significant that Glasgow has her heroine turn to an Irish American for help, but the name change from O'Grady to Dinard is a fictional representation of the attempt to avoid the anti-Celtic prejudices common in nineteenth- and early-twentieth-century America by eliminating obviously Irish names.[2]

Though Gabriella is a successful worker and single mother, she realizes, "Yes, I've missed life." Then after several years of living alone she notices a red-haired man who "was doubtless devoid of those noble traditions by and through which, her mother always told her, a gentleman was made out of a man—the traditions which had created Arthur and Cousin Jimmy as surely as they had created George and Charley," traditions that necessarily produced at least as many bad or weak men as good ones (367-68). Archibald, Gabriella's son, is immediately drawn to Ben O'Hara, but Gabriella's initial assessments of O'Hara are predicated upon the Tidewater views of her upbringing and therefore are hostile.

"I dare say he has a great deal of force," she tells her maid, "but you must admit that blood tells, Miss Polly" (391). The remainder of the novel reinforces this truth but not as Gabriella believes, for she has confused "blood," the heritage of culture, the vein of iron in her soul, with the veneer of Anglo-Norman civility that coats both the violence of Charley and George and the ineffectiveness of Arthur.

Gabriella develops a grudging respect for O'Hara through her talks with him, discovering that he was born into the direst poverty and that he despises sanctimonious hypocrisy above all else, but "never for an instant would it have occurred to the granddaughter of that sanctified snob, Bartholomew Berkeley, who despised the lower orders and fraternized with the Deity in his pulpit every Sabbath, that the red-blooded and boisterous O'Hara—the man of force and slang—could by any accident usurp the sacred shrine where the consecrated relics of her first love reposed" (437).

Gabriella begins to overcome her social prejudices when George arrives "home" to die from his acute alcoholism. O'Hara steps in to handle the D.T. fits, and Gabriella realizes, "even Arthur [whose Celtic name may suggest why he is the epitome of the best man that could be produced by Richmond's Anglo-Norman society] would have appeared at a disadvantage beside O'Hara at that moment" (445). After observing O'Hara's strength of character, Gabriella feels "suddenly humbled." Eventually, the combination of Archibald's adoration, Polly's admiration, O'Hara's empathetic handling of George, and his stories of his childhood and his wife's morphine addiction all contribute to Gabriella's realization that O'Hara "had never lost a natural chivalry of mind beside which the cultivated chivalry of manner appeared as exotic as an orchid in a hothouse" (480).

The novel concludes with Gabriella's proclamation to O'Hara, "I'll come with you now—anywhere—toward the future" (529). This has been the purpose of the novel. Glasgow's heroine is a representative wealthily raised Southern woman of the post-Reconstruction period who searches for a worthwhile future. The men of her Tidewater South, aping an anglophilic chivalry that denigrates women and masks violence, a mere "cultivated," and therefore to some degree unnatural, chivalry, are all failures. "Glasgow does not find in the South," writes Anne Goodwyn Jones, "an image of manhood that can heal by unifying energy and virtue, physical potency and intelligence, nature and culture" (262). What is significant is that the man who qualifies as the soulmate to Gabriella's vein of iron is the child of Irish immigrants in New York City, who, like the Celts in the South a century and two earlier, went to the Western frontier to make his fortune. Through this union Glasgow suggests the importance of cultural similarities. Gabriella, whose vein of iron marks the preeminence of the Irish in her, finds the culturally Anglo-Norman men of her native Richmond to be at best ineffectual. The Irish American born in New York, however, is the man with whom she can build a future. Note especially that religious differences carry no weight here. Gabriella's background is Irish Protestant, presumably a socially restricted Episcopalianism, and O'Hara's is Irish Catholic, but the difference is so meaningless to Glasgow as to be unworthy of any discussion. The suggested cultural similarity, the need to mate with another who possesses the vein of iron, overrules differences of religion, social status, and place of birth.

Linda Wagner views *Life and Gabriella* and *Virginia* (1913) as novels telling a similar story about native Southern women facing problems created by sexism. She further argues that through the novel's title, the heroine of *Virginia* should be seen as widely symbolic (8, 41). If this is so, then Gabriella must also be a symbol of Southern womanhood. Read this way, *Life and Gabriella* suggests that Southern men, choosing to live by the culturally false dictates of the Anglo-Norman Tidewater, have failed Southern women, at least those who have maintained the Celtic vein of iron in the soul, and those are the Southern women in Glasgow's works with the greatest strength of character. The result is that the female symbol of the South must, in order to have a future, mate herself with the child of impoverished Irish immigrants. Paradoxically, the Southern lady possessing the "vein of iron" finds cultural renewal among the "wild" Irish Catholics of the forbidding northern city.

Barren Ground (1925) is similar to *Life and Gabriella* in that it is also a novel that relates the arduous though ultimately successful struggle of a Southern woman to overcome the obstacles of a sexist society. More than even Gabriella Carr, Dorinda Oakley eventually creates a life for herself independent of the dictates of the Anglo-Norman hierarchy of her native eastern Virginia. Glasgow writes of the thirty-eight-year-old Dorinda, who is five years into her marriage to Nathan Pedlar, "her happiness was independent . . . of the admiration of men, and her value as a human being was founded upon a durable if an intangible basis. Since she had proved that she could farm as well as a man there was less need for her to endeavor to fascinate as a woman" (375-76). As in *Life and Gabriella*, Glasgow in *Barren Ground* links her heroine's search for an identity independent of Anglo-Norman society to her Gaelic cultural heritage.

Queen Elizabeth County, the setting for the novel, is a rural county in the eastern half of Virginia that was originally settled primarily by "sturdy English yeomen." The descendants of these non-wealthy Englishmen, however, do not dominate the county. "A few stalwart farmers of Scotch-Irish descent," Glasgow writes, "rose above the improvident crowd of white and black tenants, like native pines above the shallow wash of the broomsedge. These surviving landowners were obscure branches of the great Scotch-Irish families of the upper Valley of Virginia" (6). At the novel's opening, the most flourishing farm in the Pedlar's Mill community is Green Acres, owned by "James Ellgood, whose mother was a McNab" (6). John Calvin Abernethy, Dorinda's great-grandfather, planted his family in the low country, and "with the gradual running to seed of the Methodists in the community, the Presbyterian faith sprang up and blossomed like a Scotch thistle in barren ground" (8). Mrs. Oakley transmits tales of the family's Irish ancestry to her daughter (102-3), and Old Matthew Fairlamb, the wisest man in the community, "had never lost his shrewd Scotch-Irish understanding" (14).

Dorinda's fortunate fall, as is Gabriella's, is into love with a worthless man. The object of her affection is Jason Greylock, the spoiled son of the area's only doctor and largest landowner. Though the surname appears to be English, Glasgow writes that the old doctor "resembled an inebriated Covenanter" (6), suggesting at least a partial Scottish or Irish Presbyterian heritage. Jason perhaps alludes to his family's possible Gaelic ancestry in telling Dorinda that his father has a "will of iron" (90). Whatever the family's ethnic origin, Jason Greylock, who has been educated elsewhere and plays the role of Cavalier gentleman condescending to the lowly around him, is devoid of positive character. He tells Dorinda during their "courtship," "you put something in me that I need. I don't know what it is—fibre, I suppose, the courage of living." After Dorinda tells Jason that she'll go anywhere with him, Glasgow writes of her heroine: "her body straightened as if its soft curves were molded by the vein of iron in her soul" (113). The juxtaposition of this reference to Dorinda's vein of iron with Jason's revelation that she has something he needs in order to live a worthwhile life suggests that the hole in Jason's life is his lack of the Gaelic vein of iron, something he can acquire only by marrying and honoring Dorinda.

When Jason, who has seduced Dorinda after a marriage promise, suddenly marries Geneva Ellgood, Dorinda, like Gabriella, turns inward to the vein of iron. After old Doctor Greylock tells her of the marriage, Dorinda appears impassive: "All individual differences, all the acquired attributes of civilization, had turned to wood or stone; yet the racial structure, the savage fibre of instinct, remained alive in her" (149). Dorinda's "racial structure," "the vein of iron in her nature would never bend, would never break, would never disintegrate in the furnace of emotion" (170). Though she is overcome by despair, Dorinda feels that she possesses an "essential self . . . superior even to the conspiracy of circumstances which hemmed her in," and this "essential self would assert its power and triumph over disaster. . . . She could never be broken while the vein of iron held in her soul" (180).

After Nathan's death, Bob Ellgood, whose Scots-Irish ancestry may explain partially his lifelong admiration for and attraction to her, begins to court Dorinda. She, however, is more concerned with attempting to understand how she, a "ruined" woman from a land-poor Southern family at the turn of the century, had avoided destruction:

> After all, it was not religion; it was not philosophy; it was nothing outside of her own being that had delivered her from evil. The vein of iron which had supported her through adversity was merely the instinct older than herself, stronger than circumstances, deeper than the shifting surface of emotion; the instinct that had said, "I will not be broken." Though the words of the covenant had altered, the ancient mettle had still infused its spirit. (459-60)

The "ancient mettle" is Dorinda's Gaelic heritage, and though the religious covenant of Gaelic Presbyterianism no longer holds meaning for Dorinda, the cultural heritage, which is independent of any specific religious belief or practice, provides the center for her life. Her hardy individualism is predicated entirely on her ancestry, her Scottish and Irish family heritage.

Dorinda is the archetypal female Southern agrarian heroine. In facing the future and creating a new life for herself, she does not attempt to discard or even modernize her essential self. Unlike the community-less, hollow, materialistic modern man fearfully envisioned throughout *I'll Take My Stand,* Dorinda searches deep within herself for her identity and her strength, and they are both the Gaelic vein of iron, a center that holds against the evils and the life stifling abstractions of the modern world.

"Her eighteenth novel is in some ways her richest," Linda Wagner writes of *Vein of Iron,* which was published in 1935 (94). The novel's protagonist is Ada Fincastle, the daughter of a former Presbyterian minister who has lost two congregations due to his philosophical writings. The family is from Ironside village in Shut In Valley at the foot of the Appalachians. As Donald Akenson could point out, the family name would be considered English by most, but the Fincastles are of Irish Presbyterian ancestry: "Scotch-Irish, people called the pioneers, though after they were driven out of Strathcylde they had stayed to themselves in Ulster, and had seldom or never crossed blood with the Irish" (19). This segregation of Gaelic tribes, perceived or actual, will be important in the novel's resolution.

The Fincastles reinforce their emphasis on the family's Scottish heritage, both Highland and Lowland, at every opportunity. John, Ada's father, tells his sister Meggie, who is writing a letter to a distant relative in Scotland, to declare that Ada "has eyes like the Hebrides" (7). John regularly reads chapters of *Old Mortality* aloud to the family, and Ada wants to name her doll Flora, the "prettiest name in the world" (23, 30). Other than the Fincastle line, the family members stress the Graham heritage most. Margaret Graham Fincastle, John's grandmother, "infused a romantic legend, as well as an aristocratic strain, into the Fincastle stock. There was a cherished tradition that the Graham ancestor who had fled from Scotland to Ireland in 1650 was a near kinsman of the great Montrose" (39).

The novel traces Ada Fincastle's search for meaning and happiness in life. It opens in her childhood and closes as she faces middle age, finally at peace with herself, her past, and her future. The love of Ada's life is Ralph McBride, who has "an Irish strain in his blood. Mother said this gave him his charm and his amused, friendly manner" (71). Not only is the McBride family presumably of Irish Catholic heritage, even though the family members have been Presbyterian for some time, but Ralph's paternal grandmother, Molly O'Boyle, "had come from Ireland when she was a child." Barney McBride, Ralph's father, dead before the birth of his son, had married "Rebecca Muirhead, of a dour Scottish family" (113). This mixing of Gaelic cultures often divided by religion both explains Ralph's character and furthers the fictional exploration of the Gaelic basis for Southern society Glasgow had begun in *Life and Gabriella*.

Ada's world begins to collapse when Ralph is forced to marry Janet Rowan, the daughter of the wealthiest family in the village. At a party, Ada, spurred on by Janet and others, begins to fight with Ralph over his drinking moonshine. Ada's anger pushes her to leave, and when she takes the firm stand not to allow the men in her life to act inappropriately toward or with her, Ada, like Gabriella Carr and Dorinda Oakley, senses that the "vein of iron far down in her inmost being, in her secret self, could not yield, could not bend, could not be broken" (135). The next morning Ada discovers that Janet, pregnant by someone she cannot or will not name, had invited Ralph into her room, after which she screamed because she allegedly had seen a mouse. The Rowans and Mr. Black, the minister, then convinced Ralph he must marry Janet. Ralph "had sacrificed himself, and her also, to a last rag of chivalry, to a tradition in which he did not even believe" (166).

Like Gabriella, Ada finds the Anglo-Norman chivalric codes to be destructive. *Vein of Iron,* however, features fewer criticisms of Tidewater culture and mores than *Life and Gabriella* and focuses more on criticizing Southern Calvinism, which derives almost exclusively from Ireland and Scotland. After Janet has "lost" the baby and had an affair, Ralph comes home, and he and Ada spend two days together in a cabin before he reports for military service in the First World War. They find that their love is stronger than ever, even though Ralph has become cynical. A conversation between them provides a key to the novel:

> "I'm always waiting for punishment. I suppose I'm still incurably Presbyterian."
> "Or Irish?' she laughed. "Perhaps an Irishman makes a bad Presbyterian."
> "Or a Presbyterian a bad Irishman." (220)

The significance of this playful exchange is revealed later when Ada visits Mrs. McBride with the hope of discovering whether Janet's divorce has been granted and if Ralph has been shipped overseas. During her conversation with the woman, who had become increasingly puritanical since her husband's death, Ada realizes, "religion could be a bitter and a terrible thing!" Mrs. McBride, she senses, finds "a thrill of cruelty in the Christian symbols of crucifixion and atonement" (239). Gaelic Calvinism—Presbyterianism—is seen in this novel as primarily negative, but the reader should be careful not to confuse the organized religion with its practitioners, not to assume Glasgow's criticisms of a church she sees as ossified and culturally and doctrinally wrong to equal condemnations of the Scots-Irish Virginians. These Southern descendants of Irish and Scottish immigrants may all have the vein of iron, but if so it is due, Glasgow says through fiction, to the maintenance of family traditions, local folklore, and a sense of self, not to specific theology, and certainly not to Calvinism, as Dorinda discovers in *Barren Ground.* Ada is faced with re-creating that family tradition in the modern world: "Was the past broken off from the present? she mused, or did that vein of iron hold all the generations together?" (248).

The answer that Ada will eventually discover is yes, the vein of iron will hold all the generations together if the individual works to maintain it. Before Ada can marry Ralph, however, the family must face a crisis: Ada is pregnant. The family has already become pariahs due to her father's opposition to America's entrance into World War I, and illegitimacy further isolates them. In addition, Ada is isolated within the family as her grandmother understands neither her willingness to sleep with Ralph nor her lack of shame in bearing his child before they are married. The family's financial misfortunes (John no longer has students to teach) and its new status contribute to a move to Queensborough, a city in eastern Virginia. Though the move offers the prospect of a better financial future once Ralph returns, Ada realizes, "in Ironside, poor as they were, they had built upon rock. Now in Queensborough, it seemed to her, life was an air plant, springing up out of emptiness. Vapor it was yesterday, and vapor it would be again tomorrow" (227). The rock—and the reader should not overlook the New Testament allusion—is not Presbyterianism but Celtic family and cultural heritage, a rock that translates poorly if at all to the modern city run according to Anglo-Norman cultural values and attitudes.[3]

Though Ada, sounding like a quintessential agrarian, hopes she and Ralph can "build a home in the wilderness of the machines as their forefathers had cleared the ground and built a home in the wilderness of trees" (278), and during the boom of the 1920s the family prospers financially, her dream cannot be realized in Queensborough, a world away from the family's roots—roots necessary to the vein of iron. Ada appears to understand this when she hopes they can save enough money to repurchase the manse, the Fincastle family home in Ironside, "for this had been her secret dream ever since she had lived in the city. To go back, not now, but some day when they had prospered and saved" (290).

Linda Wagner believes "one must, at some point, connect the character of Ralph McBride—impractical, volatile, 'Irish,'—with the men in Glasgow's own life" (99). Her assessment is not only that Ada has been failed miserably by Ralph but that somehow Ralph's Irishness explains his lack of character. As already noted, Ralph begins to turn cynical after the community treats him unjustly concerning Janet Rowan. This cynicism grows as a result of his service in the World War: "I'm not so sure civilization is worth saving," he quips (287). Furthermore, Ralph is unfaithful to Ada, and he does fail to honor fully his obligations to his family in other areas.

That, however, is only half the picture, and failure to understand that Ralph is Ada's proper mate can lead to confusion about the novel's conclusion. For example, the one act of Ralph's impracticality that is directly linked by Glasgow the author, as opposed to scholars, to Irishness is positive. Unwilling to ask for charity, the Hamblens, an elderly couple, kill themselves during the Great Depression. They do not leave sufficient funds for burial, and Ralph offers half of his weekly salary to defray the costs. John Fincastle is glad Ralph "was still capable of a magnificent folly. It was the Irish in him." (416). This unsolicited willingness to aid the less fortunate and to attempt to restore a sense of dignity to those stripped of it by the forces of the modern world is more characteristic of Ralph than his failures, and it is why Ada loves him.

John Fincastle's own magnificent folly paves the way for the family's restoration. He had turned from organized Christianity to philosophical writing "that owed nothing to the dynamo" because he could not affirm unswerving belief in all Presbyterian tenets. "Perhaps in some distant future," he muses, "man might turn away, disillusioned, from the inventive mind, and human consciousness might stumble back again along the forgotten paths of blessedness and mystic vision" (110-11). Considering his emphasis on family heritage, Fincastle's "inventive mind" refers to the scientific, empirical, theoretically-dogmatic in religion as well as to technology, and his "forgotten paths of blessedness and mystic vision" suggests the religious heritage of the Celtic church, which may well be imbedded in his vein of iron. As he meditates on this, he acknowledges the blessedness in nature, "not only in beauty; it is in the little things also."[4]

After he realizes that death is near, Fincastle wonders whether he has been failed by philosophical speculation: "He was more at home nowadays with the humblefolk . . . who spoke neither the hollow idiom of facts nor the dead tongues of the schools, but the natural speech of the heart." "Pure philosophy," he acknowledges, "is a wordless [and we should recall that the Apostle John declares Jesus to be the Word] thing," and if wordless, it must also lack something essentially human (426-27). This revelation, that much of his life and most of his intellect have been wasted, forces him to conclude that he must return home to the manse to die because "only in Ironside could he find the freedom to sink back into changeless beatitude, into nothing and everything" (452). Fincastle returns to Ironside and enters the ruined gate leading to the now dilapidated manse, but like Moses, whose arrogance or impatience or frustration had led him to strike the rock, Fincastle, whose arrogance or impatience or frustration had led him away from a family-based Christianity into the vain speculations of philosophy, will be denied the promised land. The first death blow "stripped him of all that he had once thought of as his immortal part, as his inviolable personality. Nothing remained but a blind faith in some end that he could not see, in some motive he could not understand" (454).

That "end" is the salvation of his family. The city was monster machine enough, but the Depression had further dehumanized it. Ada senses in the autumn of 1932, "distraught, chaotic, grotesque, it was an age . . . of cruelty without moral indignation, of catastrophe without courage" (373). Her grandmother had told Ada, "even in the wilderness Scotch-Irish housekeepers seldom became slatterns. If you have the proper pride, you may keep nice among savages" (138). Indeed, when the esteemed German philosopher Hardenburg comes "to pay homage to one of the greatest among living philosophers," Fincastle observes of his sister Meggie, serving as hostess, "never had she appeared so natural, and yet so dignified. The mountain poise had not deserted her. His mother had never lost it, and beyond his mother—how far beyond!—he remembered the noble bearing of that grandmother who had been Margaret Graham, walking on her bare feet through the drenched grass" (424-25).

The family may have maintained its pride, but it had lost its bearings. Fincastle's trip home to die not only forces his family members to return, but it allows them the time to step back from the lifeless existence of the modern city to reflect on what they really want and need. Looking at the manse, Ralph initiates the possibility of staying there, and Ada adds that her father's insurance money could purchase the place. When she over-simplifies the work required to repair the manse and have enough to eat by suggesting they would have it easier than their pioneer ancestors, Ralph injects his comical Irish cynicism to bring Ada back to reality: "it takes conviction to set out to despoil the wilderness, defraud Indians of their hunting-grounds, and start to build a new Jerusalem for predesti-narians" (460). When the decision to return is made, Ada has:

> a sense, more a feeling than a vision, of the dead generations behind her. They had come to life there in the past; they were lending her their fortitude; they were reaching out to her in adversity. This was the her-itage they had left. She could lean back on their strength; she could recover that lost certainty of a continuing tradition. (461)

Having Ada rediscover the strength of her heritage in the midst of the Depression suggests that *Vein of Iron* should be seen as a novel of encouragement for the South in the midst of its greatest crisis since the War Between the States and Reconstruction. Just as Glasgow's fictional vision sees the Scots-Irish as necessary to taming and expanding the Southern frontier, the symbolic family representing the strength of Southern character required to survive the Depression and to begin the process of re-building is of Gaelic heritage. At the novel's conclusion, the marriage of Ralph and Ada also assumes symbolic significance. As noted, Glasgow suggests that the Scots-Irish had mixed little with the Irish before migrating to the South, leaving them the weakened descendants portrayed in the novel: the Calvinist fanatic Mrs. McBride, the society-worshipping Rowans, the ineffectual philosopher Fincastle whose brilliance cannot be tolerated by Presbyterianism. Ralph brings to this dour Scottish breed, as Glasgow sees them, the other half of Gaelic culture that they have suppressed: ecstatic joy; wild, satirical humor; and selfless impracticality, especially when someone is in need. Glasgow was not alone in emphasizing this perceived difference between Scottish and Irish temperaments. Woodrow Wilson, a native Southerner of Glasgow's generation, saw the Scottish and Irish halves of his Gaelic heritage as quite different. "To his Scottish ancestors," Arthur Link writes, "he attributed his introspection, seriousness, and tendency toward melancholy. To his Irish forebears he attributed his occasional gaiety and love of life" (5).

Ranny, the son of Ralph and Ada, who vows he will do something about all the hungry people when he grows up, is the fruit of Glasgow's fictional mating of Irish and Scots-Irish. He is the Southerner of secularized, mixed dour Calvinist and boisterous, Catholic Irish ancestry Glasgow portrays as the hope for the future. And the novel closes on an optimistic note with Ralph and Ada silently viewing the manse: "he reached out his arm, and while she leaned against him, she felt the steady beating of his heart as she had felt it—how long ago?—when they were lovers. Never, not even when we were young, she thought with a sudden glow of surprise, was it so perfect as this" (462).

Like Simms, Glasgow was raised in a part of the South almost desperate to demonstrate that the white Southern heritage lay in the "gentility" of Anglo-Norman Cavaliers. Also like Simms, she revealed in her fiction that the descendants of Celtic immigrants were essential to Southern culture. *Life and Gabriella* makes no claims concerning the predominance of Irish culture in the South, but in having its symbolic heroine be a Southern woman of Irish heritage who turns away from the products of the Anglo-Norman Tidewater culture to Ben O'Hara, Glasgow acknowledges a connection between the best of Southern culture and Ireland. *Barren Ground* is the story of a woman overcoming adversity by discovering her inner strength: the Scots-Irish vein of iron. In declaring that "a few stalwart farmers of Scotch-Irish ancestry" came to dominate the county after the War Between the States, which had destroyed the economic hegemony of the Anglo-Norman South, Glasgow suggests the shift in the Southern power structure to the descendants of Celtic immigrants. *Vein of Iron* further highlights the strength of character Glasgow sees as inherent in the Southern descendants of Irish immigrants and suggests that the best and the strongest of Southern character is formed when Irish Protestant and Irish Catholic are mated.

Chapter V

The Big Bear:
William Faulkner

Like Old Ben, the gargantuan bear in *Go Down, Moses,* William Faulkner casts his shadow over a magnificent demesne. The historical and social breadth and depth of his life's work means that if any study of themes, ideas, or cultural patterns in Southern letters is to be considered valid for the entire culture, it must include an examination of Faulkner. Fortunately for the scholar and general reader interested in pursuing the Celtic-Southern thesis as important to Faulkner's fiction, Joseph Blotner opens his biography with a chapter on the novelist's family background. "Faulkner used to say," Blotner writes, "that the principal family lines were Falconer, Murray, McAlpine, and Cameron," a quartet of Scottish surnames (3). What Blotner fails to note is that Kenneth McAlpine, whose first name indicates a P-Celt or Welsh family connection, was the Irish king of the Gaelic or Q-Celt speaking northwestern coast of Scotland who in A.D. 843 amalgamated his kingdom with that of the Picts to the east (Fitzroy McLean 21).

This uniting of the Irish, or Scots, who first began a migration to the land that would be named for them "in the third and fourth centuries of our era," with the Picts, a shadowy Celtic tribe whose primary P-Celt, or older Continental Gaulish, language and culture may have been mixed with those of non-Indo-European peoples,[1] created the Scottish nation (Fitzroy McLean 15; Mackie 16). A Faulkner as proud of his Scottishness as Blotner reveals may have known of his possible, though distant, relationship to the Irishman who forged the Scottish nation, and this knowledge, in turn, may have been the reason that Faulkner played up his Scottish background while all but ignoring the Irish and Welsh not only in his own family but also in both Oxford and his fiction (Blotner 4-7). Blotner closes this brief chapter on "The Beginnings" of Faulkner's family with a statement that addresses the ultimate importance of the novelist's genealogy: "Perhaps when a man asserts an ancestry as strongly as William Faulkner did the Scottish, this is as important, if in a slightly different way, as would be a sheaf of parchment documents from any herald's college" (7).

In the realm of Celtic studies, Oxford University archaeologist Barry Cunliffe, who over the past two decades has become one of the premier authorities on Celtic culture, writes of the problems in deciding who today can truly be labeled Celtic: "Perhaps the only real definition of a Celt, now as in the past, is that a Celt is a person who believes him or herself to be Celtic" (267).[2]

Whatever the actual bloodlines, Faulkner's self-identity was Celtic, specifically Scottish; though, of course, for the Highlanders, Faulkner's distinct Scottish background, Scottishness was and is basically equivalent to Irishness in cultural terms (McDonald, "Preface" xl-xli). Padraig O Snodaigh cautions those evaluating the current political violence problems in Northern Ireland, "A major consideration to be borne in mind with the [Protestant] plantations and migrations in the 17th century is the extent to which the population movement from Scotland to Ulster was within what had been, and to an extent continued to be part of a single culture" (26). J. P. MacLean affirms, "the inhabitants of Ireland and the Highlands of Scotland were but branches of the same Keltic stock, and their language was substantially the same. There was not only more or less migrations between the two countries, but also . . . an impinging between the people" (41). Roger Blaney says that since the sixth century A.D. "Ulster shared a common language and culture with Gaelic Scotland, a relationship which still survives" (2).

Indeed, the native language of the Scots, Gaidhlig, is a regional, dialectical alteration of Gaeilge, or Irish. The Highland speaker of Gaidhlig today will have little trouble understanding a speaker of Ulster Gaeilge from Ireland's County Donegal. The Gaelic folk culture of the Hebrideans was and is closer to that of the Gaelic folk culture of Synge's Aran Islanders than to that of the Scottish Lowland farmers, whose folk culture, while still Celtic, may be marked by the original Cymric, or Welsh, inhabitants who composed *Y Gododdin,* a work called by Kenneth Jackson "The Oldest Scottish Poem," in the first half of the seventh century (56-67, 186-91; Mackie 19-20).

The fact that Faulkner saw himself as Scottish would be of minimal importance if he had never made use of his Celtic heritage in his writings. But Blotner points out that two of Faulkner's most important families, the Compsons and the Sartorises, are of Highland origin and fled

Scotland in the face of the cultural genocide the English began to inflict on the Highlands after the 1746 Battle of Culloden (5).[3] The McCaslins, another "noble" Yoknapawtapha clan, and the McCallums, a thematically significant poorer family, are also both Scottish in origin, as is the most extensively used of Faulkner's major characters, Gavin Stevens, a man bearing a double Scottish name (Douglas 170, 185). Stevens, also the best educated of Faulkner's characters, is well aware not only of his own Celtic heritage, but also that of much of the rest of Yoknapatawpha County, hence, by implication, the South. In *The Town,* Stevens describes the area's settlement:

> Then the roadless, almost pathless perpendicular hill-country of McCallum and Gowrie and Frazier and Muir translated intact with their pot stills and speaking only the old Gaelic and not much of that, from Culloden to Carolina, then from Carolina to Yoknapatawpha still intact and not speaking much of anything except that they now called the pots "kettles" though the drink (even I can remember this) was still usquebaugh. (316-17)

The "translated intact" suggests that these Scottish immigrants brought their Celtic folkways with them. The drink, of course, is the Irish contribution to alcohol development: Whiskey. "Usquebaugh," a term Faulkner probably learned from "his great grandfather Murray [who] spoke Gaelic and lived to be a hundred" (Blotner 3) is a Scottish modification of the standard Irish *uisce beatha,* meaning literally "water of life."

Cleanth Brooks, perhaps the most prolific and acclaimed Faulkner scholar, recognizes an affinity between Faulkner and his South, on the one hand, and a Celtic land and its major modern poet on the other. He acknowledges that Yeats' "Ireland stands over against London much as Faulkner's South stands over against New York," a recognition of the basis of the Celtic-South, Anglo-Saxon-North dichotomy outlined by McWhiney and McDonald. Brooks notes, "an Irishman like Sean O'Faolain senses at once the similarity between the two provincial cultures," and he affirms, "any Southerner who reads Yeats' Autobiographies is bound to be startled, over and over again, by the analogies between Yeats' 'literary situation' and that of the Southern author" (*Yoknapatawpha* 2-3).

Fifteen years later, Brooks remained enamored of the similarities between Ireland and the South. He declares, "Yeats's view of man in relation to nature and history is rather surprisingly like Faulkner's" (*Toward* 342). Writing before both the historical-cultural scholarship of the Celtic-Southern thesis and the similar work of David Noel Doyle and David Hackett Fischer, Brooks cannot be expected to recognize that the analogy he senses is one deriving from cultural migrations, and he restricts his analysis to noting the "historical conditions true for both Ireland and the South—defeat in war, economic stagnation, and a colonial economy," as well as " a vigorous folk culture" (338). Those similarities, of course, apply also to Poland, Lithuania, Serbia, Croatia, and the Ukraine, but because even minimally significant numbers of Slavs never became Southerners, there is no cultural connection between the South and Slavic Eastern Europe. Just as it would be foolish to try to claim Slavic cultural origins for Southern culture because of similar historical circumstances, it is foolish, certainly after the work of Grady McWhiney, to ignore the massive wave of late seventeenth, eighteenth, and early nineteenth century emigrants from Celtic lands to the South and attribute the many striking cultural similarities between the South and Celtic lands to similar historical circumstances.

Because it masterfully treats virtually every major issue and theme important to Southern literature, *Absalom, Absalom!* (1936) is perhaps Faulkner's best and most important work. Considering the importance Faulkner himself saw in his Scottish ancestry, it should come as no surprise that this novel makes use of Celtic heritage and folkways. The problem for many readers is that unlike some of Faulkner's other novels, *Absalom, Absalom!* does not belabor the Culloden to Carolina to Yoknapatawpha path. As a result, readers ignorant of Celtic culture, those who unquestioningly accept the English imperial contention that the Irish, Scottish, and Welsh are not culturally separate but are provincial adjuncts to Anglo-Saxon culture, will not recognize Faulkner's use, whether intentional or growing naturally out of his Scottish identity and the South's folklore, of Celtic cultural concepts. It is only through an understanding of these concepts that a reader may fully comprehend the importance of not only the tale of Thomas Sutpen but also the impact that tale has on Quentin Compson and, to a lesser extent, on Shreve McCannon.

Quentin, the novel's central consciousness, and the reader both initially hear Sutpen's story from Miss Rosa Coldfield, and unwary readers may find their perceptions of Sutpen adversely and irrevocably colored by Miss Rosa. Though he had never been known to mistreat anyone, with the possible exception of the French architect, and the reader is never definitively told what deal brought him to Yoknapatawpha or what the architect's compensation was to be, Miss Rosa sees Sutpen only as a demon, an ogre. Among Sutpen's positive qualities are that he served valiantly, not cravenly, in the Confederate army, he refused to participate in night-riding after the war, and he was a sufficiently good father so that all three of the children raised in his house, especially Clytie and Judith, whose characteristics are foreshadowings of those in Faulkner's Nobel Prize speech, become honorable, caring adults. To attribute the children's proper raising to Ellen would be foolish, and not merely because the children look like Sutpen. As Cleanth Brooks notes, "Ellen, is silly, superficial, in love with money and position, and finally too trivial to arouse much sympathy" (*Toward* 292). Mr. Compson's later revelations help balance the picture, but for many readers, Miss Rosa's violently biased assessments determine the way that Sutpen is perceived. In order to grasp Faulkner's total presentation of this larger-than-life figure, a reader must first recognize the author's comments on Miss Rosa and her inability to assess Sutpen's character and motives.

The foremost obstacle to Miss Rosa's comprehension is her background, her ancestry. Her father, Goodhue Coldfield, whose name suggests his personality and value system more than that of any Faulkner character except Flem Snopes, was, according to Miss Rosa, "a Methodist steward, a merchant who was not rich . . . who neither drank nor hunted nor gambled" (20). Though his puritanical conscience will not permit him to amass the kind of fortune that Flem acquires, Coldfield shares with Snopes the values dictated implicitly by the Protestant work ethic, foremost of which are to equate the acquisition of money—at least by one's own people—with a state of moral justification and never to waste money. As General Compson told his son who would tell Quentin, Coldfield's objections to the war were not philosophically based, "not so much to the idea of pouring out human blood and life, but at the idea of waste: of wearing out and eating up and shooting away material in any cause whatever" (83). Coldfield, a culturally English Methodist, would no more comprehend the Irish and Scottish risings for national independence than he understood the reasons Southerners sacrificed everything for a cause linked to their cultural/familial identity.

Unlike her father, who starves himself to death rather than sell goods to the soldiers and supporters of either faction, Miss Rosa revels in the high romance of the war. The paradox is that though she views the Confederates as heroes of immense majesty, Miss Rosa is nonetheless her father's daughter, and not only is she also puritanical, but her puritanical attitudes lead her to abhor Sutpen, an actual Confederate officer. As Quentin envisions her childhood, Miss Rosa's life is and always has been "grimly middleclass." Her rearing, then, instructs Miss Rosa to view Sutpen's hunting parties, Sunday afternoon muscadine wine drinking with Wash Jones, racing to church, and, especially, fighting with slaves for sport, activities that McWhiney's chapters "Pleasures" and "Morals" link to the South's Celtic cultural origins, as barbaric (*Cracker Culture* 105-45, 171-192). If Goodhue is culturally puritanical English merchant class, his younger daughter aspires to be a culturally Anglo-Norman Cavalier lady but is bound by what she has been bequeathed by her father.

Faulkner's narrative reveals Miss Rosa to be wrong about key events and character judgments on a couple of occasions, and to move beyond Miss Rosa's furious bigotries, the reader must address these faulty assessments. Miss Rosa informs Quentin that Sutpen would not, after his marriage to Ellen, visit the Coldfield home "because since papa had given him respectability through a wife there was nothing else he could want from papa, and so not even sheer gratitude, let alone appearances, could force him to forego his own pleasure to the extent of taking a meal with his wife's people" (28).

This view, that Sutpen had only used Coldfield for monetary purposes and had no concern for family, is mollified by Mr. Compson, who reveals that the reason the child Rosa rarely saw Sutpen at Sutpen's Hundred is "the aunt would have arranged the visit to coincide with his absence" (62). Here it is the Coldfields who avoid meeting Sutpen as family on his turf. The explanation for this, and for Sutpen's preference to spending a day drinking and talking at the Holston House than to eating with the Methodist steward (63), lies in Coldfield's puritanical nature. As a hunter, drinker (though never drunk), sport gambler, fighter, and racer, Sutpen is to Coldfield both a sinner and an uncivilized ruffian. A lesser man, one worried about the superficial respectability and pretension demanded of Coldfield's petit bourgeois Anglo-Saxon shopkeeper beliefs, would have completed the family unit hypocritically for all in town to see. But Sutpen, who arrived in Jefferson as though "created out of thin air" (32), is repeatedly linked to Greek tragedy, and such a man is above both the pretense of playing the role of chastened, well-groomed son-in-law and the need to confront a disapproving father-in-law and his sister.

Miss Rosa's smug sense of Coldfield moral superiority over Sutpen, an attitude she best expresses by telling Quentin that Sutpen's decision to have his family attend church was "to at least give Ellen one chance to struggle with him for those children's souls" (23), is revealed to be purblind. Among the virtues for which she praises her father is that he had no "slaves except two house servants whom he had freed as soon as he got them" (20). This, at best, half-truth creates a vision of Coldfield as humanitarian, especially when compared to Sutpen, whose slaves work with him to clear a wilderness. But later that evening, Mr. Compson, in preparing Quentin for the visit to Sutpen's Hundred, tells his son that Coldfield had not freed the slaves who had come to him "through a debt;" he had set up a pay scale "putting them on a weekly wage which he held back in full against the discharge of their current market value" (84). While the hope of slaves buying themselves out of bondage was offered, Coldfield's chief interest was the full payment of a debt, not humanitarianism. Either his pay was too low or the assigned market value too high, or perhaps he docked pay too many times as when he would visit Ellen (66), but Coldfield's slaves earned freedom only by escaping and following Federal troops, as did Sutpen's (84-5). In this, as in other matters, Coldfield is very much the self-justified, hypocritical, reforming Anglo-Saxon Puritan, whose cultural values are antithetical to the South.

Mr. Compson, whose views of Sutpen and Coldfield are more inclusive than those of Miss Rosa partly because they have come principally from his father, presumably Sutpen's closest friend, is fully aware of Coldfield's pharisaical nature. In addition to revealing the story of the slaves, he also tells Quentin that Coldfield had been Sutpen's full business partner in whatever it was that allowed him to furnish the empty house (44) and that Sutpen had agreed to take full responsibility should the venture fail (259). But the most damning comment made on Coldfield's moral system comes in Mr. Compson's discussion of the wedding. Coldfield, at least in Jason Compson's view, regarded religion as a business: "[Coldfield] intended to use the church into which he had invested a certain amount of sacrifice and doubtless self-denial and certainly actual labor and money for the sake of what might be called a demand balance of spiritual solvency, exactly as he would have used a cotton gin" (50).

But Miss Rosa's small-shop-keeping, Methodist background is insufficient to explain her continued obsessed fury in 1909. The answer lies in her romantic coloring of the South alluded to earlier. Whether her romanticism was due to a rebellion against her father's capitalist religion, a fascination with the grandeur in which she believed Ellen lived, reading of romances, a blind acceptance of the Tidewater Cavalier myth, or a combination of reasons, Miss Rosa, still a teenager, had already begun "writing a schoolgirl's poetry about the also-dead" (65). While her father, lacking the courage to speak his peace, hides in his attic to avoid the war, Miss Rosa writes "heroic poetry" about the Confederate soldiers (68). The attitudes expressed in these poems, one can only assume, would be the modern anglophonic version of chivalric. Her Confederates would not possess and act on the sense of honor of an Andrew Jackson, a man considered by David Noel Doyle to be the symbol of antebellum Irish America (xvii) and like Sutpen a gaunt, red-headed, harshly realistic, magnetic Southerner, a man who must have been as horrendous to Goodhue Coldfield as was Thomas Sutpen. Miss Rosa's Confederate soldiers certainly would be Southern versions of Tennyson's Victorian Anglicized, epicene Arthurian knights; they would have possessed the manners and attitudes not of soldiers, particularly flamboyant ones living in a culture essentially Celtic, but of middle-class Protestant Sunday school girls. In short, Miss Rosa's Confederates would have had little relationship to the actual soldier in gray.

When Sutpen, who, Miss Rosa concedes, "had fought for four honorable years for the soil and traditions of the land" (19) and who brings "home with him a citation for valor in Lee's own hand" (68), arrives home from the war, his sister-in-law is living in his house, but he so little knows or notices her that Judith must tell him her name (159). Eventually, Sutpen not only observes Rosa, but he proposes to her. When, two months later, he expands his proposal in an attempt to fight his encroaching mortality,[4] Miss Rosa flees in horror back to town (162-168). Certainly Sutpen's suggestion is insulting and lacking in human compassion, but it does not explain fully Miss Rosa's life of fury. The romance does. The chivalric hero must not only possess charm and decorum, but he must love from afar. Sex is to be imagined, and may even be longed for, but not practiced or discussed, at least openly. Miss Rosa's childhood view of Sutpen as an ogre had been supplanted by her romantic coloring of all Confederates, especially officers cited for valor. Sutpen should be, to live up to the falseness of the Tennyson-type take on the chivalric code, almost above sexual interests, and when, in desperation for a son in his old age to carry on his name, he amends his proposal, Miss Rosa's romanticism crumbles. In many ways, Miss Rosa is the self-deluded Southerner who wants to apply the false myths of the urbane Anglo-Norman Cavalier gentleman to the non-coastal South and is horrified at meeting a largely representative Southerner whose desires and hopes are too earthy and selfish, a man too hurt by being born into dire poverty and too hardened by working his way out of it, to be chivalric in the sense understood by those fed on a diet of genteel English poetry.

Sutpen may have proposed to Rosa as much to take care of his wife's now-orphaned son as to acquire another son, and I have not doubt that once he realized her for what she is, he could have concocted the proposal deal to shock her into leaving his house.

Though it is necessary to discredit Miss Rosa's interpretations, it is relatively easy to do so, and many readers will continue to view Sutpen as a demon impervious to family and horrifically hungry for land and power. To deny that Sutpen is guilty of these human shortcomings would be to have missed why he must be cut down by his own retainer, but to conclude that Sutpen is simply a soulless or utterly immoral man, a Flem Snopes of an earlier age, is to fail to recognize the magnificence in which Faulkner cloaks him. Like an Heroic Age champion possessing near deific powers, Sutpen "rode into town out of no discernible past and acquired his land no one knew how and built his house, his mansion, apparently out of nothing" (11). His eyes possess "a quality at once visionary and alert, ruthless and reposed" (33). Sutpen's slaves and his closest friend recognize his majesty: "As General Compson told his son . . . while the negroes were working Sutpen never raised his voice at them, that instead he led them, caught them at the psychological instant by example, by some ascendancy of forbearance rather than by brute fear" (37).

Though Miss Rosa feels that Sutpen's physical manifestation of greatness is an act, that he "contrived somehow to swagger even on a horse" (16), General Compson recognizes that the swaggering is "without braggadocio or belligerence" (48); it is natural, and it reflects the strength of character necessary to fight his way out of abject poverty without stooping to illegal means, to quell a slave rebellion, to begin again in the wilds of Mississippi, to serve valiantly in the military past age fifty, and to attempt yet a third beginning, this one in the face of local devastation and at age fifty-eight.

The key to explaining Sutpen, and hence the novel, is to recognize how Faulkner describes Sutpen's fall after interspering heroic descriptions of his protagonist in the midst of Miss Rosa's outraged condemnations of him, creating a picture of the culturally impotent and sterile raging against the virile. This image is mirrored in the fifty-man posse's following Sutpen all day before finally arresting him (48) and the cringing way in which the crowd attacks him at the wedding (56-7), and then describes Sutpen's fall. Far from a villain, Sutpen is a tragic hero whose death is bound up with his life. To grasp Sutpen's tragic flaw, and to understand Faulkner's fascination with a man ruthless, if innocent, in so many ways, the reader must first understand the importance of Scottish heritage to Faulkner, which has been noted, and then discover how he employs aspects of Celtic folkways in *Absalom, Absalom!*

Sutpen tells his background to General Compson while hunting for the runaway French architect, and Quentin relates the information to Shreve and the reader. "Sutpen's trouble," Quentin asserts, "was innocence," and the reader's task is to discern Faulkner's import in having his hero described thus. Sutpen was born and raised in the Scots-Irish culturally dominated Appalachian Mountains of what in 1863 became West Virginia. The people live "in log cabins," and the primary occupation is hunting. This the average reader can easily accept, but Quentin's elaboration of the mountain culture that produced Sutpen may seem a childlike, romantic vision of Eden, albeit a violent paradise:

> where he lived the land belonged to anybody and everybody and so the man who would go to the trouble and work to fence off a piece of it and say "This is mine" was crazy; and as for objects, nobody had any more of them than you did because everybody had just what he was strong enough or energetic enough to take and keep, and only that crazy man would go to the trouble to take or even want more than he could eat or swap for powder and whisky. (221)

Students of Celtic culture, however, will recognize not only the primacy of hunting and the proximity of small-scale violence (Chadwick 122, 131), but also the emphasis on the individual accomplishing something on his own. Estyn Evans writes of the Scots-Irish cultural patterns that became integral to Southern frontier life, "another cultural trait which characterised the backwoodsmen and has Ulster antecedents was the practice of 'striving,' the performance by rival workers of prodigious feats of strength and endurance" (81).[5] Perhaps more important is that readers also perceive that Sutpen's Blue Ridge culture accepts basic Celtic tenets of land ownership.

P. W. Joyce notes that to the Irish, "in theory the land belonged not to individuals, but to the tribe," or extended family unit (I, 184), and Nerys Patterson labels Celtic land ownership as that of "fraternal partnerships" in conjunction with the clan and accepts Geoffey Keating's gloss that such arrangements were to guarantee that all members of a clan, and not simply the wealthy, would have a stake in the society's defense and maintenance (154-55). The Celtic culture brought to the New World by the soon-to-be Southerners includes, at least in Faulkner's vision of the Appalachians, a sense of family community with the land, and though, as Joyce reveals about Ireland (I, 185), men do own land, their principal responsibilities in land management are familial and communal, not individual. Sutpen's people, therefore, would be foolish to attempt to take what is culturally accepted as belonging "to anybody and everybody."[6]

Sutpen's putting away of his first wife further reveals the extent to which his innocence is Celtic. When he discovers, after the birth of a son, that his wife is in some way flawed, enough so as to warrant a divorce, Sutpen acts calmly and rationally:

> I merely explained how this new fact rendered it impossible that this woman and child be incorporated in my design, and following which . . . I made no attempt to keep not only that which I might consider myself to have earned at the risk of my life but which had been given to me by signed testimonials, but on the contrary I declined and resigned all right and claim to this in order that I might repair whatever injustice I might be considered to have done by so providing for the two persons whom I might be considered to have deprived of anything I might later possess; and this was agreed to, mind; agreed to between two parties. (264)

One of the most interesting peculiarities about early Celtic society is the prominence given to women, one that at times almost approaches equality with men (Chadwick 115, 135-6; Patterson 21). One result of such attitudes was divorce laws that declared women, specifically in terms of property, to be equal to their husbands, as is observed by Joyce:

> If the couple separated by mutual consent, the woman took away with her all she had brought on the marriage day; while the man retained what he had contributed. Supposing the joint property had gone on increasing during married life: then at separation the couple divided the whole in proportion to the original contributions. (II, 9-10)

Though he is living in a society denying women such egalitarian treatment in divorce, Sutpen operates according to Celtic tradition. Because his wife presumably had contributed virtually all the marital property, Sutpen, in Celtic marriage terms a *lanamnas fir for bantinchur* or man supported on the property of his wife, gives it all back, retaining only a minuscule portion, that which he earned. The reader should note General Compson's response. Himself a descendant of Gaelic Celtic immigrants, Compson calls Sutpen's divorce settlement "justice." Cleanth Brooks's assessment notwithstanding (*Toward* 297), the general's sympathies are with Sutpen's attempts to ameliorate a situation that grew out of his being deceived. Compson is shocked only that Sutpen would be innocent enough to expect a woman, in this case a non-Celt, to accept this hard justice as the cost of her intentional deception.

The Sutpen who in many ways acts nobly in the annulment is the same man who ultimately destroys himself, and the reason for the adult attitudes that eventually topple his family lie in his boyhood move from the Appalachians to the Tidewater. To recognize this perspective, the contemporary reader must not allow our age's Enlightenment racial views to so cloud his vision that he sees Sutpen not as a man misled, but as a non-liberal on race relations and thus evil.

The Tidewater, even more than the Charleston, as noted by David Hackett Fischer, was the site of the small but immensely wealthy Anglo-Norman Cavalier settlement in the South that served as the base of that group's political and economic hegemony. The difference of cultural attitudes between Sutpen's Celtic mountain world and the Tidewater's self-conscious attempts, at least among portions of its gentry, to emulate Anglo-Norman squirearchy is significant. The adolescent Sutpen, a youth possessing the "latent insubordination" of Celts, who left the Appalachians knowing only physical tests to measure men's worth, "lifting anvils or gouging eyes or how much whisky you could drink then get up and walk out of the room" (226), discovers that in the Tidewater, unlike in his native culture (228-29), ownership is used aggressively, that possessing certain things, such as slaves and a mansion, indicates social superiority and perhaps moral superiority as well.

When he is turned away from the Big House's front door by the slave—a member of a group he comes to despise not because of racism as we know it but because the slave defines property which demarcates class in such a way that even the slave of the Anglo-Norman considers him inherently inferior—Sutpen "went into the woods." He does not consciously plan a walk; he naturally heads to "a place where game trail entered a canebrake and an old oak tree had fallen across it and made a kind of cave where he kept an iron griddle that he would cook small game on sometimes" (233). In this secret place hidden by an oak, the sacred tree of the Celts, Sutpen meditates on his predicament. A recent etymology of the word "druid," the class of religious and intellectual leaders of the pre-Christian Celts, defines the term broadly as "the man by the sacred oak tree who knew the truth" (Delaney 92), but Sutpen leaves his oak-guarded haven without insight.

To utilize a popular, simplistic phrase, Sutpen suffers culture shock. He leaves a society operating primarily on Celtic standards and morals and lacking a true Celtic nobility for leadership, a society in which he has value based on family, place, and individual achievement, principally courage and physical skills, and he rudely is thrown into a culture in which he has no significance.[7] This is certainly not to claim that Celtic society is not materialistic. Francis Byrne notes that rank in ancient Ireland, both within the family and the larger political units, "depended on wealth as well as birth, and it was possible to rise or fall accordingly" (51). And ancient Celtic society was an hierarchical, slave-holding one (Chadwick 111-122). In fact, Thomas Cahill says of the pagan Irish during the final two centuries of the Roman Empire, whom he feels converted to Christianity en masse without appreciable bloodshed because of widespread recognition of the social evils emanating from the slave trade, "in the [early medieval European] slavery business, no tribe was fiercer than the Irish" (37).

If, like the essentially English Tidewater world, Sutpen's native Celtic culture accepts slavery and some semblance of aristocracy, however mobile within the larger clan, how then could he be said to suffer from culture shock? There are two keys. First, unlike most cultures, Celtic culture apparently always has been remarkably open to, even supportive of, debate and questioning by all classes, even of the most powerful. Cahill says of Columbanus, a sixth-century Irish missionary working primarily among the Germans, chastising the pope in a letter:

> This swaggering behavior has confounded historians, prompting them to wonder if perhaps Columbanus was a little off his rocker. But I think we may chalk up his attitude to his Irishness. (He even boasts to Boniface of "the freedom of discussion characteristic of my native land.") In chilly, cityless Ireland, men worked in close cooperation by day and slept side by side at night. Even the king was one's intimate. . . . To Columbanus, the pope was one of the brothers, a father abbot worthy of respect, by all means,—but also in need, like any man, of an occasional jab in the ribs. The jab might even be one's religious duty in a manner of speaking. (190)

In turning him away from the door as if he were a mangy, perhaps even rabid, dog, the Big House slave teaches young Sutpen that his Appalachian-Celtic world view marks him as born inferior to Anglo-Norman planters and perhaps to their house slaves.

Second, unlike the Anglo-Norman culture in which property may be all, in which name may be purchased (as in Thomas Hardy's *Tess of the D'Urbervilles*), Celtic culture ultimately stresses the importance of family,

as opposed to family name. Byrne declares, "there was no system of primogeniture: land was shared equally between brothers; but the head of
the senior line was the *cenn fine* [head of family or clan chieftain], who
represented the family in all its affairs" (49). Though Celtic society is
ordered aristocratically, the sense of extended family links together peoples of differing educational levels and wealth, a concept that largely
explains the relative ease of class relationships in the antebellum South
and after. In a note, James Leyburn acknowledges that the Highlanders,
romantically misconstrued by the Victorians as a people of absolute
authoritarian lords bossing a horde of unquestioning peasants, lacked
meaningful social classes, which

> was one reason they were regarded as uncivilized [by 16th-18th cen-
> tury Englishmen]. The Highland clan resembled a large family. . . .
> The chief was not "upper class"; he was rather the leader who tradi-
> tionally made decisions and took responsibilities. As kinsman to all
> members of the clan, he rarely tried to lord it over them. (14)

Sutpen's eventual decision, which, significantly, is not made in the
oak cave, his embarkation into his tragic flaw, is to compete with
Tidewater society on its terms. Eugene Genovese quotes Brazilian historian Fernando Henrique Cardoso, "Freedom in slave society is defined
by slavery. Therefore, everyone aspired to have slaves, and having them,
not to work" (*World* 6). Except for the latter part of Cardoso's assertion,
which Sutpen's Celtic "striving" heritage overrules, Thomas Sutpen
accepts that to be accounted worthy as an individual, a leader, and an
example among men, in his political and economic society he must
become a slave owner: "You got to have land and niggers and a fine
house to combat them with" (238). There is no suggestion here of family, no thought of love of wife and children, no mention of honoring his
ancestors, only a desire to accumulate sufficient wealth to erase the
future threat of insulting embarrassment. In general human terms,
Sutpen's "design" is cold, calculating, and mechanical. In specific
Celtic terms, it is anti-family, hence anti-life and immorally doomed to
failure. A word commonly used to describe Sutpen's design is "abstract,"
and abstractions have little place in Celtic, or Southern, society.[8]

Perhaps the best physical manifestation of Sutpen's abstraction is his
house. The plantation home built by W. J. Cash's prototypic Southern
planter is relatively large, but its construction was somewhat haphazard,
and it is basically "just a box, with four rooms, bisected by a hallway, set
on four more rooms bisected by another hallway, and a detached kitchen

at the back" (16). Gerald O'Hara's Tara, built almost identical to Cash's description, is characterized by Louis Rubin as "an ample, rather plain affair of no particular style, added to as the family's needs require" (*Gallery* 32). Unlike these homes, Sutpen's house is not organic. Rather than growing out of and around the Celtic family, it is conceived in abstraction and built before Sutpen marries a second time. It is fitting then that the crumbling symbol of Sutpen's abstraction, a house he has named after the Tidewater tradition of "a King's grant" (16) not after the Celtic tradition like Tara and Rowan Oak, Faulkner's home, which was built by Irish native Robert Shegog, should go up in flames to end Sutpen's legitimate line.

But the abstraction itself does not destroy the House of Sutpen; rather, Sutpen's attempt to ignore his responsibilities as a Celtic *cenn fine* both destroys the line and brings about his own death. Sutpen's adolescent encounters with black slaves determine his view of the race. Though he will not allow the mere thought of black blood to threaten his design, Sutpen is not a thorough racist in our sense of the term. As Rubin notes, "when the dynasty is not involved, he displays no racial prejudice whatever" (*Gallery* 33). This attitude extends to his daughter Clytie, who is not only raised in the house but is involved in important family decisions. In the Tidewater, Sutpen learned to see blacks as the toys of wealthy white men; they are subservient, menial, wealth and comfort providers. Since a white daughter would be largely subservient to her father anyway, Clytie poses no threat. But Sutpen's son and heir could not be so tainted.

As Brooks observes, two other Yoknapatawpha planters, Carothers McCaslin and John Sartoris, father mulatto children, but only McCaslin's son by his own mulatto daughter is relevant to Sutpen's case (*Toward* 298). Old Carothers does what Sutpen does not: acknowledge on some level his son with black blood. McCaslin's legacy, though it is a mere pittance, acknowledges family, which is especially essential because he too is of Gaelic Celtic ancestry. Sutpen's rationale for not doing so with Charles would lie in his views of blacks learned first in the Tidewater. He would see Charles as not just tainted but also as illegitimate. Since important information had been withheld from him, the marriage contract could not be legal, leaving Charles as illegitimate. While many Christian European societies might not have recognized the illegitimate, Celtic civilization did. P. W. Joyce states of the re-dividing of family land after a death, "those members of the sept who were illegitimate getting their share like all the rest" (I, 197). In terms of acknowledging illegitimate children, McCaslin acts as a Celt, while Sutpen, following the lead of Tidewater society, acts as a non-Celt. It is no mere coincidence that Shreve, himself bearing a Gaelic surname, conjectures that all Bon wanted was acknowledgment from his father (326-333).

Earlier I labeled Sutpen a largely representative Southerner, which seemingly puts me at odds with both Brooks and Rubin. Sutpen is largely representative in that he is of Celtic origin, Quentin's conjecture about the first Sutpen being a transported English convict to the contrary (222).[9] But as Brooks and Rubin both note, Sutpen is set apart from most of Yoknapatawpha society. The other Celtic landowners, to some degree even General Compson, see Sutpen as different. What they intuit is that Sutpen has betrayed much of his Celtic sense of community. Yes, he is a flamboyant Gaelic hero worthy of the poetry of Yeats, but he ultimately fails to found a thriving Gaelic clan because he ignores essential Celtic patterns of responsibility to family.

Sutpen's omission is not restricted to Charles. The Celtic extended family includes retainers, and Sutpen is killed by his last adherent. Wash Jones serves Sutpen for decades, drinking with the great man not only in the scuppernong arbor in good days but also providing companionship after the war. Even as he decides he must kill Sutpen for violating their relationship, for again refusing to acknowledge and accept his illegitimate child, Wash, according to Quentin via Mr. Compson, sees the old, broken Celtic chieftain now all but bereft of family and possessions as "bigger than all them Yankees that killed us and ourn . . . bigger than this whole county that he fit for . . . bigger than the scorn and denial which hit helt to his lips like the bitter cup in the Book" (287).

In a statement that reveals the sense of pride a Celtic retainer holds for the *cenn fine*, Wash acknowledges he has not actively participated in greatness, but, he says, "at least I was drug along where he went" (288). The basic Celtic sense of leadership is perhaps best presented in summation in the medieval Welsh tale *Branwen Verch Lyr*, the second of the *Four Branches of the Mabinogi*. Facing a river and with no observable means to cross it, Cymric soldiers ask their leader Bendigeidvran (Blessed Bran) what should be done: "'Nit oes,' heb ynteu, 'namyn a uo penn bit bont. Mi a vydaf pont, heb ef'" ("There is nothing," said he, "but that he who is a head [chief] would be a bridge. I myself will be a bridge," said he). In short, the Celtic leader is to serve, not be served as if he were some sort of demigod, and when he no longer successfully serves those under his charge he is to be removed as surely as a bridge that is no longer safe for those who use it.[10] Richard Weaver is one scholar who has recognized that the Southern sense of loyalty is at least in significant part Celtic in origin, due to the South's strong infusion of Celtic blood. The Scotch-Irish immigrants who filled its uplands brought along their natural clannishness and their habit of passionate devotion to a chieftain. This was to express itself in the hero worship accorded men such as Lee, Stuart, Jackson, and Forrest, an intense, personal loyalty, which took little account of reverses and crowned its subjects with something of the divinity that doth hedge a king. (162)

There is no contradiction here. Wash honors Sutpen to that degree and still must strike him down for his failures as surely as the Cymry obey Bendigeidvran's order to decapitate him after he had failed them and been wounded, for the maimed, spiritually and emotionally as well as physically, Celtic leader becomes the impotent Fisher King whose sterility blights the entire land. Sutpen—the *penn*, the head or chief—allows himself to be struck down before he blights the land.

Wash's attitude is the one with which the reader should leave the novel. It is not likely that Faulkner, who saw himself as a proud Highland Scot living in America, would intend the reader to view Sutpen as villainous, even anything less than tragically heroic, for Sutpen is the only named Faulkner character to be the child of a monolingual Gaelic speaker from Scotland (241). But neither does this mean that the reader is to approve of Sutpen's actions. Faulkner's Gaelic consciousness could not sanction Sutpen's ruthless design, which in its inability to recognize the primacy of family actually renders invalid any attempt to originate a great Gaelic clan, but it could provide an understanding. The Scots who fled Culloden did so in the face of English attempts to obliterate their national culture. Though theirs was certainly more violent, these Highlanders suffered from a cultural collision similar to that faced by Sutpen after he was turned away from the Big House. Sutpen's story is then a variation of the Culloden to Carolina to Yoknapatawpha theme, but it is the only one in which the Gaelic *cenn fine* is himself the central focus of a tragedy. It is the only one in which the Gaelic *cenn fine* destroys himself by adopting a mode of behavior unacceptable to Celts.

Paradoxically, Sutpen's greatness is triggered by the same event that forms the tragic flaw that ultimately forces a retainer who respects him, who believes that his chieftain "will make hit right," to decapitate him. Quentin, a Southerner of Celtic ancestry who attempts to understand himself as a part of his heritage, reveals the paradoxical quandary that will ignite Sutpen's drive and eventually topple him:

All of a sudden he discovered, not what he wanted to do but what he just had to do, had to do it whether he wanted to or not, because if he did not do it he knew that he could never live with himself for the rest of his life, never live with what all the men and women that had died to make him had left inside of him for him to pass on, with all the dead ones waiting and watching to see if he was going to fix it right, fix things right so that he would be able to look in the face not only the old dead ones but all the living ones that would come after him when he would be one of the dead. (220)

Sutpen's Celtic sense of honor had been insulted, requiring a response. Note that Quentin sees the insult as reflecting not simply on Thomas Sutpen but on all his ancestors and possible descendants, a sense of family extended over time identical to that envisioned by Ada Fincastle in *Vein of Iron.* As Nora Chadwick writes of Celtic society, "the individual counted for little in law. It was the kinship group which was ultimately responsible for the actions of its individual members" (113). As a Celt, Sutpen's primary obligation is to family, past and future as well as present. When he fails this Celtic responsibility, a failure born out of a youth's inability to fathom an alien culture, Thomas Sutpen creates his own fall.

Absalom, Absalom! is Thomas Sutpen's tragedy, but the novel's structure forces the reader to include the roles of Quentin and Shreve in a final analysis. The Miss Rosas, the Southern Biddys and Paudeens, are innately incapable of understanding the tragedy of Heroic Age figures. But Quentin and Shreve are of Gaelic heritage; they should largely understand and appreciate. There is, of course, a vast difference between the two that is most easily explained by Quentin's Southern, specifically Yoknapatawpha, rearing, which makes Sutpen's story immediate, and Shreve's Canadian background, which isolates him from even the larger American context. But the fact that each carries a Scottish surname suggests that their cultural baggage should be somewhat similar. An Anglo-Saxon Yankee or Canadian might want Quentin to "tell about the South," but he likely would not have listened to and participated in the protracted Sutpen story. Shreve, though he begins by injecting facetious remarks and ends by withdrawing while Quentin continues the fight in his soul, becomes almost as involved as the Southerner.

In wanting to understand, Shreve tells Quentin, "it's something my people haven't got. Or if we have got it, it all happened long ago across the water and so now there ain't anything to look at every day to remind us of it" (361). This statement and Quentin's reply, "You can't understand it. You would have to be born there" (361), demonstrate the validity of the Celtic-Southern thesis. *Absalom, Absalom!* is the story of a tragic hero whose flaw is his failure to honor his culture's sense of family obligations, who cannot say "my son" to a child with black blood and then take responsibility as the head of clan. The Canadian of Scottish ancestry who is living in a non-Celtic society cannot comprehend, but the Southerner, who lives in an essentially Celtic culture, understands in his heart as well as his mind.[11]

Louis Rubin feels that Quentin is horrified that such a man as Sutpen "was possible" in the antebellum South (*Gallery* 38). The reason for this horror is that Quentin, a descendent of Gaels who fled English bigotry and persecution, must realize that the plantation system, predicated on chattel slavery of blacks, repeats similar horrors of human exploitation, only this time the Compsons and Sutpens are in control.[12] Though Sutpen is set apart from most of Yoknapatawpha society, the evil that brings him down is present in the culture. Dirk Kuyk writes of Sutpen's "design," "he meant, I believe, not merely to acquire a dynasty but to acquire it so that he could turn it against dynastic society itself" (17). Translated into cultural terms, Kuyk's assessment is correct: Sutpen meant to establish a dynasty in accordance with the Celtic cultural patterns of his Appalachians. His tragic flaw was to allow the hoped-for ends to justify the means, to ape the Cavalier Tidewater pattern, the only one that he can associate directly with sufficient wealth and power as to protect him, even as he was dismissing it by refusing to play fully according to its rules. Eugene Genovese writes of M. E. Bradford's view of an antebellum Southern ethos to "acquire freeholds, and with them, the status and self-respect appropriate to Englishmen," "it assumes that those who could acquire property thereby positioned themselves to exercise free will to choose the good" (*Southern Tradition* 4). *Absalom, Absalom!* reveals the potential tragedy lurking in such a world view, one foreign to the young Sutpen.

Forrest McDonald closes his prologue to *Cracker Culture* by declaring of Celts, "in a manner of speaking, their entire history had prepared them to be Southerners" (xliii). In *Absalom, Absalom!*, William Faulkner utilizes his Scottish heritage to examine the tragic implications of the South's Celtic legacy: The failure of the South's "warrior aristocracy," men possessing "a preoccupation with physical prowess, a spirit of naive bravado and rivalry, a jealous regard for personal honour, and a strict and often quixotic adherence to a code of primitive chivalry" (MacCana, *Literature* 27) to honor the Celtic sense of family. The Celtic-Southern thesis allows readers to see that Sutpen's "innocence" is his Celtic cultural heritage, making him truly innocent when confronted, rudely and hostilely, with Anglo-Norman culture. The greatest cultural achievement in *Absalom, Absalom!* is that Faulkner dramatizes the tension in the white South between the minority mandarin Anglo-Norman Tidewater culture and the majority Celtic culture, and Sutpen's personal tragedy, embracing, however inadvertently, the Cavalier ethos, is emblematic of the South's tragedy and the South's failure.

Chapter VI

The Celts of the Kentucky and Tennessee Mountains: Caroline Gordon

In *Cracker Culture*, Grady McWhiney refers to an article by Ellen Churchill Semple titled "The Anglo-Saxons of the Kentucky Mountains." He observes that Harry M. Caudill had re-examined Semple's data and concluded that she "should have called her article *The Celts of the Kentucky Mountains*" (4). Unlike the scholars and novelists discussed previously, Caudill's principal focus was on the Welsh in the South, not on the Irish and Scottish: "The 1984 [Welsh] telephone directory . . . is astonishingly similar to the name listings of that portion of Kentucky which begins about thirty miles east of Lexington and continues to the Big Sandy and the Virginia line."[1] Furthermore, McWhiney notes that Caudill's name analysis suggests, "all but 6 of the 112 Kentucky counties named for persons have Celtic names" (4).

During the last two decades of her life, Caroline Gordon (1895-1981) worked on a family memoir titled *A Narrow Heart*. She considered this nonfiction work important because of her awareness of the significance, the indispensability, of family and family history to the individual in the South. Veronica Makowsky, Gordon's biographer, writes, "her claim that 'the story of their lives . . . is the story of my own' is true; she made it her own in her life and fiction, and, to some extent, she also made the story" (4). In one of the three sections of the never-completed work that Gordon published during her life, she announces that she was raised on "a farm of not more than four hundred acres, lying on the southern border of Kentucky, so near the state line that to this day I hardly know whether to call myself a Kentuckian or a Tennessean" ("Cock-Crow" 554). Gordon's life's work was an exploration and analysis of the Kentucky and Tennessee hill farmers and farm town residents of her own heritage, a fictional exploration covering Southern history from the first colonizing of the lands west of the Appalachians to the generation living through the Great Depression.

Like William Faulkner, Gordon was keenly aware of her Celtic ancestry, and she, too, often used her family members as models for her fictional characters. Makowsky notes that Gordon emphasized her Scottish Lowland ancestors as perpetrating wanton violence:

> The Adam of Gordon who appears in the ballad has always seemed to me a proper 'father image' for the entire clan. The ballad records that as the weather turned cold, he remarked to his followers that it was time to seek winter quarters. He and his followers therefore 'drew up' to the nearest 'hold.' The lord of the manor was away from home. His lady appeared at the window and in her frenzy yielded to Adam's smiling promise that he would take care of the bairn she threw down to him. The child she threw down was a girl child of two or three, so rosy and plump that Adam, as he spitted her on his sword, observed that this was the first child he had ever regretted treating in this fashion. (4-5)

In Ireland, the family continued this pattern, with some of them becoming essentially English government sponsored and sanctioned anti-Catholic terrorists, "helping Cromwell loot Irish churches, so that, Gordon wrote, 'like many traitors in those days, they were rewarded for their services to their country by the gift of an Abbey'" (5). In addition to the pillaging and plundering, and the peacetime pursuits of hunting and gambling, the Gordons had another side: theological and scholarly zeal. This, a family historian argues, not the ransacking of Irish Catholic churches, earned the Irish Gordons the abbey at Newry (Makowsky 5).

"Early in the eighteenth century," Makowsky writes, brothers James and John Gordon "emigrated to Virginia where they continued to display the family's conflicting inclination toward accomplishment and piety on the one hand and sport and dissipation on the other" (6). The descendants of the Gordon brothers are prime examples of the shift in the South from a region dominated by Anglo-Normans to a land defined in many ways by Celtic immigrants and their progeny. James Gordon, son of the original John and named for his uncle, "began the family's climb to achievement by serving as a delegate first to the Virginia assembly and then to the Virginia convention of 1788 which ratified the federal constitution." William Fitzhugh Gordon, James' son "was a general in the War of 1812 and served as a delegate to the Constitutional Convention of 1829-30. He is best known for his career in Congress where he fought what he viewed as the excesses of Jacksonian democracy" (Makowsky 6).

In Gordon's view, her mother, Nancy Minor Meriwether Gordon, also derived from Celtic antecedents. Though the surname Meriwether, or

Merry Weather, is in origin a nickname, and presumably an English one (Bardsley 528), Caroline Gordon was insistent on the veracity of the family legend that her mother's people were ethnically Welsh, not English. There are two possible explanations for this apparent problem. First, as we have seen, many Celtic peoples in the seventeenth, eighteenth, and nineteenth centuries Anglicized, even completely altered, their surnames, some complying with governmental decree and others attempting to avoid anti-Celtic prejudices in both the United Kingdom and North America. Meriwether may have been a name chosen by a Welsh family to stave off discrimination either from the English rulers of their land or from the Anglo-Norman rulers of the colonial South.

Second, the English Meriwether family may have been given land in Wales for service to the crown and, like the medieval Normans in Ireland, quickly became more Welsh than the Welsh, in which case their descendants immigrating to the South would have brought with them a thoroughly Celtic folk culture, one preserved in family stories about its heritage. Equally possible is that, though the Meriwethers were English, they had married Celtic women or women in the South of Celtic ancestry whose identities had been stamped on the family more forcefully and thoroughly than those of the male English heritage. The eighteenth-century Irish poet Brian Merriman, whose "Cuirt an Mhean Oiche" ("The Midnight Court") is the most influential Gaelic poem of its time and whose exact ancestry is not known but who is assumed to have been "the illegitimate son of a country gentleman" (O Tuama 221), should be kept in mind when discounting the Meriwether story of its Welsh cultural heritage and identity.

Apparently unaware of either the cultural differences between the English and the Welsh or the violently discriminatory social conditions of the seventeenth and eighteenth centuries that led to a mass emigration of Celts, Makowsky believes that Gordon's imagination had created "a sort of fairy tale" about the Meriwether Welsh origins.[2] According to Gordon, the Welsh Meriwethers were "of low stature, dark complexioned, round headed." The founder of the Southern Meriwethers, "Nicholas Meriwether, called 'the Welshman' in family legend, sent to Virginia three of his gnomic sons. . . . There they established themselves on land which, tradition tells us their father had received between 1652 and 1654 in return for money which he had furnished Charles the Second when he was attempting to establish himself on the throne" (11). A descendant, known as Nicholas Meriwether II, was a schoolmate of Thomas Jefferson under William Douglas, who was born and educated in

Scotland and had come to Virginia to tutor James Monroe. This Nicholas, who would win distinction in the French and Indian War, would later marry Margaret Douglas, his teacher's daughter (11-12). Dr. Charles Meriwether, the son of Nicholas and Margaret Douglas Meriwether, was sent to Scotland to complete his education, and in 1811, he traversed the mountains with his wife and son to settle in Kentucky (Makowsky 14-15).

Penhally (1931) is Gordon's first novel, and in it she initiates the major theme of her literary career: A fictional exploration of the hill Southerners of Kentucky and Tennessee largely through a reworking of her family's stories. *Penhally* is the account of an extended planter family, whose farm may be small by Tidewater or Delta standards but not so by those of the rolling hills South, from the years before the War Between the States to the Roaring Twenties. Like Faulkner's *The Sound and the Fury, Penhally* chronicles the fall of a landed Southern family, with Gordon's novel focusing on the complexities of inheritance and entailment, as well as on familial and cultural betrayal for materialist gain and social advancement. Also, unlike its Mississippi counterpart, Gordon's novel emphasizes the family home, which is its titular object. In contrast to Sutpen's Hundred, the Llewellyn home is one built organically around the family: "originally Penhally had consisted of square block with a big hall running through it. On each side of the halls there were two enormous rooms. . . . As time had gone on they had added two wings, one on each side of the house, and an L in the back" (11). Nor is the design and layout of Penhally unique to Kentucky Llewellyns: "The old place in Virginia had been like that, a long gray house, set in the middle of an oak grove. It was fated that a house should be built like that" (1-2).

The design is not an abstract vision of an alienated artist architect; it is organic: "Douglas said that all the really good houses in this section had not been built but had evolved—from the double log cabin with the dog run down its middle. . . . The whole thing had a line and a character that the more pretentious houses did not have" (260). The Llewellyn house, its clan seat, is a physical representation of the family and its independence and healthy growth.

Though war fever sweeps through the area, Nicholas Llewellyn is opposed to secession. "We came west to get land," he declares. "And now we've got it. Land is a responsibility. When a man's got land he isn't free to follow any fool uprising that comes along. He's got people dependent on him" (95). This warning born of the Celtic fear of having more land taken from them by a victorious army—one that should be kept in mind by those who label people in Celtic lands non-Celtic if they choose not to support nationalist risings and a warning that in the aftermath of the military defeat of the Confederacy would sound like a prophecy—takes on added meaning when Gordon has a prominent Southerner from outside the immediate vicinity know of both Penhally and the Llewellyn family. Gen. Albert Sidney Johnston, who is riding a horse bred and donated to the Confederacy by Ralph Llewellyn, Nicholas's younger brother, when he, Johnston, is killed at Shiloh, discusses the family with John Llewellyn, the son of Jeems, the third Llewellyn brother: "the general had made him sit down, had called him Jack, and asked him about all the family; had even joked about the quarrel between his uncles Ralph and Nicholas" (106). Penhally, it seems, is one of those antebellum family homes that is to be recognized as symbolizing the South and Southern culture. Frederick McDowell writes that the Llewellyn home, "in its flourishing state before the Civil War and in its fall from power after the Reconstruction, is a symbol for the South, the antebellum way of life, and the attenuated survival of southern traditions in the present" (14).

In her presentation of the war, Gordon links recent Irish immigrants to the Appalachian mountaineers, which coalesces with the Celtic-Southern thesis. A sergeant from the rolling hills of Kentucky, who sounds like the rare Southern Know-Nothing Nativist, "hated mountaineers. He thought they didn't make good soldiers," that their fierce individualism diluted military discipline. Likewise, "the sergeant despised the Irishmen [natives of Ireland, not those with distant Irish ancestry], too, for 'furriners.' The sergeant was a fool. A duck-legged, bullet-headed fool from Barren County. There was not a better fighting man in the whole squadron than Jerry O'Donnell" (104). O'Donnell, who had been born in Ireland (164, 166), "was always running around after Perry" (108). Nace Perry, the squadron's best shot, a man who "picked out the button he wanted on a man's coat when he fired" (105), is a mountaineer banjo player and fiddler. O'Donnell befriends him because of the unspoken similarities between them that each senses, and he watches over him because Perry has "nostalgia," the War Between the States version of post-traumatic shock syndrome. Eventually, Perry is able to shake O'Donnell and kill himself, and it is the Irishman who requires that prayers be said at the burial (109).

At the end of the war, Jerry plans to head to Kentucky, where his "mother's brother from Donegal" lives, and John Llewellyn persuades him to detour by Penhally. There the Irish Confederate marries "Molly Bracy, the miller's granddaughter" (170, 163), and his daughter will have "the map of Ireland spread all over her face" (165).[3] Chance Llewellyn, John's grandson, admires the elderly O'Donnell and spends as much time with him as possible. Chance's grandmother Lucy also "liked old Jerry. And it was not that O'Donnell had gotten around her with his Irish blarney. She genuinely respected him" (166). The clannish Llewellyns, who are loath to admit any outsiders into their close-knit circle of family and friends, embrace Jerry O'Donnell primarily because he is Irish. Having married either cousins or occasionally natives of Scotland almost exclusively since their arrival in Virginia, the Llewellyn family has presumably retained most of its Celtic cultural characteristics, and in Jerry O'Donnell they recognize a fellow Southerner of undiluted Celtic heritage. O'Donnell is the natural man to be accepted as the Llewelyn's most respected and befriended retainer.

The fall of the house of Llewellyn is due ostensibly to entailment, but the ordered inheritance of Penhally is not the primary cause; the growing lack of family identity in the modern South is. Lucy Llewellyn is Ralph's daughter, and in accordance with family tradition she marries her cousin John, who receives Penhally from his bachelor uncle Nicholas. Lucy, in many ways a person of stronger character than her husband, "was prouder of her 'blood,' as she called it than any human being he [Chance] had ever known. . . . Llewellyn was the name of an ancient Welsh king. Llewellyns would tell you that they were Welsh." Though the Llewellyns have preserved stories of their ethnic and cultural origins, some of the more distant members of the family believe they know better: "Old Cousin Woodford, who was a genealogist, said that that was nonsense. They were English" (232). Cousin Woodford is representative of the "educated," perhaps specifically post-bellum, South becoming fully American, and therefore less Southern, and refusing to acknowledge that even Southerners bearing names linked directly to Celtic history and fighting to save Celtic culture and phonetically incapable of being Anglo-Saxon in origin have a Celtic heritage, one that defines them.

In the story "The Petrified Woman" Gordon treats this theme humorously. A wealthy cousin who has spent his entire adult life in St. Louis speaks at the Fayerlee reunion and declaims upon family lineage from royal non-Celts. That evening, his speech is belittled by family members who know their true heritage. "'They are mostly Scottish people,' Cousin Eleanor said, 'descended from Edward the Confessor and Philippe le Bel of France,'" which sends Cousin Marie into giggles. "But it *is* just like a book," she says (*Collected* 12-13). The family members not ruined by modern American education created by Anglophilic Yankee school-marms get the joke.

Formal education comes under close scrutiny in *Penhally*, with Gordon linking it directly to the Llewellyn loss of family identity. Chance recognizes that the modern educational system of the area is hostile to Southern culture and is, therefore, hostile to Southern families. He thinks of Little Nick, the son of his older brother Nicholas, who has never been impressed by or interested in the family stories:

> He had gotten to talking in that funny, quick way, too, since they had sent him east to school. Or perhaps it was English. They said that those schools were all run on the English plan and all the masters were English. They evidently took a lot of pains with the way the boys talked. He had heard Little Nick say things the Southern way and then correct himself. (270-71)

Note that Chance sees a connection between Yankee ways of talking and being educated and English ways. These non-Southern ways are not merely non-Llewellyn, non-Welsh ways, but they are destructive of the Southern, Celtic ways. The modern educational system, Chance apparently feels, teaches Southerners to be ashamed of their heritage, teaches them to search desperately for some Anglo-Saxon or Norman ancestry to claim and to refashion themselves to fit that culturally mandarin false heritage.

Penhally concludes with Chance killing his older brother, who had sold Penhally, the house and land that physically symbolize the family, so that the farm could be turned into an exclusive hunting club. Chance, who from his early childhood had been moved by the Llewellyn family stories, senses that his brother's turning the family home into a personal profit for modern social climbing is emblematic of the death of the Southern family. If Penhally is symbolic of the South, then the cultural meaning of the Llewellyn family tragedy is that when the Celtic South loses its Celtic identity, as does the second Nicholas Llewellyn, and embraces an Anglo-Saxon vision of itself, it will have lost its system of roots. And without a true identity, it will turn on itself. Frederick McDowell notes that Gordon was similar to the Vanderbilt Agrarians in her horror of the modern "disintegration she saw in North and South alike" (5). *Penhally* reveals that Gordon at the beginning of her career believed the best way for the South to fight the "modern chaos" was to retain its "Welshness."

In subsequent novels, Gordon continued to reveal the importance of

Celtic family origins to her hill Southerners. One of the central characters in *The Garden of Adonis* (1937), perhaps her most overtly Agrarian novel, is Ote Mortimer, who, through his mother Nora O'Donnell Mortimer, is the great-great grandson of Jerry O'Donnell. Ben Allard, the novel's other central character and related to the Llewellyns, thinks of this family tenant-farming his land, "All the Mortimers, the O'Donnells, rather, had Irish turns of speech. But it was not that long since they had come over from the old country" (25). Ote is, to Allard, apparently a cut above his siblings because he inherited his mother's Irishness, not his father's Englishness. "The O'Donnells," Allard muses, "were probably better stock than the Mortimers. Joe [Ote's father] looked much more like a poor whiteman than Ote did" (24).

The Lewis family in *The Women on the Porch* (1944), landowners comparable to the Llewellyns and Allards in both holdings and Gordon's autobiographical origins, tell their history back to "the original settler, who had obtained all this land as a Revolutionary grant, a son of old 'Irish John Lewis,' who had to flee the old country as a young man because he had killed his landlord" (21). Gordon's choice of Lewis as the surname of her fictionalized family on the Tennessee side of the border probably reveals her knowledge of the alterations of Celtic names, for Charles Bardsley relates that Lewis is an Anglicized form of Llewellyn (480). If people, operating on the Anglophilic sense of history taught in the schools, refuse to believe that the Llewellyns are ethnically and culturally Celtic, they most likely will be incredulous to hear anyone suggest the Lewises are Celtic. In using two forms of one Celtic surname to label her most autobiographical characters, Gordon calls attention both to the alterations of Celtic names, which leads many to assert boldly that the people in question simply cannot be Celtic in any sense, and to the fact that surname alterations cannot change basic cultural or ethnic origins and heritage.

Green Centuries (1941) is in many ways Gordon's most ambitious and accomplished novel. In it, she traces the opening of Kentucky and Tennessee to white settlement in the late eighteenth century. Her protagonist is Orion—commonly called Rion, which suggests the Gaelic name Ryan—Outlaw, a younger friend and hunting companion of Daniel Boone. The novel opens in 1769 in a settlement on the Yadkin River approximately four miles from Salisbury, North Carolina, and it concludes in East Tennessee in 1779 with the Cherokee militarily defeated and the colonization of Kentucky and Tennessee imminent. Though he has found new lands and entertains the hope of settling on a large farm in a valley across the mountains, Rion Outlaw feels hollow at the novel's close. Rose Ann Fraistat believes that "in the pioneers' savage trek westward, they have ravaged the continent . . . and in so doing have inevitably destroyed themselves. Cassy's despair and the emptiness that Rion feels at the end of the novel are examples of that same melancholy afflicting all those without allegiance to a social and religious community" (54). What Fraistat, who hopefully is not so blinded by theory as to actually believe that the original pioneers of trans-Applalcahia "ravaged the continent," fails to see is that Gordon's persistent use of characters who are Celtic immigrants and the descendants of those Celts suggests that a deeper meaning may be uncovered concerning *Green Centuries,* one predicated not on relatively contemporary emphases upon environmentalism but on the importance of Celts to the development and expansion of Southern culture.

Rion has little knowledge of his family's heritage. His father, "Malcolm Outlaw had been a man grown when he came to America and he had married comparatively late in life. Rion knew that he had landed at Charleston and had gone out from there trading with the Sapona Indians" (43-44). Though Malcolm has no discernible past, he is well respected in his settlement and among men of learning. When Rion was six years old, a mysterious man who believed the Southern Indians to be the Lost Tribes of Israel visited and addressed Malcolm as "Master Outlaw." Though the Outlaws are Presbyterian and Malcolm had disliked the Reverend Dawson, the English-born Episcopalian priest "sent over here right after the Act for the Establishment of an Orthodox Clergy" (33), he is respectful of Frank Dawson, the curate's son and the area schoolteacher: "it was the learning that Malcolm Outlaw bowed to. He maintained that a man with learning was twice the man that he was without it" (30).

The catalyst for Rion's eventual flight toward the Smokies is John Findley, a man with a "wild Irish laugh." He stops at the Outlaw cabin attempting to locate Daniel Boone, a former hunting companion. Findley wants to search for the gap through the mountains leading to Kentucky, the rich land Boone had seen three years earlier while serving as a soldier. Boone and Findley secure financing for the expedition, but Rion is refused the loan he needs to purchase a horse. Denied the opportunity to explore with Boone, Rion turns his energies to local politics. He is sworn in as a Regulator, a secret organization working to undermine the colonial tax and military structures, which favor the Anglican church and the Anglo-Norman gentry at the expense of the mass of settlers. When two captured Regulators turn king's evidence, Rion leaves for the mountains with Frank Dawson, Frank's sister Cassy, properly Jocasta, soon to be Rion's common-law wife, and the German-born merchant Jacob Wagner and his wife Elsa. Gordon's portrayal of Wagner's involvement in the Regulator movement coalesces with historical scholarship on the importance of Celtic immigrants to the eighteenth-century South. David Noel Doyle writes, "the Regulator rising was predominantly Scotch-Irish, although not exclusively: Germans, everywhere when ungathered tending to assimilate to the Ulster majority, joined them" (135). Not only does Gordon's German immigrant, unbound from his cultural fellows, follow the lead of his Celtic neighbors, but his flight with them suggests the Celticization of non-Celts on the Southern frontier that the McWhiney-McDonald Celtic-Southern thesis advocates and that was suggested by George Tucker's Edward Grayson. German emigrants to the South became Southern culturally and politically as they followed the leads of their Celtic neighbors.

Captivated by the tales of pioneers he had heard, Archy, Rion's younger brother, secretly follows the group. When Archy is caught, Rion demands that the boy return home. But Archy continues to follow at a distance until he is too far from home to return alone. Archy's fever to explore does not subside when Rion allows him to stay. Rather, he wanders ahead, and soon after discovering buffalo dung, he is captured by the Cherokee. Archy's life as a Cherokee provides a contrast to that of his pioneer brother. Fraistat believes that "unlike the hopeless existence of the pioneers, the Indians' life—as Gordon conceives it—secures the individual in meaningful relationships with others" (52). Gordon's Cherokee are decidedly anti-white because they recognize that the pioneers are inherently destructive of the forests—such as clearing to plant—and game the Cherokee live on. But there are some whites they embrace as brothers. Dark Lantern, the woman overseeing the captured Archy and the wife of Atta Kulla Kulla, hates whites, but "her husband called the white man, John Stuart, brother. . . . And her son, the Dragging Canoe, loved Alexander Cameron, the agent, as he loved no other man" (239). Just as William Gilmore Simms saw the Scots-Irish as the preeminent Indian traders in part due to their ability to treat Indians with respect, Gordon's Cherokee accept as brothers only those whites of Celtic ancestry.

In addition to marking the prominence of Celts in the eighteenth-century Indian trade in the South, Gordon reveals that Rion Outlaw, her prototype of the Southern frontiersman, is a Celt, regardless of the

Anglo-Saxon sound of his surname. When Rion tells a man named Hogg his own name, the man retorts, "that ain't your name. You look like a red Highlander to me. More likely MacGregor or MacIntosh. Your folks got in some trouble in the old country and had to leave. Took the first name that came into their heads and stuck to it from pure contrariness. Just like you'd do today" (304).

Somewhat later, Rion is visited by James Adair, the mysterious man who had sojourned with Malcolm Outlaw years before. Adair tells Rion that he is indeed a MacGregor and that his father was "out in the fifteen," which means that Malcolm MacGregor Outlaw had fought for the Scottish Stuarts in the 1715 Jacobite Rising, a failed attempt that Caruthers suggests spurred large numbers of Scots to emigrate to the South. It means that Malcolm served under Rob Roy, the most famous MacGregor chieftain and possibly the most famous legendary modern Scot. J. D. Mackie reveals that the MacGregors, outlawed in the seventeenth century for a combination of anti-Campbell, anti-English, and anti-Williamite activities, "were deprived of their civil rights until 1774" (273).

After Adair's revelation, Rion, for the first time in his life, possesses a family history, and he realizes that "he had joined the Regulators in the same way his father had joined the Jacobites" (414). Simms had seen the Celts as the primary instigators behind the small Southern revolts that eventually would lead to 1776, but Gordon goes a step further. She links the Southern revolts against the crown to the desperate struggles of Celts in their own lands to maintain their cultural identity and heritage and a sense of independence. By implication, Gordon would have us see the Rob Roys, Celtic people made outlaw by the English Crown and Parliament, as an indispensable background of the American Revolution.

As a Jacobite fugitive from a proscribed clan (410), Malcolm MacGregor would have to choose a new surname, preferably one sounding un-Celtic. "Outlaw" not only signifies what he was quite literally in the world of WASP empire, but it also is emblematic of the entire eighteenth-century wave of Celtic emigrants to the South. Whether they were Scottish Highlanders, Irish Catholics, Scots-Irish or Scottish Lowland Presbyterians, Welsh Dissenters, or truly nationalist members of the Church of Ireland or the Church of Scotland, even if they had never opposed any of the victors in the English power struggles, these Celts were all outlaws from the persecutions and discriminations of the Anglophonic, Church of England, Anglo-Saxon-Norman rulers of the British empire. In order to protect themselves and their children, they would have to hide certain Celtic cultural characteristics and portions of family histories, and that would be done first with a surname change, which then would be pointed to by late-twentieth-century scholars as "proof" that they were ethnically and culturally English.

Because they have seen no significance in the author's Celtic ancestry, Gordon's critics have failed to recognize that Rion's unquenchable desire for land far away from redcoats and crown tax collectors, or any other centralized government with the power to destroy the individual, is a cultural trait born of the genocidal horrors faced by Celtic peoples, especially in the seventeenth and eighteenth centuries. In addition to Rion and the Scottish Indian traders, Gordon's pioneers include Charles Robertson, a man with a "broad Irish face," brother of James, both of whom played central roles in the traversing of the Cumberland Mountains and the settling of Middle Tennessee; James Adair, who "derived from the historic Irish house of Fitzgerald. Indeed Fitzgerald was his true name," who was born in County Antrim, Ireland (Williams vii-viii); and Daniel Boone, the descendant of Quakers from the southwest of England and from Wales who settled in America first in "the village of North Wales in Gwynedd Township," Pennsylvania. Daniel's mother was "Sarah Morgan, a descendant of the early Welsh inhabitants" (Lofaro 2), and the Boones steadily moved south and west, farther from English and Anglo-Norman Tidewater control.

In Thomas Sutpen, William Faulkner created a tragic hero of the antebellum South for the twentieth-century South, one whose failure to live by Celtic codes of conduct is his tragic flaw. In *Green Centuries,* Gordon provides the eighteenth-century origins of that tragedy, which were left unstated by Faulkner. Rion and his fellow Celtic Southern pioneers are "without allegiance to a social and religious community" because they have been stripped of it by successive English governments destroying local Celtic freedoms in order to strengthen the Empire's central control, increase its wealth, and guarantee it a steady supply of cannon fodder. As Cassy dies, Rion experiences his tragic realization: "like the mighty hunter, he had lost himself in the turning. Before him lay the empty west, behind him the loved things of which he was made" (469). Rion's understanding further highlights the importance of *Penhally.* The Llewellyns, who had maintained their Welsh identity in Virginia, built a home that symbolized the Celtic family in the South, a sense of family predicated upon place and spirituality, and it lasted until the twentieth-century owner lost his Welsh identity and so was happy to turn the family legacy into cash. At the conclusion of *Green Centuries,* Rion finally has the self-knowledge he needs to start anew without being destructive. *Green Centuries* is a tragedy, but like *Antigone,* it is a tragedy of hope, one in which the survivor may use his tragic realization to better himself and those around him. In that sense, Rion Outlaw MacGregor symbolizes the settlement of Kentucky and Tennessee.

Green Centuries also features a discussion of religion that marks the movement from Southern religion being dominated by Gaelic Presbyterianism and the primitive Baptist church, with their stern, unrelenting emphasis on predestination, some to salvation and others to damnation, to evangelical Methodist, Free Will Baptist, and Disciples of Christ and churches of Christ, that, to different degrees, proclaim man's free will and resulting accountability. Grady McWhiney notes that "British Celts, before they migrated to the American South, generally had been Presbyterians, unchurched, or nominal Catholics" (*Cracker* 188). Rory Fitzpatrick, emphasizing the frontier as at least partial catalyst, believes that the revivals in America, first that of Methodism in the 1730s and then especially the Great Revival beginning in Kentucky in 1799, "destroyed the predominance of the Presbyterian church in the South. In thousands the Ulster settlers became Baptists. The Revival also weakened the structure of all Protestant institutional churches and laid the foundation for the incredible diversification of religious beliefs and practices in the modern United States" (117).[4]

When James Adair visits Rion, he is accompanied by Jonathan Murrow, a frontier evangelist born in Glasgow (430). Murrow declares, "I left Philadelphia a Calvinist. I am now a follower of Arminius" (408). The reader may conclude that Murrow merely rejects the Calvinist doctrine of double predestination, but Cassy, raised an Episcopalian, declares of the belief in infant damnation through Original Sin and the resulting need to baptize infants, "don't seem reasonable now, does it?" This querying assertion causes Rion to remember Andrew Wallace who "held that infants are neither saved through baptism nor lost through it. His father [Malcolm] said that was Arminianism" (409). As befits a Celt, Murrow's conversion came in the forests: "it was on the journey through the wilderness that my faith changed. . . . I can no longer subscribe to the doctrine of salvation by election" (408). Gordon also notes that Quakers in the colonial South tended to become Baptists. When Rion refers to the Yadkin River area as "Baptist country," Cassy recalls the many Quaker settlers. "They'd come there Quakers," Rion responds, "but they didn't last. Take the Boones. They was all Quakers when they came there twenty years ago. Now all Boones worship at Trading Ford chapel" (408). Because most Quakers in the early South were from Wales or the southwestern part of England near Wales, they found religious conversion relatively easy because it was very much about cultural reconnection.

Considering the importance of religion in her works, especially after her conversion to Catholicism, Gordon's brief revelation of the Celtic backgrounds of Southern Christianity in *Green Centuries* should not be underestimated or downplayed. *The Strange Children* (1951) is Gordon's "most closely autobiographical novel" (Makowsky 191), and, not coincidentally, it focuses, fictionally, on the spiritual awakening of Gordon and her husband, Allen Tate, and features religious figures of Irish ancestry. The novel is set at Benfolly, a farm outside Gloversville, Tennessee, and a fictionalization of the Clarksville, Tennessee, home in which the Tate family lived briefly during the 1930s. Benfolly had been purchased by Steve Lewis's brother so that Steve and his wife could concentrate on their writings.

Makowsky believes, "the intensely autobiographical nature of this novel indicates that Caroline was using it to judge the Tates' earlier life from the perspective of her conversion" (192). In contrast to the essentially skeptical Lewises are Terence McDonough, who got religion under a hickory tree (291-2) and is a snake-handler, a fundamentalist sect advocating the continuing literal enactment of Mark 16: 17-18, in which believers baptized by the apostles are said to be able to pick up serpents, and Kevin Reardon, a Catholic who recently has had religious visions. Lucy Lewis, the daughter of Steve and Sally, is the novel's central consciousness, and she feels that "when Mr. MacDonough or Mrs. MacDonough said 'Jesus' you felt as if He were in the next room. And when she was down there listening to them, she felt the same way" (108). In contrast, Lucy feels that her parents' academic discussions, including those concerning the Bible, are but "Fiddle . . . Fiddle . . . Faddle . . . Faddle. . . . That's all their talk was" (115).

Fraistat believes, "*The Strange Children* implicitly argues that spiritual insights are best articulated and given form by the Roman Catholic Church" (118). That was certainly Gordon's belief by the time she wrote the novel, and it may be her ultimate meaning in *The Strange Children,* but Steve Lewis's vision, a necessary first step for his conversion and the novel's climax, occurs after he has witnessed one of Terence MacDonough's services. What is culturally significant is that the two viable spiritual options Gordon sees open to twentieth-century Southerners, at least in *The Strange Children,* are what for convenience sake I will call fundamentalism—a firm, Bible-centered Christianity as opposed to a bourgeois, social-gospel Protestantism—as exemplified by a man of Irish ancestry and an intense, traditional, mystery-seeking Catholicism, likewise exemplified by a man of Irish ancestry.

Gordon's presentation of these two possibilities, which many continue to see as violently contradictory, is a Southern revelation of the continual symbiotic interaction between Irish Catholics and Protestants, even in the religious sphere. David Noel Doyle, analyzing the cultural impact of Irish emigration to the United States, predicted in 1985:

> the pro-family orientation of residual Protestant Irish culture in America has finally shifted many of them from their traditional political apathy in the southern locales, just as many Irish Catholics show signs of similar concerns: to a historian of the Scotch-Irish, this is less surprising than many might expect . . . their common fears may yet help produce a 'last hurrah' of common purpose which could vindicate their tenacity of remembered descent, and—with other men and women of good will—restore in morals and manners, not in rhetoric, the substantive theism of the republic that trusts in God. The politicians would follow wanly only as the results become evident. ("Catholicism" 216)

Perhaps academics are slow to recognize the significance of Irish America in no small part because "the conservative, skeptical often cynical Irish," regardless of religion, doubt "the natural goodness, perfectability of man, inevitability of progress tenets of the Enlightenment" and recognize "a dark side of human nature, the existence of objective evil, and the impact of irrational forces on the human personality and the historical process" (McCaffrey, "Irish-American" 178). Like most Southern writers, the devoutly religious and the lukewarm, Gordon adheres to this pre-modern philosophy, and its options for the seeking soul are displayed in both Kevin Reardon and Terence McDonough, each of whom in his passionate conviction stands against the "strange children" of the modern world who would pull people from God in the name of materialism or modern art and scholarship, which is what the scoffing, childishly self-indulgent Tubby does.

A rich Yankee spendthrift and socialist, the poet Tubby McCollum works for the magazine *Now* and is the epitome of the novel's title. Like the "strange children" of the Bible, Tubby's mouth speaks "vanity" and his "right hand is a right hand of falsehood" (Psalm 144:8, 11), for he seduces the wife of his friend. Unlike Sally's Uncle Fill Fayerlee who is a non-believer driven to examine Scripture for truth, Tubby is interested in Scripture only to mine its rich language for use in his own writings, for which he will be paid handsomely.

Robert Brinkmeyer is a prime example of the contemporary professor openly hostile to both Terence MacDonough and Kevin Reardon. He labels the MacDonoughs and their fellow worshipers "fanatic religious fundamentalists" (*Three* 101) and says of Tubby's declaration that Reardon has become cracked in the head, "his observation seems fair" (*Three* 102). To accept Tubby's view of Kevin Reardon is either to miss Gordon's presentation of Tubby as quick to believe the psychiatrist's belief that his friend's religious conviction is but a mask for "latent homosexuality" (37) and then as sufficiently immoral to abscond with that friend's wife or to accept those actions as reasonable, even moral. It is the passionate belief, the non-lukewarmness, the refusal of both MacDonough and Reardon to embrace modern skeptical liberalism and its materialism that bothers Brinkmeyer. He ultimately dubs MacDonough as the worse of the two primarily because of the snakes, the faith handling of which he sees only as "wild and disordered" (103). Brinkmeyer's hostility is both philosophical-theological and social. Kevin Reardon may be an embarrassment among the modern artists and professors, but Terence MacDonough is uneducated poor white Southern, worthy only in the eyes of those like Tubby, and his contemporary academic defenders, of condescendingly amused voyeurism.[5]

Like Gordon, Professor Dennis Covington has recognized the spiritual and moral integrity of snake handlers and the faith's origin as a reaction against the excesses and the moral relativity and vacuum of the Industrial Age. "Snake handling . . . didn't originate back in the hills somewhere," Covington writes. "It started when people came *down* from the hills to discover they were surrounded by a hostile and spiritually dead culture" (xiii-xiv). That culture is the one represented by Tubby and modernism in *The Strange Children*, the one from which Steve, Sally, and Lucy will be saved by the combined efforts, actions, and words of Kevin Reardon and Terence MacDonough, who builds a brush arbor for the meeting that Reardon admires as "like something out of the Middle Ages" (107). There we see the link between Celtic Catholic and Celtic Protestant, between Celtic medieval and modern, allied against the forces of modern materialist skepticism.

Nor should readers minimize the importance of man's proper relationship to nature as sign of his spiritual rightness in Gordon's works. If the presentations of Jonathan Morrow, Kevin Reardon, and Terence

McDonough, all of whom respect God's nature and man's rightful place in it, fail to persuade in this regard, Gordon's portrayal of John Calvin in "A Walk With the Accuser" should not. As he is about to be chief party to burning at the stake Michael Servetus, once a correspondent and a fellow Protestant Reformer (though a Unitarian one), Calvin looks out upon the beauty of the Swiss mountains:

> The glory of God reveals itself everywhere, the mountains echo his name, those grasses beneath my window laugh up at Him. Truly, the whole created earth is God's visible theater. But we must not take too much delight in His manifest and familiar works. For those of us who are called to election have our part to play in His theater which is not visible to the fleshy eye. And woe to us if we fail to play our parts! (*Collected* 303)

Gordon here reveals her sense of Calvin's hubris that led to an autocratic theocracy: His belief that his role is somehow above God's creation, superior to the world of flesh and blood human beings. Terence McDonough knows better, as does Kevin Reardon.

Revealing the cultural bigotry that continues to press the notion that the eighteenth-century English evangelical revival of Episcopalianism determined the Great American Revival, which means that the cultural origins of American religious belief and practice, especially evangelical Christianity, will be considered all but exclusively English, Marilyn Westerkamp notes, "without doubt, one hundred years before Whitefield began to preach, Ireland experienced its own awakening," one replete with shouting, swooning, panting, weeping, and boisterous singing. "This awakening established traditions of revivalism and enthusiasm, traditions that would inform the course of Irish religious history and, through immigration, American religious history for the next four centuries" (16).[6] Whether Calvinist or Arminian, the Great American Revival was triggered, Westerkamp demonstrates, by "large scale migration from Ireland" and the descendants of those immigrants moving increasingly into the Southern and Western frontiers; where large numbers of Irish settled, passionate, Scripture-centered revivalism took root (14). Just as Gordon portrays Celts as the pioneer determinants of the Kentucky-Tennessee hill culture, she sees Irish forms of Christianity as both the primary determining religious heritage of the South, certainly the hill South, and the possibilities for Southerners in the modern world to maintain the sense of community necessary to mitigate the spiritual stultifications inherent in the modern age.

Chapter VII

The Agrarians,
Southern Families, and the War:
Stark Young, Allen Tate,
and Andrew Lytle

One of W. J. Cash's condemnations of the South is that it was a culture in which the descendants of Celts, fed on an extreme romantic individualism, convinced themselves of the actuality, or at least of the need to accept the validity, of a false myth: the English country squire as Southern cultural originator and prototype. Driven by his thesis, Cash misread virtually all of Southern literature, including that of the Agrarians, the group he singled out for special chastisement as purveyors of a romanticized myth that he recognized as crippling and paralyzing the South. The Agrarians, in summation, were attempting to define what was good in Southern culture, and therefore what should be saved from the force of modernization and its technological God of Progress; they were not focused on cultural origins. They did, however, occasionally mention the South's cultural genesis, and while they often pointed to ancient Greece, Republican Rome, and Scotland, they also mentioned England. Frank Owsley declares of the South's settlers, "most of them were of the yeomanry, and they were from rural England with centuries of country and farm lore and folk memory" (69). Five years after the publication of *I'll Take My Stand*, Allen Tate avows in "The Profession of Letters in the South," "the South came from eighteenth-century England, its agricultural half; there were not enough large towns in the South to complete the picture of an England reproduced" (*Essays* 526).[1] In his autobiographical reminiscence *The Pavilion* (1951), Stark Young, though he earlier had stressed the "deep Scotch sense of life" characterizing Southerners, asserts that it is the landed English families "from whom we drew our standards" (170).

Acknowledging the few nods to Scotland, we must conclude with Cash that in their essays, which derive from somewhat abstract and theoretical musings on current events and world politics, perhaps especially the rise of the overtly anti-Christian modern state[2], the Agrarians did label

Southern culture as something deriving largely from England. This may be explained as necessary: If the Agrarians were to be successful in their attempt to convince twentieth-century Americans, three generations weaned on tales of the violent Union threatening ingrates with their poverty and illiteracy, of the inherent values in Southern culture, they would need to link that culture to one all Americans had been taught by both pedagogues and politicians to admire. Republican Rome, with its focus upon "clan" membership and its agricultural basis as necessary to the worthwhile society, could serve as an historical reference point, but Southerners clearly could not be physically descended from Romans. Late-eighteenth-century England, a period after the horrors of the seventeenth-century wars and before both the wars of the French Revolutionary and Napoleonic eras and the full squalor of the Dickension Industrial Revolution, meets the criteria, especially as it presents Southerners as being part of the mandarin American WASP culture.

But this reasoning, however valid, is ultimately of little significance. Because Southern culture is one predicated on its folkways, abstract academic articles and theoretically based, politically defined essays are less valuable in determining the genesis of Southern culture than creative works of literature deriving from Southern folkways. And the Agrarians, like Glasgow and especially Faulkner and Gordon, wrote fiction born out of family and community folk tales and knowledge of local histories. Theoretically, the Agrarians might find the eighteenth-century English squire in Southern culture as a type of antebellum planter, but their fiction declares that the best of Southern culture is Celtic in origin.

Like Faulkner, another native of north Mississippi, Stark Young identified all but exclusively with his Scottish Highland ancestry. Studiously aware of his family heritage, Young chose to focus his fiction on the McGehees. "Affectionate as Young was toward his father's family," John Pilkington declares, "his ties to the Youngs were never so strong as his feelings for the McGehees on his mother's side" (*Stark Young* 3). Pilkington summarizes the McGehee migrations into Mississippi:

> The ancestor of the American branch of the family, James McGregor, a younger son of the McGregor clan in Scotland, had emigrated to Virginia early in the seventeenth century and changed his name to McGehee. For several generations, the McGehees accumulated wealth and position in Prince Edward County, Virginia; but soon after the American Revolution, Micajah McGehee (1745-1811) moved his wife and children to a settlement along the Broad River in Georgia. (*Stark Young* 4)

Micajah's children, raised in the northeastern corner of Georgia, adjacent to both the Scots-Irish South Carolina upcountry and the heart of the Appalachians, continued the trek west: "three of the boys, Edward (1786-1880), John (1789-1870), and Hugh (1793-1855), drove their wagons into Mississippi. Edward and John became Stark Young's great-uncles; Hugh was his grandfather" (*Stark Young* 4). Like Caroline Gordon's fictional Outlaws, the McGehees of both Young's actual lineage and his fiction are dispossessed and exiled Scottish Highland MacGregors who changed their outlawed surname to deflect Crown-Parliament and Anglo-Saxon hostilities.

The most insightful single work of criticism of Young's fiction remains Donald Davidson's introduction to the 1953 edition of *So Red the Rose*, a novel originally published in 1934. Davidson's article is nascent Celtic-Southern thesis literary criticism. Though some of his views are apparently influenced by the ancient bigotry (perhaps by way of Matthew Arnold) that the culturally Celtic is poetically wild and undisciplined, and therefore in dire need of Anglo-Saxon reason and moderation, Davidson recognizes a distinct difference between Southerners who are culturally eastern Virginia English and those who are Celtic. He also recognizes that Young presents the McGehees as his epitome of Southern familial culture at its finest:

> For Stark Young, the McGehees are the embodiment of that kind of person, with a continuity of memories going back to the time of their ancestor, who as THE McGregor, head of the Scottish clan, when it was outlawed by Cromwell and forbidden the name. The "aristocracy" of the McGehees . . . is not the point. But the continuity of memories, the code, the tradition of the land are of utmost importance. (xii)

Davidson argues that the novel's two principal families, while connected by marriage, represent different cultural strains in the South. The McGehees are "Celtic rebels" against the power of the ruthless, modern, centralized Imperial Nation, personified in the novel by William Tecumseh Sherman and in the McGehee's past by Oliver Cromwell and William of Orange. That modern, centralized state is intent on forcing allegiance even if that means using armies to terrorize civilian populations and achieve total destruction of folkways and cultural identities. The McGehees are fictional "exemplars of the frontier wanderings that peopled the old Indian country of the trans-Appalachian South" (xix). "The Bedfords," Davidson declares, "seem to represent a strain more definitely English, in certain ways, than the McGehees" (xvi), and

Malcolm Bedford, he believes "does suggest . . . a kind of Mississippi extension of the English country gentleman" (xvii). Finally, Davidson believes, "the decline and death of Malcolm Bedford constitute, in dramatic epitome, an indirect representation of the decline and death of the Confederacy" (xxxi). Symbolically, Young suggests that the last vestiges of the Virginia Tidewater South were killed during the war, but the Celtic South, personified in Hugh McGehee, lived on, its survival due not only to its numbers but primarily to the "Celtic intuition" Davidson attributes to Hugh McGehee, and by implication the historical "Celtic" ability to survive crushing military defeat and the violent persecutions that inevitably follow.

As in the works of Faulkner and Gordon, house names are immensely important in *So Red the Rose*. The Bedford home is Portobello, named for the house of certain Virginia antecedents. Malcolm Bedford explains the name of Hugh McGehee's home: "as a matter of fact that house was built a hundred years ago by a Scotchman. He called it Dundee, but nobody could pronounce it to suit him so he changed it to something or other, and then Hugh changed it to Montrose" (8-9). Young displays the significance of the name Montrose near the novel's conclusion. After discussing politics and economics with Mr. Mack, a Yankee investor who believes only in cash nexus, Hugh remembers telling his son Edward, killed at Shiloh, about James Graham: "The Earl of Montrose had been a Presbyterian, and so was that McGehee ancestor, the McGregor who led his clan to fight along with him; but they did not belong to the barbarous party of the Kirk" (386). In fighting for Scottish Presbyterianism and in support of the National Covenant, Montrose was fighting against English Archbishop Laud's imposition of liturgy and formal structure on the Scottish church, and partially against the vestiges of French influence over Scotland; in fighting for the Stuarts and against the Solemn League and Covenant, Montrose was defending Scottish heritage against Calvinist ideologues who, in the name of theory, gladly would destroy nation by allying with fellow ideologues from another country with a history of conquering their nation.[3]

The lesson Hugh had taught Edward is the primacy of familial, cultural, and local political connections over theoretical, ideological, and expansive political associations, for the latter three are abstract and bloodless and therefore lifeless. But that is only the first part of the instruction. The remainder of the story had concerned Montrose's execution, which he had faced with such dignity that the jeering crowds had been silenced. The, perhaps unintended, lesson here, one that Hugh at this moment of his recall has grasped fully, is that it is better to die for the right cause than to destroy your soul by submission to and cooperation with tyranny. He remembers Edward's saying, "and we fought for him" (387), and then pushes the memory away, for it certainly must then appear prescient: Edward and his general had fought and died in a losing cause opposing militarily forced government centralization.

The inevitable symbolic death of the English-country-squire-type Malcolm Bedford is foreshadowed in the dinner discussion following Edward's funeral. Commenting on the death of Gen. Albert Sidney Johnston, Mrs. Wilson, an Irish native who speaks "in her pretty Irish voice," avows, "Sir Walter Scott will be the ruin of the South, so much so I'd take my oath on it." Then she explains herself: "I mean this chivalry obsession," and "chivalry's dead, and we'll have to learn that fact in the South, or we won't stand a dog's chance" (208). Young at this point calls attention to the contrast between his two principle families; Hugh McGehee "knew what she meant," but Sallie Bedford "disliked Mrs. Wilson." Malcolm, very much the transplanted Tidewater Cavalier, believes after Bull Run "that nothing would conquer the Southern spirit and that the war would be over in three months" (156). Malcolm dies with the fall of Vicksburg, which to Young, because it meant the Union controlled the Mississippi, spelled the inevitable defeat of the Confederacy. On his typhoid deathbed, Malcolm attacks government officials in both Richmond and Washington for policies that mean horror to multitudes, but he never approaches an understanding of the philosophical issues at stake much less a tragic self-perception.

Though *So Red the Rose* features approximately one dozen major characters, Hugh McGehee ultimately becomes the novel's point of reference. It is Hugh who, in commenting on Sherman, condemns the Federal position on philosophical grounds: "all our family were Union men, but the Union is not a religion; it's a mutual agreement" (308). He believes that the metamorphosis of the Union into something at least comparable to a sacrosanct secular religion is an ideological threat to both true religion and extended family, and ultimately to true democratic freedom. As Reconstruction begins, Hugh "saw the war only as in the line that had begun in England with the Industrial Revolution and was moving onward toward its peak. This planter civilization had been in the way of it, had to be destroyed. Just that" (396).

The cost of that "destruction" is displayed during the gutting and burning of Montrose. The night before the devastation, Agnes finds her husband reading the back of an ancient book, "recipes, cures for one thing and another, that had been in the family for generations. The first recipes were written down in the time of James V, father of Mary Stuart" (318-19). He is muttering "something of which she seemed to make out only the words 'my father and his father'" (318). As the house burns, Hugh observes the officer in charge "standing with the ancient recipe book in his hand . . . . He would scan a page, then tear it and crumple the paper in his hand, scan another page and do the same thing; and then as the flames began in one corner of the room, he hurled the book in them. More than any of the rest this angered Hugh" (325).

The house and land may be restored, but the three-hundred-year-old recipe book, a direct link to the McGehee heritage, is irreplaceable. The meticulously slow, knowledgeable destruction of this priceless historical document by the Union officer reveals that Young considered the Union war effort to be more than an attempt to maintain a coerced Union and to lay the foundation for the end of American slavery; it was also, however unwittingly, an attempt to exterminate the South's knowledge of its independent ancestry dating from before Jamestown, of its Celtic heritage.

At this point, Young's thematic, as opposed to merely autobiographical, use of characters of Celtic heritage should be understood. As victims of the earlier Cromwellian and Hanoverian "displacements" in the name of progress, Celts had lost wars of defense to larger, better-equipped invaders, and somehow had survived the resulting "reconstructions" with their cultural identities intact, if altered a little, and their politics skewed. Their Southern descendants possess, as Edward attempts to define it before the war, "this inner thing of feeling and goodness" (25) deriving from the sense of clan, which provides not merely the sense of family connectedness but also a sense of place and a sense of religion, the three of which are responsible for the Southern sense of honor. Hugh attempts to explain it to Edward before he leaves for war, "it's something to know that you were loved before you were born" (150). He adds, "it's not to our credit to think we began today, and it's not to our glory to think we end today. All through time we keep coming into the shore like waves—like waves. You stick to your blood, son; there's a certain fierceness in blood that can bind you up with a long community of life" (150-51). As long as the McGehees, and thematically they represent the ideal of Southern culture to Young, possess self-knowledge—not a solipsistic modern scholarly knowledge, but a knowledge of family history and heritage and of the individual's place in the scheme of creation—, they are unvanquishable in the things that are most important.

Because Edward's death leaves Hugh without a male heir to carry on the family name, some readers may conclude that his line is to be seen as necessarily terminated, as was Malcolm Bedford. This is not so, and not simply because Lucy McGehee is a brilliant young woman (181). Among other positive qualities, Young portrays Hugh as a prescient teacher. He tells Edward before the boy departs for war:

> I was wondering about my father's grandfather when he came over here from Virginia. There was his father, the MacGregor, and his mother's father, the MacDonald; and the great Montrose was dead—the MacGregors outlawed, losing their name; there were two sons, this was the younger one. He was leaving Scotland forever—I was wondering if it broke his heart—just broke his heart. (156)

It is as teacher that Hugh acquires a symbolic son: Duncan Bedford. When he returns home from the prisoner camp, Duncan feels he can tell no one in his family about the "boundless trust" men developed for General Lee because they could not understand it. But "there was one man who would understand it, and that was Hugh McGehee" (375). Hugh warns Duncan of the self-centered Mr. Macks—and the probable Gaelic origin of the name is significant, for it reveals that Young was not a simplistic ethnic chauvinist. Not only was Young well aware of the viciously parvenu Cotton Snobs of Natchez but that people of Hugh's ethnic background certainly can be proponents of selfish acquisition and self-indulgence and can become thoroughly modern English culturally—, "the morally irresponsible industrialists who were rising to power in the American heartland" (Genovese *Southern Tradition* 67) to whom "the land's no more than stocks and bonds," a view of man's relationship to land that Hugh believes must lead inevitably to seeing one's own character as just "a quick turnover for what can be made" (395), will dominate this new imperial nation built upon forced governmental unity. More important is Hugh's instruction to the young man that what Southerners "would do better to speak of would not be what they have had but what they have loved" (395). At the close of this conversation, Duncan, who considered Edward a brother, "understood that Hugh meant he was to be like a father to him and Duncan to him a son" (397). Duncan Bedford, educated by his symbolic father, will perpetuate the McGehee knowledge and sense of clan, which eventually will produce Stark Young.

Allen Tate's biographer, Radcliffe Squires, reveals that the "Tates originally came to America from County Antrim, Ireland and were likely of both Lowland Scottish and Irish ancestry" (15). Another progenitor of Allen Tate was Robert Allen, who arrived in Port Tobacco, Maryland, in 1690 as an indentured servant. George Fraser Black discloses the origin of the name Allen—alternately spelled Allan, Alan, Alun, though this last may originate separately—one found throughout Scotland and common also to Ireland and Wales, as Celtic, the name deriving from both Gaelic and Breton, the P-Celtic language of Brittany (14).

While Tate's paternal heritage is the epitome of Grady McWhiney's development of Cracker Culture—Celtic immigrants who steadily move westward away from Anglo-Norman dominion until they reach the mountains or move beyond where they can establish their own communities—his distaff ancestry linked him to wealthy Tidewater families: "Tate's mother was born in Fairfax County at 'Chesnut Grove,' an old farmhouse built on the land of 'Pleasant Hill,' a mansion burned in the Civil War, and used as the setting of Tate's novel *The Fathers*" (Squires 14). One of Tate's more prominent ancestors was Major Benjamin Lewis Bogan, "a grandson of Colonel Fielding Lewis of 'Kenmore,' Fredericksburg, Virginia; he was the prototype of Major Lewis Buchan in *The Fathers*" (14). Bogan is the Irish surname O Bogáin (MacLysaght *Surnames* 31), and Lewis, as opposed to Louis, is "used by the Welsh as an Anglicanism of Llewelyn" (Bardsley 480). Even Tate's "genteel" Tidewater heritage, like that of the fictional Gabriella Carr, includes the descendants of Celtic immigrants.

Thomas Daniel Young notes that the original title of Tate's fiction was "Ancestors of Exile": "thinly disguised autobiography, this work intended to point up the differences between the two basic strains that had developed the South—the Tidewater Virginia aristocrats and the energetic southwestern pioneers" (x). Translated into ethnic-cultural terms, Tate planned a large novel of epic sweep that would encapsulate the conflicts between Anglo-Norman Cavaliers and the descendants of Celtic immigrants. *The Fathers* (1938) is a work of more narrow scope than the planned "Ancestors of Exile," but it retains, however obliquely, the critique of antebellum Tidewater Anglo-Norman culture that must have been a focal point of the planned work.

In the LSU Press edition of *The Fathers* (1977), Tate includes two stories from his work on "Ancestors of Exile" that help inform the novel. He reveals that two characters in "The Immortal Woman" are Little Jane Posey and Dr. Lacy Buchan of *The Fathers* (312). The other story, "The Migration," has no such direct correlation to *The Fathers*, but it is thematically related. It also is such a paradigm of the Celtic-Southern thesis that had McWhiney and McDonald known of it they could have used it as a fictional representation and summation of their theory. The first-person narrator of the story is Rhodham Elwin, who in 1851 St. Joseph, Missouri, the gateway to the Great Plains and to the Pacific coast, tells the story of his family's migration, a movement that spread Southern culture from the coastal states to northwestern Missouri and perhaps beyond. He declares of his family, a group that like a Celtic clan includes people of different surnames, "we are all over the West" (317).

Rhodham's father was born in 1742 in Ireland's County Antrim, the home of Simms' father and of *The Irish Emigrant*'s Owen McDermott and Emma Oniall as well as the Tates of the author's ancestry. Though the Elwins were poor Scots-Irish tenants, "my father said his great-grandfather was a Scottish laird, but I place little confidence in legendary tales" (318). The social status of a Lowland laird, which was roughly equivalent to that of a Highland chieftain, was possible, for the seventeenth- and early-eighteenth-century religious and political wars in Scotland created social upheaval leading to impoverishment and emigration even of the nobility, as Caruthers suggests in *The Knights of the Golden Horse-Shoe*. Rhodham's skepticism may be due primarily to his having been raised in the Anglo-Norman-dominated coastal South, where imagined noble ancestry served as an excuse for both injustice and failure and, perhaps, where nobility could be conceived as impossible except among Anglo-Normans.

Rhodham's mother, also a native Irish Protestant, declares of a Tidewater lady who "bowed indifferently" in public greeting, "'a true powderhead that can't spell her name or do the rule of three.' It was the Scots bluestocking in her," Rhodham explains of his mother's unflappable sense of self-worth, "and that I think is what has made us a great people, strong and self-reliant, and different from the English strain that takes things as they are" (323). The Celt, possessing an inviolable sense of self long determined by a strong sense of family community and history, tends to recognize no one as inherently or by right of property or governmental power or favor his superior. This will to achieve, which includes the desire to found new communities free of Anglophilic and anti-Celtic governments and cultural prerogatives, Rhodham suggests, was necessary to the settlement of the old southwest.

The Elwin migration away from the Southern coast is to evade both the Anglo-Norman social policies and political and ecclesiastical hegemony. Rhodham's father's "hatred of the established [Episcopal] church in Virginia, to which he grudgingly paid tithes, was backed up by a long antagonism, bred in him for six generations, against everything British and nearly everything that was established" (320). "It was the remains of feudalism," Rhodham declares of the Norman client relationship not predicated on extended family as is the Celtic clan system, "in Virginia that my father came more and more to dislike" (323). When the family decides to move to North Carolina, a state that in comparison to Virginia was relatively free of Anglo-Norman dominion, the oldest son goes instead to the Valley of Virginia, where, Rhodham announces, "his son is now a Christian gentleman and distinguished lawyer" (324). The Elwins, who symbolize the eighteenth-century Celtic immigrants in the South, rise in two generations to prominence in Scots-Irish-dominated western Virginia.

The remainder of the Elwins settle in the Halifax district of Edgecombe County. "All the people round about were like us," Rhodham declares, "Scotch-Irish, high-minded and God-fearing families who put Christian character and kindness before rank and position" (326). He adds of the low country gentry, "these young women were beautiful and ignorant, and had neither the strong sense nor the education of our girls; but the young planters, though they were effeminate looking, were highly educated men, most of them having been to school in England" (326).[4] Like Glasgow, Rhodham sees the intellectual, and hence to some degree economic, subjugation of Southern women as culturally Anglo-Norman, and like Simms he finds Anglo-Norman gentlemen cultivated and well educated but prone to the indolence of extravagance and to an androgyny, one that does not preclude war service, horsemanship, and mastery of dueling weapons.

Like George Tucker's Edward Grayson, Rhodham recognizes the Scots-Irish as promoters of Southern education. They establish the first school in the area and hire as a teacher "a wandering Irish man. . . . He was a learned man but given too much to rum" (331). Rhodham's narrative also reveals the development of the Southern sense of extended family, which is similar to a loosely knit Highland clan. The families in the local community, who worship together and intermarry, became "one family," Rhodham asserts, so much so that they all migrate together to Tennessee under the leadership of the Elwins. This Celtic-clan-type movement is similar to the migration of Caroline Gordon's Llewellyns and their allied kin, and it explains Piedmont and trans-Appalachian Southern social relations, which are predicated primarily on family ties rather than on estates. Of particular interest to the Celtic-Southern thesis is the fact that none of the surnames in the Elwin group would be considered by name analysis scholars as Celtic. In addition to the Irish Elwins, "there were the Wilkersons and the Maxeys, families not more than twenty years out of Ireland" (331). Symbolically, this Elwin-led clan begins its migration west from an empty Anglican church: "there were many of these deserted churches in Virginia and the Carolinas at the time" (334).

Rhodham also understands that his family's migration and its successes are representative of a larger cultural trend: "the west had been conquered by the Scotch-Irish" (345). Though they had the money and the leisure to mount expeditions and found new communities, the indolent, somewhat epicene Tidewater Anglo-Normans "waited for men of my own blood to plunge into the wilderness" (345). Rhodham acknowledges that not all the pioneers were Celtic, but, he suggests, the mass migration was a phenomenon inspired by Celts. Of special importance to Southern literary studies is Rhodham's angry revelation that "the younger sons or the broken-down heads of the Tidewater families got into their coaches, and their ladies constantly in silk dresses and French shoes, drove politely into the new country to ruin that land also with tobacco" (345). Rhodham, whose father is happy that Tennesseans own so few slaves compared to coastal Southerners, here specifically sees the Anglo-Normans as ruining the land by having slaves clear-cut and plant immense acreage, but his denunciations of their social injustices throughout his narrative suggest that he fears more than future played-out fields. The Anglo-Normans bring with them their folkways and their attitudes, and these, Rhodham feels, lead inevitably to misuse of power, which, for the Southern novelist, presents opportunities to examine tragedy. In carting to northern Mississippi the Anglo-Norman Tidewater sense of plantation and high society based on property holding, Thomas Sutpen brings inevitable tragic destruction.

The Fathers, set in northeastern Virginia just before and during the first weeks of the War Between the States, is the story not of an Anglo-Norman family, but of a Celtic family that has lost its identity and embraced the Tidewater ethos. Hence the meaning of the title: The narrator Lacy Buchan searches in his old-age memories for both his own primary father figure and the fathers who planted the twentieth-century South. Lacy reveals the Buchan loss of identity by declaring that his great-grandfather was "a Scots adventurer who ordinarily must have followed his compatriots west of the Blue Ridge had he not won the hand of Mary Armistead the very year of his landing, I think 1741" (4). Not only does Benjamin Buchan sever himself from his people, but the family does not consider his immigration sufficiently important to retain the exact year in their memories. A "Scots adventurer," however accomplished, is an embarrassment in the family tree of Cavaliers. Mary Armistead's father disapproves of the marriage to his death, after which "the name Buchan, obscure in origin, became assimilated to that unique order of society known latterly as the Virginian aristocracy" (4).

Had the Buchans not been blinded by Anglo-Norman bigotries, they would have searched Scottish history and found that their surname is "obscure in origin" only to the culturally intolerant Anglo-Normans and those under their spell. Isabel of Fife, the Countess of Buchan, ceremonially crowned Robert the Bruce King of Scotland in 1306, an offense for which the English and the Anglo-Norman warlords allied with them punished her by imprisonment in a cage (Fitzroy McLean 40).

If Lacy's knowledge of his Buchan heritage is minimal, that of his mother's ancestry is negligible: "of my mother's people I know, first-hand, much less. She was Sarah Semmes Gore of the Valley of Virginia; on the Gore side, Scotch-Irish; on the Semmes, of Maryland stock that had migrated to the Valley around 1800" (4). Like Benjamin Buchan, she is assimilated; she "became a pure Buchan—in all but religion," retaining her Presbyterian faith but evidently transmitting nothing of her folkways to her children. When George Posey enters their lives, the Buchans, who like Glasgow's Berkeley family are Celts weakened by living in the Tidewater and embracing its Anglo-Norman culture, are a typical wealthy Tidewater family, using Celts—the Higgins family—for two generations as overseers of the plantation—in effect, actually working the land—and hiring Celts as teachers: Mr. McGovern and Mr. Leary. The Buchans's inability or refusal to perform their own work or to educate themselves foreshadows their dissolution due to ineffectiveness.[5]

Lewis Buchan's role as representation of the non-realistic Anglo-Norman Tidewater Cavalier is revealed in his attitude toward Hinton Rowan Helper's *The Impending Crisis: How To Meet It,* a book he apparently rereads constantly. "A dangerous book, I heard him say," Lacy discloses, "with the little truth in it that slavery was an evil, but not in the sense that Hinton Helper thought, for slavery was a great evil only to the slave owners themselves, who were depicted by Helper as prosperous barons grinding down not only the negroes but the slaveless whites" (31). Incapable of recognizing either slave desires for freedom or the injustice of his social system to the Rhodham Elwins and the pre-wealthy Thomas Sutpens, the Major sees slavery only as a personal cross men of his station must bear for the good of society. In this, Lewis Buchan holds the sense of slavery as being a type of social work, to aid and uplift the black brother, that was common among the English and Yankee WASPs, until they decided to move toward abolitionism, also to aid and uplift the black brother. Cousin John Semmes tells Lacy during the secession crisis, "it's men like your pa who are the glory of the old Dominion, and the surest proof of her greatness, that are going to ruin us. They can't understand that reason and moderation haven't anything to do with the crisis. They won't let themselves see what's going on" (124).

Men attempting to live according to Anglo-Norman codes were primarily responsible for the glories of eighteenth-century Virginia, John Semmes declares, but because their descendants are theoretically insulated from the real world, and may be driven by principles much closer to those of even the most radical reformist Yankees than they can imagine, they will not be able to act decisively to aid Virginia in the mid-nineteenth century. When fighting begins, the Major, "a man preoccupied with some private mystery," cannot even imagine the existence of the non-Tidewater South. For to him "all that country from below the James to the Rio Grande was a map"; for him the mass of white Southerners, perhaps particularly the majority non-slave owners, "did not exist" (155). The Major prefers his religious instruction from the Episcopal rector Dr. Cartwright because he is "the kind of man a gentleman can talk to," and Lacy says of him, "I believe that not even God would have dared any familiarity with papa" (97).

The man who brings destruction to the Major's myopically beautiful world, and consequently aids Lacy in building a new life, is George Posey. The Posey family, Marylanders of long-standing, had become Georgetown business people, and Lacy describes George as "a man without people or place" (179). The dislocated and disassociated Poseys have degenerated into a coterie of refined urban freaks: Uncle Jarman, whose attire is "absurdly elegant" and who lives with his "selfish intelligence" cloistered in an attic, unwilling to interact even with his family; George's mother who rarely leaves her room and whose only topic of conversation is illness; Aunt Milly George who only eats overripe bananas. But George Posey is not a villain; he is the novel's hero. Raised by a Maryland version of the Anglo-Norman Cavalier family that has evolved to its ultimate self-absorption, George is, as Susan Buchan Posey says of her husband "so fine, but he's so violent" (172). This violence is not evil; it is an attempt to discover life in the midst of zombies. Lacy avows of George, "I never knew him to do a selfish thing"[6] and "he cared nothing for money; if he did, why did he give it away or spend it so lavishly" (132), as when he buys Lacy the rifle, saves Pleasant Hill from foreclosure by purchasing it, and saves Semmes Buchan from blackmail by purchasing the widow's letters. As his infant daughter reveals in her statement at play, "Papa make money, Papa make money," George is often the absent husband and father pursuing business. But, as Lacy sees, that is not due to his love of either money or the making of money; rather, George shoulders the burden that others in his family and his wife's family have denied as they live decorously as Anglo-Norman elites.

Nothing encapsulates the romantic foolishness of the chivalric Anglo-Norman myth like the tournament, a modern playing of late-medieval knighthood. The elderly Lacy recalls of the Gentleman's Tournament Association of Fairfax County that George wins, "I saw Knights riding in armor, with feutered lances, clashing in martial combat before pavilions gaily colored, in which lay beautiful ladies swooning in the anxiety of their delight" (32). The city-raised George participates in order to feel connected to the family and friends of his best friend Semmes and Semmes's sister, the woman he has begun to court. George and John Langton, "a bold and insolent man who deemed himself an aristocrat beyond any consideration for other people" (62), each earn perfect scores. When the judges break the tie by voting for George (most likely a truly chivalric vote to be gracious to a visitor), Langton approaches George who is standing to receive his award, "raised his hand and pushed him out of the way" (68). As soon as Langton questions the ruling, George knocks him to the ground.

This is only the beginning of George's flouting of the unquestioned Anglo-Norman gentilities. At first, he plays along with the ceremony honoring him as victor and his chosen lady as queen. But with wreath in hand and ready to crown Susan, George momentarily freezes: "He stood before her and bowed, and lifting the wreath as Susan leaned forward to receive it, according to custom, on her head, he hesitated, looked around him, and then dropped the wreath into her lap. He drew himself up to his full height and laughed!" (70).

The initial response of most readers, including those who find the tournament absurd rather than quaintly romantic, is probably anger at George for publicly embarrassing a young lady. But close reading reveals that Susan apparently is not shamed. "She turned her head to Mr. Broadacre," Lacy recalls, "and I saw her lips move, and Mr. Broadacre's mouth fell open as he stood again erect" (71). Evidently, Susan herself ridicules the ceremony or at least endorses George's actions, leaving the master of ceremonies, who had addressed the crowd as "our English squires," stunned and looking "frantic."

Tate's direct linkage of Tidewater Virginia Anglo-Norman culture to attempts to relive medieval chivalry and its tournaments should not be glossed over. First, though it is possible that many people would be drawn to staged versions of jousting tournaments in order to try to recapture a pre-modern sense of family, religious, and cultural heritage that could stand against modern deracination, the staging of such games means no more than does the contemporary staging of medieval feasts and jousts, in which many of the participants are fully content with modern senses of family, religion, and community; they are "vacationing," rather like the people in the movie *Westworld*. In that sense their dress and mannerisms are adult versions of children's playacting games, and they may be used to avoid facing the harsh realities that require attention.[7]

Second, Barbara Tuchman reveals that fighting was the knight's "substitute for work" (66). Tournaments originally served as war games of a sort and were defended as such, but "the impulse was the love of fighting" (67). At the heart of chivalry in late medieval practice (as opposed to its ideals and its at least partial origin in the Celtic sense of honor), Tuchman suggests, was a blood lust that must be satisfied in tournament if not war, and the tournaments became larger and more numerous as knights were required to perform fewer actual military duties. "The less he had to do," Tuchman says of the knight, "the more energy he spent in tournaments artificially re-enacting his role" (67). The tournaments were the Super Bowls, NBA playoffs, Olympics, and world championship boxing matches of their time and place, "attracting crowds of bourgeois spectators from rich merchants to common artisans, mountebanks, food vendors, prostitutes, and pickpockets" and acquiring such reputations for savagery, immorality, and criminality that the Dominicans eventually "denounced them as a pagan circus" (67).

It is this "pagan circus," which artificially recreates medieval knight warfare for sanitized viewing, that George Posey recognizes as ridiculous for adults to take seriously, to play. It is such a society, one in which "knights" who lack sufficient work because they live off the sweat of others—black slaves and landless and even landowning but slaveless whites—and have failed to identify the Vikings and Saracens who threaten their world, play violent games out of a combination of boredom and enjoyment, that Tate presents as an enticing artifice that must be replaced if the society is to avoid slipping into total decadence. The positive chivalric qualities that the most sincere promoters of the Tournament wish to nurture through the event are not under attack from Tate. What he apparently senses is the fact that unless those martial chivalric values are tied to a strong sense of pre-modern Christianity and family life, especially that of the Celtic extended family in which retainers have claims of blood that supercede claims of economics and shared upper class sentiment, then the tournaments and the culture fostering them will tend to produce men like John Langton.

George's response to Langton's challenge is another refusal to participate in Anglo-Norman games he knows to be valueless. George accepts the duel but names the place as "the upper end of the pavilion" (72). When Jim Mason suggests that "some less public place" might be preferable, George retorts, "I don't want a less public place. . . . I'd prefer the Court House yard" (73). He is unwilling to participate in the masking of Anglo-Norman violence; George prefers honesty and truth, and if the Tidewater code sanctions violence even to death over a sporting incident, he would have the public know and be forced to acknowledge it. At the site, George promptly takes a practice shot, demonstrating his excellence with a pistol, and then tosses the gun aside. Rather than kill John Langton, he strikes him so hard in the face that the half-drunken bully falls unconscious (75). George's concept of accepting a challenge is not chivalric, and it is condemned by Jim Mason, but the culturally Celtic, back-country Southerners, like Thomas Sutpen, would approve, for George demonstrates his courageous superiority twice, with the second being close and personal.

Susan also approves of George's refusals to play the Cavalier game. She announces in front of the Broadacres and Langton's sisters that she intends to marry George (78). After the 1860 burial of Mrs. Buchan, George says to Lacy about the mourners, who represent every genteel family in the area, all of which would have been well represented at the Tournament, "by God, they'll all starve to death, that's what they'll do. They'll do nothing but die and marry and think about the honor of Virginia. . . . I want to be thrown to the hogs" (107). Recognizing that the Anglo-Norman chivalric code, which these people equate with "the honor of Virginia," is a lifeless abstraction unconnected to real living, George declares that it is preferable to be rooted about by an earthy animal devoid of human consciousness and smeared with negative stereotypes (an animal central to Celtic mythology) but unquestionably alive than to live according to Tidewater mores.

John Langton and Lewis Buchan each represent one-half of the Tidewater Cavalier symbol, and as such each must die so that a new South, one predicated not upon the selfishly violent abstraction of chivalry recreated for play in the nineteenth century, may take precedence.

Langton is the active Cavalier, a dashing horseman and shot who believes that Anglo-Normans are born to ride roughshod over other peoples. Totally self-indulgent, he has no interest in the Code unless it facilitates his taking what he desires when he so desires. The epitome of the bad sport who misuses power and authority to harm those who have proven themselves equal if not superior to him, Langton deserves his end. After conniving to refuse George a captain's rank in the regiment George has armed out of his money, and then repeatedly insulting him, Langton, Tate's symbol of this half of the Cavalier, gets his face blown off by the man he has persecuted (301).

Major Buchan symbolizes the intellectual or theoretical half of the Tidewater Cavalier. Unlike the honestly selfish Langton, he is an idealist. The Major studies issues, and he genuinely cares for those under his charge. But, as Lacy's narrative reveals, his "goodness" is primarily for himself. The Major lives in a dream world in which he can refuse to recognize both the violence of the John Langtons and the selling of his own slaves to keep him from losing any of his property. He is a fictional representation that in the truly paternalistic Old South "the relationship of master to slave, in itself an extension of father to perpetual child, could be reconciled to the cash nexus only imperfectly" (Genovese, *World* 121).

Perhaps more insidious, behind his gentlemanly courtesy lies blind tyranny. In favor of maintaining Virginia's place in the Union, the Major writes to Lacy, then at George's house, "Semmes stubbornly held that he was in favor of disunion, whereupon I said, reluctantly and without passion, that he was no longer a son of mine" (177).[8] Lacy reveals, "I knew gentlemen in my boyhood but I know none now, and I know that I am not one" (216). He uses the term "gentleman" here not in our broad sense of general respect for and courtesy toward others but to signify the Anglo-Norman Cavalier gentleman. That creature no longer exists in significant numbers in Lacy's twentieth-century Georgetown, and that, Lacy feels certain, is good. "Men of honor and dignity! They did a great deal of injustice," Lacy declares, "but they always knew where they stood because they thought more of their code than they did of themselves. Papa thought more of his honor than of any of us but he did not know that he did" (21). Major Buchan is as blindly devoted to a theory of living and therefore is as anti-family as Thomas Sutpen. But the Major's story is no tragedy. Deluded by his myopic, idealized vision of life, he will go to his grave still wondering of George, "why has that young man done this thing to me?" (284).

An epiphanic moment in Lacy's growth to self-awareness occurs when he sees Union troops dressed in Victorianized kilts:

I gazed stupidly at the gaudy tartans above the knobby legs and before I knew it I was angry. These man ain't Scotchmen, I said; I'm a Scot and they're my enemies . . . the cheap Glengarry bonnets set off the hard, foreign faces. One man looked over me as I passed, and I thought: I am a foreigner to him." (187-88)

The Celtic heritage, apparently lost in the Major, claims precedence in Lacy's sense of self. He is a Scot, and he needs no romanticized costuming to demonstrate his ancestry. His grandfather, who as the son of the Scots adventurer presumably was at least partially culturally Celtic, becomes one of Lacy's spiritual fathers by appearing to him in a vision and explaining George. George is, the spirit says, "alone like a tornado" (268). Tornadoes are destructive, but they are forces of nature, and only the man hubristic enough to equate himself with God dares challenge them or label them evil. The vision revives Lacy as he attempts to reach Pleasant Hill: "It is a good thing, I thought, because I have nobody to guide me now. My grandfather was dead—dead as a herring" (269).

George Posey becomes Lacy's principal father figure, the man who guides him into an adulthood that allows him not only to serve others as a physician but also to tell about the South. George's tornado-like destruction clears Lacy's life-path of the Anglo-Norman Cavalier, leaving him free to become a twentieth-century Southerner who understands the beauty of much of Tidewater culture but who also possesses the distance from it necessary to tell of its gross inadequacies and injustices truthfully. As Tate says in his "Note" in the LSU edition, "George will permit Lacy to survive in a new world in which not all the old traditions, which Lacy partly represents, are dead" (314). The Southern traditions that are symbolically dead are those of the Anglo-Norman Cavalier as represented by John Langton and Lewis Buchan. The setting of *The Fathers* makes it all but impossible for Tate to declare in the novel that Celtic traditions survive in Lacy's twentieth-century South, but "The Migration" presents Celtic folkways as both the principle determinant of trans-Appalachian Southern culture and its resilience in the face of ever new challenges. Oddly enough, when he criticizes John Semmes's romantic vision of the coming war, George Posey uses a phrase from the Celtic hill South. "Mr. Semmes, your people," he says of the Tidewater Cavaliers, "are about to fight a war. They remind me of a passel of young 'uns playing prisoners' base" (166-67). Lacy venerates George's "memory more than the memory of any man" because George saved him from blindly following the genteel Anglo-Norman Cavalier tradition, a cultural freeing that was, Tate's fiction suggests, necessary for the Southern Renaissance.

According to Robert Penn Warren, of the many talented writers of the Southern Renaissance, Andrew Lytle possessed the most detailed knowledge of the folkways of trans-Appalachian Antebellum Southern culture:

> He knew the world of the plantation and of the deeper backcountry in the hills beyond the plantations. He knew the language, every shade of it by tone and phrase, every inflection, every hint of pain or poetry, the humor, the bawdiness, every expression of face. He knew the objects and practices of the old times, and of the backcountry, how meat was dressed, how food was cooked, how meal was ground or hominy made, what people—men or women or children—wore, how wool was carded, how shakes were split and whiskey run. He knew such things because he had the keenest of eyes, the shrewdest of ears, insatiable curiosity, and an elephantine memory; but mostly because he had a natural generosity and simplicity of heart and could stop a stranger on the road or lounge on the steps of the most desolate crossroads store and in ten minutes be swapping crop-talk or tales with the local whittlers, in perfect ease and pleasure, and with devoted attention. (132-33)

It should come as no surprise then that the protagonist in Lytle's Civil War-era novel *The Long Night* (1936) bears a Celtic surname: Pleasant McIvor. The inspiration for the novel came from Lytle's listening to fellow Agrarian Frank Owsley tell the story of his eccentric, revenge-seeking "Uncle Dink" (Lucas 66-67), but, like other Southern novelists, Lytle reshaped the folklore he heard into a work of fiction revealing some essence of Southern culture beyond the recounting of folklore and the amused revealing of eccentrics. Frank L. Owsley, Jr., aware of the "strong Celtic influence in the frontier states of the lower South," declares, "that the McIvors behaved like a Highland clan should surprise no one" (4).

After Lawrence McIvor graduates from college, he receives a note summoning him to the north Alabama hill country home of his Uncle Pleasant, a man long assumed dead by the family because "he had disappeared shortly after the Civil War" (14). Lawrence describes the McIvor farm as being run by a Highland clan chieftain, "a benevolent patriarch. He did no work of any sort," Lawrence reveals, "but directed all things with the air of a man who has done great deeds, and his family sustained this state with the most perfect discipline and pride" (19). When Lawrence arrives and announces his presence, Pleasant replies,

"I had no notion you wouldn't come" (18). Assuming that his nephew carries the Celtic sense of family, Pleasant, as a clan elder, also assumes the boy will honor his blood-bound, his family, and his commitment to heed the summons of a man he has never met.

Pleasant's nuclear family, which lives as high in the hills as is possible in Alabama, embraces Lawrence immediately. "I was not treated so much as a cousin whom nobody had seen," he says, "but as the eldest son returned from a long journey." Pleasant has isolated himself from his extended family, but, apparently, he has told his wife and children about them. Pleasant has summoned Lawrence to listen to his story, the reasons he has absented himself from his family. "What I have to say," Pleasant declares, "is not a thing I can tell my wife and children. But it is a thing that must be told. . . . And you are next of kin" (19). Like Lacy Buchan, Lawrence is a modern Southerner whose family story becomes art. Similar to Quentin Compson struggling to comprehend the Sutpen story, Lawrence, after hearing his Uncle's confessions, also learns "from other sources," eventually piecing "the story together" (20). Lawrence discloses of his narrative, the remainder of the novel, "I cannot tell which words are his and which are mine" (20), a revelation of the intertextuality of Southern folk culture, Southern history, and Southern literature, as well as of the trans-generational links of the Southern family.

The Celtic clan nature of the McIvor family is again emphasized when legal trouble in Georgia forces them to migrate. It is not merely the nuclear family of Cameron McIvor, Pleasant's father, that leaves. Much of the extended family, the clan, chooses to follow its chieftain: "Many had decided to leave with us, my three young uncles and several cousins. In this way they proposed to show their loyalty to the family head and their disgust with the way of justice which allowed an innocent man to suffer while defending himself against premeditated injury" (28).

After Cameron's murder by members of a John Murrell-type gang that has infiltrated law enforcement, the judiciary, politics, and commerce, the entire clan, including members from as far away as Kentucky, gathers to debate the matter[9]: "Some were dressed in fine cloth, others in butternut, and one rich old planter wore ancient gate breeches. Rich or poor, they had all come in because they had known and loved Cameron or because the memory of the long years was still fresh when, in the old country across the waters, they had stood up and fought the English who had crossed their borders" (62).

Note that even in 1859, the Southern McIvor clan retains its Scottish identity and the knowledge that it was displaced from its homeland because of successful English aggression. This cultural heritage of being violently dispossessed by "official" governments and ministers of justice underlies the McIvor decision eventually to strike back, in Pleasant's words, "secret death with secret death" (68), for they feel they can never receive justice, the punishment of a murderous criminal gang, in such a thoroughly corrupted system. It is especially important to recognize that the McIvor clan members do not engage in the popular misconception of a Southern feud; they do not wildly and indiscriminately attack the innocent family members and friends of their enemies, nor do they assume from the outset that the system is biased at least against them. They study, and then they stalk and eliminate only known members of Tyson Lovell's ring of murderers, thieves, and bribers.

Mark Lucas and Frank Owsley, Jr. present the two basic approaches to evaluating Pleasant's three-year quest to obtain justice. Lucas, apparently accepting of the modern embrace of the inactive, epicene Jamesian hero as cultural apex, believes that Lytle's novel sucks in readers initially approving of the reprisals in order to demonstrate the problems inherent in revenge. This simplistic approach, which ignores the Burkean maxim that for evil to thrive good men need only do nothing, leads Lucas to misread the novel's ending, and therefore its purpose. Lucas declares that after Roswell Ellis's death, "Pleasant deserts not only the army, but life itself" (65). As demonstrated by Pleasant's wife and children, the calm, stable home life, and distant neighbors who know and respect Pleasant McIvor, if at distance, Lucas's reading is wrong. His attempt to cast *The Long Night* as a novel dramatizing a dialogue between "Old Testament vindictiveness" and New Testament forgiveness (66) is not merely theologically simplistic, a modern rendition of Marcion's dualistic heresy pitting a Mosaic god of wrath against a Jesus-Pauline god offering a forgiveness amounting to license; it is Procrustean, for Lytle's novel is neither religiously determined, as are Flannery O'Connor's works, nor significantly concerned with the effects of Southern religion, as is Faulkner's *Light in August*. Rather, *The Long Night* is a novel about the interplay between the individual, the extended family, and the Southern honor code.

Owsley's perception is more sound: "In the end Lytle gives his reader a hero who has repented his sins and gone into the wilderness to cleanse himself" (4). Pleasant's primary sin is not the seeking of vengeance against violent criminals who have bribed civil authority, thereby preventing legal justice[10]; his sin is allowing desire for personal vengeance to interfere with his duty. This selfishness results in the deaths of his friend Ellis and other young men counting on Pleasant's information. The carnage of Shiloh prompts Pleasant to curtail his killings, and that should spur the reader who considers Pleasant's retreat from vengeance to be unequivocally good to look deeper, for sparing men guilty of heinous crimes committed against the unsuspecting innocent so they can participate further in the mass gore of the War Between the States is either absurd or Machiavellian ends-justify-means logic. I do not suggest that the extent of Pleasant's revenge is defensible; he has gone beyond the bounds set by his clan, ignoring the advice of his uncle Armistead (224). As such, Pleasant has sinned against the Celtic family. It is appropriate, therefore, that his penance include his maintaining a loving nuclear family until such time as he feels sufficiently cleansed to reenter the life of the McIvor clan. Pleasant completes his penance by telling his story to his nephew, who, as a modern Southerner, possesses the distance from the events necessary to shape them into a work of art explaining something unique and challenging in Southern culture.

For Andrew Lytle, the principal defining characteristic of the trans-Appalachian South is the Celtic family. *A Wake for the Living* (1975) is his narration of the family heritage for his daughters and subsequent descendants. The Celtic wake is not a mere prelude to a burying; it is a celebration of eternal life. A body has died, but, in addition to belief in the Christian afterlife, the wake celebrates death as a necessary fact for renewal, for regeneration, of the clan itself. In his *Wake*, Lytle reveals that his family origins are thoroughly Celtic:

> The Lytles (or Lytil as it was once spelled) were border people in the old country and stole sheep and women both from the Scots and English. And had to keep on the move. Seven of them were put to the horn in the debatable land for not paying their tithes. To be put to the horn outlawed you. The culprit was taken to the cross roads and the horn blown three times each way, and at a certain moment in the ceremony he was read out of the society. (27-28)

Lytle's portrayal of his family's origin is no mere unfounded fictionalizing. In Roger Blaney's list of prominent Irish Presbyterian ministers who were fluent in Gaelic and active promoters of Gaelic folk culture, Scottish and Irish, is Richard Lyttle (177).

Not only does Andrew Lytle reveal his family to have originated in the Celtic area of northern Britain, but he also declares that at least through the seventeenth century these people, who by the beginning of the modern era were primarily English-speaking and who occasionally and partially resided in England, lived Celtic folkways that dated back before the coming of Christianity. He affirms of being "put to the horn," "the genesis of this no doubt was the druidic ceremony of excommunication. This was more severe. It expelled you from both worlds, in this life and afterwards" (28). Like Young and Tate, Lytle portrays the ideal and the prototypic Southern family, the family whose values and traditions reflect the best of Southern culture they hoped to see preserved, as Celtic, not English. In Lytle's case, these cultural characteristics feature a willingness to accept the hard truth that at times the family must stand against "official" society to the point of violence else it contributes to society's perversion. That, which most often means isolation and banishment for the individual who takes it upon himself to make the stand, as it does for Pleasant McIvor, is integral to the Celtic sense of honor.

Chapter VIII

The Southern Epic and Its Sequel: Margaret Mitchell and *Scarlett*

In her analysis of Glasgow's revision of her 1928 *Harper's* article, "The Novel in the South," which she published in *A Certain Measure* (1943) as the preface to *The Miller of Old Church,* Anne Goodwyn Jones writes, "Glasgow interestingly includes Margaret Mitchell among the novelists of protest" against the mediocrity of Americanism (229-30). That Jones, whose book contains chapters on both Glasgow and Mitchell, should find it interesting rather than obvious that Glasgow would recognize Mitchell as a fellow Southern woman novelist with similar views is a condemnation of the sparse, often shoddy, politically based scholarship on *Gone With the Wind* (1936) and its author. Like the Glasgow novels discussed previously, Mitchell's fictional world centers on a strong woman attempting to define herself in a world that may be defined as sexist. Also like Glasgow, Mitchell is a Southern realist, by which I mean her realism is under-girded primarily by an unsparingly honest portrayal of Southern traditions and codes rather than by Freud and twentieth-century science and philosophy. Neither can be labeled a modernist in technique, and each is a writer keenly aware of the paradoxical importance of familial and cultural heritage to the individuality of her characters.

Professional students of literature, as opposed to general readers, are prone to dismiss Mitchell's novel as a mere bestseller because of the condescension of most academics to "popular" literature, except that which promotes their pet views. The novel's title is taken from *Slippy McGee,* a popular bestseller by Marie Conway Oemler, a Southerner of Irish ancestry. "The novel begins," Patrick O'Sullivan writes, "with a meditation on the statue of the Confederate soldier on the local monument" that is "the link between the vanishing of the Confederacy and that phrase from [Irishman James Clarence] Mangan's poem" (23).[1]

The unparalleled sales of Mitchell's novel and press interest in its being filmed and its title that is so easily misconstrued for a longing for a past that never was, can prejudice readers against *Gone With the Wind*. Readers so inclined to dismiss Mitchell's novel should be aware of the actual prejudices of scholars who have attacked and condemned *Gone With the Wind* unreservedly. The most glaring example of the myopic scholarship on Mitchell's novel, at least among those who are not overtly anti-Southern, is Floyd Watkins's *"Gone With the Wind* as Vulgar Literature."* Watkins asserts that the "novel is false to historical fact and also false to the human heart in the contemporary age" (84). He believes that "no one in *Gone With the Wind* is capable of Sutpen's tragic failure" (92). In addition to berating the novel for including a few factual errors,[2] "though most of them are negligible" (94), Watkins is hostile to *Gone With the Wind* because he senses it is primarily a work of literature most appealing to women: "the novel, after all, was written by a woman" (100).

Though Leroy Eid is a proponent of the Celtic-Southern thesis, he too misunderstands Mitchell's work. Affirming that "the novel reflected accurately in some fashion the ethnic realities of the antebellum South," he believes, however, that it "is misleading in the sense that the Celts did not dominate the ranks of the great planters as they dominated the small homesteads in the hills around the river plantations" ("Colonial" 90). Mitchell's description of Tara and its evolutionary construction makes it plain that the O'Haras do not possess a mansion: "the house had been built according to no architectural plan whatever, with extra rooms added where and when it seemed convenient, but with Ellen's care and attention, it gained a charm that made up for its lack of design" (57). In fact, the only mansion in Mitchell's fictionalized Clayton County, as opposed to the many built in Reconstruction Atlanta, is Twelve Oaks, the Wilkes home.

Darden Asbury Pyron argues that the primary reason for these continued misunderstandings concerning Mitchell's novel is the popularity of the film, which was not made by Southerners and which altered several of the novel's key themes. "Long before the film was done," he writes, "many readers had confused *Gone With the Wind* with the traditional plantation romance" (372), and that confusion was only heightened by the film's popularity.[3]

Like each writer in this study except Tucker, Mitchell is a descendant of Celtic immigrants. Though he does not state the ethnic origins of the Mitchells, Pyron, in his biography of Margaret Mitchell, does note the Celtic origins of the author's distaff heritage. "Not less than the Mitchells—even more, perhaps," writes Pyron, "the Stephenses and their allied kin were the stuff of legend" (16-17). They had emigrated first "to Calvert's Maryland in the seventeenth century" and had slowly moved south, founding a "'classical' school" in Taliaferro County, Georgia, in the early nineteenth century. Their Irish Catholic identity was reinforced by marriage: "twice in the nineteenth century, in successive generations before the Civil War, sons of Éire married into Mitchell's Anglo-American Catholic line." "These two Irishmen," Pyron asserts, "helped shape the most fundamental stuff of Margaret Mitchell's imagination" (17). The second of these, John Stephens, like the fictional Gerald O'Hara, "grew up in Ireland and joined an older brother in Georgia who ran a store" (19).

The cover of the Avon paper edition of *Gone With the Wind* advertises it as "The Epic Novel of Our Time." The blurb writer was probably referring to its sales, but I accept the novel as *the* Southern epic. In the *Reader's Companion to World Literature,* an epic is defined as "a long narrative poem in which the characters and the action are of heroic proportions." The standard attributes for epics in the West were laid down first by Homer and then his Roman imitator Virgil: "the underlying theme concerns basic and eternal human problems; the narrative is a complex synthesis of experiences from a whole epoch of man's history or civilization; the hero embodies national, cultural, or religious ideals; the style is earnest and dignified; the poem plunges . . . *in medias res*" (Hornstein 176-77). With the exceptions of beginning *in medias res* and requiring the work to be a poem, *Gone With the Wind* meets the epic criteria. Its theme of struggling through the adversities created by war is universal, and its historic period is the focal point of Southern history. In avoiding modernist techniques, which the author might have considered trendy when she began her novel, Mitchell could be seen as maintaining a dignified, traditional narrative style. Cultural myopia causes us to exclude prose from epics. Because the Greeks, Romans, and Germans all wrote their epics in poetry, most scholars have erroneously concluded that all epics must be in verse. Most pertinent to students of Irish culture is that the medieval Irish epic, *Tain Bo Cuailgne,* is prose with lyrics scattered intermittently. The modern epic language, like that of ancient Ireland, is prose rather than poetry, as James Joyce understood.

This definition of epic, however, remains incomplete. Many works of literature from a given culture could meet most, if not all, of the epic characteristics, but I know of no culture with more than two epics. This is not to say that there are not several surviving failed attempts at epics. The *Argonautica* is one, and no one considers it *the* Greek epic, a title rightfully accorded to both the *Iliad* and the *Odyssey*. The reason is that the complete definition of epic is: A work of literature containing most of the characteristics listed above and accepted by its audience, over a considerable length of time, as the work best exemplifying the unique traits of the group in question. Northrup Frye declares that myths "are the stories that seem to have a peculiar significance: they are the stories that tell a society what is important for it to know, whether about its gods, its history, its laws, or its class structure," (32-33) and, it logically follows, if myths, which are the building blocks of epics, tell essential truths about a given culture, reader response is a necessary part of the definition of epic. As Dario Fernandez-Morera says of the great books, "They have been considered great not because they have been imposed upon the hapless public by a hegemonic cabal, but because they have proved to be richer, more complex, and more stimulating sources of thoughtful feeling at different times and in different nations, often after numerous vicissitudes created by both chance and by purposeful human action" (164). Scholars driven by various modernist and postmodernist theories have failed to recognize the richness and complexity of *Gone With the Wind*.

In short, the *Iliad* and the *Odyssey* are not epics because scholars pronounced them to be so; they are epics because both Greeks and non-Greeks recognized that they defined Greek culture and character better than any other works of literature. Similarly, *Gone With the Wind* is accepted by what is easily the largest number of readers, both Southerners and non-Southerners, as the work of literature that best defines Southern culture for them. Nor is this recognition restricted to America. Blanche Gelfant reveals that Mitchell's novel had world-wide acclaim by the beginning of World War II. "During the war," she writes "totalitarian nations recognized *Gone With the Wind*'s popularity by such strict censorship that the penalty for its possession . . . was death. Nazis and Communists officially condemned it because its individualistic ideals, its expression of one's love for home, subverted loyalty to the State" (5).

The power of a fiction to inspire such cringing fear in theory-driven totalitarians (for the "vicissitudes" the Marxists and Nazis purposefully created to prevent the novel's dissemination were topped only by their efforts to prevent access to the Bible) is truly epic, and the fear was not unfounded paranoia. A former reporter for *The Wall Street Journal*, Julie Salamon reveals in her family Holocaust memoir that her mother had read *Gone With the Wind* numerous times by the beginning of World War

II and told it to fellow Auschwitz internees who liked it best of the stories told. "She would never forget," Salamon writes of her mother, "the way the book had helped her escape from Lager C, day after day, as she told the story ['Hadn't she, like Scarlett, triumphed over everything?'], in installments, to her bunkmates" (80, 120, 241).[4]

Before proceeding with an analysis of Mitchell's thematic use of her major characters, I must first take note of her minor white characters, especially those who own little or no property. If I do not, the widespread tendency to accept the condemnation of Mitchell's fiction as a romanticizing of the slave-owning South may be applied to my Celtic-Southern thesis cultural reading of *Gone With the Wind*: Mitchell is merely romanticizing her own Irish Catholic heritage. The one white trash family in the novel, a family that not only lives on Gerald O'Hara's charity before the war but after the war becomes aligned through marriage with Jonas Wilkerson, the brutal Yankee-born overseer of Tara who becomes rich during Reconstruction, is the Slatterys. Mitchell's portrait of the Slatterys is similar to that of Faulkner's Snopes tribe: "Old Slattery, who clung persistently to his few acres, in spite of repeated offers from Gerald and John Wilkes, was shiftless and whining. His wife was a snarly-haired woman, sickly and washed-out of appearance" (49). Edward MacLysaght notes that the surname Slattery derives from the Irish *slátra,* meaning "strong," which, if Mitchell had known any Gaelic, would have made her use of the name ironic (*Surnames* 200).

Will Benteen is a Confederate veteran missing half a leg who stops at Tara on his way back to south Georgia. Mitchell writes, "he had the sallow malarial face of the south Georgia Cracker, pale pinkish hair and washed-out blue eyes which even in delirium were patient and mild" (509). Will never mentions his family, and Mitchell provides no genealogy. His surname, however, is probably Gaelic. *Beinn* is one of the Gaelic words for "mountain," or "peak," as in Scotland's Ben Lomond and Ireland's Ben Bulben, and *in,* usually anglicized as it sounds— een—is a Gaelic suffix that when attached to a name makes it diminutive. Benteen, then, probably was originally a nickname meaning "little mountain." In stark contrast to the white trash Slatterys, who own a couple of acres and therefore are his social betters however slightly, Will Benteen is a landless poor white, and Mitchell knows the difference between the two classes. Benteen stays to run Tara, and though he "never displayed any energy. . . . He did things. He did them silently, patiently, and competently" (512). After Benteen has restored the farm, Scarlett realizes "Tara's bloom was not the work of a planter aristocrat, but of the plodding, tireless 'small farmer' who loved his land" (703). Though he lacks formal education, Benteen is as astute a diplomat as he is adept at farming. Stepping in to seize the moment before the crowd could vent its hostility toward Suellen for contributing to her father's death, Benteen gives the eulogy at Gerald's funeral: "He was a fightin' Irishman and a Southern gentleman and as loyal a Confederate as ever lived. You can't get no better combination than that" (710).

Mitchell's depiction of the Slatterys and Will Benteen is significant for three reasons. First, that she portrays a landless "Cracker" as the man who revives Tara and "gradually slipped into the status of a member of the family" (512) demonstrates that Mitchell was not, as Watkins claims (95), ignorant of the poorer whites of the nineteenth-century South. Second, that Mitchell has Benteen save Tara's land after the aristocratic Ashley Wilkes fails and then has him join the family reveals that she does not romanticize the South's genteel antebellum landowners. They, symbolized by Ashley, are abstracted ineffectual failures who must be replaced by the Will Benteens. Third, that her white trash family is of Irish extraction reveals that Mitchell was not an ethnic propagandist or romanticist. Rather, her vision of an antebellum Southern county with but one mansion, and that owned by descendants of Virginia Tidewater migrants, and other planters living in large farmhouses, with many of the poorer whites being of Celtic ancestry, is concordant with the model presented in *Cracker Culture*.

Also important to note is Gerald O'Hara's rise to prominence, which is similar to that of Cash's fictional prototype. He flees Ireland at age twenty-one after having killed "an English absentee landlord's rent agent" (42) and goes to his older brothers, James and Andrew, who had fled Ireland the previous year to avoid being arrested by English authorities for insurrectionary nationalist activities. The elder O'Hara brothers had opened a profitable store in Savannah, Georgia, and Gerald went to work for them. But Gerald, "with the deep hunger of an Irishman who has been a tenant on the lands his people once had owned and hunted . . . wanted to see his own acres stretching green before his eyes" (45), and eventually his steady hand at poker wins him both a slave valet and a rich middle Georgia farm that he names Tara. After ten years, Gerald becomes wealthy, and he sets out to marry a lady with a long Southern heritage to complete his status of social acceptance in his new country.

Mitchell's epic protagonist, who embodies the South much as Achilles and Odysseus combine to personify Greece, is Scarlett O'Hara, Gerald's eldest daughter. Though it is all but inconceivable to think of Scarlett as bearing any surname other than that with which she is born, not the Scottish Lowland or northern English Hamilton, nor the Highland or Irish Kennedy, nor the Hiberno-Norman Butler, and certainly not the English Wilkes, the novel focuses on Scarlett's struggle to define herself. Her father Gerald is a quintessential Celt: Loquacious, shrewd, forthright, contentious, determined, Gerald loves his land above everything else, for "to anyone with a drop of Irish blood in them the land they live on is like their mother." He adds, "'Twill come to you, this love of land. There's no getting away from it, if you're Irish" (36). Scarlett "found it comforting to be in his presence. There was something vital and earthy and coarse about him that appealed to her" (31). On the other hand, Scarlett's mother Ellen is a "Coast aristocrat of French descent." In opposition to Gerald's concrete, practical life on the land, Ellen is abstract and intangible, so much so that Scarlett confuses her with the Virgin Mary (60).

The O'Hara parents represent the two primary white cultures in the antebellum South: Gerald, the Celtic, and Ellen, the Norman, which is usually thought of in terms of the Virginia Tidewater Cavalier. *Gone With the Wind* is not merely a novel about fighting and rebuilding from a losing war, nor is it merely a cloying though ultimately heartbreaking love story; it is an epic in which the protagonist ultimately has the tragic perception that her life has been false in cultural terms. The conflict in *Gone With the Wind* concerns which of the two different cultures should be pre-eminent in the South, a conflict Mitchell embodies in Scarlett's relationships with her parents and, especially, in her love for Ashley Wilkes.

Though Scarlett loves her mother to the point of idolatry, she is Gerald's child. Ellen is able to train Carreen and Suellen, Scarlett's younger sisters, to be demure Anglo-Norman ladies, "but Scarlett, child of Gerald, found the road to ladyhood hard" (58). In the library at Twelve Oaks, Scarlett attempts to play the role but fails when Ashley says that he will marry Melanie: "then her rage broke, the same rage that drove Gerald to murder and other Irish ancestors to misdeeds that cost them their necks" (117). At the ball to raise money for the Confederate war effort, Scarlett feels that "she, Scarlett O'Hara Hamilton, alone had good hard-headed Irish sense" (173). When Rhett Butler sarcastically praises her courage for donating her wedding ring to the cause, "all that was Irish in her rose to the challenge of his black eyes" (186). In fact, it is Scarlett's untamable Irishness that attracts Rhett. He tells her of the Twelve Oaks barbecue, "it is one of my priceless memories—a delicately nurtured Southern belle with her Irish up—You are very Irish, you know" (195). Nor is Rhett the only person to recognize Scarlett's defining Irishness. Mammy, the character most in the know about personal relationships throughout the novel, thinks in the midst of her argument over Ellen's drapes, "Lordy, 'twas right funny how de older Miss Scarlett git de mo she look lak Mist' Gerald and de less lak Miss Ellen" (546).

The importance of Scarlett's Irishness is best manifested when she arrives home after the burning of Atlanta. She understands why Gerald stood on the porch and refused to allow the Yankees to burn his home: "There were too many Irish ancestors crowding behind Gerald's shoulders, men who had died on scant acres, fighting to the end rather than leave the homes where they had lived, plowed, loved, begotten sons" (411). Though she does not like Suellen and she sees Carreen as weak, they are "of her blood," and Scarlett, assuming from the incapacitated Gerald the role of clan chieftain, cannot and will not allow them to subsist on charity. When she is exhausted to the point of resignation in her attempt to provide for everyone at Tara, Scarlett recalls family stories of survival against all odds in the face of unspeakable horrors. Her Irish ancestors may have lost physically, but they were never beaten spiritually, and they never allowed themselves to be beaten culturally and then refashioned per the whims of their imperialist English overlords: "They had not whined, they had fought. And when they died, they died spent but unquenched. All of those shadowy folks whose blood flowed in her veins seemed to move quietly in the moonlit room. And Scarlett was not surprised to see them, these kinsmen who had taken the worst that fate could send and hammered it into the best" (421). Scarlett's vision includes the French Robillards and Prudhommes on her mother's side, but the vision itself is Irish. It marks Scarlett as Irish in clan, for the Celtic sense of family, as understood by both Glasgow's Ada Fincastle and Faulkner's Quentin Compson, considers both ancestors and descendants as important as the living.

While Scarlett is culturally Celtic, Ashley is an Anglo-Norman gentleman. Upon being told by his favorite child that she wants to marry Ashley, Gerald blusters, "Our people and the Wilkes are different. . . . The Wilkes are different from any of our neighbors—different from any family I ever knew. They are queer folk, and it's best that they marry their cousins and keep their queerness to themselves" (34). The reason for the differences of the Wilkes family from the majority of Mitchell's antebellum middle Georgia farmers is revealed in the novel's opening chapter. Brent Tarleton tells his brother Stuart in reference to Ashley's love of Europe, "you know how the Wilkes are. They are kind of queer about music and books and scenery. Mother says it's because their grandfather came from Virginia. She says Virginians set quite a store by such things" (16). Unlike the rest of their neighbors who are living a culture that Grady McWhiney would label as essentially transplanted Celtic, the Wilkeses, descendants of Tidewater Virginians, are culturally Anglo-Norman Cavaliers. In the Tidewater or in Charleston or Savannah, the Wilkeses would be in the majority culture and the O'Haras, MacIntoshes, and Tarletons would be, regardless of education or wealth, crackers, hillbillies, or peckerwoods. But in the rest of the South the Wilkeses are "queer." Appropriately then, after the end of the war the almost androgynous Ashley, whose proper mate is the hipless epicene Melanie, waxes poetic on the *Gotterdammerung*, the fatalistic Germanic death of the gods (527).

Scarlett's tragedy is that she refuses to listen to her father and throws her life away thinking she loves Ashley. In the midst of the war, she considers him "still a young girl's dream of the perfect knight," an early hint that deep-down Scarlett knows Ashley is false (214). While attempting to keep the family together in the war's last days, Scarlett realizes, "everything her mother had told her about life was wrong," yet she persists in her dream of Ashley much as her mother had done with her memory of Philippe Robillard (434). Though Scarlett's intensity to have Ashley wanes—after being kissed by Rhett "the quiet face of Ashley Wilkes was blurred and drowned to nothingness" (835)—she does not realize fully the mistakes she has made until after Melanie's death when Ashley admits to her that his wife was his life. Scarlett then understands that Ashley "never really existed at all, except in my imagination. . . . I loved something I made up, something that's just as dead as Melly is. I made a pretty suit of clothes and fell in love with it. . . . I kept on loving the pretty clothes—and not him at all" (1016).

In contrast to Ashley is Rhett Butler. Though Butler might appear to be a distinctive Anglo-Saxon surname, MacLysaght informs that it is "always called *de Buitleir* in Irish. . . . One of the great Anglo-Norman families which, however did not soon become hibernicized like the Burkes etc. Mainly identified with the Ormond country. It is now very numerous in all the provinces except Ulster" (*Surnames* 38). Though the Norman Butlers may not have become almost immediately more Irish than the Irish themselves, as did many other Norman families in Ireland, they eventually did become culturally assimilated, as witness William Butler Yeats.

As already noted, Rhett is first attracted to Scarlett because of the

Irish character that he senses defines her. While still a blockade runner, he informs her why he left Charleston and is not a Southern patriot: "I didn't conform and I couldn't. And Charleston is the South, only intensified" (240). Rhett knows that the Anglo-Norman chivalric code of Charleston (which will produce its own John Langtons), a code he sees most of the rest of the South aping, is false and stultifying, and he has no desire to save it, unless, of course, there is a profit to be made. With the fall of Atlanta, though, Rhett rushes off to join the Confederate army, which offers no possibility of financial remuneration. The change is abrupt, and Mitchell does not belabor an explanation. Rhett, however, does tell Scarlett his reason: "because, perhaps, of the betraying sentimentality that lurks in all of us Southerners. Perhaps—perhaps because I am ashamed" (389). This shame, which cannot be about feelings of cowardice, for Rhett has risked his life repeatedly as a blockade runner, may be due to a realization spurred by his knowing Scarlett and Gerald. Most of the South may desire the genteel trappings of Charleston, which would serve as a great mark of *class,* but most of the South is the O'Haras and Benteens, not Charleston. Such an insight would explain Rhett's sudden desire to accept his "quixoticism" and serve as a Confederate infantryman when the war is all but lost.

The brief friendship between Gerald O'Hara and Rhett supports this reasoning. Fearful that this older man may harm his recently widowed daughter's reputation, Gerald, on a visit to Atlanta, decides to have a talk with Rhett. They return in the early morning hours, drunk and singing. Gerald wants to teach Rhett the "Lament for Robert Emmet," but Rhett would like to delay the lesson for another time:

> "Sing it I will and listen you will or I'll be shooting you for the Orangeman you are."
> "Not Orangeman—Charlestonian."
> "'Tis no better. 'Tis worse. I have two sister-in-laws in Charleston and I know."

The Orange Order is a fraternal organization of Irish Protestants, most of them Dissenters (non-Anglican Episcopalians), founded in 1795 with the purpose of protecting their religious rights in a predominantly Catholic land, and it became almost immediately an organization associated with violent persecution of Irish Catholics. Not surprisingly then, a Scots-Irish ancestry is sufficient to put Gerald on his guard, eyes peeled for potential attack: "The MacIntoshs were Scotch-Irish and Orangemen and, had they possessed all the saintly qualities of the Catholic calendar, this ancestry would have doomed them forever in Gerald's eyes" (48-49). But, surprisingly, Gerald sees Charlestonians—and the reader should recall that Gerald's sisters-in-law are Catholic—as worse than Orangemen. The reason, perhaps, is that Gerald instinctively senses that Charlestonians, Catholic or Protestant, are culturally somewhat different from him and that the Scots-Irish, however rabidly anti-Catholic some are, are culturally similar, if not identical. This also explains his instant friendship with Rhett. Though born in Charleston, Rhett is not culturally Anglo-Norman, and he prefers the Celtic folkways of the non-coastal South. When Rhett agrees to try to take her home to Tara to escape the burning of Atlanta, Scarlett senses a similarity between her father and Rhett: "So gentle, so quiet, so devoid of mockery, it did not seem Rhett Butler's voice at all, but the voice of some kind stranger who smelled of brandy and tobacco and horses, comforting smells because they reminded her of Gerald" (380).

At this point we must recall that as an epic protagonist, Scarlett O'Hara is, to some degree, a symbol of the South. Nor should a female Southern personification be startling. In opposition to the English John Bull and the Yankee American Uncle Sam, the South, like Ireland, is always seen as female. Scarlett's story then is not merely a personal love tragedy; it reflects a larger cultural tragedy. On her way home to try to explain her realization to Rhett, Scarlett says to herself, "I've never been able to see the world at all, because Ashley stood in the way" (1022). She tells Rhett of mistakenly believing she had loved Ashley, "It was—well, a sort of habit I hung on to from when I was a little girl" (1028). Scarlett and Ashley are representative of the two primary cultures of the white South: respectively, Celtic and Anglo-Norman cavalier. Scarlett, Mitchell's embodiment of the South, tragically rejects what she truly is, her Irish heritage, in an attempt to become what she is not, an Anglo-Norman lady. Her inability to see herself and her world for what they are guarantees that she will lead a life false to herself. Her desire to have Ashley symbolizes the South's blinding itself to reality by playing Cavalier. Rhett sums up the issue in his attack on Scarlett for believing that Ashley could manage Tara, "You'll never make a farm hand out of a Wilkes—or anything else that's useful. The breed is purely ornamental." He concludes, "Strange how these illusions will persist even in women as hard headed as you are" (628).

Scarlett has a recurring dream during her marriage to Rhett. It is of her great hunger while living at Tara after the war, and in the dream she runs through a mist, hoping to find security. She does not know, however, for what she searches (856). The night of Melanie's death and her tragic realization, Scarlett must walk home in a thick fog like that in her nightmare (1020). What she desperately searches for in the dream is love, and the familial security it will provide. That love is personified in Rhett, and the fog that blinds her step is the illusion of the Cavalier gentleman, personified in Ashley. If the basis of the majority Southern culture is Celtic, then attempting to play the role of "ornamental" cavalier is false, as is the South's desire to be that Anglo-Norman gentleman. The South's tragedy, in Mitchell's vision, is that its Celtic hardheadedness did not prevent it from choosing the pretty illusions of cavalier gentility, which include a cavalier defense of chattel slavery and the caste system that goes with it. The South, like Scarlett, blinded itself to reality, and thereby lost what was most precious to it. The Southern tragedy personified in Scarlett is then similar to that personified in Thomas Sutpen.

Mitchell's epic is one in which her Irish symbol of the South almost destroys herself by refusing to be what she is—Celtic—and in chasing a false culture that appears to be more refined, one that is self-deluded by its wealth and its failure to see the destructions necessary for its wealth and comfort. But Mitchell ends the novel on a note of optimism. Scarlett will return to Tara, a farm founded by an Irish immigrant and, after being ravaged during the war, restored by a "Cracker," to recoup herself before attempting to win back Rhett. When she overhears the girls talking about her at the Twelve Oaks barbecue, Scarlett immediately wants to return to Tara, and following her miscarriage, she goes to Tara to recoup herself and returns reinvigorated, "the unhealthy pallor had gone from her face and her cheeks were rounded and faintly pink" (123, 972). The symbolic importance is apparent: Tara, which is located in Gerald's native County Meath, is the traditional capital of ancient Ireland; Tara is the spiritual center of Irish culture. To atone for her mistakes and prepare for her future, Mitchell's symbol of the South must return to the roots of her Irish culture.

Because they define certain significant cultural characteristics, epics belong more to their audiences than to their authors. Just as it would be ridiculous for us to condemn Aeschylus, Sophocles, and Euripides for stealing Homer's epic Trojan War material, it is unwarranted to condemn the existence of the sequel to *Gone With the Wind*: Alexandra Ripley's *Scarlett* (1991). Though to some *Scarlett* may be tainted due to its being a commissioned novel, and therefore as much a capitalist enterprise as an endeavor to create art, it is no more corrupted than any other literary work whose author hopes to make money. The Greek tragedians wrote their versions of epic material with the hope of winning prizes and earning a living, and Virgil certainly was not above accepting sponsorships. In fact, Western belletristic literature, if not all world literature, was from its infancy agonistic.

Whatever may be concluded about Ripley's skill as a novelist, she does recognize the primary cultural significance of *Gone With the Wind*, that Scarlett's Irishness is indispensable to her character, and Ripley makes it the focus of *Scarlett*. After reinvigorating herself at Tara, Scarlett commences her mission to win back Rhett's love. Feeling beaten, Rhett has returned to his family in Charleston, and Scarlett follows him. There she discovers why Rhett despises Charleston society. Though Charlestonians are great snobs, Scarlett learns that Rhett's mother's family, the Ellintons, who are old Charleston, are in origin quite common: "the first Ellinton to settle in colonial America was part of the shipload only because he had won a land grant in a wager with the owner as to who could drink the most ale and remain standing" (142). The Anglo-Norman elite of Charleston, then, acquired their property and wealth much as did Gerald O'Hara, the Celt they deem inherently socially inferior. In an attempt to arouse Rhett's love through jealousy, Scarlett flirts with Middleton Courtney. Her friend Sally Brewton, assuming that Scarlett, like so many of the Charleston ladies, is unfaithful to her marriage vows, attempts to explain to her the "proper" ways in which a married lady conducts an extramarital affair: "this is an old city with an old civilization. . . . You can do anything you like provided you do it discreetly. . . . You must make it possible for others to pretend they don't know what you're doing." Scarlett is astonished at the institutionalized hypocrisy of Cavalier gentility: "I don't want to be civilized, she thought with despair" (273).

Scarlett's realization of the significant differences between the Anglo-Norman South and the Celtic South is furthered in her visit to Savannah for Ellen's father's birthday. There she meets her cousin Jamie O'Hara, who invites her to visit the rest of the clan. At first, Scarlett is startled. The O'Haras have no servants, the residents of the three households move freely in and out of each of the homes, and "all the adults played parent to all the children" (348, 409). When Maureen, Jamie's wife, tells Scarlett that there will be music, she cringes: "my grief, I've sat through one musicale already in Savannah" (349). But this music is Celtic, and its exuberance invigorates Scarlett as much as her visits to Tara. As she leaves, Scarlett asks whether she will be invited back, and Maureen replies: "there's no inviting done here. We're all a family, and you're a part of it. Come anytime you like" (355).

In contrast to the O'Hara clan is the Robillard family. Scarlett's grandfather is a humorless tyrant who goes out of his way to make his two suffering daughters, as well as Scarlett, miserable. The lifeless house is run with clockwork precision, a far cry from the spontaneity of the O'Hara homes. Aunt Pauline reveals the anti-Irish prejudices common to many non-Irish Catholics: "'everyone knows that the Irish take certain freedoms with the laws of the church. You can't really blame them, poor illiterate nation that they are,' she crossed herself piously" (358). When Scarlett informs her grandfather that she intends to stay with the O'Haras, he retorts, "You don't mind sleeping in the parlor with the pig, I take it" (373).

Her second visit with the O'Haras ignites the beginning of the change in Scarlett that is necessary before she can win back Rhett's love. She realizes that "the O'Haras shared love and happiness as freely and unconsciously as they shared the air they breathed." This allows her to "shed the artifice and calculation that she'd learned to use in the battles for conquest and dominance that were part of being a belle in Southern society" (380). In Ripley's vision, Scarlett's tragic realization at the conclusion of *Gone With the Wind* was the beginning of a lengthy education process, not an epiphanous, complete self-knowledge. It is only after spending time with her O'Hara kin that Scarlett senses the link between Ellen, the Anglo-Norman South and its belles, and her own misery: "At that moment Scarlett's near-worship of her serene, self-contained mother shivered and suffered a tiny crack, and she began to free herself of the guilt she'd always felt because she couldn't live up to her mother's teachings. Perhaps it was all right if she wasn't a perfect lady" (381).

But the glitter decorating the Anglo-Norman Cavalier myth and the power of anti-Celtic prejudices are strong, especially in juxtaposition, and Scarlett momentarily slips back into the role for which her mother had prepared her. Pierre Robillard wants her to be the chatelaine of his house, and he smears the O'Haras by declaring that Maureen had once been "barmaid in an Irish saloon" (386, 388). It takes another society gala to convince Scarlett that her mother's family's ways are not her ways, and she leaves abruptly to visit Jamie and Maureen and meet a cousin from Ireland, Colum. Ripley writes of Scarlett, her "essential self was as much her heritage from her father as was her name," and Colum's stories of the original Tara and her ancestral homeland inspire her. "Now her instinct," her Irish heritage, "and her training," as an Anglo-Norman lady, "were at war" (398).

Scarlett's "instincts" will win, due in no small part to Colum. He informs her of her Irish family and the history of its nation. Scarlett's embrace of family is such that "she had put aside her class pretensions without noticing their departure" (416). Discovering that her grandmother, Katie Scarlett O'Hara, will soon turn one hundred, Scarlett decides to visit Ireland rather than return to Charleston:

> She hated Charleston. The drab dresses, the interminable calls and committees, the walls of politeness that shut her out, the walls of decaying houses and broken gardens that shut her in. She hated the way that Charlestonians talked. . . . She hated their secrecy—the dance cards and receiving lines and the unspoken rules that she was supposed to know and didn't, the immorality that they accepted, and the hypocrisy that condemned her for sins she never committed. (434)

Most of the rest of *Scarlett* takes place in Ireland. Evidently, Ripley's vision of Scarlett's path to earning Rhett's love requires more than an acceptance of her Irish identity and her Savannah Irish cousins; she must return to the original Tara. The boat on which Scarlett sails to Ireland "soon had a full complement of passengers who boarded at Boston and New York, but they didn't seem like Yankees at all, Scarlett thought. They were Irish and proud of it" (444). These recent immigrants returning to their homeland for a visit have not become fully Anglicized; therefore, they are not "like Yankees at all," the implication being that they are much more like the Southern Scarlett. Once in Ireland, Scarlett confronts, and discards, the English squirearchy myth of the South: "where did she come up with that idea that a plantation is the same thing as . . . an English manor?" (481).

When Colum takes Scarlett to Tara, "something ancient and pagan stirred deep within her, and the barely tamed wildness that was her hidden being surged hotly through her blood" (491). She purchases Ballyhara, the former O'Hara estate held in Irish Protestant Ascendancy hands since the Battle of the Boyne in 1691, and her work to aid her family earns her their respect as "The O'Hara," the *cenn fine* (556). Through a set of extraordinary circumstances, Rhett re-enters her life in Ireland. Ripley's Rhett owns a plantation outside Charleston, and its name spurs Scarlett to ponder the possibility of Rhett's also being of Irish heritage: "not far from the city of Kilkenny, she saw the name Dunmore Cave. And Rhett's plantation was called Dunmore Landing. There had to be a connection" (664). When the violence of English rule in Ireland encompasses her (Colum is a Fenian organizer working for national independance), Scarlett leaves Ireland with Rhett once again at her side. As Mitchell suggests symbolically at the conclusion of *Gone With the Wind*, in order to be worthy of Rhett, Scarlett must return to the roots of her Irish heritage. Ripley's heroine does just that.

Even if *Gone With the Wind* could not be seen as the Southern epic, its mass appeal to white Southerners suggests that it strikes an important cultural chord. Speaking of the nineteenth-century Savannah area, the coastal South and therefore more Anglo-Norman than Celtic, Mitchell affirms, "America, in the early years of the century, had been kind to the Irish" (44). It is astonishing that the Irish Catholic Scarlett O'Hara could be so widely accepted in the fundamentalist Protestant South[5] as the portrait of a realistic, admirable, though certainly morally faulty and failing, Southern woman. Only the Celtic-Southern thesis adequately explains it, for then the mass of white Southerners, regardless of religion, would be of Celtic cultural ancestry too. Their multi-generational embracing of Scarlett is not only as a fellow Southerner of Celtic migrant heritage struggling against great odds, but as their cultural epitome. Through this portrayal of the daughter of an Irish immigrant as the symbol of the South, Mitchell's novel presents a powerful criticism of the minority mandarin Anglo-Norman culture of the Southern coast. And the near universal acceptance of that fictional criticism as true, particularly the passionate approval of Southerners, is a powerful refutation of the myth that white Southern culture is English in origin.

Indeed, *Gone With the Wind* recognizes the passing of that culture's hegemony over the South to the descendants of Celts. Pyron calls the Jonesboro Road episode, the flight from burning Atlanta toward home, the novel's "seminal episode" that provides "the overarching themes of the novel itself" (265). When Rhett leaves her for his stint as a soldier, Scarlett is "now on her own on the Jonesboro Road" (Pyron 267). Without Rhett to lean upon for comfort and strength, Scarlett must face the desolation and the nighttime threats with only her own cultural baggage to aid her. After foraging at the destroyed Twelve Oaks, Scarlett sees the Wilkes mansion "rise before her eyes as it had once stood, rich and proud, symbol of a race and a way of living. Then she started down the road toward Tara . . ." (428).

St. Patrick, the Celtic Church, Crypto-Catholics, and Southern Fundamentalism: Flannery O'Connor

Much has been written on the paradox that staunch Roman Catholic believer and practitioner Flannery O'Connor chose to write her stories of modern man's struggles with salvation primarily about fundamentalist Protestants.[1] Robert Mildar believes:

> In repudiating what she regarded as the predominantly ethical mainstream of American Christianity, Flannery O'Connor was returning not to the Catholic tradition but to the evangelical Protestantism of the Reformation and the seventeenth century, a Protestantism whose lineal, if shrunken, descendants were the backwoods prophets of the modern South. (803-4)

In addition to wondering why a modern "fundamentalist" is more "shrunken" in any way except absolutist power than an English Puritan intent upon annihilation of Irish Catholics, and a few other groups as well, the O'Connor reader must remember that she considered sincere fundamentalists part of her Catholic world. In a letter to Sister Mariella Gable, O'Connor declares of Mason Tarwater, "Essentially, he's a crypto-Catholic. When you leave a man alone with his Bible and the Holy Ghost inspires him, he's going to be a Catholic one way or another, even though he knows nothing about the visible church" (*CW* 1183).

Though the paradox is obvious to O'Connor, her critics have struggled with it, tending to see it as either odd or a mere fictional device concocted as a contrast for furthering her themes. Sara Mott agrees that "Preston Browning has rightly termed this 'convergence of Catholic dogma and fundamentalist Protestant belief . . . a peculiar mating'" (219). Louis Rubin recognizes O'Connor's affinity with fundamentalists because "they alone, she implies, are willing to confront evil" (53),[2] but he believes that "in the primitive fervor, and also the error, of fundamentalism she perceives the waste and the horror of that spiritual integrity" (55). Rubin, like a some-what diluted modern Marcionite, prefers to see a contrast between a God of Wrath and a God of Love.[3] Similarly, Robert Brinkmeyer finds in O'Connor "a violent wrenching of extremes not only between secular and divine, but also between two diametrically opposed systems of faith" ("Closer" 6).[4]

The reader who, like these critics, is confused by O'Connor's treatment of fundamentalists must remember her Southern heritage and its importance to her writing. In the last month of her life, O'Connor responded to a query about the influence Nathaniel West had on her: "The South anyway has much more to do with it; also Catholicism" (*CW* 1215). Her wording suggests the preeminence of her Southern heritage in the development of her art over her specific theological beliefs (including rejection of *sola fide* and the concept of an invisible Elected church within a visible church that led to Protestant denominational theology) and Southern culture is paradoxical; O'Connor is both a zealous Roman Catholic and a staunch defender of her fundamentalist characters, whether they are defined properly as Protestants or as nondenominational Christians.[5] The O'Connor reader, then, should strive to understand how and why O'Connor sees fundamentalist believers and prophets as crypto-Catholics rather than struggle to find a meaning for a contrast she does not intend. O'Connor's Irish heritage, with its ineluctable traditions and nexuses, provides the key.

Sally Fitzgerald, a longtime friend of the author, says that by 1800 "Savannah had begun slowly to burgeon as a Catholic center, soon after restrictions on admission ceased to be enforced" (380-81). The many Irish Catholic families that settled in Georgia, Fitzgerald asserts, were "assimilated into Georgia life and became an integral part of it," "retaining as their single difference from their neighbors in Sharon, Savannah, Augusta, Atlanta, and Milledgeville, an allegiance to the Catholic faith they brought with them at the outset" (377-78). Note that Fitzgerald does not see these Irish Catholics as becoming assimilated into the predominately Protestant Scots-Irish settlements of middle and north Georgia by losing their cultural traits. Church affiliation is the sole distinguishing point between these two culturally Celtic peoples. Also important to note is that in Flannery O'Connor's line these Irish Catholics often bore family names that would *seem* to many observers to be Anglo-Saxon and therefore mark their bearers as culturally English: Cline, Harty, Semmes, Treanor (378, 384).

The Celtic church, Christianity as practiced in Celtic lands during the early Middle Ages, the most important branch of which was Irish, was simultaneously backwater and conservative, both theologically and culturally, and the most energetic and successful in Western Europe[6]:

> From the founding of Clonmacnoise in 548 to the founding of the Irish monastery at Ratisbon in 1090, the Irish were a powerful influence in the western church. Toynbee claims for them a degree of cultural superiority in western Europe during all this time, and while that may be too bold a claim, the known facts prove a very high level of piety and of scholarship at home and abroad. (Dillon 323)

In his mid-twentieth-century history of Christianity, Earle Cairns, writing from a Calvinist vantage, agrees with Toynbee, declaring that the Irish church—culturally and theologically conservative—for centuries "led in scholarship and the evangelization of Europe" (177).

Though the Celtic churches were largely responsible for the conversion of the Germanic pagans and the establishment or intellectual expansion of centers of learning throughout northern and western Europe, as well as a few as far south as Italy and as far east as the Ukraine, it was often at odds with Rome. The early-fifth-century Pelagian controversy (the denial of inherited original sin and predestination as taught by Augustine, and the belief among certain Pelagians that man without God's grace could earn salvation) was largely Celtic in origin, and the Celts later were forced by Rome to alter the dating of Easter and to adopt the Roman tonsure (Morris 4, 12). These, however, were not the only differences:

> The overall ethos, which was reflected in organizational habits arising from the tribal background, was the bone of contention. These made the Celtic church independent and threatened the growing power of the Romans. In Ireland the spiritual adviser or soul friend . . . was primary, rather than the ecclesiastical authority of the Bishops. . . . These habits gave extreme autonomy and individuality to each foundation . . . . Rites, customs and so forth differed locally, and there was no central organization. (Bamford 178)

In addition, the Irish church accepted, perhaps preferred, married clergy and apparently practiced immersion rather than pouring or sprinkling (Lonigan 34).

Patrick, the traditional founder of Irish Christianity, was a British Celt, whose descendants today are both Welshmen and the partially, perhaps predominantly, culturally Celtic residents of northwestern England.

What we know of Patrick largely comes from his "Confessio," an attempt to argue his case for his mission in Ireland, which also presents his defense against charges that he had foregone a role assigned by Rome to preach among pagans as he felt directed by God to do. As Celts unconquered by the Roman Empire, the Irish would require a conversion different from many other peoples (De Paor 44). As a Celt, Patrick was able to minister in such a way as to establish a firm Christian base in Ireland. "To outsiders," Paul Lonigan writes, "he was controversial, ignorant, erratic, 'irregular' in his ministry. From his point of view, his work was God-appointed and necessarily adapted in style to the unusual circumstances of dealing with an untamed, rural, warrior-oriented aristocracy" (23). Though he does not make the direct connection, Lonigan presents Patrick as remarkably similar to a fundamentalist evangelist preaching in a land similar in several ways to the rural, small town South.

In contrast to the man of the romantic mythologies who cast the snakes out of Ireland and played with shamrocks is the real Patrick: a prophet whose "counter . . . to charges of sin [presumably 'sins' of refusing to follow dictates from hierarchical officials in Rome] is that of election" (Lonigan 21). That Patrick could have held his own with O'Connor's prophets or against their detractors, fictional and academic, and would have seen eye to eye with Mason Tarwater on many issues may be observed throughout the "Confessio":

> So then, be amazed, you great and small that fear God, and you clerical intellectuals, listen and take stock. Who raised me up, a fool, from the midst of those who seem to be wise and learned in the law and powerful in speaking and all else, and inspired me in preference to others, execrated as I am by this world, to prove fit to help (if only I could!), faithfully, with fear and reverence and without complaint, the people to which the love of Christ brought and gave me for the rest of my life, if I am worthy; in short, to serve them sincerely and with humility? (43)

The answer to Patrick's protracted question is that God, not any person or group of people, raised him, and because of his Divine calling Patrick can tolerate the belittlement he receives from those who despise and dismiss him for being "countrified": "He who wants to can laugh and jeer, but I shall not keep silent nor keep hidden the signs and wonders which have been shown me by the Lord many years before they took place, as He knows all things, even before the world began" (50-51).

Had these words come from the mouth of an O'Connor prophet, many O'Connor critics would see them as evidence of tension, or perhaps as playful dialectic, between her Catholic vision and the fundamentalist non-Catholicism of many of her characters. But, paradoxically, they are the words of the most famous Roman Catholic saint: Ireland's patron, and, therefore, O'Connor's patron as well.

An ostensible problem in using the heritage of the old Celtic church, which, however uniquely, was connected to the Roman Catholic Church, to evaluate O'Connor's use of Southern fundamentalists is the sacramental tradition. The gap that contemporaries may feel between Catholic and fundamentalist based on sacraments as necessary for grace is not necessarily accurate historically. In the first of his five volumes on the development of Christian doctrine, Jaroslav Pelikan recounts a number of major conversions that arose from nothing more than Bible study (oral as well as written) throughout Christendom up to Francis of Assisi. He then concludes: "The attention to the sacraments in dogmatic theology [presumably Roman Catholic as well as Protestant] has failed to do justice to the place of the doctrine of the word of God, proclaimed but also written, within the total doctrine of the means of grace in the second and third century" (162).

A greater difficulty is the tendency of those adhering to postmodernist assumptions to assign their prepossessions even to writers whose entire oeuvre was created to reject earlier forms of moral, philosophical, or theological relativism. Robert Brinkmeyer in *The Art and Vision of Flannery O'Connor* argues that O'Connor's fiction is a dialogue between "raging fundamentalist" Yahwist and "sympathetic Catholic" that syncretizes a pure Yahwist vision with the world (73). Brinkmeyer utilizes Herbert Schneidau's *Sacred Discontent: The Bible and Western Tradition* to define this unadulterated Yahwist or fundamentalist. As best revealed, Schneidau believes, in the Old Testament prophets, the Yahwist "judges his society only by losing his sense of brotherhood with it" (17) and is an anti-mythological desacramentalizer of all in this world, especially the works of man, for only Yahweh, the God who created everything and cannot be captured in image or idol or ritual or building, is sacred.

Schneidau sees Christianity as historically evolving away from pure Yahwism to a syncretism that would have been unacceptable to an Old Testament prophet. Christians "went out to meet the Gentiles on their own ground," Schneidau declares, "and in so doing made out of Christianity a gigantic mythological structure whose saints, feasts, cults, and concepts have long been known to have pagan origins or parallels" (35). As can be seen in both the quotes from Patrick and its disputes with Rome, as well as in literature such as "St. Patrick's Breastplate,"[7] the

Celtic Church was focused primarily on capturing and maintaining the Yahwist vision, not on sacramental ritual or church hierarchy.[8] In discussing Christianity in early medieval Scotland, J. D. Mackie writes, "'The Celtic Church gave love, the Roman Church gave law': the epigram is as true as most epigrams, though doubtless both churches gave both" (26). As Mackie observes, the ethos of the Celtic Church was passionate belief and practice and love of God and God's revelation, while the Roman Church, even by the fifth century, had begun to focus increasingly on church law and order, on governmental hierarchy.[9]

O'Connor's fundamentalist prophets are likewise Yahweh centered. Specific sacraments, other than baptism, and denominations apparently mean little to them in their wrestlings to understand and serve Yahweh. This is not to claim that O'Connor was a syrupy ecumenist. As she informs Dr. T. R. Spivey in a letter, "you will find that the doctrinal differences between Catholics and Protestants are a great deal more important than you think they are" (*CW* 1102), and "the Catholic," she writes to Cecil Dawkins, "using his own eyes and the eyes of the church (when he is inclined to use them) is in a most favorable position to recognize the grotesque" (*CW* 1035). The Protestant, by implication, tends to be "out of context." To Alfred Corn, O'Connor declares that "liberal Protestantism," as opposed, presumably, to a more fundamentalist non-Catholicism,[10] had promoted relativity, which had led to personal feeling and desire being elevated over studious examination of theology and philosophy, which had led people to believe that "God has no power . . . and that religion is our own sweet invention" (*CW* 1166). But these theological, denominational, philosophical differences are not, except by implication, the primary religious focus of O'Connor's fiction; Yahwist belief versus modern materialist, scoffing, quibbling disbelief is her focus.

It is, however, important to emphasize that the Celtic Church was from its inception more Yahwist than Roman in ethos. In a recent interview concerning his overview of the intellectual contributions to Western Civilization of the first centuries of Irish Christianity, Thomas Cahill says of Patrick, "He's the first person to create a non-Roman form of Christianity, and the way he did it, he didn't try to bring all the Roman practices with him. He reduced Christianity to the gospels and planted it in Ireland; he brought them a much more diverse form of Christianity than the Romans would ever have allowed" (Basbanes J6).[11] The Celtic Church was, Cahill believes, "the first de-Romanized Christianity in human history, a Christianity without the socio-political baggage of the Greco-Roman world" (148).

Liam De Paor's assessment is virtually identical. Patrick's "remark-able achievement," he declares, "was to found a new kind of church, one which broke the Roman imperial mold and was both catholic and bar-barian. And he broke the Roman church mold by going among the pagans" (95). In other words, Patrick emulated the apostles and preach-ers of the first century, not the Roman hierarchy of his day, which was faced with a crumbling Imperial government and growing social disor-der. And though centuries of Roman Catholic legislation altered the structure, and perhaps the sacramental emphasis, of Christianity in Ireland, the more Yahwist than Roman ethos of Patrick persisted in Ireland at least well into the nineteenth century. "Prefamine Irish Catholicism," historian Lawrence McCaffrey declares, "had been loosely structured, 'racy of the soil,' more Irish than Roman in content and style" (*Irish Diaspora* 74).

Flannery O'Connor considered that Irish Catholicism, which tradi-tionally "has included more cultural identity than theology" (McCaffrey "Irish-American" 180-81), to be "passed on from generation to genera-tion" in her own family (*CW* 926). Perhaps especially important to the topic of O'Connor the Catholic and non-Catholic fundamentalists in her fiction is that she made this comment to Caroline Gordon, another Southern writer greatly interested in religion and morality, one who had converted to Catholicism, in the context of discussing the growing num-ber of her family members leaving the Roman Catholic Church. And to Sally and Robert Fitzgerald, O'Connor distinguishes between "European Catholics" and "Irish Catholics," saying of the latter in the South, "a great many of them are going to the Baptist church three months after they get here" (*CW* 939). Perhaps they did so not primarily for theologi-cal reasons but because of cultural connections.

The Violent Bear It Away is concerned with the passing of the prophet-ic vision, God's calling, to the next generation. What is most important is that Mason Tarwater looks only to his family to find a successor. The "tribal background," the clan structure of Celtic society, certainly helped steer the Celtic church toward a structure that would reflect all aspects of the culture: One organized according to both family lineage and heritage and place that physically grounds the clan and its history. Nora Chadwick observes that at its zenith the Celtic church in Ireland was a "federation of monastic communities, each with its paruchia under the supreme jurisdiction of the 'heir' (*conarb*) of the founder-saint" (203). Paul Lonigan more explicitly denotes the importance of family to the Celtic church. Irish families found it "exceedingly advantageous . . . to establish a trust whereby the foundation would retain identity with the endowing family, continue to operate as a religious unit of that family, and elect, whenever available, as ruler of that community a descendant of the original endowing family" (41).

Mason Tarwater apparently is not a member of any Protestant denomination. O'Connor says, "He is not typical of a group . . . of the Southern Baptist or the Southern Methodist" (*CW* 1183). This is not to declare that we could not infer from his words and actions into which general theological camp he would most easily fit; rather, it is to point out that Mason exhibits no interest in any church organization beyond his local, family-based congregation. In his foreword to the English translation of his *Les chrétientes celtiques*, Dom Louis Gougaud explains:

> The title has been changed because the English language contains no word corresponding exactly to the French *"chrétiente,"* used in the sense of a Church in process of formation and as yet imperfectly organized, such as were those Christian communities of the Celtic world in the early Middle Ages whose history is sketched in this book. (vii)

To Gougaud, a modern continental Roman Catholic monk, a church lacking a governing structure reflecting some kind of centralized political system is "imperfectly organized." Mason Tarwater, perhaps like Patrick, would care little for Gougaud's emphasis, for it suggests the preeminence of human structure, of human political establishments, in the quest to maintain the Yahwist vision. And, as O'Connor writes to Sister Mariella Gable, "anything the human being touches, even Christian truth, he deforms slightly in his own image. Even the saints do this" (*CW* 1182).

Like Patrick and the subsequent peripatetic Irish monk-saints, Mason Tarwater is a bachelor without children to inherit his rural religious see, and he turns to his nephews to train a worthy successor (Hughes 35, Chadwick 204-05). The Celtic clan structure, at least for purposes of inheritance, is based on a common great-grandfather (Chadwick 112-14). After his failure to save Rayber, a failure that haunts the old preacher until his death and one for which he accepts complicity (*CW* 333-34), Mason Tarwater has but one hope for a successor to spring from his clan: his grand-nephew. Immediately upon seeing the baby, "The voice of the Lord had come to him and said: HERE IS THE PROPHET TO TAKE YOUR PLACE. BAPTIZE HIM" (*CW* 376). Perhaps most important in understanding the inextricable connection of old Tarwater's senses of family and religion is that he raises his successor with his surname though the boy is double-distaff removed from the Tarwater name.

Old Tarwater understandably makes family history the center of the boy's education: "at least once a week, beginning at the beginning, the old man had reviewed this history through to the end" (*CW* 366). Though he would "mince no words" in labeling both his sister and his niece "whores," old Tarwater respects and has pride in his family. Rayber's father, a soulless, modern insurance huckster who would "sell you a policy against any contingency," even losing the soul, is, Mason believes, largely to blame for his son's adolescent denial of his salvation: "It was not to be wondered at, the old man would say, that the schoolteacher was no better than he was with such a father as he had" (*CW* 367). But Rayber is also a Tarwater, and even if from a "whore," good blood will tell eventually. "'Good blood flows in his veins,' the old man said. And good blood knows the Lord and there ain't a thing he can do about having it" (*CW* 368). Rayber, who uses a monkish asceticism to fend off both the perpetual tug to believe and the irrational surges of love with which he is occasionally bombarded, also recognizes the unshakable importance of family: "The affliction was in the family. It lay hidden in the line of blood that touched them, flowing from some ancient source, some desert-prophet or pole-sitter, until, its power unabated, it appeared in the old man and him and, he surmised, in the boy" (*CW* 402).

Not only does the Tarwater prophetic vision mirror the Celtic church in familial organization, but the Tarwaters taken as a pair are remarkably similar to Patrick in ways other than the previously cited rhetoric. As noted, Patrick sees himself as God's elect, not merely saved but saved to do something important. Francis Marion Tarwater is similarly convinced of his personally-called salvation, but O'Connor gives it a comic twist that makes it part of her attack on modern secular education: "The boy knew that escaping school was the surest sign of his election" (*CW* 340).

Patrick's mission is dictated by God's visions. First, he is told by "a voice" to flee his enslavement in Ireland (44), and then he is instructed by visions to begin his Irish mission (45-46); Patrick apparently acted and then presented the beginnings of his work for approval by established churchmen. Similarly, the Tarwaters are personally instructed by God, not by hierarchical officials of a Protestant denomination. In addition to being instructed to baptize his successor, old Tarwater is commanded to flee the city to save the future prophet with Godly rearing at Powderhead (*CW* 332). At the novel's conclusion, Francis Marion Tarwater accepts the vision to "GO WARN THE CHILDREN OF GOD OF THE TERRIBLE SPEED OF MERCY" (*CW* 478).

There are further direct analogues between Patrick and Francis

Marion Tarwater. The boy is either fourteen or fifteen depending upon which of the ages O'Connor provides for old Tarwater is valid (*CW* 331, 375). At the time he was kidnapped into slavery in Ireland, Patrick also was in his teens, "almost a boy without any beard" (43). One of the charges against which the "Confessio" is aimed is left ambiguous. It is something Patrick "had done as a boy one day. . . . I do not know, God knows, whether I was fifteen years old at the time, and I did not believe in the living God, nor had I done since earliest childhood; but I remained in death and unbelief till I was severely chastened and in truth humiliated by hunger and nakedness, and every day too" (46).

After discussing the possibilities in light of the standards of the era, Thomas Cahill concludes, "My guess is that the sin was murder" (113). If this conjecture is correct, both Patrick and Francis Marion Tarwater take life before they preach eternal salvation from death.

His sin, Patrick feels, of not having been a fully believing, practicing Christian was punished by being taken into slavery, which awoke him to accept God's will. Similarly, the adolescent Tarwater upon first seeing Bishop Rayber's mentally handicapped son knows that he has been called, but he fights the desire to baptize his cousin until the moment of baptismal drowning (*CW* 388-89). Like the Patrick who confesses, "I did not go to Ireland of my own accord, until I was nearly at the end of my strength" (47), it is not until after he has been raped, when he, like Patrick, is "humiliated by hunger [and Patrick here, I believe, alludes to the Bread of Life] and nakedness," that Tarwater is scorched by God's truth (*CW* 472). The rapist, who is called "the stranger," is, like Tarwater's inner stranger, a facet of Satan. This recalls an incident in Patrick's flight from Irish slavery. "Now that same night I was asleep," Patrick says of traveling with a group of pagans, "and Satan attacked me violently, something which I shall remember as long as I am in this body" (45). I am not suggesting that Patrick's rather vague wording means necessarily that he was raped, but I am proposing that young Tarwater, as was Patrick, is shown through a Satanic attack that "even the mercy of the Lord burns" (*CW* 342).

One of the most important aspects of Celtic culture is affinity with nature. A pagan Irish king was married symbolically to the land, and pre-Christian Celtic religious sites were centered in the forest or beside bodies of water (Chadwick 111, 147). The Celtic church retained this cultural trait, typically shunning the grandiose in favor of simple structures in the midst of nature as preferable places in which to hold worship services. Christopher Bamford declares, "the Celtic, or as it is also called, the British[12] Church has always represented an ideal for those who have known of it. . . . 'If the British church had survived," wrote H.J. Massingham, "it is possible that the fissure between Christianity and nature, widening through the centuries, would not have cracked the unity of western man's attitude to the universe" (169).

The Tarwater family prophecy is similarly rooted in nature. After realizing that Rayber has been using him, Mason receives from God "a rage of vision [that] had told him to fly with the orphan boy to the farthest part of the backwoods and raise him up to justify his Redemption" (*CW* 332). When old Tarwater is downcast by his failure to save Rayber, "he would wander into the woods and leave Tarwater alone, occasionally for days, while he thrashed out his peace with the Lord, and when he returned, bedraggled and hungry, he would look the way the boy thought a prophet ought to look" (*CW* 334).

After hearing his great-uncle expound upon his freedom from the bondage of sin through Jesus, Tarwater "even felt he could smell his freedom, pine-scented, coming out of the woods" (*CW* 342). In his attempt to save the seven year old Rayber, old Tarwater exposes his nephew to nature, and when his father comes to take him home the youth imagines an escape into the nature "where he had been born again" (*CW* 371). Listening to the Carmody revival, Rayber recalls watching his father, the modern atheist salesman, cross the field at Powderhead to take him back to town: "He had let himself imagine that the field had an undertow that would drag his father backwards and suck him under" (*CW* 409).

Tarwater, attempting to flee the call of salvation in the city, is stunned to discover a park in town, so much so that "as they approached it, the boy paled as if he were shocked to find a wood in the middle of the city" (*CW* 417). His first calling to baptize Bishop occurs in the city park, a refuge of nature in the midst of the mechanistic city: "They had only entered it when he felt a hush in his blood and a stillness in the atmosphere as if the air were being purged for the approach of revelation." As they enter deeper into the park, Tarwater begins "to feel again the approach of mystery" (*CW* 431). At the Cherokee Lodge, only thirty miles from Powderhead, "Tarwater stood for a moment, his head lifted sharply as if he detected some familiar odor moving from the pine forest across the lake" (*CW* 424). After accepting his calling, Tarwater "stooped and picked up a handful of dirt off his great-uncle's grave and smeared it on his forehead" (*CW* 478), thereby linking nature, family, and Christ-centered religion.[13]

The nature emphasis in the Celtic church was not equivalent to modern nature deification; rather, like Jesus's references to the beauty and power of nature, it drew man's attention to both the Creator and man's own fleshly mortality that binds him to the mundane and the ephemeral. The all but imponderable magnificence of the creation, the Celtic church ethos suggests, forces man to acknowledge Yahweh as the only source of meaning and to accept himself as important only because Yahweh created him in his image to do his will. Francis Marion Tarwater's problems arise from his rejecting this view of man's relationship to the rest of Yahweh's creation. He desires a call "untouched by any fleshly hand or breath" (*CW* 343), which, in its repudiation of both the Yahweh-created flesh and the interconnections among people, is but a version of the modern non-believer's self-sacramentalizing. Especially when we recall that Rayber is as horrified at the thought of the flesh of his mentally retarded son as is Tarwater and that each would have a "calling," a mission of teaching, that avoids human contact, we are not unjustified in seeing that O'Connor may be suggesting through fiction that the Gnostic heresies of Docetism and Cerintianism lead directly to Socinianism and from there to Rayber's militant modern atheism. Appropriately then, for this appears to be the one thing that spurs him to accept his calling as humble but uncompromising servant, the boy who flees toward Powderhead believing he has saved himself from "trudging off into the distance in the bleeding stinking mad shadow of Jesus, lost forever to his own inclinations" is raped in the woods (*CW* 464-65, 471).

Just as those who embrace the natural world are saved or are capable of being saved, those hostile to God's nature in both the world of the Celtic church and *The Violent Bear It Away* are damned. In contrast to old Tarwater, who loves his humble home set so deep into the woods that the dirt road is distanced from the front door by a grove of trees and a cornfield, is the adult, anti-Christian Rayber, who finds the very thought of crossing the forest to get to the house distasteful (*CW* 443). Rayber discovers neither peace nor understanding nor community in the backwoods: "the forest rose about him, mysterious and alien" (*CW* 444). In contrast, Bishop, God's idiot who is labeled by his father "a mistake of nature" (*CW* 403), is mesmerized by his first trip deep into nature: "he lifted his face to stare open-mouthed above him as if he were in some vast overwhelming edifice" (*CW* 444). His father, who has warred against being born again, against being converted and becoming like a child (*CW* 451), though he senses that the trees "belonged to an order that had never budged from its first allegiance in the days of creation," reduces God's natural temple to monetary value (*CW* 445), suggesting that he is the modern equivalent of those whom Jesus cast out of the temple.

That Tarwater's ambivalence toward his rearing eventually will be resolved in his accepting his calling is suggested in his responses to machines, the technological marvels modern man uses not only to subdue nature but also to justify belief in man rather than God. The boy, proud of having been born in a car wreck (*CW* 353), admits to the salesman Meeks that he has no knowledge of machines (*CW* 383). Tarwater berates Rayber's hearing aid, asking his uncle, "Do you think in the box" (*CW* 396). The adolescent insult proves to be prophetic, for Rayber, who is frightened by the message he hears, turns off his hearing aid when Lucette Carmody's preaching pierces him (*CW* 415). At the Cherokee Lodge, Rayber attempts to seduce Tarwater into adoration of the modern world with a plane ride. "Flying," the school teacher declares, "is the greatest engineering achievement of man . . . " The boy, who has flown with Mason at a fair, retorts, "I wouldn't give you nothing for no airplane. A buzzard can fly" (*CW* 438). His response reveals both that his common sense tells him man's technological achievements cannot better God's creation and that he, though hostile to the modern world of machine worship, still must be burned clean before he will accept his calling to preach and baptize as just another of God's creations.

Rayber desires "some enclosed garden," a nature controlled by man and not regulated by God, in which to teach Lucette Carmody the error, as he sees it, of her firm, committed belief in Jesus (*CW* 420, 414). The schoolteacher's metamorphosis from a saved seven year old into an ineffectual, intellectualized modern, militant agnostic is perhaps best revealed in the scene in the Cherokee Lodge as he waits for Tarwater to act. He remembers that after being forced back into town he had "expected any moment that the city would blossom into an eternal Powderhead," that God's nature would give rebirth to man's spiritual life. But as a godless modern adult, "he sensed that he waited for a cataclysm. He waited for all the world to be turned into a burnt spot between two chimneys" (*CW* 454). Appropriately, Tarwater's "stranger," the Devil inside him, the Devil to whom he listens, sees no value in nature: "What would he [Rayber] want to come out here for—where there's nothing?" the stranger asks Tarwater (*CW* 352).

Flannery O'Connor was not ignorant of the heritage of the Celtic Church, at least in its more popular, modern, Catholic Church-approved form. Arthur F. Kinney notes that O'Connor owned—and marked—D. P. Conyngham's *Lives of the Irish Saints: From St. Patrick to St. Lawrence O'Toole* (53). Thomas Cahill observes that in his "Letter to Coroticus" Patrick alludes to Matthew 11:12, the source of the phrase "the violent bear it away":

> In the Gospel story, the passionate, the outsized, the out-of-control have a better shot at seizing heaven than the contained, the calculating, and those of whom this world approves. Patrick, indeed, seems to have been attracted to the same kinds of oddball, off-center personalities that attracted Jesus, and this attraction makes him unusual in the history of churchmen. (123)

In a footnote, Cahill also remarks O'Connor's attraction to such forceful, "off-center" Yahwist personalities (123).

Perhaps O'Connor's readings inspired her to recognize similarities between the heritage of Irish Catholicism and the beliefs and practices of Southern Bible inerrantists, or perhaps O'Connor sensed a deep cultural connection between Ireland and the South. Nadine Brewer argues of O'Connor that "for all her orthodoxy, no where is her profound understanding of her country [the South] more evident than in the unerring delineation of Protestantism" (103). Brewer also suggests how the Irish Catholic O'Connor could so naturally understand and even identify with Southern fundamentalists: "the population of the South is largely Celtic in origin, 'of all Western strains the most susceptible to suggestions of the supernatural'" (105). Though she appears unaware of its implications, this insight allies Brewer with the Celtic-Southern thesis.

If this thesis is valid, the paradox O'Connor readers must grasp is that white Southern fundamentalists, though not Roman Catholic, are her people culturally: essentially, Celts altered by New World conditions. As seen in relation to Caroline Gordon's fiction, Marilyn Westerkamp's *Triumph of the Laity* reveals the validity of this approach to understanding the cultural significance of early American frontier religion and, by implication, its largely Southern twentieth-century successors. We tend still to view the eighteenth-century evangelical reformation of Episcopalianism, out of which was born Methodism, as the chief, if not sole, determinant of certainly the Southern wing of the Great American Revival. But Westerkamp notes, "without doubt, one hundred years before Whitefield began to preach, Ireland experienced its own awakening," one that "established traditions of revivalism and enthusiasm, traditions that would inform the course of Irish religious history, and, through immigration, American religious history for the next four centuries" (16). The Great American Revival, Westerkamp demonstrates, was triggered by "large scale immigration from Ireland" and the descendants of those immigrants moving steadily into the Southern and western frontiers (14).

O'Connor's affinity then for Southern fundamentalists is not due merely to a similar recognition of evil, and it does not represent a startling contrast in her work. Nor, as Ralph Wood believes, is it because O'Connor's Catholicism is so strongly orthodox "that she makes even her Protestant characters its advocates" (16). Mason Tarwater's beliefs and actions certainly are not in full accord with the strictures of the Roman Catholic Church. Thomas Landess suggests that the religious defining characteristic of the South is one found in both Ulster Scotch Presbyterianism and Irish Catholicism (160). If this is so, then the spirit of supernatural, fiery Catholicism that is culturally grounded into O'Connor's Irish heritage is the same supernatural, uncompromising fundamentalism of her prophets, and those who would argue that O'Connor's Catholicism is the basic culture out of which she writes must remember that she emphatically declares, "the Church is not a culture" (*CW* 857). "There are certain conditions necessary for the emergence of Catholic literature," O'Connor avows, "which are found nowhere else in this country" (*CW* 854). Robert Mildar reasons, "if old Tarwater is to be included among the census of Catholics, natural or otherwise, we are left with a Catholicism without Church or sacraments or priesthood, predicated solely upon the Bible and the individual's immediate confrontation with God—a Catholicism remarkably like Evangelical Protestantism" (805). For O'Connor, Southern religion, which tends to be passionate in its belief, is determined primarily by fundamentalists who, like Patrick, see "religion Biblically," and she believed, "the fact that Catholics are not accustomed to seeing religion Biblically is a deficiency on the part of Catholics" (858). The preponderantly non-Catholic South paradoxically reinforced in Flannery O'Connor a vision of Christianity that is analogous to the spirit and practice of the Celtic church, which, like old Mason Tarwater, could be labeled "crypto-Catholic."

Thus far, I have not addressed the ethnicity of the Tarwaters. As we have seen repeatedly, people of Celtic ancestry, people who are culturally Celtic, often do bear surnames composed of prosaic Anglo-Saxon syllables. Anglicization of the conquered, forced directly by law or restriction to opportunities or name "simplifying" census takers and forced indirectly by fear or threat of economic or educational ostracism, to seem to be as English as possible explains most such names; marriage of non-Celts to Celtic women whose children were culturally Celtic explains the rest.

O'Connor frequently uses names to suggest basic character traits; Haze Motes and Mrs. Hopewell are two prime examples. Because she writes in the English language, O'Connor, to achieve her desired effects with readers most easily, must use Anglo-Saxon root words to construct names. Considering "Tarwater" as such a name, we could focus on the fact that "tar," perhaps associated with the Devil's burning stench or at least with the world's griminess, and "water," necessary to baptism, do not mix, or we could conclude that O'Connor suggests that the tar will perhaps hold the baptismal salvation in place even when someone resists, as does Francis Marion Tarwater.

But this does not mark the Tarwaters as Irish in any sense. William Butler Yeats's poem "The Seven Sages" does. This poem in which the seven aged men speak alternately about their family brushes against and ties to the intellectual and cultural glories of eighteenth-century Protestant Ascendancy Ireland is included in *The Collected Poems*, the 1952 reprint of which O'Connor owned (Kinney 127). The Third Sage declares that his great-great-grandfather, "Drank tar-water with the Bishop of Cloyne" (236). The Bishop is George Berkeley, Church of Ireland theologian and philosopher, who was previously discussed in this study in relationship to Ellen Glasgow's fiction. In the 1740s, a dysentery epidemic raged in a rural Ireland largely bereft of medical professionals, and the majority of the afflicted were peasants unable to afford any care not administered charitably. Berkeley, recalling an American Indian preventative for smallpox derived from tar, "studied the chemistry of his day, and found out how to eliminate from the infusion the thick and nauseating elements, and to run it off clear" (Luce 200). After experimenting first on himself and then on family volunteers, Berkeley, receiving no financial remuneration even to cover his costs, dispensed tar-water to all takers.

Quoting from *Siris*, Berkeley's philosophical treatise on tar-water, A. A. Luce concludes that the effort was principally spiritual:

> "the luminous spirit lodged and detained in the native balsam of pines and firs is of a nature so mild and benign, and proportioned to the human constitution, as to warm without heating, to cheer but not inebriate, and to produce a calm and steady joy like the effect of good news. . . ." That result links physic and metaphysic, experiments and speculation, science and philosophy, and explains why Berkeley penned this treatise which, as has been truly said, begins with Tar-Water and ends with the Holy Trinity. (205)

The tar-water, according to the anti-materialist, theologically conservative Berkeley, who sees God as "omnipresent, immediately operative in nature around us, and intimately present to our consciousness" (Luce 44), brought the good news, the gospel of the Christ risen, its inventor believed or certainly desired and hoped, to the people of Ireland; it was principally about the Holy Trinity and the saving of souls, not the saving of earthly lives. Whatever their actual ethnicity, O'Connor's Tarwaters, natives of the Celtic emigrant filled hill country of north Georgia and Tennessee, are as culturally Irish Christian as was the Bishop Berkeley-created tar-water that produced "a calm and steady joy like the effect of good news."

Chapter X

The Shanty Irishman in the Civil Rights Era South: Pat Conroy

In at least one significant area, Pat Conroy is the most popular and best known contemporary Southern novelist: Film interpretation of his work. With the exception of *The Boo*, a first novel that he published at his own expense in 1970, each of Conroy's works has been translated to the screen. *The Water is Wide* (1972), Conway's non-fiction treatment of his year as a public school teacher on the all-black Daufuskie island off the South Carolina coast, was made into the 1974 film *Conrack*. The novel *The Great Santini* (1976) was made into the 1979 movie called *The Ace*, which was later released with the novel's title, and *The Lords of Discipline* (1980) appeared on the screen in 1983. And most successful as a film, both critically and commercially, is *The Prince of Tides* (1986), a 1991 release that was nominated for seven Academy Awards. Conroy also has written an original teleplay, *The Unconquered* (1989). This work, with its title reminiscent of Faulkner's *The Unvanquished*, is the real-life story of the Richmond Flowers family of Alabama. Like Conroy's fiction, *The Unconquered* includes an exploration of both the 1960s Civil Rights movement and the importance of sports in the South.

In the essay "Mama and Me: The Making of a Southern Son," Conroy reveals his immediate heritage. His mother came from "tar-paper shacks in Alabama," and her favorite book was *Gone With the Wind*. "When my mother married a Conroy, whose family originated in the Irish county of Roscommon," he writes, "she thought she was being true to the spirit of her one heroine, O'Hara. She remembered the O'Hara name and that Scarlett was Irish, wildly, proudly, demonstrably Irish" (125). Donald Conroy, a career Marine, brought to his wife's vision of *Gone With the Wind* "the primitive howling of Chicago," "the memory of coarse streets and the discriminations of Studs Lonigan" (125). Perhaps because of his non-Southern paternal heritage, coupled with the rootlessness of a military childhood, or because of his mother's "religious" devotion to *Gone With the Wind*, Pat Conroy, unlike most Southern authors, has yet to write a novel set before his own life. His "postage stamp of native soil" is the South Carolina low country, primarily in the area from Charleston to Beaufort, which is home to a Marine Corps air station, from the 1960s, the decade in which Conroy graduated from both high school and college, to the present. In terms of the Celtic-Southern thesis, Conroy's works present the Irish Southerner as both the future chronicler and the moral arbiter of the Civil Rights-era South.

The titular character of *The Great Santini* is Wilbur "Bull" Meecham, a native of Chicago who is a career Marine fighter pilot. He had met his future wife, Lillian, an Alabama native then living in Atlanta, during World War II, and, with the exceptions of Bull's overseas duties, the family has always lived in the South. The catalyst of the novel's actions is Bull's transfer from the Mediterranean to a base in Ravenel, South Carolina, in the summer of 1962. Conroy's narration of the drive from Atlanta, where Bull's wife and children had stayed with Lillian's mother while he had been in Europe the past year, to the South Carolina coast reveals to the reader Bull's unequivocally anti-Southern prejudices. When his wife asks why he has placed a .22 pistol on the dash, Bull responds that because they are in the Deep South in a time of racial turmoil and revolution, he might have to shoot "some wild nigger" (29). Later, when Bull meets Arrabelle Smalls, the woman hired to be Lillian's maid, Conroy writes, "if there was a single group in America that Bull had difficulty with over the simplest forms of address, a group as mysterious to him as children, it was southern blacks" (114).

Bull's anti-Southern hostilities are not restricted to blacks. When Lillian, in reprimanding him for publicly using the word "nigger," informs Bull that she has been raising their four children to be ladies and gentlemen, Bull declares, "there ain't nothing in this world that makes me puke faster than a southern gentleman." Lillian responds that as a Marine colonel Bull is both an officer and a gentleman, to which he growls, "I'll remind you that I'm not a pansy southern gentleman" (30). Though they have been raised exclusively in the South, the Meecham children have no distinguishable trace of a Southern accent; their father, literally, has beaten it out of them because "a southern accent sounds dumb anywhere outside of the Mason-Dixon line" (49). The Yankee marine is not completely successful, however: "he could exorcise the language of the South, but he could not purify his children of the experience that tied them forever to the South, to the strange separateness, the private identity of the land which nourished and enriched their childhoods" (49-50).

Bull's disgust with a South he considers inferior may appear initially to undercut the Celtic-Southern thesis. After all, he is a descendant of Irish immigrants. However, unlike the recent Irish immigrants to Boston whom Alexandra Ripley's Scarlett finds similar to her sense of Southerness, the Meechams have been in the United States for more than a century, all of it in the urban Midwest, where its modern American Irish Catholic identity could grow without encountering non-Catholics of Irish heritage and where they would be pulled to become cultural WASPs with Irish surnames and at least nominal Catholic religion. Bull, rather like one of Flannery O'Connor's Modern agnostic characters, is mesmerized by trains because "the destiny of his family in Chicago was wedded to the movement of trains through the Midwest. If the potato was symbolic of the Meecham family's flight from Ireland, then the freight train was the lucky talisman of their redemption in the new world" (45). When the family settles into its off-base rental home in Ravenel, Bull insults their first visitor, an elderly woman. After informing Mrs. Earline Grantham that her first name "sounds like something you put in your crankshaft," Bull proceeds to tell her that his great-grandfather, a draftee, had fought for the Union, or "the winners" as Bull dubs them, during the Civil War (106). This attitude is manifested in his disdain for "Dixie," which he labels "a loser's song" (35).

Bull Meecham, then, is the descendant of Irish immigrants, but the family's century-long residence in the North with its assumptions of intellectual and moral superiority, coupled with the family's traditional work on trains, which only heightens the sense of rootlessness, had molded Bull Meacham into an anti-Southern Yankee whose actual senses of religion, family, and community are restricted to the globe-trotting military of the USA. Irish primarily in surname origin—Bull reveals no knowledge of an interest in his heritage or its folkways—and indoctrinated into the American myth of success, financial as well as military, equaling the just and the desirable, Bull Meecham is apparently all but incapable of understanding or appreciating the South.

Conroy's vision, however, is not that simplistic. Bull's primary tangible opposition to the South is that he sees it as a place denuded by visions of genteel grandeur. Lillian furthers his hostility with her romanticized distortion of the South. She is saddened that after all the years spent in the South, it still has not "touched" her husband: "the gentility, the courtliness, none of it" (102). Conroy emphasizes Bull's role as destroyer of Southern genteel romanticisms when the Meechams arrive at the house Bull has rented. Lillian declares it reminds her of Tara, and Bull responds, "I remind myself of Rhett Butler. A real ol' stud horse" (61). This intentionally comic statement and his earlier slur on the "Southern gentleman" as a "pansy" combine to reveal that Bull's hostility to Southern culture is because he finds the Anglo-Norman gentleman, the cultural apex for most Southerners, including his wife, to be effeminate. Rhett Butler, evidently, he sees as something else entirely, something worthwhile.

Bull eventually does spend time with a group of ordinary Southerners, and he comes to like them. Feeling "that a Marine commander should establish a good rapport with the civilian population of the local town," Bull begins eating breakfast at Hobie Rawls's grill. Though "it was no easy task for a stranger to become a regular at Hobie's" because the regular customers were also "regulars to the town and their family names were on street signs and monuments," Bull "liked the restaurant immediately" (190). As descendants of historically prominent coastal Southerners, the regulars at Hobie's probably all have Anglo-Norman ancestry, but rather than play Cavalier with its class snobbery, they live average small-town Southern lives. Recognizing this, Bull respects them for their sincerity, for their individualism that is bound inextricably with senses of place and history. The mutual acceptance between the outwardly anti-Southern Yankee marine and the lifelong sons of South Carolina is such that when Bull's plane goes down, the regulars at Hobie's lead the civilian search.

If Bull is something of a southside Chicago-Irish Rhett Butler trampling through the sacred groves of the Anglo-Norman Southern myth, then Joe Varney, the Ravenel base's commanding officer, is his Ashley Wilkes. Bull tells Virgil Hedgepeth, his best friend, "do you know that guy is starting to have an English accent and the nearest he was ever stationed to England was Arlington, Virginia" (86). What Bull despises about Varney is "his aristocratic posturing: The clipped, slightly British pronunciation of words, the carefully manicured nails, the bloodless smile, the natural condescension, the refined air of the aristocrat" (91). After her husband's death, Lillian reveals the origin of the hostility between the two Marines. Joe Varney had wanted to marry her, and he "was transferred thinking I was going to wait for him until the war was over." But in the interval, Lillian met Bull Meecham, and though "he had no idea how to conduct himself at an affair with ladies and gentlemen present. He was pushy and boorish" (527-28), Bull won Lillian away from Varney.

Though Lillian feels the need to promote the Anglo-Norman genteel myth throughout her marriage, she decided to marry not a Southerner attempting to be a mid-twentieth-century embodiment of that myth but an Irish American. In his essay, Conroy suggests that his mother's marriage to his father was a mixing of both "metaphor and geography" and that she chose the Chicago Irish marine to emulate her beloved Scarlett. The same may be said of Lillian Meecham, but there is more than merely life emulating art here. The bond between Lillian and her violent, coarse, decidedly non-genteel husband is too strong to be simply the girlish acting out of a movie fantasy. Though she, like so many white Southerners raised in an aggressively Anglophilic culture, evidently needs the Anglo-Norman myth to reassure herself of the South's nobility and worth, Lillian perhaps sensed that the Joe Varneys are false and certainly intuited that the coarse Bull Meecham was, for all his many faults, the better man.

The novel takes its title from Bull Meecham's family nickname, but its main character and primary focus is Ben, the oldest child. The year covered in the novel is Ben's senior year of high school, and his maturation requires him to understand the father who pushes too hard and in so doing becomes abusive. *The Great Santini* is a *künstlerroman*, a novel in which the protagonist recognizes that his calling is to the pen. Walking home from a Catholic catechism class, Ben asks his sister, "do you think either one of us will ever write, Mary Anne?" (222). Mary Anne is not optimistic, but Lillian has already placed her son on the road to becoming a writer.

In addition to inspiring him with the love of words, Lillian encourages Ben to go fishing with Toomer Smalls, Arrabelle's son who sells fish, crabs, flowers, and honey from a wagon drawn by a mule. "In a way, Ben thought," of Toomer's "wailing summer canticle" he "sounded like a priest chanting during a Mass for the dead" (124). On the night of the junior/senior prom, Lillian tells Ben that she had encouraged him to spend time with Toomer because "he was all the South used to be and all it should still be and all it's never going to be again. So is Arrabelle. You can look into her face and see a most glorious and noble history of pain and even of victory" (500). Spending time in nature with Toomer, whose name evokes the memory of Jean Toomer and his *Cane* (1923), is necessary for Ben to become a chronicler of the contemporary South. On the drive to Atlanta after the funeral, Ben finally makes peace with his father's memory, and this peace will free him to be the Southern son his mother wants and to write about his experiences, to chronicle the contemporary Southern family and its South.

Through Toomer's troubles with Red Pettus, who finally pushes his bullying too far and kills the black man, Ben confronts the inherent injustice of the Jim Crow segregation system—not to the blacks who rape and murder at rates far above those of whites[1] but to the Arrabelles and Toomers. Conroy's next novel, *The Lords of Discipline*, focuses on the young Southerner of Irish ancestry facing social injustice and acting decisively to uncover it and end its terrors. The first-person narrator is Will McLean, whose Gaelic surname with its historical ties to Scotland rather than Ireland again suggests the lack of significant cultural distinction between the two. His story, told from the vantage of many years distance, is set in Charleston, South Carolina, in the middle and late 1960s, centering on the 1966-67 school year, Will's senior year at the Carolina Military Institute, a thinly disguised fictionalization of the Citadel, which is Conroy's alma mater.

Will avows, "I define myself this way: I am the son of Thomas Patrick McLean of Savannah, Georgia" (3). Like Mitchell's O'Hara clan, the McLeans are part of that city's sizeable Irish Catholic community. His mother is from Dahlonega, Georgia, a small Appalachian town most infamous as the center of the gold rush on Cherokee lands that would lead inexorably to the Trail of Tears. Of the South of Broad Street area of Charleston, the home of the city's old, wealthy families, Will reveals, "my flat Irish features often shamed me as I walked in their midst. . . . I bobbed precariously on the immigrant flood; I smelled of Kilkenny, the back seats of station wagons, and the chlorine of YMCA pools" (18). When Will tells his name to Annie Kate Gervais, a South of Broad girl in hiding because her boyfriend, also South of Broad, had dumped her when she got pregnant, she responds, "a Hibernian. The Irish drink too much and they are never serious" (56). Though she eventually will come to despise him for befriending a "shamed" woman unfit for South of Broad society, Annie Kate, in her recognition of Will's kindness and willingness to sacrifice himself for others, says, "'you have a very Irish face . . .' observing me closely" (105). The Bear, Col. Thomas Berrineau, Commandant of Cadets, facetiously refers to Will as "a sloppy shanty Irishman from Georgia" (224-25).

It is Bear who thrusts Will into the situation that will eventually, as he sees it, make a man of him. Tom Pearce, the first black cadet in the Institute's history, has enrolled for the 1966-67 school year. Afraid that some of the cadets might go beyond even the wide parameters of hazing at a military school in order to drive Pearce away, Bear chooses Will, who, though he has never risen beyond the rank of private, is apparently the cadet most respected for his integrity by the commandant, as his "liaison" with Pearce. Bear mentions that The Ten, a secret group believed by many cadets to exist but labeled a myth by the school's Administration, might instigate trouble. Will gives no credence to the stories of The Ten until a plebe named Poteete kills himself. Because he is overweight and he cries whenever he is verbally hazed, Poteete is widely regarded by the cadets as a disgrace to the school, and there is a concerted effort to make him quit. Fearful of his father, the boy refuses to leave the Institute. But one evening, Poteete snaps and plans to commit suicide. He tells Will that his spirit was broken when he was taken off campus by cadets, which is illegal, to "the house" where he was terrorized. Later in the year, Bear tells Will that a "10" was painted on the door of another plebe who mysteriously left school. All of this recalls to Will the story of Bobby Bentley, a plebe in his class who also vanished with rumors of The Ten circulating.

In order to avoid bringing further attacks on the plebe deriving from anger at his having a special protector, Will devises a method of secret communication with Pearce. Whenever he needs to contact McLean, Pearce is to leave a note in the library copy of Oswald Spengler's *The Decline of the West*, which, Will avows, has never been checked out. The only problem with the system is that as a basketball player Will must make road trips. To cover for his absences, he asks his roommates, Tradd St. Croix, a Charleston native, and Mark Santoro and Dante Pignetti, a pair of Northerners, to check the book. At the close of basketball season, a frantic Pearce contacts Will to ask why his last four notes had not been answered. Also, Pearce informs Will, a man had come behind him, ordered him to leave school, and used his finger to draw the number ten on the plebe's back.

The continuing rumors of The Ten induce Will to broach the possibility of the group's existence with Col. Edward T. Reynolds, a professor of English history and the author of the history of the Institute. An obese man, Reynolds "was a quintessential gentleman, courtly in the finest sense, with a troubled, endangered civility rooted in the bruised mythology of the Old South" (273). The people Reynolds, a proudly bigoted man who despises virtually every ethnic and national group in the world, "primarily blamed for the decline of Western civilization and culture was the Irish Catholics" (274). As a historian, Reynolds is "not blind to the faults of the English; a more bloodthirsty, rapacious, and brutal people never existed on this planet." But the English, he feels, have a gift for governing, and it has been left to them "to enforce a system of laws on inferiors like the Irish" (275).[2] Reynolds views Ireland as a land bereft of, among other accomplishments, art, philosophy, and theology, and he considers the Irish to be an absurd people who love freedom yet "lack the mental capacity to comprehend what the essence of freedom truly means" and therefore are "incapable either of self-rule or of accepting the hegemony of their superiors" (276).[3] To convince Will of the sincerity of his bigotries, to make sure that the student does not confuse the jocularity with satire or mere bombast, Reynolds declares, "I absolutely loathe the Irish. . . . I only wish Cromwell had been less lenient in his dealings with these pitiful and contemptible brutes" (354), an honest admission of the longstanding Anglo-Saxon desire to exterminate Celtic culture.

Fearful that the myth of The Ten might be true, Will asks Colonel Reynolds why there was no mention of the group in his history. Acknowledging that in addition to the standard rumors he had attended funerals of two prominent graduates at which the wreath had ten white carnations, there was a cage holding ten white doves, and a $10,000 scholarship gift to the Institute was announced, Reynolds nevertheless affirms that as The Ten's existence could be neither demonstrated conclusively nor disproven, a scholar would not mention it. He does, however, inform Will of a rumor concerning The Ten that Will has yet to hear: It has sworn never to allow a woman or a black man to graduate from the Institute. "'There are times, Mr. McLean,' Reynolds intones, 'when I hope with all my heart that The Ten does exist and . . . that they are true to their ideals'" (285).

As Reynolds has always been scrupulously honest even with his most violently bigoted pronouncements, Will feels no need to doubt his source. Thus, when Reynolds asks Will to meet him after his Palm Sunday service at the prestigious Episcopal church, Will assumes that he is to be reprimanded for thus far failing to earn an A in English history. After Reynolds assures Will that he has no interest in Will's classroom performance—"You are an Irishman and a scoundrel, Mr. McLean, and I cannot expect you to master the sweep and scope of an alien and enemy culture" (354)—he confesses that he had previously misled Will. He had found a written reference to an unnamed secret society, and when delivered to the school's press, his history had featured a chapter on the rumors about The Ten. Each disappeared under mysterious circumstances. Reynolds then declares of The Ten, "I believe they exist and I am afraid of them" (356).

At this point, the reader may begin to sense the dichotomy set up by

Conroy. Reynolds, the suave, well-connected, highly educated Anglo-Norman from the South Carolina low country, is not merely an insufferable bigot; he is also a coward hiding behind the myth of the sophisticated, urbane Cavalier born superior to others by group ancestry. Will McLean, conversely, possesses both the vision and the courage, though he too is terrified at several points, to uncover the plot. In defending his views of the inherent superiority of the English and inferiority of the Irish, Reynolds declares that he is not concerned with birthplace: "I'm talking bloodline. I'm talking about origins. I'm talking about racial patterns that have emerged in groups and have been catalogued and studied for centuries" (276). What Conroy suggests in *The Lords of Discipline* is that if these ethnic traits have survived in the South, then those of the Irish, however humble their socioeconomic origin or current status, are morally preferable to those of the societal mandarin Anglo-Normans for they include courage when outnumbered and outgunned and a tendency to risk everything to fight a recognized injustice, and not merely when they bear the brunt of that injustice.

This contrast between Will and Reynolds, however, is not the extent of Conroy's cultural analysis. For all his verbal abuse, Reynolds is more pitifully ineffectual, like an inactive Jamesian protagonist accepting the way of the world, than he is evil, and it is the nature of evil in man (at least in white men) as it manifested itself during the Civil Rights-era South that is Conroy's primary concern. "The city of Charleston," Will affirms, "in the green feathery modesty of its palms, in the certitude of its style, in the economy and stringency of its lines, and the serenity of its mansions South of Broad Street, is a feast for the human eye" (1). Charleston is simply "the most beautiful city in America" (2). Will comes to know the city through his roommate Tradd St. Croix, scion of a still wealthy and powerful family of Huguenot origins that has long since traded away its French heritage and Calvinism for the genteel Episcopalianism of the Anglo-Norman coastal South. Will is so enamored of the beauty of the St. Croix mansion and gardens and of the city as a whole that he informs Abigail St. Croix, Tradd's mother, "I'm going to mold my life on the St. Croix family" because "I want my whole life to be infected by beauty" (261).

Will's maturation enables him to recognize that "Charleston is a dark city . . . whose covenants and secrets are as powerful and beguiling as its elegance, whose demons dance their alley dances and compose their malign hymns to the side of the moon I cannot see" (1). Tradd St. Croix, like his father before him, is a member of The Ten, and he, with his father's blessing and afterwards his mother's defense, has participated in illegal and immoral activities that have led to two deaths and the near destruction of Will's college career. In his final confrontation with Abigail and Tradd, Will exclaims, "all this beauty around you. This house, your flowers, your fine silver, your antiques, your music, your perfect life. Such beauty, such stunning beauty, but you missed it, Abigail, you missed seeing the corruption . . . that has grown up around you" (489).

The cultural point made by Conroy's fiction is understood more fully by focusing upon the novel as a critique of Charleston by Savannah, Will's hometown and the second city of Southern coastal elegance. Each is a city filled with old mansions, but the cities took differing paths historically in race relations, in no small part, Conroy's fiction suggests, because the Irish came to play a major role in the full cultural life of the latter and not in the former. In the nonfiction novel *Midnight in the Garden of Good and Evil,* journalist John Berendt presents a Savannah native who declares St. Patrick's Day to be a High Holiday for the city. Berendt also notes that, led by mayor Malcolm Maclean, Savannah moved easily into the Civil Rights era, so much so that in 1964 Martin Luther King, Jr. designated it "the most desegregated city in the South" (50, 42). Conroy's fictional member of the Savannah Maclean clan attempts to bring to Charleston, a city that like Professor Reynolds is hostile to toward Celtic heritage, a similar awareness of the self-defeating nature of modern racism, which began with Anglo-Saxon desires to exterminate Celtic cultures if not necessarily all Celtic peoples.[4]

Like *The Great Santini, The Lords of Discipline* is a *kunstlerroman.* When General Durrell, the Institute's president and a member of The Ten, asks Will derisively what he believes his place in school history will be, he responds, "I plan to write that history, sir" (484). His eventual history, the story of his own growth to manhood, necessarily involves a recognition of the evil inherent in the Anglo-Norman South that has cast a net of fear and paranoid suspicion over the Institute, an evil not of blood but of an unquestioning acceptance of a surface beauty that masks violent injustice. Like Thomas Sutpen, Will is enamored of the Anglo-Norman mansion, its pristine grounds, and the power underlying it. But unlike the Faulkner character, Conroy's protagonist is not a tragic hero because he realizes the horrible truth about the Anglo-Norman Southern myth in time to strike a blow against it. The difference is significant, for it suggests that Conroy sees the Southerner of Celtic heritage as the South's moral arbiter, as the white Southerner whose history of being discriminated against first and foremost by the English and then by both

Yankee WASPs and the wealthy Anglo-Norman South will ultimately facilitate his acting decisively to help create a New South of greater racial and ethnic justice.

Moreover, Conroy's work brings Southern literature full circle from William Gilmore Simms. The antebellum Charlestonian could recognize the indispensable role of Celtic immigrants and their descendants to the development and expansion of Southern culture and Simms did parody the Anglo-Norman South, but, perhaps because he was himself anxious to be accepted as an equal among the South-of-Broad Charlestonians, Simms either could not recognize or refused to acknowledge any inherent evil, even serious defect, in its social systems. Conroy, whose first book was published one hundred years after the death of Simms, reveals that evil while acknowledging its attraction. And that attraction, which provides a way to avoid slurs (hillbilly, redneck, cracker, peckerwood, even honky in our own time) on being Southern, or more specifically on being back country Southern, is the catalyst for much of the South's tragic nature. Unlike any Simms character, Will McLean comes to understand that much of the beauty of the Anglo-Norman South was built upon a commerce deriving from the bartering of human beings. Not coincidentally, Tradd St. Croix's father's first name is Commerce.

Conroy does not address the issue, but his linkage of Charleston's Anglo-Norman-Huguenot wealthy elite to mere commerce, to business grubbing, should remind students of American history that the Massachusetts Bay Puritan colony was, in effect, little more than a land speculating company transported in its entirety—directors, stockholders, books—to a new land in which it would be free to mix predestinarianism, a nascent form of laissez-faire capitalism, and its concept of theocracy without accountability to the claims of the past and its traditions. Whether the focus is the Puritan or the Anglo-Norman Southern "gentleman" who defines himself and his world by his possessions, Southern literature provides numerous examinations of the spiritual and moral costs that accompanied the development of the English colonies into the States that united and eventually, with the push of war, centralized into the imperial nation in which we live, using force of arms to remake the world in the image of the Yank. Conroy, like no insignificant number of other Southern writers, has utilized characters of Celtic ancestry to foil Englishness.

Chapter XI

The Phoenix Rising from the Ashes: James Everett Kibler

Increasingly over the past thirty or forty years, it has been easy to pick up novels advertised as Southern literature that are largely indistinguishable from novels produced by and about any other region of these United States. Yes, the novels almost invariably will have been written by someone who resided in the South at some point, and they will have Southern settings. But most of them will read as if the setting does not matter, as if it were easily interchangeable with any suburb in Ohio or Southern California or even Connecticut. These novels are often Southern only superficially; most of these works display senses of history, family, community, morality, and Christianity that are far more redolent of New England, New York, and Hollywood than they are of the South, even today's South. To a small degree, this reflects demographic changes in the South as more non-Southerners move in, many of them dripping with contempt for Southerners and Southern culture, and more native Southerners, including some of pre-Civil War lineage, embrace modern America in all its secularizing international imperialist glory and mad-dash for consumerist heaven.

Ironically, the renaissance of real Southern literature, literature that accurately and unapologetically depicts Southern culture, rather than being merely southern in geography and Yankee WASP Reform in spirit, may have begun with a college professor. It is almost too poetically perfect that James Kibler be a South Carolina native whose academic specialty is William Gilmore Simms, for Kibler then brings us back to the father of Southern literature in a way that is different from, and ultimately more important than, Conroy. Most significant is that Kibler is a native of the Carolina upcountry, of the part of South Carolina dominated by Scots-Irish, and that bastion of conservative Celtic heritage is the source of his creative writing. Kibler's blooming as a significant man of belletristic literature began with his determination to chronicle the history of the family that built the antebellum farmhouse he bought to restore. The resulting work, *Our Fathers' Fields,* won the 1999 Fellowship of Southern Writers Award for Nonfiction.

In some ways, Kibler's book presents a continuation of the New England WASP Puritan versus Cavalier view of American culture. That view falsely sees almost all white Americans before the massive influx of post-Great Famine Irish Catholics as English, with the only divisions being class and religion. It does, however, at least recognize that from the early colonial era whites in the South were significantly different in cultural terms from whites in the North, where slavery was also legal and virtually all American trans-Atlantic slave traders lived. It therefore forces us to acknowledge that the Anglo-Saxon Puritan is alien and preponderantly antithetical to Southern culture. Kibler notes of the Hardys, the family whose ancestral house he restored, "Theirs was not the New England Puritan ideal of John Winthrop's City on a Hill, but instead the Southern dream of a fertile, pleasant valley" (7).

As the Hardy name is Norman and the family holds a pedigree stretching back to the *Magna Carta,* it is natural to associate them and *Our Fathers' Fields* with the WASP Puritan versus Cavalier thesis: The Hardys were epitomes of the Norman Cavalier South besieged by violently reforming Puritan fanatics. But even Kibler, who clearly respects the Hardy ancestry, makes the understated case that the Celtic-Southern thesis explains far more about the South. First, he notes that, as McWhiney and others have documented indisputably for the entire non-coastal South, the Norman-surnamed Hardys were a distinct minority in upcountry South Carolina to the majority of Celtic, mostly Scots-Irish, ancestry (14). Kibler also notes that almost all the other families of distinction in the area, with whom the Hardys socialized, worshiped, and intermarried, were from Celtic lands: Eppes, Caldwell, Maybin, Rogers, Douglass, Beard, Renwick, Lyles, Sims, Glenn. Nor should anyone assume that these families were either ignorant of or hostile to their Celtic ancestry: "Although both John Rogers Sr. and Jr. were said to have 'loved the virgin beauty and freedom of the hills of Carolina, yet their hearts yearned for ole Ireland'" (211).

Ignorance of and hostility to Celtic ancestry grew in the South beginning with Reconstruction and mushrooming in the early twentieth century, as Southern children were indoctrinated with anti-Celtic, pro-Puritan WASP propaganda in government schools. The result, seen today in even many genuinely conservative pro-Southern Presbyterians and Baptists who at least romanticize and defend Anglo-Saxon Puritans as long as they murdered and stole and raped traditional conservative cultures while still devout Calvinists, is that most Southerners of Scots-Irish and Welsh ancestry came to see themselves as Anglo-Saxon if only because they had been trained to equate Protestant with WASP.

Kibler's book helps show how the Puritan versus Cavalier thesis is at best partial.[2] His list of Anglo-Norman traits that defined the Hardy family (14-15) is worlds apart from the traits that both McWhiney and David Hackett Fischer have seen as defining the ethnically pure Anglo-Saxons of southeastern and east central England. If the traits that define the Anglo-Normans of western and northern England, where large numbers of Celtic peoples remained after Anglo-Saxon conquests, are often diametrically opposed to the traits that define the ethnically pure Anglo-Saxons, then the cultural traits that define those English Normans cannot be truly Anglo-Saxon; their "Englishness" must be culturally something that is far from pure Anglo-Saxon. As those traits sound rather French, the natural assumption would be that what makes Normans from the west and north of England culturally different from pure Anglo-Saxons is the French heritage. That is reasonable, especially as most Norman families in England spoke French as their first language to at least the beginning of the fifteenth century.

That, though, merely begs the question, for we then must consider why French traits are often diametrically opposite those of ethnically pure Anglo-Saxons (and all northern Germans). The answer is Gaul. Though the Germanic Franks, who had centuries of economic and cultural contacts with Gauls before ruling the land, conquered and politically unified and gave their name to the language and the nation, and Normans were also Germanic, Gaulish Celtic cultural traits remained predominant in France. That is the reason that the Gaul Vercingetorix is the archetypal French hero and that Charlemagne filled his court with Irish scholars and Irish-trained English scholars. He came to realize that as long as they remained fully culturally Germanic, the Germanic tribes he ruled, such as the Saxons, would not rest until they destroyed French culture. That also is the reason that while Kibler's list of Hardy family Norman traits clashes with cultural traits of the pure Anglo-Saxons (as well as with Prussians and Hessians), it fits rather smoothly and naturally with both French and Irish/Scottish traits.

The main division in Western European culture is between Celtic and Germanic ways and identities (recall that Celtic and Latinate are so closely related linguistically that they are perhaps best seen as one group). England's Puritans, who were Calvinist versions of pristine Anglo-Saxon culture, hated and wished to exterminate the Norman houses in the west and north of England primarily because those Anglo-Normans, like their kin who had become more Irish than the Irish, had adopted much, perhaps most, of the Celtic cultural worldview and its outward characteristics. It is the same reason that virtually all Anglo-Norman families fit easily and naturally into parts of the South in which peoples of Celtic ancestry are the vast majority. It is the same reason that English Puritans saw Scottish and Irish Calvinists (Calvinists who still would be required to *purify* by losing all Celtic cultural traits and identity and to *reform* by becoming culturally Anglo-Saxon—or be destroyed by righteous, progressive WASP Puritans) as fit only for being cannon fodder against Catholics and Stuart adherents. It is the same reason that New England Puritans despised Scots-Irish Presbyterians as inherently inferior by ethnicity. As historian Clyde Wilson has phrased it, it is a Yankee problem that plagues America,[3] and Yankee culture is Anglo-Saxon culture in America: the pure culture of the ethnically pure WASP.

Kibler is aware of these implications and, to his great credit, does not flinch from them. He writes of the Hardy family livestock practices, "These facts place the Hardys within the Celtic tradition of herdsmen as explained by historian Grady McWhiney. Although they were Anglo-Norman rather than Scots-Irish [actually, through mothers, they were approximately half Celtic], their manner of homesteading was analogous to the Celtic" (114). As he eases into his conclusion, Kibler suggests, "Maybe it is a Celtic thing with us, after all, the mythic and archetypal knowledge that sees us through" (392).

Child to the Waters (2002) is Kibler's volume of short fiction. It is dedicated *"To my Connelly kin,"* which is important in light of the significance of Margaret Mitchell's use of Tara, which Alexandra Ripley explores further, and the connection of the Connelly clan to County Meath, in which sits Tara. The volume's title is an intriguing play on lines from the William Butler Yeats poem "The Stolen Child," which concerns the relationships among humans, the fairy world, and art. Kibler's volume obviously is the work of a man steeped in lyric sensibility. In fact, it may be best to refer to it as a series of prose poems that serve the purpose for Southern culture that many Yeats works served for Irish culture in its fight to survive the onslaughts of imperial Anglo-Saxon culture.

Southern literature, when it is worthwhile, is a folklore, folk-culture-based literature. It is built from, and is rooted in, old tales and talking:

Family and community histories told in both verse and prose, mostly informal and unpolished. In addition to a keen awareness of the centrality of land and place, and Southern identity and emphases that are bound to land and place (without which you will have Southern geographic writing but not Southern literature), belletristic Southern literature requires Southern folksong and oral history and discussion of politics and preaching, not necessarily in the works but behind them as trusses. *Child to the Waters* is a fictional presentation of that truth, one that calls for a new generation to take up the mantle that the vast majority of contemporary creative writing and Southern literature professors and editors at publishing companies and literary journals have declared deservedly dead.

The opening paragraph in the prelude is, in both language and philosophy, something that Yeats could have penned: It calls for readers to reject as false "the rules that govern the modern mind, so rigidly shaped by reductive science . . . " The volume's subject is *art,* which (if it is art grounded in the eternal verities and family, land, and history) is a necessary antidote to the modern religions of empirical materialism and economic acquisition that spawn endless Dantean hoarding and wasting. Art is not religion, nor can it replace religion, as was proven by the failed cultural legacy of what I call "high modernists." But art—which does entertain, though not cheaply and superficially—is necessary to a healthy, vigorous culture—certainly to one that is not focused on Mammon. And it is such cultural renewal for the South that Kibler strives to encourage.

"Stories for Christmas, or Willows Like Wands" shows us that art is necessary to "travelers," those who make no permanent home, but it warns that art not connected to place and family (which is the vast majority of art that today is promoted and praised) ultimately will use up the world rather than replenish it. "Fair Grace by the Eddying Pool" presents the power of folksong. "A Perfect Day for Tyger Fish" provides examples of both art deriving from the natural world and the necessity of art and its meanings being passed down in the family. "The Wee One's Alphabet Blocks" declares that the poet is necessary to *dream* the story fully, to see the truth and its significance. "A Knight of the Sheep," with its title that suggests especially medieval Christian culture, concerns daydreaming, art, and eternity, linking them ultimately with Irish culture. The absence of art, which has been replaced by consumerism in our modern become postmodern world, is revealed humorously in "Transistorized Resurrection" to produce inanity and worse.

"Quar" is the tale of furniture-maker Mazen Prysock, whose craft is an art that requires of him such focus that he is seen by the community as "quar": Queer, meaning odd, not like the normal ordinary man who works only to make a living and acquire stuff. In a materialistic society the "normal" man works to consume and satisfy his every fleshly desire. Kibler furthers the theme of the necessity of art by having Prysock and his physically ugly wife produce a beautiful daughter, who sings beautifully to her father's fiddle, which he made. The community, in its limited way, comes to take a type of pride in these "quar" folk. Indeed, Kibler says by contrast, any community that does not welcome and honor such "quar" folk will culturally and spiritually desiccate itself. Most important about this tale in terms of the Celtic-Southern thesis is that the Prycosk daughter, who symbolizes the art that her parents give to the community, art which they require in order to be something more than another mass of cash nexus moderns, is named Deirdre. "Quar" calls readers to recognize that man does not live by bread alone. It also suggests that the Southern art that both best nourishes the Southern soul and best represents its culture will reveal its Celtic sources or cognates. Though the name Mazen Prysock does not sound Irish in the least, when Mazen reproduces, his child, a symbol of Southern art at its most beautiful as her father is a symbol of the Southern artist, is named for one of the great tragic heroines in Irish literature.

As the book's title suggests, Kibler sees the possible reinvigoration of Southern culture as best explained by, and perhaps inextricably linked to, Irish cultural and national survival and renewal. "Singin' Billy, the Song Catcher" is a piece about William Walker, who in 1835 published the widely influential *Southern Harmony,* which is very much the genesis of Southern folk and church music—that of the whites in the Piedmont and Appalachian areas—being collected and distributed, and then determining most of America's popular music forms. Kibler's fiction has young Billy hearing music in all aspects of Southern life: nature—animal and plant and weather and geography—livestock, work, his mother's hum. The storyteller says of Billy's mother's songs, which stirred in him the desire to write and collect the music of his South, "They began in the wet, bright greens of moss-covered mounds on Meath's broad brow and Armagh's hills. They carried the magic of pipes and harps, of jigging reels, and the sidhe—the language of blue crags and Tara's misty far dells" (51).

County Meath, in which sits Tara, the seat of the High Kings of ancient Ireland, is seen as the symbolic cultural and historical center of Ireland. Because of the life and work of St. Patrick, County Armagh (located in today's Northern Ireland statelet) has been seen as the spiritual center of Ireland since the early Middle Ages. All that understood, the meaning of this passage in Kibler's tale should be obvious: The Southern folk and religious music that continues to reach the world and has been instrumental to much belletristic Southern literature derives straight from the cultural, historical, and spiritual heart of Ireland. If that is the case, then any revival of Southern culture must reconnect with those Celtic roots fully. Deny—from ignorance (cultural, familial, or theological ignorance) or greed or fear or lust for Empire: The reason matters not—those Celtic roots, and you participate in the murder of Southern culture as surely as the man who chops the roots or denies life-regenerating water kills the mighty oak.

"The Golden Cup and Bowl" is as important in this regard as "Singin' Billy, the Song Catcher." In it, Kibler presents a stinging picture of the contemporary South while holding out hope. Odell (note the Celtic name) visits the Cullen place (more Irish in the South) and tells a dream. Kibler's story is a Southern version of the Yeats play *Cathleen ni Houlihan,* the single most influential work of literature to inspire early-twentieth-century Irishmen to rise for their culture's survival and for national independence. Odell's dream, which is narrated to Hamp Cullen, is about a poor old woman who comes to his door. Hamp Cullen's name recalls both Wade Hampton, the chief South Carolina Confederate hero, especially to the Scots-Irish upcountry, and the medieval Irish hero Cuchulainn. Hamp Cullen is an impoverished, dispossessed cultural descendant of both the worlds of Wade Hampton and Cuchulainn.

Odell knows the old woman generally but has never talked to her. Odell listens to her, but he does not understand, not even when she tells him that what she requires is passion. When Odell has finished with recalling his dream, Hamp asks his friend what that story means, and Odell honestly replies that he has no idea. Worse, he is ready for a nap. Because the old woman is the personification of the South seeking for any men worthy of serving her, just as Cathleen ni Houlihan is the personification of Ireland raped and impoverished by English conquering and rule (which included laws aimed at cultural genocide), the apathy shown by both Odell and Hamp is damning. It represents the average Southerner of the past forty to fifty years, including those of significant Irish ancestry. Their ignorance is not their fault, not entirely, for they are products of a government school system and popular culture, both of which harbor great animus against Southern culture. But their apathy is their own doing. Once the moment of grace has come, he who rejects demonstrates his worthlessness, and this pair, typical modern era Southerners focused on daily routine and modern conveniences, are too lazy, or perhaps tired and broken, to try to understand. To them, a tale is mere diversion: pleasant, ephemeral, signifying nothing.

The hope is that Rob-Emmet Cullen overhears Odell's tale, and his response is the only way Southern culture will be spared from extermination:

> He pondered on it long and well and riddled and reriddled night and day, year passing into year. With memory's clearer eye, no strange old woman then did he see, but young lady fresh in bloom and walk of queen. And when he grew a man, turned from his father's fields by alien culture's ways, he sought and found this same lost lady's cup, and filled to brim with all his soul and passion up. (171)

The significance is not restricted to one child's acceptance of the old woman's calling. His name is that of Robert Emmet, an Irish nationalist who was executed by British officials in 1803. In the dock, Robert Emmet declared that no man should write his epitaph until "my country takes its place among the nations of the earth." In "The Golden Cup and Bowl," Kibler calls not merely for Southern cultural revival based on its Celtic sources, but also for Southerners to hear the pleas of our Cathleen ni Houlihan.

The most fun story in *Child to the Waters* is "The Revenge of the Great House." Contemporary academia and publishing are revealed in all their anti-cultural, cliché-ridden barbarity. Kibler presents a pure urban editor ("books were his game"—and games are for children and light passing of time) who loves Thoreau and Harriet Beecher Stowe and seems to cringe from any contact with life lived on the land. Those who know the real Thoreau, who is discussed briefly in the tale, will understand that the editor has chosen well.

Bob, Kibler's author and farmhouse-restorer character, sees not merely the editor and his historian sidekick but the whole culture war as spawned by Puritans "in their Mather-created Cities-on-Hills." Bob sees Anglo-Saxon Puritans as men who "had always despised their own nature as men and hated all others for not hating themselves" (94). As befits a tale in such a book, "The Revenge of the Great House" ends with focus brought back to Ireland and to Yeats. In thus doing, Kibler says that we, Southerners and other Americans, have but two basic cultural models, only one of which we may choose. Either we will take the path of Anglo-Saxon Puritanism, which has led inexorably to ever-grasping

Leviathan State cultural barbarity, including the thanatos syndrome Walker Percy sought to analyze, or we will take the path of Celtic culture with its emphases on family, history, religion, and land, bound insuperably in Celtic knots.

One of Kibler's best works is the novel *Walking Toward Home* (2004). It is an Agrarian novel, one in which readers slowly are brought to see a need for a cultural renewal based on families and local communities living close to the land. Unlike the Agrarian novels of Caroline Gordon, Kibler's work does not feature discussions of his characters' ethnic ancestries, but Celtic heritage is central to the novel's moral. *Walking Toward Home* is set in upcountry South Carolina in 2002-03, primarily in Clay Bank, an unincorporated farming community. The traditional world of Southern community and manners, Southern senses of family and history, tenuously survives in the midst of rampant consumerism and adoration of American Democracy as The Last, Best Hope for Mankind (thus as the church outside of which there is no salvation), which produce little, save increasing numbers of T. S. Eliot's Hollow Men and C. S. Lewis's Men Without Chests.

Walking Toward Home is a Christian novel in that the antidote to the moral chaos and cultural decay is presented as traditional, pre-modern Christian belief and practice that envelops the whole life. The Christian vision is not anti-Puritan in the sense of direct rejection of Anglo-Saxon Puritan cultural heritage as being nefarious (which is the case with *Child to the Waters*), but it is anti-puritanical in the sense that Kibler's main character, the autodidact farmer Chauncey Doolittle, recognizes the primacy of non-Calvinist, non-*sola fide,* conservative High Church thinkers such as Dante, Eliot, Lewis, G. K. Chesterton, James Agee, and Flannery O'Connor to both dissection of the malady and application of remedies.

In addition is that Chauncey advocates the rebirth of community rituals tied to seasonal celebrations that historically served to mesh family and church into a community using holidays—whether sanctioned by church or civil government—not primarily for personal pleasure but to ponder both the life cycle, of generations and not merely of an individual, and the Christian mysteries, to reinforce through ritual the defining sense of intergenerational Christian community acting for eternal purposes. Implicit in Kibler's presentation, especially in light of his hostility to Puritans as destroyers of traditional conservative cultures as seen in *Child to the Waters,* is that the Calvinist-Anabaptist drive to "purify" and simplify both church services and community celebrations based on their Low Church *sola fide* exegesis of Scripture, in which anything they failed to see as perspicuously sanctioned in Scripture was damned as pagan that must be destroyed, led not to the reinvigorating of Christian communities that both Calvinist and Anabaptist leaders asserted but to a type of endlessly reforming anti-cultural anti-intellectualism that was necessary for the rise of the Social Gospel and resulting loss of ancient Christian dogmas and for the cultural void in communities and individuals that has been filled with soul-numbing consumerism, faith in the secular State, and insatiable hedonism.

Kibler stakes out the importance of this cultural awareness by titling his second chapter *All Saints Eve.* Chauncey recognizes that it is the thirtieth of October, and his mind searches the significance: "It was in days-long-since-past that the wise ancients felt that on this holy day the line between living and dead was weakened and often sometimes removed, yes, completely erased. It was then that the dead could walk unabashedly next to the living" (32).

All Saints Day on the Christian calendar derives from the pre-Christian Celtic celebration of their New Year,[4] which began with the first of November. Because Celts, like ancient Hebrews, saw the day as beginning at nightfall, the New Year actually began on what those with a Roman sense of calendar saw as the night of October 31. Pre-Christian Celts believed that at each of the seasonal changes, and especially at the New Year, the otherworld creatures, the fairies, were free to walk among men.[5] In Christian times those folk cultural beliefs became invested with an awareness of the Christian belief in a communion of saints across time, of the necessity of living Christians seeing themselves as bound inextricably with the dead saints and the yet to live. As that theology matched perfectly with Celtic familial philosophy (such as that which Scarlett O'Hara realizes), the Christianizing of Celtic New Year was easy and natural. The loss of it, save in the de-Christianized vulgarly materialistic form that we have, and other traditional Christian community rituals and festivities is part and parcel of the cultural, and ultimately spiritual, void that Modern man desperately fills with whatever he fancies will whet his appetite and scratch his itches.

That modern American culture is the antithesis of Celtic culture, Southern culture, traditional Christian culture, and families generally is highlighted by the discussion at Kildee Henderson's country store about Chauncey's having seen a motor home with a bumper sticker reading, "I'M SPENDING MY CHILDREN'S INHERITANCE." Kildee, whose surname is Celtic and the first syllable of whose first name is Gaelic for "church," observes that such retirees are not merely wasting money for one time, "but all the substance of the land for more than just a few, and for more than one isolated time. This spending's for a long, long time, and for more generations than one" (185). Chauncey concludes of what the liberal media has dubbed the Greatest Generation, that which lived through World War II and afterwards fashioned America even more fully to its Welfare State tastes, and its spoiled children, "A perfect and fitting saying for the 'Me Generation,' still just as selfish as they've been all their lives, and they'll never change. Great squanderers they are" (185-86). As the country store, down-home philosophical analysis of one of the major symptoms of the modern malaise-unto-death winds down, Chauncey, "as he frequently did," offers "up a prayer that man be spared the logical consequences of his folly. Then Chauncey had a strange vision of Dante's ninth circle in hell, where traitors to their kin lay half buried in ice, up to the pubic shadow, where the doleful souls were sounding their chattering teeth like storks" (190-91).

Here, Kibler deftly suggests that the hoarders and wasters in the fourth circle of Dante's *Inferno* are, at least in their Modern American versions, equal to the ninth circle treacherous to kin in the magnitude of their sin. Personal greed and childish, boastful self-indulgence, which define much of modern America, are sins against both descendants and ancestors.

The theme of the necessity of community-wide ritual to protect from cultural ravages from without, of ritual linked directly to both families and church, culminates with the novel's closing chapters. Chauncey, after learning the extent of the crass materialism in the area ("Boosterism reigned") and visiting a nearby large town with a college that is simultaneously progressively liberal and reflexively supportive of any American military adventuring, realizes that the actual religious fruit of the Anglo-Saxon Puritan City on the Hill, which acquired near-full control of America's intellectual future, and determining sway over America's spiritual future, with the Union victory in the War Between the States, is modern indifferentism and Unitarian-universalism: "The land flying these thousands of secular flags [the Stars and Stripes, which unlike the Confederate Battle Flag is in no way a Christian symbol] had gone from the Church of Your Choice to the God of Your Choice—poly-theism at best, in keeping with a tolerant, multicultural plan" (230).

After querying why people today "are so hell bent on destruction" (244), Chauncey's active mind recalls that December 13 is St. Lucia's Day, a day to draw the attentions of men to light out of darkness, which is sorely needed in our world. This thought leads him to recall hearing from his grandfather about community Christmas rituals, which have ancient European origins and were largely victims of the culture war waged by the puritanical, that had died during the twentieth century, as the South became more American and less Southern. In participating in the community Christmas ritual, the people

> gave thanks, prayed for a fruitful year, drove the demons back to their dens with loud song and dance, caroled, feasted, loved dearly their neighbours, family, and friends, and hoped for the blessing of peace, among themselves and all men. Death and rebirth were factored in all that they did. . . . Chauncey longed for some such ritual again. He grieved its passing as if the death of one of his close kin. It was sorely needed in these impoverished, antiseptic times, when harsh, brutal forces of darkness ruled the diminished day, and the light seemed wholly to have given up its fight. (257-58)

No ineffective dreamer, no more than he is a passive acceptor of the cash-nexus cultural and spiritual hemlock hawked incessantly as cure-all, Chauncey decides to work to make his dream a reality, to revive old Southern traditions and rituals, and their European antecedents, that will be essential to preserving all that is best about Clay Bank.

And Celtic heritage lies at the heart of Kibler's vision for a Southern community to save itself from being homogenized and consumerized out of cultural existence. One of Chauncey's friends since childhood is Triggerfoot, who is something of a Sut Lovingood character in his community status and ability to puncture the sanctimoniousness and pretensions of the "respectable" class. After Triggerfoot has been cheated and betrayed by the area's boosters for progress and their town-church "he-pillars" and "she-pillars," and then has exacted his revenge, Chauncey thinks, "The world's absurdity could only be expressed by Triggerfoot's own theatre of the absurd" (137-38).

Later, Triggerfoot tells a story to children about area church bells. Each church has bells with a unique sound. First Scots church bells Triggerfoot says "rang true and rang long" (156). The past-tense verb is correct, for the bells of First Scots, which had "strengthened the sons to take up the plough or to measure and mend," had been "melted for shot and ball in defense of the land" during the War Between the States. While other churches that had likewise melted bells for the defense of their country acquired new bells, "No new bell would then ring from its [First Scots] towers again till the freedom of land, till the curse of invader would lift with his leaving and the people be free. Other churches had restored their bells; but First Scots had made its decree" (157).

Triggerfoot doubles his cultural meaning with the continuation of the tale. Finnuala, who "had no protector, for her father and brothers died in the hard war," is widow before her marriage in that her betrothed also dies in the attempt to repel the invader. She is wooed by a "usurping suitor [who] was the best of the invaders," but Finnuala will be as true as First Scots. Her virtue is rewarded with her being turned into a swan:

> It is said she's to wander until old First Scots' bells ring out again and on her mystic far lake, she can hear their fair sound. And that can only be when the curse of the land then is lifted, and it is free. Then she will be transformed back to her own, released, and the same faithful soldier in grey will be released from his bonds to bend face to her own in a kiss. (159-60)

In having Triggerfoot repeat, in Southern form, an Irish tale concerned with that land's resistance to military conquering and cultural and religious "reform" leading to cultural genocide perpetrated by the WASP conquerors, Kibler emphasizes the central cultural point he made in *Child to the Waters*: Southern folklore and history derive straight from Celtic sources and thus any worthwhile survival of Southern culture will require the reinvigorating and honoring of Celtic heritage.

To get back home, Kibler's novel says, Southerners are best served walking, rather than mindlessly careening at ungodly speeds that prevent any awareness of what is passed and what threatens, and they must reacquire much of what culturally has been slowly lost over the past century and a half, especially community rituals that bind family and church, past and future with the present. And indispensable to it all is the knowledge that First Scots has remained faithful and culturally points the way home, praying for the release of Finnuala that can only come when Southerners themselves are equally faithful and are bound in a communion of saints from which they will draw strength and renew meaning.

Conclusion

The term *metanarrative* is one prominent in recent literary theory. It signifies the overarching story that includes and largely defines all other stories told by a culture. The South, I believe, has a pair of metanarratives: Christianity[1] and what Faulkner saw as the Culloden to Carolina to Yoknapatawpha migration, the flight, the never fully ending exile, of culturally Celtic peoples west away from persecution toward a place where they might carve out for themselves freedom: a place to serve as home. These twined metanarratives are symbolized most vividly in the Southern rendition of the St. Andrew's Cross flag: the Confederate battle flag that is both a Christian and a Celtic symbol.[2]

That Scotland's flag is the basis of the most prominent and most reviled symbol of Southern culture points to Scottish history as a locus of Southern history. The wars by the English to conquer the Scots and force them to accept rule from London and eventual extinction of their culture and identity, the last of which ended at Culloden, were battles in a long cultural war, for imperial hegemony on the English side and for national freedom on the Scottish side, that crossed the Atlantic with immigrants and in America came to blows with the War Between the States. The shooting wars have not been replayed, but the cultural wars to obliterate, or at least make permanently subservient, the Celtic cultures continue.

That raises an interesting issue, one that I do not believe has been treated by any historian and should be examined in depth. I assert that the American Revolution was an unwieldy alliance composed of two groups with long-term goals that were incompatible. The Northern part of the Revolution was an attempt to further the Puritan part of English culture, which is culturally and theologically anti-traditional with a strong bent toward democratic tyranny and imperialism. The Southern

253

part of the American Revolution was a conservative revolution that could be said to promote an American version of the political and cultural philosophy expressed in the Scottish *Declaration of Arbroath* (1320). That the descendants of those Southerners would embrace their own form of the St. Andrew's Cross as they were fighting for freedom from a government dominated by Puritan values, a government culturally and economically injurious to them, is a mystery only to those who see the world exclusively through the eyes of English culture and refuse to consider Celtic culture and history.

In his fictionalized personification of the rise of the late antebellum South's "ruling class," W. J. Cash provides an outline of the life not of a descendant of Anglo-Normans given immense land grants by the Crown but of an Irish immigrant, once almost penniless, in the "Carolina upcountry." When he dies in 1854, the local newspaper eulogizes him as "a noble specimen of the chivalry at its best" (17). The language reveals that Cash saw the antebellum South as a land attempting to convince itself that, regardless of its Celtic heritage (which Cash derided in a different way from his derision of noble Anglo-Norman pretensions), it was the last refuge of Anglo-Norman Cavalier lords and ladies and, perhaps more important, that its "successful" people were embodiments of the Cavalier legacy even if they were Celtic immigrants. Most scholars of the South, including those who emphasize Anglo-Saxon over Anglo-Norman, have accepted this myth-making as reality, but Southern novelists from the antebellum Old South to the contemporary New South, and most especially the novelists of the Southern Renaissance who used their distance from the epic events of nineteenth-century history to create a literature that recovered the origins of both the best of Southern culture and of its tragedy, modern novelists utilizing family histories and community folklore, have looked behind the Cavalier myth to discover the indispensable role of Celtic immigrants and their descendants to Southern culture.

Simms suggests that the vital Southern folklore that will lead to a great literature is Irish, and Caruthers implies that the preferable Southern nobility, a natural nobility that proves itself by appealing neither to a list of genealogy and hereditary titles and privileges nor to a monarch but by exploring and settling and creating new communities, derives from Scottish immigrants, not from the Anglo-Norman first families of Virginia. Faulkner, Gordon, and Mitchell all link a lack of knowledge of, respect for, or adherence to, the Celtic heritage to Southern tragedy. Young believes all that is best in Southern culture springs from the extended Southern family of Celtic heritage, and Tate suggests that the Anglo-Norman Tidewater sense of family had to fail, perhaps lie in crushed defeat like John Langton or Major Buchan, before the writers of his generation, the Southern Renaissance generation, could create the great literature Simms predicted. Gordon and O'Connor connote that the fervent Christianity that has shaped and defined so much of the culture of the non-coastal South since the early antebellum national era is culturally Irish in origin. Glasgow and Conroy both see Celtic heritage and especially identity as the matrix of individual success and the hope of a better, more just future. Conroy's use of The Ten, the exclusive Skull and Bones-like club that exists only to maintain privileges and benefits for one group that are denied to other groups, a club utterly contemptuous of individual achievements and merit among whites of Celtic ancestry as well as violently hostile toward blacks, provides a fictional analogy to the Cavalier myth; though it is widely pronounced a myth, many not only believe but choose to act upon the myth and thereby harm both individuals and the whole of Southern society.

Peter Beresford Ellis, a novelist and non-academic writer of historical, cultural, and linguistic works on Celtic peoples and their folkways, postulates that the standard popular and scholarly presentations of Celts are similar to those of American Indians. "The real history of the American Indian," he writes, "did not have an impact on popular consciousness until Dee Brown wrote *Bury My Heart at Wounded Knee: An Indian History of the American West* (1970). For the Celts, such an act of rehabilitation in history has yet to be made" (*Celtic Empire* 205). Though the first half of his assertion is overstated—the widespread, if romantically skewed, American fascination with American Indian resistance leaders and the moral costs of expanding the United States into "new" Indian territories began long before 1970—Ellis is correct in the second half of his claim.

King Arthur is a prime example. No one, not even the most fervid yet racist white admirer, claims Sequoyah, Tecumseh, Cochise, or Chief Joseph as a WASP, but Arthur, whether purely mythological or based on a real leader or series of leaders, is the British Celtic resistance warrior against the Saxon barbarians who has been lifted from his Celtic origins. The process began with Henry II, but it was powered toward completion by Edward I who based his claim of overlordship of both Wales and Scotland on Arthur's rule of the whole island as recorded in Geoffrey of Monmouth's *History of the Kings of Britain*: "Arthur, the champion of the

British people [Celts] against the heathen English invaders, had been received into the Valhalla of his enemies and was henceforth an English worthy" (Ashe 110). This fictional denial of Celtic heritage by requisitioning it by and for a people claiming, and presumed by many others, to be more worthy of its glories reached its apex in T. H. White's *The Once and Future King* (1958), the basis of the wildly popular musical *Camelot* that was so important to 1960s American liberal mythology. White's novels form a fictional tetralogy in which Arthur is presented as the quintessential romanticized Anglo-Norman lord served by loyal Saxons (longsuffering in their being mistreated by the Norman overlords) and troubled by inherently contemptible and peace-savaging Celts.[3]

As long as scholars, editors, journalists, classroom teachers, and entertainment promoters allow such cultural usurpation to pass unquestioned as representative of the truth, there can be no "act of rehabilitation" for Celtic peoples; they will remain fixed in popular stereotypes as either the dead though perhaps romanticized past's incarnations, frustrating or cutely lovable anachronisms, or Irish Republican Army or Ulster Defense Association and Ulster Freedom Fighter terrorists. The descendants of Celtic immigrants to the South, suffering indirectly from these bigotries against Celtic peoples and their cultural contributions, have had their importance minimized and often denied, but a portion of it may be found in Southern novels, if only readers will recognize and acknowledge the cultural significance, and not toss Celtic identity under an indiscriminate pile of "British" or European culture.

Eugene Genovese takes W. E. B. Du Bois to task for doing that. Though Du Bois's focus is not specifically Celtic heritage, it is directly applicable to the Celtic-Southern thesis because of what McWhiney defines as a Celtic sense of leisure that came to predominate among white Southerners (8, 41-50, 72-74, 78-79). In attempting to explain through comparison the concepts of time and work ethic held by the black slaves, Du Bois lumps all whites into a category of Anglo-Germanic Protestant work ethic, which Genovese labels a "costly error" because of the obvious non Anglo-Germanic work and leisure sensibilities of the Irish, Italians, and Slavs, to name but three white groups obviously non-WASP (*Roll* 311).

Also important is that scholars in their efforts to promote multiculturalism not ignore Celtic peoples and their cultural contributions to the United States because of the headlong trend to emphasize non-European peoples. William Piersen does just this in *Black Legacy*. Recognizing that most characteristics of white Southern folkways are not English in origin, Piersen automatically assumes they must be African (73, 161, 172). He declares:

> So much of the southern code of honor would have made sense to Africans: autocratic rule, the need for revenge,[4] the value of hospitality and gregariousness, the prestige given to eloquent oration, and the respect for ancestors. All of these values were far more common in West Africa than in nearby New England. (170)

The Celtic-Southern thesis also distinguishes that these cultural traits (with the exception of autocratic rule, which is no small part of English political heritage and a primary reason for the American Revolution) are not central to English culture, but its proponents recognize the obvious fact that not all whites in the United States are Anglo-Saxon. Each of these Southern cultural characteristics that Piersen, guided by the Afrocentrism that theoretically tells him he need consider nothing save African origins, claims must be African simply because they are not English are now, and always have been, essential to Celtic culture as distinguishing and defining traits. The hundreds of thousands of Celtic immigrants in the colonial South and their millions of nineteenth-century descendants did not need to "borrow" these cultural traits from any group of people. They were, to use a maxim found in all Celtic languages and common in the hill South, bred in the bone of Celtic peoples for more than two millennia before becoming Southern.

Piersen's book, which includes promotions of hereditary class elitism and of negative stereotypes of non-genteel, non-wealthy white Southerners (x, xii, 74-75, 97, 163), provides an excellent example of the ludicrous ends scholars often come to when ignoring Celtic heritage in their attempts to explain Southern culture. In a note, Piersen declares of the Rebel yell, "it seems likely that the rousing yell that made southern soldiers distinctive was influenced by the African-American tradition of black dancers bellowing a bloodcurdling yell before leaping to the center of a dance ring" (248). Piersen does not explain how a vocal part of black group dancing was transformed into a battle cry and a hunting and sports yell used all but exclusively by, perhaps long before, the middle of the nineteenth century and since by white Southerners, most especially by hill Southerners, whose lands were populated with the fewest black slaves in the South and were the havens for the mass of Celtic immigrants and their descendants. Had Piersen bothered to look at Celtic culture rather than to allow his Anglocentrism to truss his Afrocentrism, he would have found what Grady McWhiney and Perry

Jamieson found. In discussing Celtic warfare from the Greco-Roman era to Culloden, they affirm, "note that yelling—indeed a special kind of yelling—was an intrinsic part of the Celtic charge" (190), and this type of yelling also was ritualized into Celtic hunting and herding (191). And the two are directly linked in Celtic culture. Nora Chadwick finds that Celtic "warfare had characteristics more akin to those of hunting than to true wars of aggression or defense" (131).[5]

Finally, if Piersen were familiar with modern Irish literature he would know that no Southern novelist has written a better definition of the Celtic-Rebel yell than has Irishman Liam O'Flaherty. *The Informer* is the story of Gypo Nolan, a simple brute of an Irish revolutionist who turns informer. When he believes he is in the clear, Nolan sings forth in the urban streets he finds alien: "It was that peculiar yell that mountaineers will utter in the west of Ireland, when the fair is over in the district town and night is falling, as they issue from the public-houses, bareheaded and wild-eyed, dragging their snorting and shivering mares after them by the halter. . . . It was like a challenge to mortal combat issued to all and sundry" (75).

Especially important, I think, are the theoretical implications of Piersen's work. In revealing that Margaret Mitchell's fictional world is, like that of the more widely academically praised Southern writers of her generation, "a brawling, democratic, egalitarian frontier" (246) that assaults the perception of contented, static social classes in the Lost Cause of the Last True Nobles Romance notions of the Thomas Nelson Page generation, Darden Asbury Pyron says that the plantation romancers had set their stories chiefly in the coastal (non-Celtic) South and "had chronicled the lives of aristocrats identified with vast estates, slavery, and the knightly order of *noblesse oblige*" (241). Those of the Southern Renaissance generation would swallow no such chivalric fairy tales, and they declared open war on what they saw as unrealistic, paralyzing nonsense: "In New Orleans, youthful heretics launched their 'little magazine,' *The Double Dealer*, in 1921 with broadsides against 'the storied realm of dreams, lassitude, pleasure, chivalry and the Nigger.'" The following year, the Fugitive poets in Nashville initiated their own rebellion with proclamations against "the high-caste Brahmins of the Old South" and the "treacly lamentations of the old school" (242-43).

The Double Dealer's "broadside against the storied realm of . . . the Nigger" is far from a white supremacist diatribe; it is an attack on the plantation romance, which required house slaves, and some drivers or head field slaves, of noble, royal African ancestry. These black slaves often saw themselves as inherently culturally superior to the masses of whites, whom they pitied as "poor white trash," and they respectfully served their somewhat more inherently genteel and noble masters in an alliance of born nobles over the rabble and as the most visible means by which the wealthy, large-plantation owners demonstrated their superiority, their hegemony. As noted by Eugene Genovese and countless scholars of Celtic heritage, the first English prejudice and the most deeply held is not against blacks but against Celts, and wealthy WASPs using black servants to keep Celts down in their place may be a cultural meaning of the literary use of "noble" black slaves. The young Thomas Sutpen may be the unparalleled fictional example of the non-wealthy white Southerner learning that his lack of money and social position will mean that not only rich whites but those blacks who serve them, and perhaps serve with rather than under if only in their own minds, will see him as beneath notice or concern, unworthy not merely of entering the front door but of knocking upon it, that many, perhaps most, black people will look upon and treat him with a contempt curiously like that of many whites looking upon and treating blacks.

Hugh Thomas notes that until the advent of the eighteenth century, black slaves in North America were largely domestic workers. At that time, tobacco growers in Virginia and rice and indigo growers in the southern part of Carolina began emulating the sugar plantations of the Caribbean and South America. One economic result of their moves to expand chattel slavery and to work larger masses of land with slave labor was "the small independent farmer began to fail, as had happened in Barbados and elsewhere in the West Indies when those colonies had embarked on growing sugar" (258). Understood in this light, the plantation romance seems little more than an elaborate, and perhaps psychologically necessary, fictional justification of the system as one both protecting blacks from whites too ignoble to appreciate them and explaining why the masses of whites did not own slaves, why they were not "noble" and therefore could not reasonably expect to be treated as full equals by the owners of large plantations and numbers of slaves, by the elite.[6]

Advanced to our own time, this alliance may be seen in the academic left, in white liberals, Marxists, feminists, and postmodernists allied with Afrocentrists in sweeping contemptuous attacks against the non-genteel white South. In his book, postmodernist Michael Kreyling claims that there is no Southern tradition, no Southern culture, except for white racism, "the main body of the culture" (176). He labels both Stark Young and Margaret Mitchell "propagandists" and dismisses all opposition to Richard Wright's predictable negative portrayal of white characters as some form of racist attitude, either violent or unaware and insensitive, as proof of ubiquitous white Southern racism, and declares that advocates of "cracker culture," which he sees not as Celtic but as the entire non-wealthy white South, are one with Theodore Bilbo, are racists (180). In direct contrast to David Harvey's definition of the ideal postmodernist stance, Kreyling refuses to allow white Southerners "to speak for themselves, in their own voice," refuses to accept their voices "as authentic and legitimate." Rather, Kreyling, playing Herbert Marcuse's "repressive tolerance," attempts to silence the voices of the white South by declaring that those voices are racist; therefore those voices should not be heard but condemnations of them, by those like Kreyling, should be heard endlessly.

Except for the desire to serve their owners and masters, which he has transformed into a different kind of black longsuffering of less "noble" whites who control them, Piersen's race and cultural views of the South are remarkably similar to those of the Thomas Nelson Page school, certainly to its excesses. The South once possessed, according to each school, a genetically determined minority nobility superior to other people, and that nobility of race, birth, bloodlines, political alliance, and tradition, not of individual deed and accomplishment, was wronged by ignorant and envious masses of the culturally unwashed (culturally Celtic) whites, which was the South's tragedy. The meaning cannot be overemphasized today: What passes for contemporary black-focused civil rights is bound inextricably with ethnic-racial hatred for the white South and desire to exterminate its culture.

Eugene Genovese is but one of countless scholars over the past three decades to have contributed to an indirect denial of the importance of studying Celtic cultural contributions to the South. Genovese rightly declares of studies of black and white Southern tendencies toward physical and verbal fervor in worship, "The frequently heard assertion that the blacks merely copied the whites may be left aside as unworthy of discussion." Hard on the heels of this automatic rejection of culturally biased simplicity, Genovese declares, "If one must choose between the two separate tendencies, the view of Dr. DuBois, according to which the style of the poor whites had been a 'plain copy' of the blacks, easily holds the field" (*Roll* 239). As Marilyn Westerkamp's detailed study reveals, emotional worship characterized by shouts, swoons, and loud singing and bodily movements considered outrageous to most English observers, as well as to most Irish Catholics and Irish Episcopalians, were typical of Revival Irish Protestantism a full century before the Wesley-Whitefield reform of Episcopalianism, which was the spur of mass Christianizing of black slaves in North America, which would be necessary for black worship styles to become incorporated into the worship patterns of whites. At a minimum, tens of thousands of culturally Celtic peoples brought this type of worship with them to the American continent by the middle of the eighteenth century and therefore had no need to copy blacks or any other ethnic group. For Genovese, who does state that "black and white responses reinforced each other" (*Roll* 239), to give preference to Du Bois's claim is not merely to honor black African cultural tradition transferred from pantheist paganism to Christianity; it is to take no stock of the heritage of Celtic peoples and their contributions to the development of Southern culture.

Much of the academy's dismissive, at times almost hysterical, hostility toward the Celtic-Southern thesis is due to its inherent refutation both of the chivalric myth of the Thomas Nelson Page school, with its Brahminic elite by birth, landed property ownership, and title (which allows so-inclined specialists to feel that their area is one defined by proper lofty social station), and of the Marxist myth so dear to the American academy of the last four decades, with its elite of the dictatorship of the alienated intelligentsia [the "elite" according to Herbert Marcuse] standing in lieu of the proletariot.[7] This link between two theoretical systems many of us would assume to be standing at loggerhead extremes of the spectrum is not original with me. Barbara Tuchman, for example, writes, "Chivalry was regarded as a universal order of all Christian knights, a trans-national class moved by a single ideal, much as Marxism later regarded all workers of the world" (65).

The Celtic-Southern thesis is Burkean conservative both in its honoring appreciation for local historical and cultural traditions, including those of peoples legally denied any semblance of equality, like the Irish Catholics and black slaves being shipped across the Atlantic of Burke's era, a folk cultural respect that activist trans-nationalism must dilute to be successful, and in its stressing individual merit rather than group merit, group rewarding and punishing. It remains to be seen whether the contemporary academy will become truly tolerant of such non-leftist approaches.[8] After recounting his researches into the attempts of academics, journalists, and editors to silence those who would acknowledge the almost countless plagiarisms of Martin Luther King, Jr., Theodore Pappas concludes: "No more evidence is needed; the verdict is in: nothing is more intolerant of a diversity of opinion than a 'liberal' society touting the virtues of tolerance and diversity" (175).[9]

At this point, it may be helpful to reemphasize that the proponents of the Celtic-Southern thesis, as well as the many proponents of studies of Irish Catholics and their cultural contributions to the United States, have no record of making claims of Celtic cultural connections that are demonstrably false. There is, for example, no Celtic-Southern thesis supporter who suggests that FDR really was a Southerner of Welsh ancestry, nor has a Nora Chadwick claimed that ancient Greek philosophy and artistic motifs were stolen from Celts. However, in *Long Day's Journey Into Night* (1955), Eugene O'Neill presents drunken Irish American actor James Tyrone as having convinced himself that Shakespeare was Irish Catholic.[10] Such falsification, sometimes deeply and even violently believed, to protect the wounded spirits of people belonging to groups long derided and persecuted can be expected.

The problem becomes serious when such beliefs are not derided but instead are defended and ultimately promoted in the name of group education and self-esteem. *Mary Lefkowitz's Not Out of Africa: How Afrocentrism Became an Excuse to Teach Myth as History* (1996) details the falsification of classical history and cultural studies by Afrocentrists, most of them teaching at American universities, to claim that Socrates was black and an Egyptian Master Mason; Moses was an initiate into black Masonic Mysteries from which he stole most of the Pentateuch; Aristotle stole his philosophy from the library at Alexandria and Democritus copied his philosophy from books stolen from Egypt by Anaxarchus though the library was built after Aristotle's death by Greeks and Democritus died years before Alexander's invasion, facts unimportant to Afrocentrists and their apologists; the likely fictional Aesop (described in ancient accounts as having a dark complexion and a flat nose and deriving from Asia Minor) was a black man if for no other reason than his status as slave; Cleopatra was black (which claim Lefkowitz traces through the footnotes of Afrocentric texts to find cited in a *Ripley's Believe It or Not*); the ancient Egyptians (automatically assumed to have been black Africans) invented flying; Hannibal, regardless of the Phoenician origins of Carthage, was not a Semite but was black because the city was located on the continent of Africa; and a massive white conspiracy hides all these "facts" from the world. Lefkowitz concludes that this pro-black, "civil rights"-promoting faux scholarship is racialist, mere race-promoting, and therefore damning other races, "fictive history of the kind developed to serve the Third Reich" (50).

Lefkowitz, using as her basis for analogy a hypothetical course to teach the ancient Jewish claim that Plato learned his philosophy from Moses to help a conquered and persecuted group feel better about itself, says that many American universities have concluded that "it does not matter whether what is taught is true, or is supported by warranted evidence, because a diverse point of view, with a laudable social goal, has been presented" (163). Discussing Clayborne Carson's attempts to excuse Martin Luther King, Jr.'s plagiarisms, Theodore Pappas says, "Such statements, in essence, say the end justifies the means, that if one steals for the right reason—whatever 'right' might mean—then the vice is excusable if not sanctionable and commendable" (56). If for no other reason than limited resources, every such class taught or book or article published that falsifies history for contemporary political goals or alliances means something else must be omitted, perhaps something that will demonstrate the errors of those predicated upon false and bigoted premises to promote particular social and political and non-white racial goals deemed laudable by today's hegemonic academic left. The diverse point of view that would recognize significant Celtic cultural contributions to the South is not seen by the powers in academia as a laudable social goal, and therefore its validity carries little weight, particularly when it is attacked by promoters of social goals deemed laudable; that allows Afrocentrists and Anglocentrists alike to claim with near impunity that their preferred groups of study made all the significant contributions to the development of Southern culture.

No such charges of attempted falsification and cultural usurpation as those proven by Lefkowitz, and many others, may be raised against either the Lawrence McCaffreys and Charles Fannings trying to study Irish Catholic contributions to America, principally Northern urban areas, or the Grady McWhineys and Forrest McDonalds trying to study the contributions of Celtic immigrants and their descendants in the South. Even with official MLA scholars DiPietro and Ifkovic erroneously claiming that Celtic immigrants came to the United States from Germany, no scholar of Celtic culture has declared Mozart and Beethoven, Kant and Hegel, Goethe and Mann as Celts. If anything, each of the two primary scholarly groups studying Celtic heritage in America is too clannish to care much for the other and, as befits people spending time immersed in Celtic heritage, too proud of Celtic differences from the accepted modern Western European, increasingly Germanic defined, patterns to make false claims of them, or any other peoples, for Celts. Their stand is that culturally Celtic peoples came to

America among the earliest settlers and in significant numbers and like all groups brought their unique folkways—folkways and cultural contributions that did not die upon reaching American shores and in some cases thrived. The former cannot be denied due to copious immigration records, but most academics and journalists continue to deny the latter, just as many once denied the relevance of recognizing and studying Native American, sub-Saharan African, and Jewish cultural survivals in and contributions to these United States.

Regardless of whether scholars finally acknowledge in course offerings and general textbooks the Celtic contributions to American culture, the impact of Celtic heritage on and in the South will continue to be explored in Southern literature. Ernest J. Gaines has a white character acknowledge that the Irish language lies at the heart of Southern culture, but Alex Haley goes further. In *Queen* (1993), he reveals that there is an indispensable Irish-Southern element in his own ancestry: His grandmother Queen Haley was half Jackson, her grandfather Jackson having been born and raised in Ireland. A defining part of the Alex Haley story, perhaps one equal to the Kunta Kinte legacy, began in Ireland. Haley's role as epic fictional author of the African American search for roots makes his paternal, part-Irish heritage, and his maternal part-Tom Lea "cracker" heritage, symbolically significant: It suggests that Celtic heritage may be an important, if minority, component in much of the best of African American culture in the South.

John Ehle's *The Winter People* (1981), set in the North Carolina Smoky Mountains, presents Philadelphia-born Wayland Jackson, a clock maker, a craftsman whose work marks time and therefore the connections to and responsibilities toward both past and future, who stumbles into the life he was meant to lead. The novel's chief conflict concerns the hostility between the Wrights, who see themselves as the more civilized, and the Campbells. William Wright always has used a Campbell servant, which "appeared to please him immensely" (37), but orders his children to have nothing to do with any Campbell, a family he believes capable of any and all horrors.

The quick, vicious Campbell feud many readers may expect when Cole Campbell is killed around Wright land never materializes. Instead, the Campbells investigate slowly and carefully, and within three days come to all the correct conclusions and then accept something other than at least one Wright life to pay for the Campbell life taken. The reader sees the Campbells not as mindlessly bloodthirsty but as justly stern, sees Young Wright as more unsettled and irresponsible than any

Campbell, and sees Gudger Wright, who allowed the freezing Cole to die, as more vicious than any Campbell save Skeet, whose behavior gets him banished by his uncle. At the novel's conclusion, it is Drury Campbell, the wrongly maligned clan chieftain, who goes to the Wrights' store and initiates peace, giving more than he receives, even though he then holds all the advantage and desires nothing from the Wrights. The Campbells, the most Celtic of these mountain clans, when not treated as backward, unthinking creatures who must be forced into line, when treated with honor, prove to be magnanimous. The novel concludes with mountain clans expanded and Wayland Jackson, bearing a prominent Scottish Lowland name, among his people, the first people among whom he has felt at home.

William Wright muses upon the cultural traits of the various mountain families but seems uncertain of his own ethnic origin. Ehle provides the answer in *The Land Breakers* (1964), his novel tracing the earliest white settlement in the mountains south of Watauga. Mooney Wright, who moves from Pennsylvania indentured servitude south and west and eventually into the Smokies in 1779, had been born and raised in Ulster, "a land settled by the Scots, so they were Scots, really, and were called Scotch-Irish" (3).

Appalachian feuding is also the subject of Annabel Thomas's *Blood Feud* (1998). The novel, however, is set not in a Southern state but in a part of Little Dixie, in fictional Colerain County "in the Appalachian mountains of southeastern Ohio" (1). The families at war with one another for almost a century are the Clemmers and the Kilkinnys. The Kilkinneys, the first syllable of whose name is Gaelic for "church," "came of Scotch-Irish stock and, while they were opposed to slavery, they bridled at government laying down rules as to what a man could or couldn't keep on his own land" (8). For the anti-slavery Kilkinnys, support for the Confederacy certainly was not to expand or even preserve chattel slavery; it was a stand against a centralized government expanding its powers into the daily and economic lives of citizens. The war, the origin of the feud, guarantees that the Kilkinnys will lose virtually everything they own. "Truth to tell," says Winnie Clemmer, the novel's first person narrator, "the Kilkinnys had started out at a disadvantage. During the war, union troops heading south laid waste most of their farms, ran off their cows, and stole their horses and mules" (8). The Kilkinnys, then, stand not merely for the many peoples of the lower midwest whose principal cultural ancestry is Celtic but also for the mass of white Southerners of Celtic ancestry, non-slave owners who were the political and economic victims of the scorched earth Union war effort and the waving of the bloody flag of the Union following the War.

The persecutions and hatreds directed to the Kilkinnys are not exclusively due to their having supported local democracy and states' rights, including the right to secede, against the increasing centralization of Federal government power. Charlotte Clemmer, Winnie's aunt, "was clan historian. So far, she'd traced the Clemmer family back to Anglo-Saxons who'd routed the Celts, the Kilkinnys' forebears, out of England and chased them up into Scotland and over into Wales and Ireland" (60). The Clemmers despise and oppress the Kilkinnys because they are Celtic, and then slur them, the fair-skinned and often dark-haired Kilkinnys, as mixed race, Gypsys, Indians, Mexicans, and even Africans, because they are not Anglo-Saxon (18). The Clemmer-hounding of the Kilkinnys proceeds in each generation from the 1860s until the beginning of World War II. The full economic exploitation of white Southerners by victorious Union supporters is played out against the Kilkinnys by the Clemmers. First, the Clemmers use government taxes and their control of banks to acquire Kilkinny farmland (9). Then, they use the coal mine as source of kingly wealth to build various Clemmer-owned businesses while the Kilkinnys who work the mines suffer black lung, the loss of virtually all they earn to the Clemmer Company Store, and finally the deaths of dozens when the mine collapses due to inadequate safety measures (26-28, 61). Finally, the Clemmers agree with Charlotte that a Kilkinny-free valley is in their best interest and begin a denial of any employment, which they expect will result in Kilkinnys losing their meager land holdings, under which the Clemmers hope to find minerals to sell to the federal government planning for its entry into the war in Europe (74, 129).

It is important that the heads of the two feuding families be compared. John Kilkinny, whose wife was murdered when Clemmers burned down the Kilkinny church, is a deeply Christian leader of his clan. His potter's shack is the center of the Kilkinny community, a place where Kilkinnys see that one of their own can create and earn a living without dependency upon being given a menial job by a Clemmer or the government controlled by Clemmers and their allies. Equally important, the potter's shack is the gathering spot where Kilkinnys tell stories and play mountain music, a music so powerful that the young Winnie tells John, "They make such a sweet music . . . that if I didn't know them to be devils, I'd take them for angels" (56). In a sermon, John sums up the basic differences between the Clemmer sense of family, with its emphasis upon possession and exclusion by a combination of Anglo-Saxon identity and wealth, and that of the Kilkinnys, in which the Celtic emphasis upon the individual's actions and abilities predominate: "I know it ain't where I live nor what I own nor who my kin is tells me my worth. It's what I do shows who I am" (86). Not long before he is murdered, John says of his hopes for a more just future, "I mean a change in the way men live together, not jest a change in who bosses and who gets bossed" (140).

Charlotte Clemmer recognizes that John Kilkinny is the key to breaking irrevocably Kilkinny staying power and lectures the Clemmer church to go after the potter. "'A clan without its chief,' she says, 'is easy to beat. If we can break the hold he and his sons have on the rest of the family, we can rout the lot of them'" (78). Charlotte evicts John from his shack, hoping that will end the Kilkinny sense of independence. As vicious as Charlotte is, her twin Cap, Winnie's father, is worse. In contrast to John Kilkinny, Cap is an atheist who uses the organization of church to effect his terrorist goals, which include his having been the one who burned the Kilkinny church and murdered John's wife (131). Cap sets up the final round of deaths by torturing a Clemmer, the new preacher. Fergus Kilkinny, John's son and the leader of the Kilkinnys who strike at Clemmer economic targets, wears a Confederate jacket, one that he loses in flight from Clemmer authorities. "'He'd lost his Confederate jacket somewhere,' Winnie says, 'and made a sorry sight with only tatters to cover him'" (138). The man who tars Clemmer preacher Parker T. Law wears Fergus's Confederate jacket, and Winnie recognizes the man as her father (151-52). Cap is aware that prejudices against the South, the Confederacy, and unapologetic culturally Celtic peoples means that his disguise will work to increase hatred of Kilkinnys. Cap's final horrors are the castration and lynching of Fergus and the cutting off of the tongue of Davy Kilkinny (178-79, 183), the boy not only loved by Winnie but also the singer whose tales keep alive the memories of the Kilkinny heritage as Celts and as Confederates unwilling to be silent slaves of Clemmer Anglo-Saxon, Union "justice." Destroy the folk and family histories and identities, which is done best by destroying those who know them, Cap intuits, and you most easily make the victims of government supported ethnic-regional hatred utterly defenseless.

Blood Feud opens and closes with references to the medieval Irish tale "The Pursuit of Diarmuid and Grainne." That guarantees that the reader lacking biases will focus upon the Irish origins of the Kilkinnys. Equally important, I think, to the fact that this novel links the persecution of Celtic-origin Southerners with a hatred of the Confederacy and perhaps all of white Southern culture is that it also may be seen as an

American comment on the English-government-created statelet of Northern Ireland.

First, the Clemmers refer to themselves as a "clan," which suggests either that they too have a Celtic origin or that they are also culturally hill Southern, which is culturally Celtic. Second, Coleraine is a city in Northern Ireland important to the Ulster Protestant sense of superiority, a city near the Giant's Causeway, which legend says was created by Finn MacCumaill to reach his rival Finn Gall in Scotland. Third, the novel's framing tale is one in which a thoroughly Celtic man, Finn MacCumaill, chases relentlessly to the death another thoroughly Celtic man. Thomas may be using Appalachian feuding not merely to reveal the historical, political origins of Southern feuding and the vicious prejudices against Southerners and lower midwesterners of Celtic heritage but also to comment on Northern Ireland, a land in which two "clans" fight to the death, the one claiming to be Anglo-Saxon and therefore superior and inherently correct and reaping benefits from fighting for a Union that in return has guaranteed its hegemony over the defeated; the other refusing to be defeated or to accept inferior status, its folkways, its arts, surviving in the face of generations of centralized government attempts to obliterate them. As Winnie discovers, the Clemmers, beyond the feud, are in origin basically the same people as the Kilkinnys, only the Clemmers have become so bound in a political identity of ethnic exclusion and superiority, one that is essentially false ethnically but once believed and acted upon for generations becomes true in practice, that they have become as cold to the touch as their mausoleum. The Clemmers, who allow no singing in their church, are spiritually and artistically, as Davy tells Winnie, "dead as lead." The Kilkinnys, the unabashed Scots-Irish, the unapologetic Celts, in contrast are "all of us alive and kicking" (81).

More important than Ehle's undercutting of Appalachian feuding stereotypes and perhaps equal to the importance of Thomas's presentation of Celtic heritage as the reason for hatred of and discrimination against hill Southerners is that Cormac McCarthy, born fully into Catholic Irish America and raised in East Tennessee, portrays the development of his art as culturally Celtic. *Suttree* (1979) is a picaresque in which the protagonist absorbs the folkways and lifestyles of the poorer people of the Knoxville area and then flees the city armed with the knowledge and sensibilities to write. The movement from idle wanderer to astute observer begins for Cornelius (and the Roman name derived from the Latin cognate of the Celtic Horn of Plenty is significant, perhaps suggesting an absorption of Celtic culture by others, as well as the strong similarities between Celtic and early Latin cultures that is evidenced linguistically) Suttree when he heads to the Smokies in late October, the end of the Celtic year and the beginning of renewal. Like an ancient student of Druids, he meshes into the world of nature, which all but kills him, and sees leprechauns and understands his place in creation:

> He looked at a world of incredible loveliness. Old distaff Celt's blood in some back chamber of his brain moved him to discourse with the birches, with the oaks. A cool green fire kept breaking in the woods and he could hear the footsteps of the dead. Everything had fallen from him. He scarce could tell where his being ended or the world began nor did he care. (286)

Suttree's vision, like that of the feverish Scarlett O'Hara, the teachings of Hugh McGehee, and the shamed frustration of the young Thomas Sutpen, links him to Celtic generations past and present. He is the Celtic *gealt,* the madman whose insanity allows him to see and comprehend truths the sane are able to ignore; he is a Southern Mad Sweeney Astray.

Vereen Bell, whose book was the first published on McCarthy's works, sums up the American academy's failures to recognize and appreciate Celtic heritage. He notes the significance of Mother She, whom he labels a "geechee witch," perhaps using "geechee" loosely for black, to Suttree's wanderings, but he fails to note that which a modicum of Yeats knowledge would provide: that "she" and "shee" are common Anglicizations of the Gaelic *si* (*sidhe* in medieval Irish, which is a spelling often used by Yeats), fairy, and that banshee is the English spelling of Gaelic for fairy woman, that the banshee wail foretells death. A reasonable conclusion, perhaps especially in light of Alex Haley's *Queen,* is that McCarthy through Mother She suggests that Celtic folkways and magic have become at least as much a part of Southern black culture as black folkways have influenced white Southerners. In this case, Mother She, helping oversee the death of his old self, is aiding Suttree in his recovering of his Irishness.

Of greater significance is that Bell, who without considering Celtic parallels labels the "tone and values" of McCarthy's treatment of man, nature, and transitoriness as "of distant Anglo-Saxon origin" (10), glosses McCarthy's use of the phrase "beyond the Pale":

> In fifteenth century Ireland beyond the pale meant outside the jurisdiction of the English monarch—hence, to the English and in fact,

unadministered and uncivilized. As the idea has relevance to
McCarthy's fiction, it refers not simply to the stubbornly unsocialized
east Tennessee mountain people about whom he writes but also to the
environment they inhabit, which is altogether unhuman. (11)

For many people today to fathom the extent of Bell's anti-Celtic bigotries, his wording would need first to be understood as if it applied to
black people. Let us say that "beyond the Pale" is a term that developed
out of English colonialism not in Ireland but in West Africa. I daresay
that the near universal response to Bell's declaration that "beyond the
Pale" meant outside the grip of the English Governor "hence, to the
English and *in fact . . . uncivilized*" and his use of the phrase "stubbornly unsocialized" to label the people of the Gold Coast would be to descry
his simplistic imperialism if not his racism. And that response would be
correct. Should not peoples of Celtic heritage in Europe and the South
receive an equal consideration?

Finally, Pat Conroy is not the only contemporary Southern novelist to
utilize a contrast between Anglo-Norman and Celtic Souths. Lee Smith's
Oral History (1983) is a novel about contemporary recoverings of
Southern heritage. A college student is encouraged by her oral history
professor to investigate the Virginia mountain heritage of her mother.
"All her life," Smith writes of Jennifer, "she looked down on her real
mother's family the way she was taught by her father and her stepmoth-
er" (16). The novel's central tale is a contrast between meddling, wealthy
eastern Virginians, symbolized by Richard Burlage, and the poor mountain people, symbolized by Dory Cantrell, the woman Richard seduces
and leaves pregnant. His flight from responsibility is an image not only
of the snobbery of the Anglo-Norman South but also of the costly
dressed, spiritually flaccid, epicene Cavalier fleeing in terror from the
fecundity of Celtic culture, an assumed impoverished culture from which
he parasitically creates a reputation. In addition to sneaking back to take
furtive photographs of the area, funded by the Works Progress
Administration and hidden symbolically by a "new English scarf,"
Burlage in old age writes his memoirs, which are published *"to universal if somewhat limited acclaim, by the LSU Press"* (285). Burlage, then,
is not merely an emblem of the formally educated, financially comfort-
able Anglo-Norman South; he also represents the complicity of the academy and its presses in this continuing bigotry against the Celtic South,
the cultural heart of which is the hill South.

Caroline Gordon also uses the surname Cantrell. Near the conclusion
of *Aleck Maury, Sportsman* (1934), Sally and Steve take the aging angler

to the Caney Fork River in Warren County, Tennessee, where they are hosted by Bill Cantrell and his family. As he and his family leave, Steve, who is presented in this novel as a more cold, clinical academic than he is in *The Strange Children,* calls the Cantrells a "nice family. . . . More like a French family than American. The way they all work together and everything so-so" (284). His academic training allows him to recognize the Norman etymology of the surname from the Old French diminutive of singer. The "logical" Steve, ignoring the facts that the Cantrells are inappreciably different from most of their neighbors and the Normans long had been recognized as becoming "more Irish than the Irish" whenever in the midst of Celts, declares the Cantrell folkways to be French apparently because they are quite different from the American ways. This is particularly relevant when we focus on Steve as a fictional representation of Allen Tate the Agrarian, because the Vanderbilt Agrarians distinguished between Southern and American cultures and ways. The scholar Steve assumes, despite the facts that there is no history of any French settlement in the hill South beyond a few isolated individuals and the only measurable French cultural survival in the South was in southern Louisiana, that the Old French origin of the name Cantrell must mean the folkways of those bearing the name are French, hence the difference from the American ways. This intricate and yet superficial assessing of Southern cultural patterns has dominated Southern studies and denied much of the South's Celtic cultural heritage, especially when the characteristics are positive.

Smith reveals the principle cultural origins of Southerners, certainly hill Southerners, bearing the surname Cantrell. Though it is a name Norman in origin, the first of Dory's ancestors to arrive in the Virginia Appalachians was Charles Vance Cantrell, an Irish native who proclaimed his Irishness "at one time" (28-29), a hint that he learned not to boast of a heritage dismissed as inherently inferior in Anglophilic America. In using a non-Irish surname to represent the Celtic origins of Appalachian culture, Smith, like many before her, suggests the validity of Normans becoming more Irish than the Irish, and in doing so she connotes fictionally why name analyses inevitably undercount culturally Celtic peoples in the South. More important, through Jennifer, who, rather interestingly, marries a non-Southern academic and remains so ashamed of her hill heritage—its raw history, and earthy stories perhaps as much as its poverty, the sum banging with harsh reality and common sense against the sheltered walls of the ivory tower—that she never returns to visit the Cantrells, Smith challenges us to move beyond our attraction to the glitter of Anglo-Norman "nobility" and recognize the power and the beauty of the Southern folk culture, and the belletristic literature that derives from it, that is Celtic in origin.

Notes

Preface

1. This is, I believe, an especially important point, for one of the general characteristics of modernism is a disdain for the past, a denial that the past is particularly relevant to the present. That attitude may be seen in the fiction of Hemingway. But Hemingway's modernist peers from Celtic America, Faulkner and O'Neill, knew that history is ever present and to attempt to dismiss it is at best an adolescent rebellion. This is an example of Celtic heritage surviving even as descendants of Celts make use of artistic and scholarly accomplishments and techniques that are in the main antithetical to the basics of Celtic heritage.

2. That most of these English novelists have had a wide audience among Southerners since antebellum times is no more an indication that the white South is purely, even predominately, English in cultural heritage than is the similar popularity of classical literature an indication that white Southerners are even in significant minority descendants of Greeks and Romans.

3. This is the same attitude that facilitates the continued false teaching that English is the oldest written vernacular literature in the non-Mediterranean European world and *Beowulf,* which was lost and only rediscovered in the early modern era and left zero trace of influence in subsequent English or any other literature, is the supreme, perhaps exclusive, epic of northern Europe. But literature in Irish is at least a century older than Anglo-Saxon literature. "Written literature in Irish," Proinsias MacCana reveals, "can be traced back to the late sixth century, and the orthographic system that made it possible was probably devised about the middle of the century" (*Early* I 1).

4. After years of looking through college catalogs and talking to both

professors and students, I have no reticence in stating that for every one class offered across the nation on Irish American literature or history or politics, there will be thirty, perhaps forty or even fifty, offered on African American literature or history or politics. Considering that Americans of Irish ancestry, which includes those of Protestant as well as Catholic background and belief, are perhaps 50 percent more than the number of African Americans, the disparity is even greater. I suggest that it reflects at best a deep-seated ignorance and resulting indifference and at worst a deep-seated ethnic contempt that masks itself by pointing to its support for courses and books that promote non-white, non-Christian cultures.

5. Sometime after I placed the first of my Celtic-Southern thesis articles online in 2001, a reader sent an email telling me about an English teacher of his who had presented "The Streets of Laredo" as a perfect example of Southern racism, for to her the song obviously had been written by someone black and obviously reflected African musical culture because it is so mournful, yet white Southerners refused to acknowledge that they were celebrating African culture in loving the song. I submit that such glaring cultural ignorance and thorough hostility to white Southerners and their European ancestors define the contemporary academic world.

6. In a 1979 BBC interview, Alexander Solzhenitsyn said that liberal Western academic culture is apologetic toward Marxism because it is based on the same materialist philosophical assumptions and that common ideological origin leads to the academy refusing to accept research that is significantly anti-Marxist (172-74). The Nobel laureate affirmed great hope, however, for the United States, "where there are many untapped, unawakened forces quite unlike those which operate on the surface of newspaper, intellectual, and metropolitan life" (175). I suggest that the Celtic-Southern thesis is one such important scholarly approach.

7. Fernandez-Morera notes that peer review can and does both prevent sound scholarship that is anti-leftist from being published and "can and does weed *in* unsound, cranky, and even fraudulent research not only in the 'softer' realms of the humanities and social sciences but even, though less often, in the case of the 'hard' sciences" (175). His assertion was proven correct the very year of his book's publication. New York University Physicist Alan Sokal published in the spring/summer issue of *Social Text*, one of the most "prestigious" journals evangelizing postmodernism, an article titled "Transgressing the Boundaries: Towards a Transformative Hermeneutics of Quantum Gravity." Sokal, who

describes himself as left of center and who worked with the Sandinistas, outlines and defends his trap in "A Physicist Experiments With Cultural Studies" (*Lingua Franca: The Review of Academic Life.* May/June 1996: 62-64). His original article was filled with absurdities such as calls for a feminist "liberatory" science and an "emancipatory mathematics," the pair helping to produce a teaching of science and mathematics freed of the dogma of facts and "enriched by incorporating the insights of the feminist, queer, multiculturalist, and ecological critiques," and a claim that even quantum gravity "has profound *political* implications." But the article was accepted by the postmodernist review, Sokal believes, because it "flattered the editors' ideological preconceptions." Likewise, I submit, much sound, even important scholarship that flies in the face of those ideological preconceptions of Marxists and postmodernists is not allowed publication by the current peer review process.

8. Solzhenitsyn was writing before speech restrictions became fashionable and common on American college campuses. Alan Charles Kors and Harvey Silverglate write of the codes, which restrict the possibility of many if not most non-leftist approaches being aired widely in college classrooms and presses, "on college campuses the drive for speech codes, for double standards in their applications, for the mechanisms of indoctrination in their rationales, and for the disciplinary systems to enforce their strictures, comes from the Left" (67). That fact is particularly important to this subject because the white South, certainly when linked to devout Christian belief and practice, has long been the favorite whipping boy of the American left.

Introduction

1. An example is Richard Schickel's review of the film *A Family Thing* in *Time*. The opening sentence reads: "Not since *In the Heat of the Night* has a good ole cracker had a culture shock like the one Earl Pilcher Jr. (Robert Duvall) receives in *A Family Thing*" (April 8, 1996: 77). As has been recognized at least since the Nazi era, the widespread, particularly public, use of epithets against an ethnic, religious, or class group serves the purpose of dehumanizing and therefore demonizing the members of that group, which serves as a justification for whatever is done to harm members of that group. More important than Schickel's film review is Thomas Sowell's presentation of a string of slurs made by various leaders of liberal movements in their eras against the poor and certain ethnic groups who are assumed to be, like the "class" Kulaks in the early Soviet Union, the reason for all failures of the policies advocated

by the self-anointed prophets of progress and the new justice. Most significant to students of Southern culture is Sowell's quoting of a letter from future literary critic Edmund Wilson, a darling of the northeastern liberal establishment at least until his generation came to be denigrated by the "new left" that came of age in the wake of 1950s McCarthyism. Speaking of his service in the first World War, Wilson declares, "I should be insincere to make it appear that the deaths of this 'poor white trash' of the South and the rest made me feel half so bitter as the mere conscription or enlistment of any of my friends" (*Vision* 122). These words of Wilson, a predictable anti-Southern liberal who took great delight in condemning the Southern racism against blacks he managed to find ubiquitous while imagining no prejudices in himself, or perhaps seeing them as fully justified, reflect the deep-seated bigotries against the South, particularly against non-wealthy white Southerners, that Campbell discusses.

2. Again, the reader should recall Marxist and postmodern denials of truth and exhortations to discover and use effective strategies, to use "any means necessary" to achieve the stated goals. The inevitable end result of such a mind set is a double standard, many of which are examined by Alan Charles Kors and Harvey Silverglate. The ACLU's Morton Halperin, discussing a case defending a California State University-Northridge student journalist who had been suspended for writing an editorial defending a UCLA student suspended for printing an editorial cartoon opposing affirmative action, "Spoke truths that academics still do not want to hear. Conservative students and opinions, he said, were the victims of bias at American campuses: 'There is a double standard, and it's a troubling matter.' 'There are no cases,' he observed, 'where universities discipline students for views or opinions of the left, or for racist comments against whites'" (181).

3. Bultman appears to be completely sincere in this call for affirmative action "justice" based on historic prejudices. Of course, the vast majority of the *rednecks* likely would prefer that no one be given official government preferences based on race rather than that they also be given such preferences. Anyone who has spent time discussing politics with *rednecks* will know that they tend to ken in their guts from common sense, if not in studied intellectual terms, what Dario Fernandez-Morera notes: "A recent book published by the openly Marxist International Publishers, for example, points out the need for still more affirmative action as 'the best path to more democracy now, on a path to socialism'" (78). Perhaps that is the reason English and American socialists, or economic democrats as many now prefer to be labeled, continue to slur the group.

4. Campbell's essentially liberal views on most political, social, and theological issues may be seen in his 1988 Peachtree Press novel *The Convention: A Parable.* Using a futuristic and renamed Southern Baptist Convention fight for the presidency of the denomination, Campbell examines the hardball politics of churches dealing with issues imposed on them from the secular world. All of what he writes would be acceptable to the majority of liberals except that his Baptist liberals, who call themselves moderates, all seem to use the *redneck* slur to designate non-wealthy white Southerners and prejudge non-wealthy white Southerners as racists.

5. Reed, most often comically, comments on the Ulster Irish heritage of the white South throughout the volume, most notably in the final essay, "A Letter to My Great-Grandfather," in which he weaves through family and regional history and heritage as a prelude to confessing that his son is engaged to an Ulster Catholic.

6. I am not, in using this quote, suggesting that Irish culture is immutable. Peoples of all ethnic backgrounds and cultures may adopt the values and mores of other cultures, eventually becoming pristine examples of the new culture. For example, other the past half-century or more, many Catholic Irish Americans have assimilated in most ways to Yankee WASP culture. David Hackett Fischer provides John F. Kennedy as an example of assimilation by immigrant families into one of the four main American regional cultures. While Kennedy certainly maintained many aspects of Irish family and Catholic religious culture, "he was also a New Englander [a culture founded by ethnically pure Anglo-Saxons] in his education, associations, prejudices, dress ways and even his speech ways" (872). If that is true of John F. Kennedy, and I agree with Hackett's assessment, then imagine how much less culturally Irish and more culturally Yankee (in one form or another) Irish Americans born twenty or more years after JFK were likely to be, when immigration from Ireland had been cut drastically and many Irish Americans had negligible contact with Ireland or native Irish immigrants to America.

Cahill's point is fully valid as long as it is understood to mean that the Irish, as with all other peoples, have cultural traits that are resistant to change and will flourish whenever able. Individuals of Irish ancestry may change their cultural values and identity (say, act and talk and think like Anglo-Saxons in order to be allowed to rise off the cellar floor in a world run by and for Anglo-Saxon cultural proclivities), but Irish culture will remain the same.

7. Scots-Irish is a problematic term. In American historiography, it

has been used traditionally to refer to Presbyterian and other non-Episcopalian Protestants from Ireland, almost all of whom were from the northern Ulster province, and most of whom were descended from Scottish colonists planted on confiscated Irish Catholic lands to serve as a Protestant buffer for the crown. I would prefer to use a term that describes these people more accurately, but Irish Fundamentalist Protestants is too cumbersome, and few Americans understand the term Dissenter. In addition, the Episcopalian Church of Ireland, not the Presbyterian Church, was the largest Protestant denomination in nineteenth-century Ireland (Akenson, *Irish* 28), and to emphasize Scottish Presbyterian heritage eases the automatic dismissal made by too many scholars, journalists, and politicians of the Episcopalian Irish from being culturally and nationally Irish. My primary objection to the term Scots-Irish is that it is too often and easily associated with people from Ireland who somehow magically are not supposed to be Irish, and therefore not Celtic culturally.

Chapter I

1. The words "Britain" and "British" are examples of the semantic difficulty faced by any scholar or general reader, especially an Anglophone, attempting to uncover the cultural contributions of Celtic peoples. Though they are widely used interchangeably with "England" and "English," they derive not from English language and culture but from the Cymric, or Welsh, word "Prydein," which in its lenited form is "Brydein." "Prydein" is a Celtic name for the island home of a Celtic people, who, interestingly, are not acknowledged as natives by the Germanic invaders, but labeled "Wealh," originally meaning "foreigner" and later signifying "slave" or "serf" as well as the Celtic natives of the island (Sweet 201). Just as the English convinced themselves that they, not those they plundered, were natives, they eventually usurped both the Celtic name for the island and the mythological Celtic resistance leader: King Arthur. In unquestioningly accepting these usurpations, scholars blind themselves to the Celtic cultural origins that often underlie modern Anglophonic folk cultures.

2. The scholarly consensus for some time has been that the Celtic language family, though a verb first language family like Hebrew, is closest to the Italic family, so much so that "some linguists have postulated a common Italo-Celtic origin for both" (Cunliffe 21).

3. Ellis's *The Cornish Language and Its Literature* (London: Kegan Paul, 1974) remains one of the most important studies of the language of

Kernow, which to the English is Cornwall, literally Kern or Corn foreigners or slaves.

4. Thomas Sowell discusses several emigrant cultures that survived intact for centuries though surrounded by a majority population. One of particular interest to Sowell is the Germans that settled in Russia's Black Sea and Volga regions in the eighteenth century, who remained thoroughly German in folkways though they supported Russia against Germany unequivocally during World War I. Only Soviet Marxist persecution of the Germans for their economic and intellectual successes and their general opposition to forced collectivization turned them against Russia politically, yet they never became culturally Russian (*Race* 59, 124). Political support for a particular nation, even over a long stretch of time, does not equal folk culture, and folk culture may survive though resented and persecuted.

5. Joshua Whatmough represents scholars who use the label "Celtic" only in the linguistic sense. In *The Dialects of Ancient Gaul* (Cambridge: Harvard UP, 1970), he declares, "the term Keltic . . . applies properly to language and language only" (15). The use of such a declaration to attack the Celtic-Southern thesis is misguided. First, Whatmough is a linguist, and that is his interest. He declares "Celtic" to be a linguistic term; he does not declare that the linguistic Celts do not possess a distinctive folk culture, nor does he deny that such a folk culture might survive after the extinction of the broad use of Celtic languages and become incorporated into the determining cultural characteristics of certain Anglophones and Francophones. Second, if scholars accept Whatmough's usage and apply it to other linguistic groups, there could be no discussion of Anglo-Saxon cultural traits after the Norman Invasion, for the term could only signify the language of *Beowulf.* The most significant flaw in Whatmough's view is that it can be used as support for those who see culture as essentially static, which means that the moment significant changes occur in a given culture it no longer exists. Cultures grow and change and adapt, or they die. Throughout this work, I will use "Celtic" to refer to folk cultural characteristics and ethnic heritage and identity.

6. Oddly, Powell (whose surname is P-Celtic) also writes that the term *Celtic* is "misapplied" in the modern world to "all manner of things to do with 'Folk Life'" (15). That he could recognize that Celtic heritage is primarily in folk culture and not restricted to linguistics and then emphasize the survival of Celtic heritage across at least eighteen centuries, various conquests, and differing geographies and finally suggest those

traits magically evaporated with the beginning of the modern United Kingdom may speak chiefly for Powell's desire for UK stable union.

7. Grady McWhiney's *Cracker Culture* features numerous examples of "racist" slurs against white Southern ways that sound as if the term "Irish" has been omitted and replaced by "Southern."

8. Bernal apparently misses a key meaning in his discussion. His intent is to suggest that "Eurocentric racism" has blinded people to seeing that the Pelasgians were non-white, which would mean that the major original foundation of Greek culture would be non-Indo-European. But his analogy fails miserably, for it is backward. English Imperial status combined with insufficient studies of language and folklore patterns may have led these nineteenth-century scholars to conclude the Celts were not European culturally, which, for some people in the era would have served as a justification for English dominion over them, but the fact is that Celts are pristinely Indo-European. If Bernal's analogy holds, the Pelasgians were a European group conquered by another, which means that rather than these conflicts indicating that Europeans have claimed for their own that which derived elsewhere, the pattern has been for Europeans to deny that certain Europeans are in fact culturally European. In other words, Bernal has it backwards: A kind of tribalism by the conquering to justify itself has led Europeans to deny the European culture of those conquered. This means that rather than having a history of making false claims for itself, European culture has a tendency to disparage part of itself and ultimately to allow others to claim for themselves that which is European. And contempt for Celtic peoples and culture is central to that process of European self-denigration and self-destruction.

9. That Bernal's familial heritage apparently includes both Irish Catholics and Presbyterians in no way lessens the fact of his slurs on all things Celtic in his mad rush to promote his theory of Egypto-Levantine origins of all Greek, and ultimately Western European, high culture. The need to include Scotland especially in his diatribe may be due partly to the importance of Scottish regiments to the British Army in the nineteenth century, but I suspect there may be more to the matter than that. Jean Markale, whose work on Celtic culture features speculative claims and analyses that are questionable, does note correctly that until at least the end of the nineteenth century the alleged barbaric whipping boy of European education was not the African but the Celt: "Fettered by the cliches of our schooldays, by statements like 'The Gauls lived in huts' we tend to believe that the Romans brought civilization to Western Europe

when all they ever did was to adapt the civilization of others to their own needs. Just as Rome owed an immense debt to Greek civilization, so the Roman Empire took from the Gauls. . . . Centuries of official culture based on an unthinking and arbitrary belief in 'Greco-Roman' models have blinded us to the basic fact that Western Europe is the legacy of the Celts." If this statement is essentially true, and though overstated (the language suggests Celts alone are responsible) I believe it is, then the Afro and/or Levantine-centrists must, in order to make their case, not merely allege the ancient Greeks either borrowed or stole all their culture from the East but also that the peoples of northern and western Europe, particularly Celts, were culturally insignificant. For if Celts are recognized as having provided major cultural foundations for what would develop into Western Civilization then all claims of Greek or Roman theft of alleged racially superior non-European cultures are blunted if not rendered irrelevant, regardless of the lack of truth in the charge.

10. The reader interested in additional studies should consult four works. Barry Cunliffe's *The Ancient Celts* is the most inclusive archaeological based study of ancient Celtic civilization, and his list of further reading is exhaustive. Nora Chadwick's *The Celts* is the most concisely informative work on Celtic culture and history. *The Celtic Connection,* edited by Glanville Price, provides overviews of the ancient Celts and of the literatures of the six Celtic languages to survive into the modern world. Peter Berresford Ellis's *The Celtic Empire: The First Millennium of Celtic History, 1000 BC-51 AD,* the title of which comes from the Roman historian Livy, is a discussion of the roles played by Celtic peoples in the development of Western heritage, much of the work relating little known information such as Celts sacking both Delphi and Rome and massive Celtic mercenary work for the Carthaginians and the Ptolemaic Egyptians. The concluding chapter of Ellis's work is essential for those inclined to view all scholarship advocating Celtic folk cultural survivals as another Ossian fabrication. Ellis, contemptuous of those who romanticize a Celtic "never-never world," reveals the lack of foundation for the two theories upholding the delusional Celto-centric view promulgated by a handful of cranks: that the Etruscan language is Celtic, and the Etruscan Celts were largely responsible for Roman civilization, and that Celts migrated across the Atlantic and determined Algonquian American Indian language.

11. That is a continuing pattern that marks a major flaw in American academia. If no English source is found, then the assumption is that the source is non-white or perhaps development on American soil with no

lineage. Such a simplistically biased approach guarantees that scholars cannot recognize Celtic cultural contributions because they refuse to consider them possible and end the search among European cultures as soon as English possibilities are ruled out or unlikely.

12. Donald Akenson likewise recognizes that this widespread religious bigotry hinders the study of Ireland and the emigrant Irish, and he stresses the Irish Catholic contributions to its perpetuation (*Small* 134).

13. In *Scottish Clans and Tartans*, Ian Grimble notes that the desire to de-Celticize surnames, which was for political reasons and did not reflect any loss of Celtic folkways, was strong even in twelfth-century Scotland, which had been overrun by Norman warlords. Of the surname More (also spelled Moore and in Scotland Muir), one common in both Ireland and Scotland and derived from the Gaelic word for "big" or "great," Grimble reveals, "when Donald, son of Michael More in the wholly Gaelic [speaking] province of the Lennox, rendered homage, his name was written Dovenal le fiz Michel More de Levenaghes" (219).

14. In a note, Akenson calls the Celtic-Southern thesis "a fascinating scholarly byway" attempting "to break out of the narrow national categories in immigration-cultural studies" (318). He approves of this scholarship because he recognizes that it undercuts long unchallenged notions centered on ethnic and religious prejudices.

15. There are those who claim that studies of ports of origin of immigrants into the United States should provide the final word on the folk cultures of immigrants. Thomas Sowell has summed up the problems with that approach. "For example, if one counts all the people who immigrated from Russia as Russians, then many [cultural] Germans, Poles, and other non-Russian peoples will be statistically transformed into Russians and any conclusions derived from such statistics will be correspondingly invalid" (256). That, for example, Ronald Reagan's ancestors made a brief stop in England and left from there for America does not lessen the fact that they were culturally Irish.

16. A weakness with this military argument is that McWhiney and Jamison fail to take into account the long history of Celts, especially when faced with overwhelming odds or almost certain defeat or after defeat, fighting what we now label guerilla warfare, sorties by small groups that then hide from their pursuers to regroup and strike again.

17. There were exceptions, of course. What is most interesting is that most of the few vociferously anti-Catholic and anti-Irish immigrant antebellum Southerners also were Unionist during the Civil War, such as Tennessee's Parson Brownlow.

18. Mitchel seems to have believed that the Anglo-Saxon propensity for perpetual war to conquer and administer the globe allegedly for perpetual peace guaranteed both cultural liberalism and cultural and moral decay, leading to eventual inward collapse.

19. I do not want the reader to assume either that Kolchin plays down the role of slavery in the "crisis" or that I have misread him. In his rejection of the general thesis that antebellum Northern Americans and Southerners were virtually identical, Kolchin declares that slavery was all important: "an increasing number of historians (including the author of this book) believe that those who have played down Southern distinctiveness have seriously understated the impact of slavery on the antebellum South" (171). The problem with Kolchin's view is that it is false to the complexity of cultural origins and transmissions. As Flannery O'Connor has written, "An identity is not made from what passes, from slavery or from segregation, but from those qualities that endure because they are related to truth" (861). If Kolchin's theoretical analysis were correct, obliterating the economic structure—chattel slavery—would have made North and South almost exactly alike in folkways, which is the point made by Louis Rubin: "If southern sectional identity were dependent on slavery, then the loss of the war and the end of slavery should have destroyed that identity" (*American* 4). The differences between antebellum North and South were not merely more complex than chattel slavery but were predicated at least in significant part by white ethnic differences summed up by the Celtic-Southern thesis. That is why the end of neither slavery nor legal race discrimination in the South ended Southern culture as predicted by many whose views on culture were clouded by basic Marxist concepts.

20. This loose grouping, common in America and generally unquestioned, is, I believe, due to the American education system that historically has declared all aspects of American culture and government to be derived almost exclusively from the Plymouth and Massachusetts Bay colonies. When writers use the term "puritan," often capitalized, scholars declare the usage to reveal Anglo-Saxon Puritan cultural heritage. Usually it does not. The term is generalized in America, and elsewhere, and should be recognized as denoting firm moral convictions deriving especially, not far from exclusively, from a fundamentalist Protestant heritage. In a broad sense, eighteenth-century Scots-Irish Presbyterian and French Huguenot communities are correctly labeled "puritan," as are many Southern Baptist congregations today, but none of them are culturally English Puritan, and some are not even Calvinist.

21. James Leyburn reveals of Scottish feuds, "in the southwest, especially, these blood feuds were violent and unending" (9).

22. This exclusive emphasis on geography may help Fischer avoid acknowledging Celtic folk culture: He sees only the northern and western geographies ruled by the English from London.

23. For me, the most interesting reference is to Walter Scott's *Rob Roy,* which is set primarily on the border. But Scott's cultural point here, and in other novels, most notably *Redgauntlet,* is that for all the local disparities and the myriad of feuds, the Highlanders, Lowlanders, and English borderers were part of one basic cultural pattern. That is the primary tragedy underlying Scott's works concerning Scotland.

24. It would be incorrect, I believe, to assume that this *need* of the Cavalier was simply to believe in a direct lineage from nobility, something far from restricted to white Southerners, national stereotypes notwithstanding. Rather, the Cavalier as image was a simple way to assert the recognition that Southern cultural heritage was not Anglo-Saxon Puritan, in fact was something decidedly antithetical to Anglo-Saxon Puritan. After all, the "Cavalier" opposition to the Puritan Parliamentarians featured Irish and Scottish Catholics and Episcopalians.

25. Amazingly, Jordan and Kaups are not the first to claim for Finns some part of Celtic cultural heritage. In 1889, Charles de Kay (note the Cymric surname Normanized) inspired by the Finnish *Kalevela,* a nineteenth-century gathering of Finnish folk tales into an epic of sorts that also inspired Jordan and Kaups, claimed that Old Irish literature revealed that the original inhabitants of what is now Europe were the Turanian peoples, of whom the Finno-Ugric language group is a subfamily. According to de Kay, the Irish are a truly composite people, a Shem and Shaun, half Finnish and half Celtic, a continuing contest between Finno-Ugrian and Aryan. Most of the aspects of the Irish he sees as positive—their sturdiness, love of soil, remarkably low crime rates outside of agrarian and national disputes, conservative retention of ancient lore, imaginativeness, wistful poetic nature, circumspection that keeps the hot-headed Celt from too much trouble—de Kay attributes to the Finnish element among them. The bad traits of the Irish are Celtic according to de Kay. What is most amazing to me about this claim is that it is based upon a race bigotry 180 degrees opposite that of the later Nazis: In this scenario, all that is Aryan, more precisely Indo-European, culturally (as opposed to Aryan equaling fair skin) is negative. Except for the Savo-Karelian area, Finns are a people who have produced little folklore or literature or music,

and this most folk-culturally rich part of Finland has produced little of merit other than the *Kalevela*. Compared to the Irish, the Finns are culturally dull and largely inactive. As all Indo-European peoples produced impressive folklore and, whenever they chose to write, great literature that amounts to much more than one epic not assembled until the nineteenth century, it is far more reasonable to assume that the Savo-Karelians stand out from their fellow Finns because they are, though Finnish speakers, significantly Indo-European in culture than it is to assume that non-Indo-European Turanian culture is the source of Irish cultural contributions. But reason has little to do with the myriad attempts to strip Celtic peoples of everything they have left, save perhaps that it is quite reasonable for the person who hates western Christian civilization, and/or wishes to continue to wage ancient Germanic war to subdue it, to want to obliterate not merely living Celtic heritage and identity but also the memory of Celtic heritage.

Nor are Finns (and the English, of course) the only people who are promoted as being responsible for key aspects of Celtic culture. In *From Scythia to Camelot* (Garland Publishing: New York, 1994), C. Scott Littleton and Linda A. Malcor claim that Arthurian literature is in origin not about Celtic Britain being despoiled by pagan Germanic invaders but is actually the tales of several Iranian speaking tribes native to the Caucasus region, a few thousand of whom moved west into Gaul, a few hundred more into northern Britain, some as allies of conquering Germanic barbarians, others, as those in Britain, as mercenaries for the late Roman Empire. Again, we have a thesis that asserts that a minuscule population of non-Celts in the midst of a majority Celtic population somehow is responsible for Celtic culture.

The question that should be asked repeatedly is: Why are there so many people bound and determined to deny that culturally Celtic peoples are responsible for anything that is culturally significant? Did Jean Markale hit upon the answer?

26. The Episcopalian Church of Scotland primarily stood firm with the Scottish people against the English onslaughts against Scottish independence throughout the seventeenth and eighteen centuries and was officially persecuted by the Hanoverians after Culloden (Fitzroy McLean 181-82).

27. This was the era of the Irish Penal Laws, the horror of which was recorded realistically—eating the children was the next logical step, not merely a satiric exaggeration—by Jonathan Swift in *A Modest Proposal*. Irishmen could be sentenced, including colonial servitude, for such

"crimes" as speaking Gaelic, practicing Catholicism, or possessing a horse worth more than the English deemed appropriate. Eibhlin Dhubh Ni Chonaill's "The Lament for Art O'Leary" (c. 1774) recounts her husband's quarrel with an English official who then claims his horse. When O'Leary refuses to acquiesce, he is outlawed and hunted (see *The Field Day Anthology of Irish Writing*. Ed. Seamus Deane. Vol. 1, p. 309). Donald Akenson sums up the economic effects of the Penal Laws by noting that by 1775 Catholics, some 80 percent of the population, owned only 5 percent of the land (*Irish* 34). For more information, see W.E.H. Lecky, *History of Ireland in the Eighteenth Century* (5 vols. London, 1892).

28. Hugh Thomas reveals that the ban on black slavery in early colonial Georgia was supported generally by the Scottish settlers and "bitterly opposed" by the "Anglo-Saxons," who in 1750 finally succeeded in legalizing chattel slavery in the colony (272). In addition to the American cross-Atlantic slave traders having been almost exclusively Anglo-Saxon, and preponderantly New England born and bred, such ethnic facts about the original pushing for the expansion of chattel slavery in the colonial South demonstrate the validity of the view, which we will see expressed fictionally by William Faulkner and Allen Tate, that plantation chattel slavery in the South was culturally an Anglo-Norman invention, one that many culturally Celtic peoples opposed whenever possible.

29. Pulitzer Prize-winning novelist William Kennedy reveals fictionally how this could be when his Albany, New York, journalist Daniel Quinn sees a photograph of a Union Army unit: "the Irish brigade, led by Batt Conners from Wexford. Quinn had ridden with them for two days and told a bit of their story: wild men all, daredevil heroes their superiors thrust into lost or impossible causes" (217). Equally important is that McCaffrey estimates forty thousand Irish-born Southerners served in the Confederate Army (*Irish* 96).

30. See especially my discussion of Faulkner's Thomas Sutpen but also my analysis of class issues in Tate's *The Fathers*.

31. British historian David Cannadine, author of *Ornamentalism: How the British Saw Their Empire* (Oxford University Press: 2002), observes that the all-powerful role of class in the United Kingdom right through the end of the Empire was such that the British elite classes openly saw and treated the preponderance of British citizens as inherently inferior "poor white trash."

32. Economist Paul Craig Roberts, a Senior Research Fellow at the Hoover Institution, has written several times warning that American

legal changes of the past fifty years, both those that apply to economics and, especially, those that create special status and privileges for certain racial groups, are ushering in a return of feudalism.

33. The sharp distinctions between lower New England and upper New England are, I submit, due in part to this ethnic component from the founding periods of the two sub-regions. It may explain part of the reason that Robert Frost, who best represents the attitudes of upper New England in literature, always had a fairly large audience among Southerners, as well as Irish Catholics, and was lauded by most major Southern poets and scholars as America's greatest poet at least of the twentieth century. Southerners tend to see affinities in Frost, which I think are deeper than mere rural settings, while seeing little more than antithesis in lower New England poets from James Russell Lowell to Robert Lowell.

34. Beyond his own writings, Mitchel is immortalized in Yeats's "Under Ben Bulben." For an introduction to his life and his writings, see John Mitchel *Jail Journal* (University Press of Ireland, 1982). Thomas Flanagan's introduction asserts, "a novel crime, treason-felony, had been created by act of parliament with the specific purpose of removing him from the Irish scene, and a jury had been packed with elaborate care to make certain that he should suffer its punishment of fourteen years' transportation" (vii). For an analysis of a brief period of Mitchel's life as a Southerner see Dee Gee Lester, "John Mitchel's Wilderness Years in Tennessee" (*Eire-Ireland* 25, No. 2, Summer 1990: 7-13). As regards the Celtic-Southern thesis, the most significant revelation in the article is that "Mitchel saw the South as the 'Ireland of this continent' . . ." (10).

35. Though Clark became very much an epitome of Irish American assimilating to Yankee WASP culture, he continued to promote Irish studies, primarily from the vantage that the Irish could be as "progressive" and liberal as Anglo-Saxon Protestants, and, in typical paradoxical Irish fashion, he became a rather ardent Irish nationalist focused on Northern Ireland. Lawrence McCaffrey sees "the Irish as the pioneers of the American ghetto, previewing the experience of almost every other ethnic, religious and racial minority that followed them into the cities of the United States" and Chicago Irish writers Finley Peter Dunne and James T. Farrell as the pioneers of "American urban ghetto literature" (*Irish* 6, 84). Charles Fanning concludes that Irish American literature, "one largely concerned with minority alienation and assimilation into a primarily urban New World environment" (1), is in quantity of quality, as well as its often coming first (think of Dunne's Mr. Dooley tales created

a half century before Langston Hughes's Jesse B. Semple tales, the former in no American literature anthology in print today and the latter in most if not all), perhaps the premier "ethnic" American literature. Yet courses focusing on Irish American literature, history, and politics are at least as rare as such courses devoted to the African American experience were in the 1950s. Clark's banquet address at the 1993 American Conference for Irish Studies national meeting, published as "The Future of Irish Studies" in *The Irish Literary Supplement* 12:2 (Fall 1993): 29, argues passionately for the need to make Irish and Irish American studies more widely available in American education.

36. Berthoff makes no mention of the cultural studies of black Southerners, and it is unclear whether he would also consider them to be inherently racist, or, utilizing a race-based double standard, laud them as promoting multicultural diversity. After quoting George Fitzhugh's declaration, "Social systems, formed on opposite principles cannot co-endure," Eugene Genovese tells a hard truth: "When a Seward, a Lincoln, or a John F. Kennedy utters such sentiments, we are called upon to applaud his moral courage and profound grasp of reality; when a Fitzhugh, a Goldwater, or a Mao Tse-tung says the same thing, we are expected to deplore his extremism, inhumanity, and lack of moral sensibility" (*World* 215-16). The only change in the academy's simplistic labeling from Genovese's 1960s writing is that now Mao and other Marxists, as well as all non-white and non-Christian peoples, are generally assumed to be among the inherently good and non-racist whose pronouncements must be understood always in a positive sense. Political and, especially, cultural conservatives, particularly when white and Christian, are inherently bad and in dire need of forced reformation.

37. As noted, Marxists and postmodernists deny the existence of objective truth and focus on developing effective strategies to achieve their chosen goals. The charge of racism can be absolutely false and still powerfully effective. The attacks upon the Celtic-Southern do not refute any facts or demonstrate any line of reasoning to be illogical; they are attempts to prevent the airing of opposition to the hegemonic vision of contemporary academia.

38. Barry Cunliffe writes, "One estimate is that in the early first century B.C. there were 300,000 Gaulish slaves in Italy alone," and this number would soon explode: "Caesar's campaigns in Gaul are estimated to have provided a million slaves, most of them destined for the Roman markets" (215, 212). That 1,300,000 Celts enslaved by the Romans during the closing century of the Roman Republic would constitute only a fraction

of Celts enslaved by Rome during its history. And those numbers do not address the violent discriminations against Celts in the medieval and modern eras. Also important to recognize, considering the climate of victimization driving much of the American academy, is that the scholarly consensus is that a mere four hundred thousand to five hundred thousand black Africans and black descendants of Africans from the Caribbean were brought as slaves to North America from its first settling by Europeans until the 1860s (Genovese *Roll* 57; Hugh Thomas 804).

39. See Marilyn Westerkamp's *The Triumph of the Laity,* which documents the Irish origin of the frontier Great Revival. Also note that like McWhiney, Mencken considers the peoples of English border counties to be more culturally Celtic than English.

Chapter II

1. Cleanth Brooks, R. W. B. Lewis, and Robert Penn Warren, the editors of *American Literature: The Makers and the Making,* write, "The transcendentalist, according to the philosopher George Santayana, in his essay 'The Genteel Tradition in American Philosophy' . . . might love and respect nature as Emerson did, but he loves it because what he takes to be nature 'is his own work, a mirror in which he looks at himself and says (like a poet relishing his own verses), 'What a genius I am! Who would have thought there was such stuff in me?'" (Vol. I. New York: St. Martin's Press, 1973: 341). The Southern love of and respect for nature, it seems to me, is largely unmarked by such a Gnostic hubris and therefore considerably less likely to be a falsely romanticized game played by intellectuals and dilettantes; rather, it is bound concretely by the natural cycles of crops, stock, and hunting and fishing so that Southerners tend not to see nature as something akin to a mystical womb from which knowledge my be gleaned by the initiate.

2. Taylor holds a similar view. "More than anyone else," he writes, "Simms became the historical consciousness of the South" (*Cavalier* 269). Joseph P. Ridgely is even closer to my position: "Simms had written a Southern literature" that explained and analyzed the South (5).

3. Perhaps Larne's greatest claim to fame was that it was the site at which the Scots under Edward Bruce landed in 1315 to attempt to rally the Irish to full rebellion against their English conquerors. Edward's brother Robert had prepared the way by sending envoys to Ireland proclaiming friendship due to sharing "the same national ancestry . . . a common language and a common custom" (Scott, 174-75). Robert's recognition of the Celtic folk ways that determined Scottish character

and heritage as much as they determined Irish character and heritage should indicate that those who claim either that only the Highlands of Scotland can be considered culturally Celtic or that to accept recognition of a common Celtic folk culture is a romanticization of the past are not fully informed. Also, the tenth-century Cymric, Welsh, poem *Armes Prydain* (Prophecy of Britain) encourages all the Celtic peoples to rally together to fight against the English for the freedom of Britain. More and more I have come to believe that it is fear that such could happen that drives the increasingly desperate attempts to deny the existence and importance of Celtic heritage.

4. Wimsatt does, however, allude to Simms's Celtic heritage as underlying *Paddy McGann,* a quote that will be used when I discuss the novel.

5. One probable origin of the Macnamara scene is the Yamasse capture of native Scot Thomas Nairne, who was tortured and burned for three days before dying. Unlike Macnamara, Nairne was a wealthy and powerful man who promoted the conversion of the Aboriginal nations to Episcopalianism and an acceptance of British hegemony. In making his fictional victim of prolonged aboriginal torture a man lacking status, Simms provides his readers with a picture of the typical victim of Southern frontier death at the hands of natives, for few children of the wealthy risked their lives among people they saw as savages.

6. "Revolutionary Romances" is the designation Simms scholars have used to label his seven novels set during the American Revolution. Like Cooper's Natty Bumppo novels, Simms's Revolutionary-era novels were not published in chronological order of historical events.

7. Katherine Walton and Robert Singleton are prime examples, but the best is perhaps Ralph Colleton in *Guy Rivers* (1834). This is not to claim that Simms fails to praise Anglo-Norman characters in his works as exemplifying true gentlemanly qualities. What is important is that he often does so when the Anglo-Norman is living the life of the backwoods crackers, like Singleton in *The Partisan* or Willie Sinclair in *The Forayers and Eutaw.*

8. For additional information, see R. F. Foster, *Modern Ireland 1600-1972* (Penguin Press, 1988): 268.

9. The change among Southerners from being an antebellum people with strong awareness of Irish and/or Scottish heritage and sympathy for the Celtic lands, including for nationalist anti-imperial revolutions, to a twentieth-century people who often saw themselves as "Anglo-Saxon" and culturally and ethnically exactly like old Anglo-Saxon New Englanders began with the schools erected in the South during

Reconstruction. As with their kin in Ireland whose children were taught to see England as their mother and who were taught to sing of being happy English children, Southerners were taught the New England Yankee Anglo-Saxon view of the world and that they too were happy Anglo-Saxons—younger brothers, as it were, of the New England WASPs, both of them the cultural, intellectual, and spiritual children of Puritans.

10. For an example, see *The Partisan,* where it is said of Dennison, "truer historian of the deeds which he beheld, never put fact on record; more faithful bard never sang in honour of brave spirits" (240).

11. As Simms himself is the author of "Dennison's" poems and the son of an Irish immigrant, this praise of the Irish Dennison is self-praise. Though beleaguered by self-doubts throughout his life, Simms also was sufficiently arrogant as to see himself as the epic bard of his country. His preface to *The Yemassee* makes that point clear.

12. This literal translation, which makes no attempt to capture the inherent musical quality of Gaelic, is that of Mary MacDonell. Note that the Scottish poet has no doubt that if victorious, the British forces will be restrained by neither law nor reason. Also, keep this reason for refusing to join the American Revolution in mind when reading my discussion of Caroline Gordon's *Penhally* and recall this Celtic warning about victorious Anglo-Saxons when contemplating Reconstruction.

13. Simms here puns on the Irish origin of the word "whiskey," *uisce beatha,* meaning literally "water of life."

14. Note that Simms does not "romanticize" his praise of Celts by seeing them as untainted with the desire to accumulate money and power. In his analyses of human character, especially in his portrayal of Celts here and of frontier violence, Simms was ahead of his time.

15. For an introduction to Simms's problems with Charleston society see Louis D. Rubin, "Simms, Charleston, and the Profession of Letters" in *Long Years of Neglect: The Work and Reputation of William Gilmore Simms.* Ed. John C. Guilds (Fayetteville and London: University of Arkansas Press, 1988): 217-234.

16. Also of interest in *The Cassique of Kiawah* is Calvert's Irish lieutenant from County Wexford who bears the "obviously" French name Molyneaux. Simms contrasts Molyneaux's Celtic honor with the English lieutenant Sam, who cares nothing for honor or fair play (29-30, 32, 296-98, 302, 481).

17. The presumed Catholicism of the deserting Irish troops in the Revolutionary romances is never mentioned. Furthermore, Edward Fitzgerald *was* Protestant. That Simms, who so clearly recognizes the

importance of Celtic immigrants to Southern culture, would find the positive fictional portrayal of Catholicism in antebellum America apparently anathema explains the ease with which linking Celtic culture to Irish Catholics exclusively would lead to Celtic Protestants "forgetting" their cultural heritage. Also, Simms's portrayal of decadent Spanish Catholicism in *Vasconselos* would be applauded by most Protestants of the era as well as any Know-Nothing-inclined readers. Though Simms himself was no common anti-Catholic bigot, his America saw nativist riots against Irish Catholic neighborhoods, including the destructions of churches, and the rise of the Know-Nothing party, which would be essential to the rise of the Republican Party. For detailed information on the subject, see Ray Allen Billington, *The Protestant Crusade 1800-1860: A Study of the Origins of Nativism* (MacMillan Company: New York, 1938).

18. Implicit throughout *I'll Take My Stand: The South and the Agrarian Tradition* is the belief in a basic difference between Southern and American cultures. For more information, see the LSU Press edition, with a preface by Louis D. Rubin.

Chapter III

1. Note the surname Douglass, which most Anglophilically educated readers will identify as Scottish and, as the clan was not known for speaking only Gaelic in the eighteenth century, as one that proves the Anglo-Saxon-Norman culture of Scotland.

2. Readers unfamiliar with Ireland who might be inclined to view this conversion of the scion of such an historically important Irish Catholic family as too improbable for fiction need only acquaint themselves with Terence O'Neill, who was the Northern Ireland prime minister from 1963-1969.

3. Readers bothered by this view, particularly those who believe it to lack merit, should consider that for every book of folklore collected from the midwest there will be at least three collected from the Arkansas Ozarks alone. Differing cultural groups emphasize different things and will succeed, in group terms, in different ways. The German response to this could be to emphasize that in comparison with them few peoples of Celtic heritage make major contributions to the hard sciences. The differences do not demarcate human inferiority or superiority.

4. Donald Akenson reveals that contrary to the commonly held bigotry, nineteenth-century Irish emigrants to America, who were more poor than their eighteenth-century predecessors and the poorest emigrants of their time, were among the most literate emigrants (*Irish* 40).

Considering that, it is reasonable to conclude that the eighteenth-century Irish emigrants, not merely less impoverished but also primarily dissenter Protestants with an emphasis upon reading the Word, would have been the most literate on the continent.

5. See page 43.

6. William Taylor holds a similar view. Tucker, he says, portrays the Tidewater aristocracy "as improvident, rash and self-destructive," with the South's future lying on the frontier. But he, oddly, considers the Scots-Irish to be very much like the Cavaliers, only "more vigorous" (317). This misreading derives, I believe, from his inability to recognize the Scots-Irish as culturally Celtic, which leaves him but to see them as plebeian Anglo-Saxons. This approach, which derives from English imperial politics and readings of culture that deny ethnicity to try to refocus energies into class alliances, which are easier to control than ethnic/national/cultural allegiances, dovetails nicely with Marxist and later postmodernist views that present class as all important.

7. Curtis Davis reveals that Bacon had been in America "only a few months" before the Rebellion and that he "had spent his youth as the spoiled child of a wealthy English squire" (140). Caruthers' fictional portrayal, so divergent from the facts, is necessary for his thematic examination of the role of Virginia Cavaliers.

8. Caruthers misdates the expedition as occurring in 1714. This would be before the 1715 Jacobite Rising.

9. The reader should note Watson's conflation of Scottish and English nations and cultures. Also, Watson sees Scott as treating only the medieval, and therefore presumably more mysteriously and enticingly romantic, era. But Scott's best novels, those exploring Scottish history, are set in the early modern era. For example, *Rob Roy* is set around the 1715 Jacobite Rising, *Waverley* around the 1745 Jacobite Rising, and *Redgauntlet* around a fictional 1760s Jacobite planned rising. These two misreadings of Scott are, I believe, necessary to the Twain-inspired attacks on Scott's influence on the South. Also, the reader inclined toward accepting the prejudices against Scott should be aware that Barry Cunliffe, after condemning the excesses of certain defenders of Celtic culture, includes Scott's Scottish novels among those to be praised and studied seriously (14-15).

10. James Webb emphasizes the geographic ties by noting that Scotland is very much like Appalachia: "difficult water barriers, sharp mountains and deep hollows, soggy moors and rough pastures, and of thin, uncultivable soil that lies like a blanket over wide reaches of granite" (35).

11. The cultural border was north of the Ohio because of the Little Dixies that had been created by the descendants of Southerners, most of whom were of Celtic ancestry.

12. See McCaffrey's *Textures of Irish America,* 17-22 and Michael Feldberg's *The Turbulent Era: Riot and Disorder in Jacksonian America.* (New York and London: Oxford University Press, 1980).

Chapter IV

1. Luce also succinctly summarizes the process by which non-Irish settlers became Hibernicized: Berkeley's "family came originally from England, no doubt; but Irish air acts quickly; one generation can alter the outlook, and Berkeley's father was settled in Ireland, if not born there" (25).

2. For a discussion of the violent discrimination faced by Irish immigrants, see Lawrence J. McCaffrey, *The Irish Diaspora in America*: 85-106. Also, Mark Twain and Charles Dudley Warner provide a comic version of an Irish name change in *The Gilded Age*: "The Hon. Patrique Oreillé was a wealthy Frenchman from Cork" (Justin Kaplan introduction; New York: Trident Press, 1964): 229.

3. Part of Glasgow's opposition to the Calvinism of her father appears to be that it, certainly by the post-Reconstruction period, fostered a dismissal of familial and cultural heritage in name of focusing on the Bible. If faith only and grace only and Bible only mean no interest in, much less promotion of, the Celtic cultural vein of iron, then Glasgow would oppose all such Protestantism as surely as she opposed the airy nothingness of the modern world.

4. For a discussion of the Celtic Church and nature, see Christopher Bamford, "The Heritage of Celtic Christianity: Ecology and Holiness," in *The Celtic Consciousness,* ed. Robert O'Driscoll (New York: George Braziller, 1982) and Anthony Duncan, *The Elements of Celtic Christianity* (Element Books Limited, 1993). The latter is particularly flawed by New Age silliness but is interesting.

Chapter V

1. The primary "proof" generally asserted by those claiming the Picts were at least partially non-Celtic was their medieval tendency toward matrilineal inheritance, a family pattern long held to be outside the Indo-European cultural umbrella. Nerys Patterson, using the work of Alfred Smyth, has demonstrated a more plausible reason for the Pictish matrilineal succession: Sons of other Celtic peoples, displaced northern Britons and especially Irish Dal Riata, intruding into Pictish kingship by marrying Pictish princesses (320-21).

2. Cunliffe's point is that Celtic heritage is about culture much more than genetics and certainly linguistics.

3. Official government efforts to destroy a folk culture in order to rule a people as part of an empire are properly labeled cultural genocide. Fitzroy McLean notes that the English government after Culloden imposed "a series of acts of policy designed to prevent any risk of a Jacobite revival *by crushing the spirit of the Highlanders and destroying the Highland way of life*" (180. My emphasis). Similar to the Irish penal laws developed a half century earlier, the Scottish discriminations included persecutions of Scottish religion, colonial servitude, and the outlawing of anything that the English deemed indicative of independent Scottish culture: Civilians bearing arms, wearing kilts, plaids, or tartans, and owning bagpipes. Scholars of the South would do well to recognize that immigrants to the South from Ireland and Scotland, regardless of specific religious and political affiliations, brought with them a sense of being members of a folk culture hunted to extermination. This is the principal origin of the white South's inherent distrust of powerful centralized government; as descendants of Celts, they possess a cultural memory of such governments attempting to destroy them in the name of "progress."

4. While it is assumed commonly that Sutpen amends his proposal in order to guarantee a son and heir before he weds, I wonder if he does not do so also knowing such will drive Rosa away. Surely in that time Sutpen would have learned that he would never live with Rosa Coldfield and could not trust her genes nor her parenting to provide him with an heir.

5. This, men challenging one another at manual labor with boasts, insults, and songs, is yet another area in which scholars finding no English example have assumed white Southerners have borrowed from blacks. Southerners of Celtic heritage had ancestors who brought this cultural trait to America with them, as did the Irish Catholics who worked on and in the railroads and canals and mines. Claiming that Americans of Celtic ancestry owe this to blacks is as foolish and as misguided as claiming that Americans of African ancestry stole this from Celts.

6. This Celtic sense of land and family means that Ike McCaslin's view of the futility, even inherent wrong, of individual land ownership may not be due exclusively to a romantic response to the Indian in Sam Fathers. Ike's stance is an extreme position, but one within the parameters of Celtic land and family. His flaw, like Sutpen's, is that he acts abstractly, according to a theory that has displaced everything else in his mind, and in so doing, he cuts off life.

7. The reader might want to compare this to Ralph Ellison's *Invisible*

Man. Though Ellison's character is not seen by Southern whites, there is in the South some semblance of community that provides stability and meaning. Once in Harlem, the Invisible Man continually confronts a world lacking sense of family community, and this outrages him, as the eviction scene best reveals. Interestingly, the Harlem blacks no more see the Invisible Man than do whites.

8. Allen Tate, in "Remarks on the Southern Religion" in *I'll Take My Stand,* declares, "abstraction is the death of religion no less than the death of anything else" (156), and Flannery O'Connor declares, "The isolated imagination is easily corrupted by theory" (856).

9. Even if transported as a convict, the first Southern Sutpen could have been a Celt, possibly even a political prisoner of the seventeenth- and eighteenth-century wars. Furthermore, "pen" is Welsh for "head," suggesting a possible Welsh origin of the name. But whatever his ethnic heritage, the first Southern Sutpen headed immediately to the Celtic backcountry.

10. This is one of those cultural similarities between ancient Hebrews and Celts that may explain the relatively quick and peaceful conversion of Celtic peoples to Christianity. The fear of kings, and religious leaders, ruling for themselves runs throughout the Old Testament. It is perhaps best summarized in Ezekiel 34:1-10 in which the prophet in Babylonian Captivity declares that Yahweh has instructed him to denounce the selfish rule that led to the conquest and deportations: "Woe be to the shepherds that do feed themselves! Should not the shepherds feed the flocks?"

11. Small Gaelic-speaking communities continue to exist in Nova Scotia, and Irish Catholics and Protestants and Scots all contributed to Canadian independence, but I doubt that there is a "Canadian culture," and if so it is too centered on the Anglophone versus Francophone clash to be Celtic in origin. Hence, Shreve must look back to Scotland to understand Celtic tragedy in America.

12. An interesting study along these lines is Donald H. Akenson's *If the Irish Ran the World: Montserratt, 1630-1730.* Using as his case the small island Monserratt, unique in that the majority of its whites were Irish, Akenson finds that the recently exploited and violently abused tend, when given the opportunity, to accept any discriminatory system as long as they are on the power side reaping the benefits.

Chapter VI

1. Gwyn Williams's *The Search for Beulah Land* reveals the extensive role played by the Welsh, often inspired to repeat the heroics of the legendary medieval Welsh "discoverer" of America, Madoc, in the settlement

of the trans-Appalachian frontier from the 1790s to the 1820s. These Welsh, carrying evangelistic Christianity as well as education and commerce, were instrumental throughout the hill South and in what later would be the Little Dixies north of the Ohio River.

2. Scholar of Irish fiction and critically acclaimed novelist Thomas Flanagan presents a fictional portrayal of equating assertion of Celtic heritage with storybook romance, which allows the entire subject to be dismissed as either a joke or a flight of wild imagination. In *The Tenants of Time*, Flanagan has Irish-born Patrick Prentiss, a Clongowes Woods College graduate, say of his interest in the Fenian Rising of 1867, "Ambushes, demagogues, famine graves. That is our history." Dick Leese, Prentiss's English friend from Oxford University days, responds, "*We. . . . Our.* Now we are getting to it. Is that how you think of it? A bit romantic, if you want my opinion of it" (152).

3. Note that the Southern Gordon uses this phrase before the Irish Catholic-born Eugene O'Neill, whose posthumously staged plays popularized it.

4. In a note Eugene Genovese, focusing on the antebellum era rather than the colonial era, says, "The widespread notion that the South was conquered by Calvinist predestinarianism is a figment of historian's imagination" (*Southern Tradition* 128). The South never was dominated in any way by Calvinists or Calvinism.

5. A few words from Solzhenitsyn may further explain Brinkmeyer's hostility to the fictionally expressed conservative Christianity of not merely Gordon but also of Flannery O'Connor. "Then, the intellectual West's sympathy for the Soviet system is also conditioned by the common source of their ideological origins: materialism and atheism. A movement openly connected with religion always alarms, if it does not scare them" (172).

6. I am indebted to Michael Montgomery of the University of South Carolina for recommending that I read Westerkamp's *The Triumph of the Laity*. I have found it invaluable in understanding both Ulster Protestant communities and attitudes and the legacy of Christianity in the South.

Chapter VII

1. Note the built-in explanation—the lack of metropolitan areas—for why the South was not like eighteenth-century England though it was supposed to have been that society reproduced. Such gymnastics always have been necessary in explanations about the South's origins. The many significant differences between the South and England of any era need

not be explained away once the importance of the South's Celtic heritage is acknowledged.

2. In his foreword to *A Novel, A Novella and Four Stories*, Andrew Lytle declares that there are "two conflicting world views" in battle in the twentieth century. What he calls "the prevailing Faustian view . . . has until recently seemed invincible. Relying entirely on the material ends as the only proper reward for action (the delusion that man can know the final secrets of matter), it defines itself as laissez faire in economics (the shift from the individual to the state does not alter this), faction in politics, social welfare in religion, relativism in history, pragmatism in philosophy. The older belief in The City of God as the end of the drama has persisted, if defensively, in the South" (xx). This foreword demonstrates the agrarian's continued hostility to both the overtly anti-Christian modern state (whether communist, fascist, liberal welfare, or corporate and moral laissez faire) and to the anti-family abstract theories that drive such states.

3. A diluted twentieth-century version of that aspect of Scottish history may be seen in Earle Cairns's history of Christianity. A graduate of Presbyterian Theological Seminary of Omaha, Cairns summarizes the Reformation in Scotland: "The middle class was firmly in political control, and the presbyterian system of church government and Calvinistic theology were adopted by the Scottish people. The French threat to English security through Scotland was forever ended, and the religious barrier to political union between England and Scotland was removed so that the two lands were united under the same ruler in 1603 and became one kingdom with one Parliament in 1707" (322). Scotland's loss of independence, the cultural ravaging of the Highlands, the economic forced migration of hundreds of thousands of Scots, and certainly the dispossession of Scottish Catholics—none of these matter, for a bourgeois Calvinism had won the day. The religious end of this mixing of Calvinism, capitalism as Protestant work ethic doctrine, and UK imperialism was that in the Victorian era, "Ignorance and indifference were, continued to be, and remain, the English working-class attitude to religion," for their choices seemed to be restricted to either "the Methodist Church of the *petit-bourgeois,* the small shopkeepers's church which became that of the well-heeled" and "the Church of England, with its lands and rents and endowments and its established position in the nation at large" (Wilson 82-83). The situation in Scotland developed more slowly, but Wilson's summation, with diluted Presbyterian churches added, well fits it.

4. Camille Paglia declares that in addition to epicene inactivity, genteel "English society is also noted for a toleration of eccentricity, a taste for sadomasochistic erotica, and a high incidence of male homosexuality, stimulated by the monasticism of public-school and university life" (549).

5. The reader should not see this as a conflict with Stark Young, who unflinchingly condemns the theoretically inspired Union desire to eradicate the planter class. Unlike the "English squire" Bedford, Hugh McGehee is an active worker on his land, so much so that Sallie Bedford condemns him as too concerned with his slaves (*So Red* 38-39). Sutpen also works and plays with his slaves to the wonderment of some and the condemnation of others.

6. George's selling of Yellow Jim, his own half-brother, appears to be selfish. But we readers only hear Jim tell the story to Lacy, and, especially considering Jim's later compulsive, violent action, it is possible that he was sold because he had caused trouble. This series of events, then, is roughly analogous to Thomas Sutpen's treatment of the French architect.

7. This means that Yankee attacks on antebellum Southern tournaments, which often focused on the displayed "backwardness" and "romantic escapism," were somewhat wrongheaded, for the tournaments may have served to help keep many Southerners, those most at play, from seeing the coming tide of reforming violence aimed at their extermination. Similarly, most Confederate soldier re-enactors, I have found, seem uninterested in most aspects of Southern culture and have great difficulty imagining that there could be any real hostility to Southern culture. Their playacting appears to serve as a type of soothing narcotic, helping them believe that their games preserve all culture that needs to be preserved and demonstrate their honor, which eventually will be recognized by those who hate their culture and its history.

8. As the stereotype of all slave owners being rabid secessionists continues even among those with graduate degrees, I think it important to note that throughout *The Southern Front* Eugene Genovese reveals that a large percentage of the wealthiest plantation owners were, depending on time period, Federalists, Whig nationalists, and Bell anti-secessionists.

9. William Gilmore Simms was fascinated by the John A. Murrell gang and used its alleged activities as the basis of several novels: *Guy Rivers* (1834), *Richard Hurdis* (1838), *Border Beagles* (1840), and *Helen Halsey* (1845). In *The Adventures of Tom Sawyer,* one of Mark Twain's villains mentions the Murrell gang.

10. Lucas asserts that Lytle's presentation of "homey" episodes in the lives of several of Pleasant's victims humanizes them. It does, but it should not do so the way Lucas feels. It should demonstrate that the most violently evil people in the world are three-dimensional human beings, and if their occasional kindness or sense of humor or concern for family mitigates their atrocities, they will tyrannize the world.

Chapter VIII

1. I had made a note to myself to locate this Southern novel linking the Confederacy to Mangan's Young Ireland nationalism, but I never got around to doing so. In a note to his introduction to volume five of *The Irish Worldwide* O'Sullivan supplies this information covering my article's lapse. I continue to be amazed at his seemingly inexhaustible fund of inter-disciplinary knowledge of Irish and Irish emigrant cultures.

2. Using that rationale, Shakespeare's history plays are also vulgar literature.

3. For a thorough analysis of just how much and how subtly David O. Selznick's film altered Mitchell's novel, transforming the story from one critical of false Southern myths to a mere romance apparently embracing those false myths, see Pyron's *Southern Daughter*, 380-93.

4. In a discussion at the University of Arkansas in October 1990, Peggy Whitman Prenshaw revealed that on her then recent tour of the former Soviet Union to speak on Southern women writers, the book that the audience at every location most wanted to discuss was *Gone With the Wind.* For somewhat similar views of *Gone With the Wind*'s merits see Leslie Fiedler's *The Inadvertent Epic, From Uncle Tom's Cabin to Roots* and Harold K. Schefski's "Margaret Mitchell: *Gone With the Wind* and *War and Peace.*"

5. I am not here suggesting that there is much truth in the widespread bigotries that assume Southern fundamentalism is violently, or even staunchly, anti-Catholic as the term is understood from modern European history. As Eugene Genovese often has noted, it was in the theologically liberal, quintessentially Anglo-Saxon northeast, not in the South, that antebellum convents were torched and Irish Catholic immigrant neighborhoods attacked.

Chapter IX

1. I am not using the term "fundamentalist" in its strict signification for dispensational premillennialist. Nor am I using it in the perverted popular meaning adopted by many academics and journalists as the

label for "uneducated" believers in Jesus as the Christ. I am using "fundamentalist" in its broad sense to designate any adherent to the New Testament who is word-centered rather than ritual- or church-hierarchy-centered; a fundamentalist Christian recognizes the Bible as inerrantly inspired of God and therefore the only ultimate word on matters of faith and practice. That definition, of course, raises problems that lead us back to the very hyper-individualistic and anti-traditional, liberal ethical mainstream of American Christianity (now certainly as much a part of American Catholicism as Protestantism) that O'Connor rejected, but it will have to suffice here.

2. As O'Connor clearly believed that Catholics were willing to confront evil, Rubin must be using the term "fundamentalist" to mean more than merely Protestant conservatives.

3. Marcionism, I believe, is necessary for liberal Christian theology, for in its dualist separation it promotes seeing a God of justice who punishes the wrongdoer as a horrible concept if not an actual evil. It is also important to consider, then, the anti-Semitism undergirding Christian liberal theology, which Rubin evidently does not recognize. In Marcionite liberal theology, the "God of Wrath" is the intolerant, punishing Hebrew Yahweh and the "God of Love" is the sympathetically all-absolving, non-Hebrew Jesus.

4. The volume of scholarship purporting to prove that O'Connor did not mean what she meant in moral and basic theological terms derives from the widespread hostile bigotries against fervent, unadultereated Christianity. "To find that a writer believed passionately in Chairman Mao, or Stalin, or Ho Chi Minh," D. M. Thomas writes of Solzhenitsyn, "was acceptable to the liberal mind; but if he believed passionately in God it caused a frisson of discomfort and doubt" (381). Rather than face their own prejudices, some of these liberal academics writing about O'Connor create systems whereby they can claim she really was something of a postmodern relativist and at least as hostile toward uncompromising Christian belief as she was toward the vicious anti-Christians in her work.

5. The emphasis placed on baptism throughout O'Connor's works, perhaps especially in *The Violent Bear It Away*, at least suggests that many of her fundamentalist characters see baptism as being necessary for the remission of sins and therefore for salvation. As the key Protestant doctrine is salvation by faith alone, which renders baptism into a form for joining a particular denomination and/or a mere symbol of the salvation that accrued previously at the moment of belief, such

characters cannot be labeled Protestants, not if Reformation theological doctrine determines the signification.

6. That is another paradox that moderns denied: Churches that are culturally and theologically conservative make converts and influence the general culture for the better, while churches that embrace liberalism and its relativist theology begin to wither, though their influence continues to move the general culture toward the telos of their theology.

7. "St. Patrick's Breastplate" may be found in *The New Oxford Book of Irish Verse,* edited by Thomas Kinsella. Thomas Cahill declares of the poem, which is dated three or four centuries after Patrick, "it is Patrician to its core, the first ringing assertion that the universe itself is the Great sacrament, magically designed by its living Creator to bless and succor human beings" (116).

8. The reader should not infer that I am suggesting either that Protestantism is, or that O'Connor believed Protestantism to be, more Yahwist than is Roman Catholicism. Anyone familiar with the so-called mainline Protestant denominations knows that to be untrue. Nor am I suggesting that the Celtic Church taught against the doctrine of baptismal regeneration, as do most Protestant denominations, or the role of bishops.

9. Considering the historical circumstances, with civil government falling into increasing ruin and murderous barbarian tribes marauding, that choice was all but necessary in order to try to protect the lives of those the Roman bishops shepherded.

10. Of course, O'Connor may mean that she sees Protestantism as inherently liberal philosophically. Richard Weaver, perhaps the most important Southern conservative thinker since John C. Calhoun, seems to have believed thus. He opens his *Ideas Have Consequences* with the assertion, "There is reason to believe that modern man has become a moral idiot," and almost immediately declares, "For four centuries every man has been not only his own priest but his own professor of ethics, and the consequence is an anarchy which threatens even that minimum consensus of value necessary to the political state" (1-2).

11. There is no evidence that Patrick did not see the other twenty-three books of the New Testament as fully inspired scripture, which in times like these must be emphasized; Cahill apparently means that Patrick discarded the accreted Greco-Roman practices that had been added to the gospel message throughout the Mediterranean world. Also, it should be noted that Martin of Tours, who became a bishop in 372, went among the pagans of western Gaul, which includes the area that

would become Brittany, and planted churches. The difference is that Martin of Tours remained within the Roman Empire, while Patrick left the Empire to convert Ireland.

12. As noted previously, the word "British" is not English; it is the lenited form of the Cymric, or Welsh, or P-Celtic name for their island, and Bamford's use of the term in no way suggests the English or their church.

13. The indispensable affinity between Irish Christianity and nature also may be seen in popular culture. The final verse of Van Morrison's "In the Garden," a song on the 1986 PolyGram compact disc/cassette of *No Guru, No Method, No Teacher,* includes:

> No Guru, no method, no teacher
> Just you and I and nature
> And the Father and the
> Son and the Holy Ghost
> In the Garden wet with rain.

Morrison's linkage of Christianity to nature is especially important, for he is an Ulster Protestant.

Chapter X

1. The Hollywood film, predictably, omitted one of the most important sections of Conroy's novel concerning race relations: The brutal rape of a white girl by a black man, which helps drive Red Pettus to his extreme. The Hollywood omission serves to distort both Conroy's harshly realistic, if liberally slanted, vision and the way that moviegoers perceive the South and race relationships.

Those who doubt the huge disparity between the races as producers of violent criminals, with blacks of all socio-economic levels per capita producing up to ten times as many violent criminals as whites, need to consult the New Century Foundation's *The Color of Crime* (Web site: http://www.amren.com/color.pdf). Dr. Walter Williams of George Mason University is perhaps the most significant black scholar to verify the research and recognize its importance; he notes that while white criminals only commit 2.6 percent of their crimes against black victims, black criminals commit 56 percent of their crimes against white victims (Web site: http://www.frontpagemag.com/Articles/ReadArticle.asp?ID=3691). That means that while the Red Pettuses are extremely rare in the real world, the back rapist in Conroy's novel is actually quite common in the real world, and it is the extremely rare former that Hollywood, academia, journalism, and politicians dwell on while all but totally ignoring the common latter.

2. It should be easy for readers to see in Reynolds' assertions the cultural-ethnic source of imperial American neoconservatism, with its self-righteous fury to slaughter worldwide to bring peace to the world through its rule.

3. Reynolds's anti-Irish prepossession is, regrettably, one that I have found all too common in the academic world, specifically in two professors whose courses I took, one a teacher during my undergraduate years and the other during my graduate student years, and in a pair of professors I have talked with at academic conferences. The reader tempted to accept Reynolds's views as valid should consult *Ireland: A Cultural Encyclopedia,* edited by Brian de Breffny. It includes brief discussions and descriptions of hundreds of Irish contributions to western culture that are usually usurped under the headings "English" or "British."

4. That means that all attempts, including by blacks, to destroy Southern culture, especially those attempts that focus on stifling knowledge of the Celtic-Southern thesis, are merely service in one theater of the continuing original modern racism.

Chapter XI

1. Likewise, I have found that offending the gods of professedly "conservative" Yankee WASP America, perhaps by refusing to worship at the shrine of Puritans or by seeing Lincoln as a tyrant or by opposing its wars around the globe to expand its cultural empire or by advocating for cultural independence from it, means ostracism from the very few outlets that it controls.

2. See the discussion of Taylor's *Cavalier and Yankee* on pages 53-54.

3. It is significant that all peoples around the world who come to distrust and fear the American government as self-righteously destructive and loathe its culture as juvenile and perverse, imperialistically so, and often come to hate American citizens, use the terms Yank and Yankee to label that which they oppose about modern America.

4. The word in Gaelic is *Samhain,* pronounced roughly *sow-in.* For decades, many puritanical American Protestants, following the lead of Anglo-Saxon Puritans in seeing everything that is culturally Celtic as of the devil, have based their opposition to any kind of Halloween celebration on the belief that "Sam Hane" is one of the names of Satan.

5. It is easy to see the origin of Halloween (from All Hallows Eve— the evening before All Saints Day) trick or treating: Children dress up as

fairies and inform local farmers that if they do not want, say, their milk pails tipped over, they must give a treat. Adults play along. Children and adults thus enact a ritual that helps bond them to one another and to the dead and the yet to live.

Conclusion

1. That Christianity is a metanarrative of the South should be an assertion shocking to none. The best example for me is the writing of Robert Penn Warren. An agnostic himself, Warren's fiction and poetry are imbued with Bible language and allusions, and many of his works open with verses from the Bible. Had Warren chosen to ignore as beneath him or to belittle exclusively this metanarrative his works would have been false to Southern culture, would have been either solipsisms or rehashes of the prejudices of high modernism. Also, that the South has at least two metanaratives, one of which is the Bible, explains to a great degree the desire of contemporary scholars to "prove" that the South and Southern culture exist only as mental constructs, principally to further the various isms fought by the New Left, for as Jean-Francois Lyotard has succinctly stated, postmodernism is defined as "incredulity toward metanarratives."

2. That understood, attacks, as well as defenses of such attacks, on the Confederate Battle Flag are attempts to dishonor if not obliterate both the South's Christian heritage and its Celtic heritage.

3. That White set his work rather nebulously in the high Middle Ages, some six centuries after the actual Arthurian age, with anachronisms from later times interspersed throughout serves to mark *The Once and Future King* as fiction designed to present an account of how modern England came to be and what it should strive to remain: Celtic culture absorbed by conquering Germans who rework it to make themselves its originators and who then shower perennial contempt upon surviving Celtic peoples.

4. The phrases "autocratic rule" and "the need for revenge" may describe West African systems of honor perfectly, but "the importance of tradition and heritage in authority" and "the need to defend family and personal honor and autonomy at almost any cost" better relate Celtic and Southern honor codes. Readers inclined to see the South as autocratically inclined should recall that the South was the basis of the broadening of American democracy in both the eras of Jefferson and Jackson and that direct democracy was so powerful in the antebellum South that Confederate officers were elected. That localist democratic spirit, very

much anti-autocratic, underlies both the South's long history of populism and its tendency to defy and oppose increased government centralizing.

5. The political desire to see American slaves as being primary determinants of much of Southern, and thereby all of American culture, is, perhaps, finally giving way to scholarship that is more reasoned. Peter Kolchin, an important authority on American slavery, writes, "Slaves in Saint Domingue and Jamaica lived in a world that was overwhelmingly black, a world in which European planters felt intensely uncomfortable and from which they frequently retreated; serfs in Russia lived in a world that was even more overwhelmingly peasant, one alien to and usually avoided by their noble masters. Southern slaves, by contrast, lived in and had to adjust to, the world of their masters" (152). When we consider that the black slaves in most areas of the South had to adjust as much to ways of non-slaveholding whites who lived in their local communities, with whom many of them would have had general community dealings, as they would have been required to adjust to their actual owners, we can sense that Piersen's claims are at best overstated, for the situation of American slaves meant that they would inevitably assume considerably more of European values than they would have a chance to impart African values and cultural attitudes to whites.

6. Ellen Glasgow's 1902 novel *The Battle-Ground* provides an interesting presentation of this subject. Major Lightfoot, a man proud that the Washingtons are a family beneath his and who disinherited his daughter for eloping beneath her station, declares that the owning of slaves is reserved for gentlemen. The major's rebellious grandson, Dandridge Montjoy, is similarly put out for dueling a "gentleman" in defense of the honor of a person his grandfather sees as a "barroom hussy."

7. I am well aware that in many, if not most, humanities academic "disciplines" postmodernist theories rather than Marxist theories are predominant, and I also recognize that while Marxism is focused on changing and destroying institutions identified as Western, capitalist, conservative, and Christian, postmodern theories are at war with all systems of thought and if they were consistent would be at war constantly with everything that is remotely Marxist. However, Marxism and the various postmodern theories are allied in that each has the same enemy it wishes to destroy in the name of its tolerance, and each has a defining history of dismissing, often refusing to answer, opposition by noting that it is spoken or written by those not of the assumed enlightened left. In addition, Marxism is the numen of postmodernism. Dario Fernandez-Morera analyzes this peculiarity of American academia, accepting the

validity of the assertions of Mike Brown, "who praised the 'thoroughly Marxist frame of reference of the enormously influential Modern Language Association'" and adding, "even without taking into account the usually unidentified traces of their thought in much of postmodern academic writing, a recent issue of the *Arts and Humanities Index* lists Marx and Lenin as the two most frequently cited sources in arts and humanities journals over a seven year period" (3; see also pages 128-29 for a discussion of how the professed poststructuralist "*multiplicity* of revolutionary *foci*" is merely remarketed, new or improved Marxism). The Celtic-Southern thesis, and to a slightly lesser degree any call for promotion of Irish American studies, is a bane of both Marxism and post-modernism because it supports none of the bigotries that define each, and because both define themselves at least partially as the essence of opposition to prejudices, according to their definitions they cannot be guilty of bigotry. Therefore, that which they condemn or ignore is lacking in merit while those who support that which they condemn or ignore must necessarily do so out of bigotries. This circular thinking that defines leftism is succinctly stated in D. H. Thomas's biography of Solzhenitsyn. Discussing the tendency of Western liberals in the late 60s to see Solzhenitsyn and Sakharov as twin liberal opponents of the "excesses" of Soviet Marxism, Thomas writes, "It was not that the former was trying to deceive anybody by a pretense of being liberal; the illusion came mostly from that peculiar complacent certainty, in liberal or left-liberal circles, that no other philosophical position is tenable" (338.). The Celtic-Southern thesis throws that "peculiar complacent certainty" of the left in Southern studies, with its seeing virtually everything as black and white, whether in race or gender or socio-economic class, a curve ball that it prefers to ignore as if its spitballs were the only legitimate pitches.

8. Dario Fernandez-Morera addresses this issue by quoting from novelist Larry Woiwode's article that originally was his speech accepting the John Dos Passos Prize for Literature. "And just as bad or worse (it's difficult to judge with the dark growing darker) is the academy's refusal to carry on discourse with ideologies or views alien to its entrenched Marxist-humanism (no oxymoron that), and the reluctance of the literary-publishing complex to take note of, much less put into print or support, the work of anyone whose views are not quite correct. If anyone is unsure of what I'm saying, I'll say it more openly, because the attitude that needs to be identified has made its way from the literary arena to grant-giving foundations to the media, and from the best universities and colleges

into every branch of public education." Fernandez-Morera also quotes from Robert Brustein, artistic director of the American Repertory Theater: "Funding blackmail is, in fact, the means by which political correctness, masquerading as multiculturalism, has proceeded to harass the world of serious art." Brustein reveals that lacking any standard of excellence because they have swallowed the Marxist line that such is an obsolete criteria set by the "repressive bourgeois," postmodern distributers of arts funding tend to base support upon "evidence of affirmative action" (19). Such a system inherently discriminates against artists, and scholars, who are not members of the approved race and ethnic and particularly left of center political and social groups.

9. Writing about the November 14 and 15, 1998 "Accuracy in Academia" conference on the hostility to conservative ideas in academia that was to be held at Columbia University, a conference shut down by heckling leftist students, liberal columnist Nat Hentoff says, "While these students are in favor of affirmative action, they oppose diversity of ideas." That is the contemporary left, particularly in the world of education: Every skin shade and sexual persuasion must be represented in rough approximation not to achievement but to population, and conservative ideas must be denied free airing and especially a presence among faculty.

10. There is significant discussion of Shakespeare as a Catholic, and as he was raised in Stratford on Avon, which in the time would have retained at least some Welsh cultural affinities, it seems to me that it is reasonable to suggest that Shakespeare may have been a secret Catholic and may have been of partial Celtic ancestry.

Bibliography

Akenson, Donald H. *Being Had: Historians, Evidence, and the Irish in North America*. Toronto: P. D. Meany Publishers, 1985.

—. *If the Irish Ran the World: Montserratt, 1630-1730* (McGill-Queen's University Press, 1997).

—. *The Irish Diaspora: A Primer*. Toronto: P. D. Meany Company; Belfast: The Institute of Irish Studies, Queen's University, 1993.

—. "The Population of the United States, 1790: A Symposium." *William and Mary Quarterly* 41, no. 1 (1984): 85-135.

—. *Small Differences: Irish Catholics and Irish Protestants, 1815-1922: An International Perspective*. Kingston and Montreal: McGill-Queen's UP, 1988.

Backman, Melvin. *Faulkner: The Major Years, a Critical Study*. Bloomington: Indiana UP, 1966.

Bardsley, Charles Wareing. *A Dictionary of English and Welsh Surnames*. London and New York: Oxford UP, 1901.

Basbanes, Nicholas A. "Forget Snakes, Remember Patrick for Literacy." *Arkansas Democrat-Gazette*. 19 March 1995. J6.

Bell, Vereen M. *The Achievement of Cormic McCarthy*. Baton Rouge and London: LSU Press, 1988.

Berendt, John. *Midnight in the Garden of Good and Evil*. New York: Random House. 199.

Berthoff, Rowland. "Celtic Mist Over the South." *Journal of Southern History* 52 (1986): 523-46.

Billington, Monroe Lee. *The American South: A Brief History*. New York: 1971.

Black, George Fraser. *The Surnames of Scotland; Their Origin, Meaning, and History*. New York: The New York Public Library, 1946.

Blaney, Roger. *Presbyterians and the Irish Language*. Belfast: Ulster Historical Foundation, 1996.

Blessing, Patrick J. "Irish Emigration to the United States, 1800-1920: An Overview." *The Irish in America: Emigration, Assimilation and Impact. Irish Studies* 4. Ed. P.J. Drudy. Cambridge UP, 1985.

Blotner, Joseph. *Faulkner: A Biography.* 2 vols. New York: Random House, 1974.

Brinkmeyer, Robert H. *The Art and Vision of Flannery O'Connor.* Baton Rouge and London: LSU Press, 1988.

—. *Three Catholic Writers of the Modern South.* Jackson: University Press of Mississippi, 1985.

Brooks, Cleanth. *William Faulkner: Toward Yoknapatawpha and Beyond.* New Haven: Yale UP, 1978.

—. *William Faulkner: The Yoknapatawpha Country.* New Haven: Yale UP, 1963.

Bultman, Bethany. *Redneck Heaven: Portrait of a Vanishing Culture.* New York: Bantam Books, 1996.

Bush, Robert. "Introduction." *Paddy McGann; Or the Demon of the Stump.* Ed. James B. Meriwether. Columbia: University of South Carolina Press, 1971.

Byrne, Francis J. "Early Irish Society." *The Course of Irish History.* Eds. T.W. Moody and F.X. Martin. Cork: Mercier Press, 1967.

Cahill, Thomas. *How the Irish Saved Civilization: The Untold Story of Ireland's Heroic Rule from the Fall of Rome to the Rise of Medieval Europe.* New York: Nan A. Talese, Doubleday, 1995.

Cairns, Earle E. *Christianity Through the Ages: A History of the Christian Church.* 1954. Second Revised Edition. Grand Rapids, MI: Academie Books, Zondervan Publishing House, 1981.

Cannon, Devereaux D., Jr. *The Flags of the Confederacy: An Illustrated History.* Memphis: St. Luke's Press and Broadfoot Publishing, 1988.

Caruthers, William Alexander. *The Cavaliers of Virginia, or The Recluse of Jamestown: An Historical Romance of the Old Dominion.* 2 Vols. New York: Harper and Brothers, 1834-35. Rpt. Ridgewood, NJ: The Gregg Press, 1968.

—. *The Knights of the Golden Horse-Shoe: A Tradionary Tale of the Cocked-Hat Gentry in the Old Dominion.* 1841. Southern Literary Classics Series. Chapel Hill: University of North Carolina Press, 1970.

Cash, W.J. *The Mind of the South.* New York: Vintage Books, 1941.

Chadwick, Nora. *The Celts.* Harmondsworth, England: Pelican Books, 1971.

Chitham, Edward. *The Brontes Irish Background.* New York: St. Martin's Press, 1986.

Clark, Dennis. *Hibernia America: The Irish and Regional Cultures.* New York: Greenwood Press, 1986.

Collins, Bruce. *White Society in the Antebellum South.* London and New York: Longman, 1985.

Conroy, Pat. *The Great Santini*. Boston: Houghton Mifflin Company, 1976.

—. *The Lords of Discipline*. Boston: Houghton Mifflin Company, 1980.

—. "Mama and Me: The Making of a Southern Son." *The Prevailing South: Life and Politics in a Changing Culture*. Ed. Dudley Clendinon. Atlanta: Longstreet Press, Inc., 1988.

Corcoran, J.X.W.P. "Introduction." *The Celts*. By Nora Chadwick. Harmondsworth, England: Pelican Books, 1971.

Covington, Dennis. *Salvation on Sand Mountain: Snake Handlers and Redemption in Southern Appalachia*. Reading, Massachusetts: Addison-Wesley Publishing Company, 1995.

Cunliffe, Barry. *The Ancient Celts*. Oxford and New York: Oxford UP, 1997.

Davidson, Donald. "Introduction." *So Red the Rose*. By Stark Young. New York: Charles Scribner's Son's, 1953.

Davis, Curtis Carroll. *Chronicler of the Cavaliers: A Life of the Virginia Novelist Dr. William A. Caruthers*. Richmond: The Deitz Press, 1953.

Davis, Richard Beale. *Intellectual Life in Jefferson's Virginia, 1790-1830*. Chapel Hill: University of North Carolina Press, 1964.

de Breffny, Brian, ed. *Ireland: A Cultural Encyclopedia*. London: Thames and Hudson, Ltd., 1983.

Delaney, Frank. *The Celts*. Boston and Toronto: Little, Brown and Company, 1986.

Dickson, R.J. *Ulster Emigration to Colonial America, 1718-1775*. London: Routledge and Kegan Paul, 1966.

Di Pietro, Robert J. and Edward Ifkovic, ed. *Ethnic Perspectives in American Literature: Essays on the European Contribution*. New York: Modern Language Association, 1983.

Douglas, Ronald Macdonald. *Scots Lore and Folklore*. New York: Beekman House, 1982.

Doyle, David Noel. "Catholicism, Politics and Irish America Since 1890: Some Cultural Considerations." *The Irish in America: Emigration, Assimilation and Impact. Irish Studies* 4. Ed. P.J. Drudy. Cambridge UP, 1985.

—. *Ireland, Irishmen and Revolutionary America, 1760-1820*. Dublin and Cork: The Mercier Press, 1981.

Eaton, Clement. "Custom and Manners." *The Encyclopedia of Southern History*. Ed. David C. Roller and Robert W. Twyman. Baton Rouge: LSU Press, 1979.

Eid, Leroy V. "The Colonial Scotch-Irish: A View Accepted Too Readily." *Eire-Ireland* 21 (1986): 81-105.

—. "Irish, Scotch and Scotch-Irish, a Reconsideration." *American Presbyterians: Journal of Presbyterian History* 64 (1986): 211-225.

Ellis, Peter Beresford. *The Celtic Empire: The First Millennium of Celtic History, 1000 BC - 51 AD*. Durham, NC: Carolina Academic Press, 1990.

—. *The Celtic Revolution: A Study in Anti-Imperialism.* Talybont, Ceredigion, Wales: Y Lolfa Cyf, 1985.

Evans, E. Estyn. "The Scotch-Irish: Their Cultural Adaptation and Heritage in the American Old West." *Essays in Scotch-Irish History.* Ed. E.R.R. Green. London: Routledge and Kegan Paul; New York: Humanities Press, 1969.

"Fairies and Druids of Ireland." *Century Magazine.* New York, Vol 37, 1889. Reprinted in *The Druid Sourcebook.* Ed. John Matthews, London: Blandford Press, 1996.

Fanning, Charles. *The Irish Voice in America: Irish-American Fiction from the 1760s to the 1980s.* Lexington and London: University Press of Kentucky, 1990.

Faulkner, William. *Absalom, Absalom!* New York: Random House, 1936.

—. *Go Down, Moses.* New York: Random House, 1942.

—. *The Town.* New York: Random House, 1957.

Fernandez-Morera, Dario. *American Academia and the Survival of Marxist Ideas.* Westport, Connecticut and London: Praeger, 1996.

Fiedler, Leslie. *The Inadvertent Epic, From Uncle Tom's Cabin to Roots.* New York: Simon and Schuster, 1979.

Fischer, David Hackett. *Albion's Seed: Four British Folkways in America.* New York and Oxford: Oxford UP, 1989.

Fish, Stanley. *Is There a Text in This Class? The Authority of Interpretive Communities.* Cambridge and London: Harvard UP, 1980.

Fitzgerald, Margaret E. and Joseph A. King. *The Uncounted Irish in Canada and the United States.* Toronto: P. D. Meany Publishers, 1990.

Fitzgerald, Sally. "Root and Branch: O'Connor of Georgia." *Georgia Historical Quarterly* 64, no. 4 (Winter 1980): 377-87.

Fitzpatrick, Rory. *God's Frontiersmen: The Scots-Irish Epic.* London: Weidenfeld and Nicolson, 1989.

Flanagan, Thomas. *The Tenants of Time.* New York: E. P. Dutton, 1988.

Fraistat, Rose Ann C. *Caroline Gordon as Novelist and Woman of Letters.* Baton Rouge and London: LSU Press, 1984.

Frazier, Charles. *Cold Mountain.* New York: Atlantic Monthly Press, 1997.

Frye, Northrup. *The Great Code: The Bible and Literature.* New York and London: Harcourt, Bruce, Jovanovich, Publishers, 1982, 1981.

Gaines, Ernest J. *The Autobiography of Miss Jane Pittman.* 1971. New York: Bantam Books, 1972.

Gelfant, Blanche A. "*Gone With the Wind* and the Impossibilities of Fiction." *Southern Literary Journal* 13:1 (Fall 1980): 3-31.

Genovese, Eugene D. "Foreword." *Plagiarism and the Culture War.* By Theodore Pappas. Tampa, FL: Hallberg Publishing Corporation, 1998.

—. *Roll, Jordan, Roll: The World the Slaves Made. 1972,* 74. New York: Vintage Books, 1976.

—. *The Southern Front: History and Politics in the Culture War.* Columbia and London: University of Missouri Press, 1995.

—. *The Southern Tradition: The Achievements and Limitations of an American Conservatism.* Cambridge and London: Harvard UP, 1994.

—. *The World the Slaveholders Made: Two Essays In Interpretation.* 1969. New York: Vintage Books, 1971.

Glasgow, Ellen. *Barren Ground.* Garden City, NY: Doubleday, Page and Co., 1925.

—. *Life and Gabriella: The Story of a Woman's Courage.* New York: Doubleday, Page and Company, 1916.

—. *Vein of Iron.* New York: Harcourt, Brace and Company, 1935.

Gleeson, David T. *The Irish in the South, 1815-1877.* Chapel Hill and London: UNC Press, 2001.

Gordon, Caroline. *Aleck Maury Sportsman.* New York: Charles Scribner's Sons, 1934.

—. *The Collected Stories of Caroline Gordon.* New York: Farrar, Strauss, Giroux, 1981.

—. "Cock-Crow." *Southern Review* ns 1 (1965): 554-569.

—. *The Garden of Adonis.* New York: Charles Scribner's Sons, 1937.

—. *The Green Centuries.* New York: Charles Scribner's Sons, 1941.

—. *Penhally.* New York: Charles Scribner's Sons, 1931.

—. *The Strange Children.* New York: Charles Scribner's Sons, 1951.

—. *The Women On the Porch.* New York: Charles Scribner's Sons, 1944.

Green, E.R.R. "Queensborough Township: Scotch-Irish Emigration and the Expansion of Georgia, 1763-1776." *William and Mary Quarterly* 17 (1960): 183-199.

Grenier, Richard. "*Braveheart*: Legacy of a People." *Readers Digest.* March 1996: 66-70.

Harris, Thomas. *Hannibal.* New York: Delacorte Press, 1999.

Harvey, David. *The Condition of Postmodernity.* Cambridge, MA: Basil Blackwell, 1989.

Hentoff, Nat. "Hecklers Outvote Ideas at Columbia University." *Denver Rocky Mountain News* 28 December 1998. 41A.

Hesseltine, William B. and David L. Smiley. *The South in American History.* New York: Prentice Hall, Inc., 1943.

"An Hibernian." *The Irish Emigrant. An Historical Tale Founded on Fact.* Winchester, Virginia: John T. Sharrocks, 1817.

Hill, James Michael. *Celtic Warfare, 1595-1763.* Edinburgh: John Donald Publishers, 1986.

Hornstein, Lillian Herlands, Leon Edel, and Horst Frenz, eds. *The Reader's Companion to World Literature.* Second Edition. New York: Mentor, 1973.

Horwitz, Tony. *Confederates in the Attic: Dispatches from the Unfinished Civil War.* New York: Pantheon Books, 1998.

Jackson, Blyden. "The Black Academy and Southern Literature." *The History of Southern Literature.* Ed. Louis D. Rubin, et. al. Baton Rouge and London: LSU Press, 1985.

Jackson, Kenneth Hurlstone, ed. With "Introduction." *The Gododdin: The Oldest Scottish Poem.* Edinburgh: Edinburgh UP, 1969.

Jefferson, Thomas. *Writings.* New York: The Library of America, 1984.

Jones, Anne Goodwyn. *Tomorrow Is Another Day: The Woman Writer in the South, 1859-1936.* Baton Rouge: LSU Press, 1981.

Jordon, Terry G. and Matti Kaups. *The American Backwoods Frontier: An Ethnic and Ecological Interpretation.* Baltimore: Johns Hopkins UP, 1989.

Joyce, P.W. *A Social History of Ancient Ireland.* 2nd ed. 2 vols. London: Longmans, Green and Co., 1920.

Kells, Mary. "'I'm Myself and Nobody Else.' Gender and Ethnicity Among Young Middle-Class Irish Women in London." *Irish Women and Irish Migration.* Vol. 4. *The Irish World Wide: History, Heritage, Identity.* Ed. Patrick O'Sullivan. London and New York: Leicester UP, 1995.

Kennedy, John Pendleton. *Horse-Shoe Robinson.* 1835. Ed. Ernest J. Leisy. New York: American Book Company, 1937.

—. "A Legend of Maryland." 1860. *The Collected Works of John Pendleton Kennedy.* Vol VII. New York: G.P. Putnam and Sons, 1872.

—. *Swallow Barn; or A Sojourn in the Old Dominion.* 1832. Rev. 1853. Ed. Lucinda H. MacKethan. Baton Rouge and London: LSU Press, 1986.

Kennedy, William. *Quinn's Book.* New York: Viking Penguin, 1988.

Kibler, James Everett. *Child to the Waters.* Gretna, LA: Pelican Publishing Company, 2003.

—. *Our Fathers' Fields: A Southern Story.* Columbia and London: University of South Carolina Press, 1998.

—. "Simms's Irish: An Address at Hibernian Society Hall, Charleston, South Carolina, 14 January, 1999." *The Simms Review.* 9, no. 2 (1999): 1-7.

—. *Walking Toward Home.* Gretna, LA: Pelican Publishing Company, 2004.

Kinsella, Thomas, ed. *The New Oxford Book of Irish Verse.* London: Oxford UP, 1986.

Kolchin, Peter. *American Slavery, 1619-1877.* 1993. New York: Hill and Wang, 1994.

Kors, Alan Charles and Harvey A. Silverglate. *The Shadow University: The Betrayal of Liberty on America's Campuses.* New York: The Free Press, 1998.

Kreyling, Michael. *Inventing Southern Literature*. Jackson: University Press of Mississippi, 1998.

Kuyk, Dirk, Jr. *Sutpen's Design: Interpreting Faulkner's Absalom, Absalom!* Charlottesville and London: University Press of Virginia, 1990.

Leary, Lewis. "1776-1815." *The History of Southern Literature*. Ed. Louis D. Rubin, Jr. et al. Baton Rouge and London: LSU Press, 1985.

Lefkowitz, Mary. *Not Out of Africa: How Afrocentrism Began an Excuse To Teach Myth as History*. New York: Basic Books, 1996.

Levathes, Louise E. "Iceland: Life Under the Glaciers." *National Geographic* 171, no. 2 (1987): 184-215.

Leyburn, James G. *The Scotch-Irish: A Society History*. Chapel Hill: University of North Carolina Press, 1962.

Link, Arthur S. "Woodrow Wilson and His Presbyterian Inheritance." *Essays in Scotch-Irish History*. Ed. E.R.R. Green. London: Routledge and Kegan Paul; New York: Humanities Press, 1969.

Lofaro, Michael A. *The Life and Adventures of Daniel Boone*. Lexington: University Press of Kentucky, 1978.

Lucas, Mark. *The Southern Vision of Andrew Lytle*. Baton Rouge and London: LSU Press, 1986.

Luce, Arthur Alston. *The Life of George Berkeley, Bishop of Cloyne*. London and New York: Thomas Nelson and Sons, Ltd., 1949.

Lytle, Andrew. *The Long Night*. 1936. "Introduction" By Frank L. Owsley, Jr. Tuscaloosa and London: University of Alabama Press, 1988.

—. *A Novel, A Novella and Four Stories*. New York: McDowell, Obolensky, 1958.

—. *A Wake For the Living: A Family Chronicle*. New York: Crown Publishers, 1975.

MacCana, Proinsias. "Early and Middle Irish Literature." *The Field Day Anthology of Irish Writing*. 3 Vols. Ed. Seamus Deane. Derry, Ireland: Field Day Publications, distributed by W. W. Norton and Company, 1991.

—. *Literature in Irish*. Dublin: Government of Ireland, 1980.

McCaffrey, Lawrence J. *The Irish Diaspora in America*. Bloomington and London: Indiana UP, 1976.

—. *Textures of Irish America*. Syracuse and London: Syracuse UP, 1992.

McCarthy, Cormac. *Suttree*. 1979. New York: Vintage Books, 1992.

McDonald, Forrest. "Prologue." *Cracker Culture*. By Grady McWhiney. Tuscaloosa and London: University of Alabama Press, 1988.

McDonald, Forrest and Ellen Shapiro McDonald. "The Ethnic Origins of the American People, 1790." *William and Mary Quarterly* 37, no. 2 (1980): 180-199.

—. "The Population of the United States, 1790: A Symposium." *William and Mary Quarterly* 41, no. 1 (1984): 85-135.

MacDonell, Mary. *The Emigrant Experience: Songs of Highland Emigrants in North America.* Toronto: University of Toronto Press, 1982.

McDowell, Frederick P.W. *Caroline Gordon.* University of Minnesota Pamphlets on America Writers, No. 59. Minneapolis: University of Minnesota Press, 1966.

MacKethan, Lucinda H. "Introduction." *Swallow Barn; or, A Sojourn in the Old Dominian.* By John Pendleton Kennedy. Baton Rouge and London: LSU Press, 1986.

Mackie, J.D. *A History of Scotland.* Second Edition. Revised and Edited by Bruce Leaman and Geoffrey Parker. New York: Dorset Press, 1978.

McLean, Fitzroy. *A Concise History of Scotland.* New York: Viking Press, 1970.

MacLean, J.P. *Scotch Highlanders in America.* Cleveland: Helman-Taylor Company; Glasgow: John MacKay, 1900.

MacLysaght, Edward. *More Irish Families.* Galway and Dublin: O'Gorman LTD., 1960.

—. *The Surnames of Ireland.* New York: Barnes and Noble Inc., 1969.

McWhiney, Grady. *Cracker Culture: Celtic Ways in the Old South.* Tuscaloosa and London: University of Alabama Press, 1988.

McWhiney, Grady and Perry D. Jamieson. *Attack and Die: Civil War Tactics and the Southern Heritage.* Tuscaloosa and London: University of Alabama Press, 1982.

Makowsky, Veronica A. *Caroline Gordon: A Biography.* New York and Oxford: Oxford UP, 1989.

Markale, Jean. *The Celts: Uncovering the Mythic and Historic Origins of Western Culture.* Trans. 1978 C. Hauch. Rochester, VT: Inner Traditions International, 1993.

Marlette, Doug. *The Bridge.* New York: HarperCollins, 2001.

Meade, Robert Douthat. *Patrick Henry: Patriot in the Making.* 2 vols. Philadelphia and New York: J.B. Lippincott Company, 1957.

Mencken, H.L. *A Mencken Chrestomathy.* New York: Alfred A. Knopf, 1956.

Meyer, Duane. *The Highland Scots of North Carolina, 1732-1776.* Chapel Hill: University of North Carolina Press, 1957 and 1961.

Mitchell, Margaret. *Gone With the Wind.* New York: Macmillan, 1936.

Newby, I.A. *The South: A History.* New York: Holt, Rinehart and Winston, 1978.

Noble, Donald R. "Introduction." *The Valley of Shenandoah.* By George Tucker. Southern Literary Classics Series. Chapel Hill: University of North Carolina Press, 1970.

O'Flaherty, Liam. *The Informer*. 1925. Preface By Denis Donoghue. New York and London: Harcourt Brace Jovanovich, 1980.

O'Grady, Kelly J. *Clear the Confederate Way: The Irish in the Army of Northern Virginia*. Marion City, Iowa: Savas Publishing Company, 2000.

O'Neill, Eugene. *Long Day's Journey into Night*. New Haven and London: Yale UP, 1955.

O Snodaigh, Padraig. *Hidden Ulster: Protestants and the Irish Language*. Belfast: Lagan Press, 1995.

O'Sullivan, Patrick. "Introduction." *Religion and Identity*. Vol. 5. *The Irish World Wide: History, Heritage, Identity*. London and New York: Leicester UP, 1996.

O Tuama, Sean and Thomas Kinsella. *An Duanaire 1600-1900: Poems of the Dispossessed*. Dublin: Dolmen Press, 1981.

Owsley, Frank Lawrence. "The Irrepresible Conflict." In *I'll Take My Stand*. By Twelve Southerners. 1930. Introduction by Louis D. Rubin, Jr. Baton Rouge and London: LSU Press, 1977.

Owsley, Frank, Jr. "Introduction." *The Long Night*. By Andrew Lytle. Tuscaloosa and London: University of Alabama Press, 1988.

"Paddy O'Flarrity." *The Life of Paddy O'Flarrity, who, From a Shoe Black Has, By Perseverance and Good Conduct, Arrived To a Member of Congress*. Washington, D.C.: n.p., 1834.

Paglia, Camille. *Sexual Personae: Art and Decadence from Nefertiti to Emily Dickinson*. 1990. New York: Vintage Books, 1991.

Pappas, Theodore. *Plagiarism and the Culture War: The Writings of Martin Luther King, Jr., and Other Prominent Americans*. Tampa, FL: Hallberg Publishing Corporation, 1998.

Patterson, Nerys Thomas. *Cattle Lords and Clansmen: The Social Structure of Early Ireland*. Notre Dame and London: University of Notre Dame Press, 1994.

Pelikan, Jaroslav. *The Christian Tradition: A History of the Development of Doctrine*. Vol. 1. *The Emergence of the Catholic Tradition (100-600)*. Chicago and London: U of Chicago Press, 1971.

Pierson, William D. *Black Legacy: America's Hidden Heritage*. Amherst: University of Massachusetts Press, 1993.

Pilkington, John. *The Heart of Yoknapatawpha*. Jackson: University Press of Mississippi, 1981.

—. *Stark Young*. Boston: Twayne Publishers, 1985.

Powell, T. G. E. *The Celts*. New Edition. Preface by Stuart Piggott. London: Thames and Hudson, 1980.

Price, Glanville. *The Celtic Connection*. Princess Grace Irish Library 6. Gerrards Cross, Buckinghamshire: Colin Smythe Limited, 1992.

Purvis, Thomas L. "The Population of the United States, 1790: A Symposium." *William and Mary Quarterly* 41, no. 1 (1984): 85-135.

Pyron, Darden Asbury. *Southern Daughter: The Life of Margaret Mitchell.* New York and Oxford: Oxford UP, 1991.

Reed, Roy. *Looking for Hogeye.* Fayetteville: University of Arkansas Press, 1986.

Renan, Ernest. *The Poetry of the Celtic Races, and Other Studies.* Trans. William G. Hutchinson. London: Walter Scott, 1897.

Ridgely, Joseph. "Introduction." *The Yemassee.* By William Gilmore Simms. New Haven: College and University Press, 1964.

Ripley, Alexandra. *Scarlett: The Sequel to Margaret Mitchell's Gone With the Wind.* New York: Warner Books, 1991.

Rubin, Louis D. *The American South: Portrait of a Culture.* Baton Rouge: LSU Press, 1980.

—. "Changing, Enduring, Forever Still the South." *The Prevailing South: Life and Politics in a Changing Culture.* Ed. Dudley Clendinen. Atlanta: Longstreet Press, Inc., 1988.

—. *The Edge of the Swamp: A Study in the Literature and Society of the Old South.* Baton Rouge and London: LSU Press, 1989.

—. *A Gallery of Southerners.* Baton Rouge and London: LSU Press, 1982.

—. "The Image of an Army: The Civil War in Southern Fiction." *Southern Writers: Appraisals in Our Time.* Ed. R.C. Simonini, Jr. Charlottesville: University Press of Virginia, 1964.

—. *William Elliott Shoots a Bear: Essays on the Southern Literary Imagination.* Baton Rouge: LSU Press, 1975.

Salamon, Julie. *The Net of Dreams: A Family's Search for a Rightful Place.* New York: Random House, 1996.

Simms, William Gilmore. *The Cassique of Kiawah.* New York: Redfield, 1859.

—. *Eutaw.* 1856. Lovell, Coryell and Co., n.d.

—. *The Forayers.* 1855. Lovell, Coryell and Co., n.d.

—. *History of South Carolina.* New York: Redfield, 1860.

—. *Joscelyn.* 1867. Ed. Stephen E. Meats. Columbia: University of South Carolina Press, 1975.

—. *Katherine Walton.* 1851. New York: Lovell, Coryell and Co., n.d.

—. *The Letters of William Gilmore Simms.* Ed. Mary C. Simms Oliphant, Alfred Taylor Odell, and T.C. Duncan Eaves. 5 vols. Columbia: University of South Carolina Press, 1956.

—. *Mellichampe.* 1836. New York: Lovell, Coryell and Co., n.d.

—. *Paddy McGann; Or the Demon of the Stump.* 1863. Ed. James B. Meriwether. Columbia: University of South Carolina Press, 1971.

—. *The Partisan.* 1835. New York: Lovell, Coryell and Co., n.d.

—. *The Scout*. 1841. Ridgwood, NJ: The Gregg Press, 1968.

—. *The Yemassee*. Ed. Joseph V. Ridgely. New Haven: College and University Press, 1964.

Schefski, Harold K. "Margaret Mitchell: *Gone With the Wind* and *War and Peace*," in *Gone With the Wind as Book and Film*. Ed. Richard Harwell. Columbia: University of South Carolina Press, 1983: 229-43.

Scott, Ronald McNair. *Robert the Bruce: King of Scots*. New York: Peter Bedrick Books, 1989.

Simpkins, Francis B. and Charles P. Roland. *A History of The South*. 4th ed. New York: 1972.

Smith, Lee. *Oral History*. New York: G.P. Putnam's Sons, 1983.

Solzhenitsyn, Alexander. *East and West*. New York: Harper and Row, 1980.

Sowell, Thomas. *A Conflict of Visions*. New York: Basic Books, 2002.

—. *Race and Culture: A World View*. New York: Basic Books, 1994.

—. *The Vision of the Anointed: Self-Congratulation as a Social Policy*. New York: Basic Books, 1995.

Squires, Radcliffe. *Allen Tate: A Literary Biography*. New York: Pegasus, 1971.

Sweet, Henry. *The Student's Dictionary of Anglo-Saxon*. Oxford: Oxford UP, 1976. Rpt. Oxford UP, 1986.

Tate, Allen. *Essays of Four Decades*. Chicago: Swallow Press, 1968.

—. *The Fathers and Other Fiction*. 1938. Introduction by Thomas Daniel Young. Baton Rouge and London: LSU Press, 1977.

Taylor, William R. *Cavalier and Yankee: The Old South and American National Character*. New York: George Braziller, 1961.

Thiebaux, Marcelle. *Ellen Glasgow*. New York: Frederick Ungar Publishing Co., 1982.

Thomas, Annabelle. *Blood Feud*. Knoxville: The University of Tennessee Press, 1998.

Thomas, D. M. *Alexander Solzhenitsyn: A Century in His Life*. New York: St. Martin's Press, 1998.

Thomas, Hugh. *The Slave Trade: The Story of the Atlantic Slave Trade: 1440-1870*. New York: Simon and Schuster, 1997.

Tindall, George B. *The Ethnic Southerners*. Baton Rouge: LSU Press, 1976.

Trent, William P. *William Gilmore Simms*. Boston and New York: Houghton Mifflin Company, 1892.

Tuchman, Barbara W. *A Distant Mirror: The Calamitous Fourteenth Century*. New York: Alfred A. Knopf, 1978.

Tucker, George. *The Valley of Shenandoah*. 1824. 2 Vols. Southern Literary Classics Series. Chapel Hill: University of North Carolina Press, 1970.

Twelve Southerners. *I'll Take My Stand*. 1930. Introduction. Louis D. Rubin, Jr. Baton Rouge and London: LSU Press, 1977.

Ver Steeg, Clarence L. *Origins of a Southern Mosaic: Studies of Early Carolina and Georgia.* Athens: University of Georgia Press, 1975.

Wagner, Linda. *Ellen Glasgow: Beyond Convention.* Austin: University of Texas Press, 1982.

Wall, Eamonn. "The Irish Voice in American Fiction." *The Irish in America.* Ed. Michael Coffey. Text Terry Golway. New York: Hyperion, 1997.

Warren, Robert Penn. "Andrew Lytle's *The Long Night*: A Rediscovery." *Southern Review,* n.s. 7 (1971): 130-39.

Watkins, Floyd. "*Gone With the Wind* as Vulgar Literature." *Southern Literary Journal* 2, no. 2 (1969-70): 86-103.

Watson, Ritchie Devon, Jr. *The Cavalier in Virginia Fiction.* Baton Rouge and London: LSU Press, 1985.

—. *Yeoman Versus Cavalier: The Old Southwest's Fictional Road to Rebellion.* Baton Rouge and London: LSU Press, 1993.

Watson, William. *Life in the Confederate Army.* New York: Scribner and Welford, 1888.

Weaver, Richard. *Ideas Have Consequences.* Chicago: University of Chicago Press, 1948.

Webb, James. *Born Fighting: How the Scots-Irish Shaped America.* New York: Broadway Books, 2004.

Westerkamp, Marilyn J. *Triumph of the Laity: Scots-Irish Piety and the Great Awakening, 1625-1760.* Oxford and New York: Oxford University Press, 1988.

Williams, Gwyn A. *The Search for Beulah Land: The Welsh and the Atlantic Revolution.* New York: Holmes and Meier Publishers, Inc., 1980.

Williams, Samuel Cole. "Introduction." *Adair's History of the American Indians.* Johnson City, TN: The Watauga Press, 1930.

Wilson, Charles Reagan and William Ferris. "Introduction." *Encyclopedia of Southern Culture.* Ed. Charles Reagan Wilson and William Ferris. Chapel Hill and London: University of North Carolina Press, 1989.

Wilson, Clyde. "The Yankee Problem in America." *Southern Partisan.* (Jan/Feb 2002): 16-21.

Wimsatt, Mary Ann. *The Major Fiction of William Gilmore Simms: Cultural Traditions and Literary Form.* Baton Rouge and London: LSU Press, 1989.

Woodward, C. Vann. *The Burden of Southern History.* Baton Rouge: LSU Press, 1960 and 1968.

Wright, Richard. *Black Power.* New York: Harper and Brothers, 1954.

Young, Stark. *The Pavilion.* New York: Charles Scribner's Sons, 1951.

—. *So Red the Rose.* New York: Charles Scribner's Sons, 1934.

Young, Thomas Daniel. "Introduction." *The Fathers and Other Fiction.* Baton Rouge and London: LSU Press, 1977.

Index